AMERICA'S
BLACK SEA
FLEET

AMERICA'S
BLACK SEA
FLEET

The U.S. Navy Amidst War and Revolution, 1919–1923

Robert Shenk

NAVAL INSTITUTE PRESS
ANNAPOLIS, MARYLAND

This book has been brought to publication with the generous assistance of Marguerite and Gerry Lenfest.

Naval Institute Press
291 Wood Road
Annapolis, MD 21402

Library of Congress Cataloging-in-Publication Data
Shenk, Robert, 1943-
  America's Black Sea fleet : the U.S. Navy amidst war and revolution, 1919-1923 / Robert Shenk.
     p. cm.
  Includes bibliographical references and index.
  ISBN 978-1-61251-053-8 (hbk. : alk. paper) 1. Black Sea Region—History, Naval—20th century. 2. United States. Navy—Foreign service—Turkey. 3. United States. Navy—Foreign service—Black Sea. 4. United States. Navy—History—20th century. 5. United States—History, Naval—20th century. 6. Turkey—History, Naval—20th century. I. Shenk, Robert, 1943- II. Title.
  DJK66.S54 2012
  359.00973'0918229—dc23
                                    2012028104
♾This paper meets the requirements of ANSI/NISO z39.48-1992 (Permanence of Paper).
Printed in the United States of America.

20 19 18 17 16 15 14 13 12   9 8 7 6 5 4 3 2 1

First printing

AGAIN, TO PAULA

Not even a little chantey survives to tell of the children carried in the arms of American sailors.

— William Ellis

CONTENTS

MAPS AND ILLUSTRATIONS

Maps

Illustrations

PREFACE

It was while we were writing our biography of Admiral Dan Gallery that my friend, Herb Gilliland, discovered the admiral's youthful diaries in the stacks of Special Collections at the Naval Academy. When I read those colorful accounts of Gallery's first four years of commissioned service, I became intrigued by the young officer's description of his six-month tour of duty at Constantinople in 1922–23, this while serving aboard the old armored cruiser *Pittsburgh*. Clearly, most Navy people relished the uproarious highlife of Constantinople's European quarter, despite some of them having just witnessed enormous human tragedies only a couple of hours' cruise away. Fascinated, I began looking into why America had sent that very small fleet to its four-year home in the Bosporus Strait to begin with.

Shortly I came across Marjorie Housepian Dobkin's fine book on the burning of Smyrna, published in 1971.[1] The story of Smyrna that she narrated was a very gripping one, resulting in the deaths of many tens of thousands and miseries beyond imagination. However, a successful evacuation of nearly 200,000 ethnic Greek and Armenian refugees did result, accomplished through the able coordination of the officers and men of the American destroyers in the harbor, even if, at one crucial point, an American civilian (rather than a naval officer) had to take the lead. I discovered in Dobkin's account that an American Navy shore patrol of several dozen men along with a civilian relief team sent by the admiral had been ashore in the city before and after the fire—and that the American relief team was the only one operating ashore.

I soon visited Dobkin in New York. Not only her encouragement but also her example of successfully searching for naval accounts beyond official reports were especially important in an early stage of this project. Her example would stimulate me to similar efforts.

However, in the beginnings of my research, I soon discovered that the Smyrna catastrophe was only one among several great humanitarian crises, tragedies, and atrocities that confronted the Bosporus-based American naval detachment in its four short years. A final evacuation of some 150,000 White Russians from the Crimea to Constantinople, this followed by a great famine in southern Russia, were late spinoffs from the Russian Revolution, for example, to which American naval vessels and naval personnel ably responded. About the same time, events were occurring deep in Anatolian Turkey (in the region known as the Pontus) that resulted in the deaths of tens of thousands of innocent Turkish minorities (chiefly ethnic Greeks). In the latter instance, two American destroyer captains recognized that they were witnessing something very terrible indeed and made fervent pleas for their admiral's intervention. Since the Navy detachment commander, Adm. Mark Bristol, was not entirely willing to entertain this viewpoint, both of these officers risked their careers by doing so.

Increasingly, it seemed to me that someone ought to consider America's Black Sea navy at book length. After all, the experience of the Black Sea Express (as Admiral Bristol's small group of destroyers were sometimes called, in imitation of the famous trans-European train Orient Express) was in several ways similar to that of the Yangtze Patrol that America had maintained in China for decades, this in roughly the same period, though on the other side of the globe. I had studied the Yangtze Patrol in my work with the papers of Richard McKenna, author of the fine novel *The Sand Pebbles*. Moreover, as the great majority of the ships that served then in Admiral Bristol's small fleet were destroyers (specifically, the type of destroyer called "four-pipers" or "flushdeckers"), it was perhaps not unimportant that I had once been a destroyer sailor myself. So, while I knew I certainly was not a novelist, and although I was a literature specialist rather than a historian (no doubt I write with more appetite for the sea story and colorful detail than some historians would appreciate), eventually I considered that I might be able to portray well the various events that took place in that long-forgotten age.

Having decided to write a book with this specific focus, I knew that it would have to include historical and political background and other discussion that reached beyond a narrow operational treatment.

One reason for a wider viewpoint than one might find in other naval histories is that early on in his assignment to Turkey, Admiral Bristol became America's chief diplomat as well as the senior naval officer in the very large region under his cognizance (virtually all of what was then known as the Near East—or what we now call the Middle East—and southern Russia, too). Therefore, not only did Bristol head up a small diplomatic team in Constantinople in addition to his naval staff, but his ship captains also were rightly regarded as the admiral's and America's representatives in most of the Turkish, Russian, and other foreign ports they visited.

As for the admiral's work at the embassy, virtually every prominent American visitor sooner or later called on Bristol, who frequently helped them in one way or another, although at the same time he did his best to "correct" their points of view. Beyond that, Bristol was always interacting both with Europeans and Turks in important ways (both Turks in the sultan's pay, and, increasingly, those with Nationalist sympathies). Bristol also met with American and other journalists (including soon-to-be famous American novelists John Dos Passos and Ernest Hemingway) whenever he could and fed them suggested storylines that might promote his agenda. I have not hesitated to listen to these correspondents and report their opinions and descriptions when it seemed particularly helpful to do so. To a lesser extent, I also often cite the opinions and writings of American relief workers, educators, businessmen, and missionaries, for the Navy people were always interacting with the other Americans in the region, and it is in some ways artificial to separate them.

A second reason that I must present a wider than usual viewpoint in this book and sometimes must delve into the general historical background in considerable depth is that, during this period, several historic events had very forcefully gripped the attention of the United States. As mentioned above, on the north coast of the Black Sea, aftershocks from the great human earthquake that was the Russian Revolution were continuing to be felt, to which Americans back home (such as Herbert Hoover, for one) felt obliged to respond. Further south, the Armenian genocide that had taken place in Turkey during World War I had awakened great compassion mixed with anger back in America, and Americans everywhere were contributing money on a massive scale to help the survivors. American relief teams were also scurrying to help.

This Armenian issue, I soon learned, was a very complex one, and discovering exactly what had happened in Turkey during the Great War itself and what was taking place in the immediate postwar period was not easy. Indeed, these issues are hotly contested today in some circles, as anyone knows who has attended (as I have) addresses by such diverse scholars on the period as Richard Hovanissian (a prominent American historian of the Armenians), Justin McCarthy (an outspoken American scholar who usually supports the Turkish point of view), and Taner Akçam (a Turkish scholar who explores Turkish sources of the Armenian genocide) and who has heard diverse modern audiences' very passionate reactions to these presentations. Furthermore, then and now, Adm. Mark Bristol's support for ethnic Turks, as opposed to the ethnic Armenians and Greeks of Turkey, has come in for considerable criticism.

For these reasons, I have done my best first to search out and then to present as clearly as I can important perspectival material, much of it not being specifically naval in subject. The long second chapter (in which many pages go by without reference to specifically naval topics) is absolutely vital for understanding the situation confronting Bristol's small naval forces, as well as the wide context into which the admiral began to exert himself almost immediately upon his arrival in Constantinople. Beyond that, in the chapter about the deaths that were occurring in the Pontus region, I purposely stray a bit from naval activities or naval reports to clarify what was going on not only right along the Black Sea coast of Turkey, at the two ports the destroyers regularly visited, but also deep in the country's interior. I am convinced that to illuminate the nature of Admiral Bristol's decisions regarding these matters (and naval officers' decisions when they attempted to influence their boss), it is necessary to describe the *via dolorosa* of the Black Sea Greeks in some detail.

One final reason that I go beyond naval operational accounts is to trace the varied nonnaval interests of the servicemen I write about. It only makes sense that, if the naval officers and enlisted men were both enthralled by the city of Constantinople, yet horrified by what was going on in some of the other places they visited, I should make clear why, and that this would require wide quotation of both official and unofficial accounts. To find such material (I was searching at the same time for witnesses of major historical events, of course, such as American naval activities during the Smyrna fire), beyond looking into all published and archival sources I could find, I also sought privately held materials. I did this by making wide use both of the Internet and the archives that are available to researchers at the Naval Academy's Archives and Special Collections.

That is, knowing that virtually all the line officers in the Navy of that time were Naval Academy graduates, and thinking that their relatives might have retained some of their letters, diaries, or scrapbooks, I searched out the names of most of the officers who had served in Admiral Bristol's small navy and wrote their relatives whenever I could locate recent addresses. This was quite a successful enterprise; thanks to all who assisted me (I note some of their names below). The material I received allowed me to portray much more fully than I could have otherwise both the operational and the routine sides of America's Bosporus-based navy. The letters, diaries, scrapbooks, photographs, informal oral histories, and family traditions that were shared with me have also helped me very much to picture the nightlife and other recreational activities in which Navy enlisted men and officers—especially junior officers—so ardently participated. Such holistic treatment of the experiences of naval people both while on duty and off is intentional on my part, for I think that after-hours activity and interests are too often left for fiction by naval historians. For example, in this duty assignment, enlisted men, junior officers, and even the white-haired commodore of a destroyer squadron decided to marry the young Russian or

Greek women they met ashore, and some of these men's decisions were force-fully opposed by the admiral himself. Hence, the unusual circumstances that so affected his men need to be explained.

Incidentally, the two collections of destroyer war diaries in private hands to which I was led or that I was sent have proved quite valuable in other ways, providing some additional evidence about the continuation of the genocide in the Pontus during the 1921–22 period, evidence that, so far as I know, had not been unearthed before.

Naturally, much of my research was more ordinarily academic, requiring me to visit various libraries and archives, for instance. Over a few years, I spent many weeks with the Bristol Collection in the Library of Congress and more weeks reading widely in the National Archives—typically taking advantage of the wonderful hospitality of Herb and Carol Gilliland near Annapolis to do so. Many thanks to you, Herb and Carol.

Besides all those who aided me at the Library of Congress and National Archives, I should say that the archivists at Nimitz Library at the Naval Academy proved very helpful, as did the people who work at the Naval Historical Division at the Navy Yard.

I also searched into a variety of university collections (sometimes in person, but often by ordering materials online or by mail), assisted by a score of expert archivists. Then, aided by the interlibrary loan people at the University of New Orleans, I read very widely in published materials. Finally, at one point my wife, Paula, and I traveled to Istanbul so I could get the lay of the land and see what might be available there in terms of scholarship or scholarly expertise. Thanks to the American Research Institute in Turkey (ARIT) for putting us up, and to the University of New Orleans English Department for helping to fund my part of that trip. UNO's College of Liberal Arts also helped with funds at one point. And thanks to the many people who met with me in Turkey and who helped make that trip most illuminating and enjoyable at the same time.

Finally, thanks to Dan Doll and Bill Still, who read early versions of this manuscript in a somewhat different form, as did Marjorie Dobkin early on (though I'm, of course, responsible for all the mistakes that remain). The strong support of this project by John Gery, Peter Schock, and, particularly, the late John Cooke of the English Department at UNO (and Angela Brown's able assistance) are also most appreciated.

Among the relatives of Turkish-era naval veterans who responded to my inquiries, I would particularly like to thank Frank and Margaret Howell. Margaret is Captain Harry Pence's daughter, and her husband, Frank, not only told me of the valuable Harry Pence papers, then still in the process of being transferred to

Mandeville Special Collections at the University of California at San Diego, but also found an institutional way to help fund my visit to that library.

Also, the help of Peter Fitzgerald, Lawrence Olsen, and Webb Trammell Jr. has been absolutely invaluable.

But thanks, too, to the following people (and others I may not remember) for sharing family letters, journals, other materials and even "family traditions" or anecdotes (one or two of which have found their way into this book), and for encouraging me in my quest, often as interesting to them as it was for me: David Bailey, Joseph Barse, Janet Brooks, Bea Buchheister, Susan Devore Chambliss, John Chanler, James P. Clay, Grace Dillingham, Anne McIver Dunn, Eugene Farrell, Joel R. Gardner, Robert L. Ghormley Jr., Alice Grinnell, Edward H. Jones Jr., Ted Libbey, Daniel P. Mannix IV, Bob Maser, Britton Murdoch, John B. Pleasants, Franklin Saunders, George Sharp, Tony L. W. Waller, Bob Watts, Ted Wellings Jr., Judy Meiselman and Banice Webber, and Carol Winckler.

Note: In describing all the regions and cities discussed, I typically use the names that were used by Americans at the time, such as Constantinople (rather than Istanbul) and Smyrna (rather than Izmir), and similarly with a host of lesser-known names. I'm afraid some of my listings of naval ranks may be a bit off target, so that the "lieutenant" I quote may in fact have been a lieutenant junior grade; it is sometimes difficult to discover (without much extra effort) when a person was actually promoted, nor does it seem all that important in most cases. And I often silently correct mistakes in spelling or punctuation in letters or journal entries.

AMERICA'S
BLACK SEA
FLEET

CHAPTER 1

THE ARRIVAL

Constantinople is noisy, hot, hilly, dirty and beautiful.

—Ernest Hemingway

For three or four years just after the Great War, many American naval officers and enlisted men would be ordered to duty at the famous oriental metropolis of Constantinople. Other Americans would come too. Typically, they would all be quite excited at the prospect.

When, in April of 1917, the United States declared war on Turkey's ally, Germany, and Turkey broke diplomatic relations with the United States, all of the ranking American Navy people had to leave, along with the entire embassy staff. Most of the other three or four hundred American residents also departed Constantinople or mainland Turkey and traveled back to the States.

Noteworthy among the few Americans who remained in Constantinople were a few dozen naval enlisted men and three officers. These men were interned in the famous crowded harbor called the Golden Horn on the steam yacht USS *Scorpion*, which had been America's station ship (ambassador's yacht) in Constantinople since 1908.[1] Although Turkish wartime regulations restricted these men to their ship, it appears that all the Navy people regularly got ashore anyway, while their officers maintained very good relations with the local authorities. Also manifesting the good feelings many Turks had for Americans, although British and French schools had been closed and turned into Turkish army barracks, the two fine American colleges in the city were permitted to continue operating.[2]

Upon the impending armistice of the Allied powers with Germany a year later, President Caleb Frank Gates of Robert College (the leader of the remaining Americans) cautioned his staff to be respectful of their defeated hosts and not to rejoice too openly.[3] Following Gates' lead, unlike other foreigners in

the city who overnight began to fly their national flags and rejoice with abandon, most Americans waited to celebrate. However, when a fleet of a hundred
British, French, Italian, and Greek warships steamed into the Bosporus Strait
on November 13, 1918, Americans joined the cheering people who lined
the hills on both sides, even though no American naval vessels were a part of
this armada.[4]

As the Allies began dividing the city of Constantinople among them—the
United States, having never declared war on Turkey, was allowed no part in
the supervisory commission—some of the Americans who had fled the country came back. However, other Americans who had remained in Turkey went
home, including all those interned sailors (some fifty of whom were said to
have taken home wives acquired in the city during or before *Scorpion*'s internment![5]). Before long, a few additional ships and officers began to arrive. Almost
all of these Navy people and diplomats as well as most of the businessmen, educators, and other Americans who, at about this time, began traveling halfway
around the world to this exotic city, were quite new to the place.

—◆—

They came primarily by sea. Ordered to Constantinople from Norfolk in early
1920, the American destroyer *Smith Thompson* fell in behind *Alden* and *Long*.
The three destroyers took ten days to reach Gibraltar, where they stopped to
fuel and provision. A very new ship, *Smith Thompson* burned oil rather than
coal, but it was oil of a different kind that interested Fireman First Class Bert
Berthelsen and his mates, who, once overseas, felt they could freely thumb their
noses at the 1919 Prohibition amendment. Back in Philadelphia in December,
the crew had found the vessel's torpedo alcohol tanks unlocked, so they drained
the tanks dry and stowed bottles of firewater throughout the ship. Upon discovering the theft, the skipper ordered the crew members to stand watch over
the empty tanks in the freezing weather. Once the ship sailed, he had seven
marines (aboard for transportation to Turkey, probably to work at the embassy)
stand guard over those same tanks, now once again filled with alcohol.

When *Smith Thompson* and its sister ships reached Gibraltar, each night the
sailors tanked up with wine, whiskey, and cognac and then took their invigo-
ration out on the "Limeys" to such a degree that the British governor-gen-
eral invited the three destroyers to move on two days ahead of schedule. As the
ships steamed eastward, some crew members sobered up enough to note that
the Mediterranean was covered with ships' lights.

A couple of days later, after passing through the Straits of Messina, *Long*
turned north for duty in the Adriatic, while *Alden* and *Smith Thompson*

continued east through the Ionian Sea. There, heavy squalls sent waves as high as the bridge and stove in watertight doors. The two ships suffered a bit more heavy weather in the Aegean before reaching Cape Helles, the famous rocky cape commanding the entrance to the Dardanelles. When Berthelsen's destroyer eventually reached Constantinople and moored alongside a tanker to fuel, crew members bought so much liquor from clustering bumboats that there were not enough sober men aboard to shift the ship to the buoy! (Or so Berthelsen reports, at least.) The skipper had to crack down again.[6]

The American destroyer *Smith Thompson*, moored at USN Buoy 2 off Constantinople in 1920, with Dolmabagtche Palace in the background. *Photo/Postcard in the Thomas Kinkaid collection, The Naval History and Heritage Command*

Naval officers came to Turkey by different routes and with a variety of outlooks. Adm. Mark Bristol took on his assignment as the senior naval officer at Constantinople with mixed feelings, but he would come to thrive in the position; shortly he would become America's senior diplomat in the region in addition to being America's naval head. Upon receiving orders to Turkey in January 1919, Bristol was helping to supervise the surrender of German naval forces in Belgium. Quickly, though, he traveled by train to the Italian naval base of Taranto, and then ordered the USS *Schley* to give him a ride via the Corinth Canal through the Dardanelles and on to the old Ottoman capital. This duty did not include the "division of armored cruisers or battleships" he had fantasized having upon making admiral, and Bristol was further chagrined that the destroyer he was riding had but one working screw. However, at least he could steam into Constantinople on a warship.[7]

A younger officer was also less than happy about his assignment. In 1920 Lt. (jg) Charles Olsen tried to swap his orders for a European cruise on *St. Louis* with a fellow officer so he could stay home near his new bride, but failed. Although he liked hiking about when the ship docked at the Azores and Cherbourg, he cared little for flirting and drinking while ashore, and he lightened his low spirits over the succeeding months by writing long letters to his wife, Edna. He did feel privileged to be the officer of the deck as the American cruiser steamed through the Straits of Gibraltar, and on coming off watch, he pounded the ship's piano a bit as the ship left the famous Rock on its port side and steamed east.[8]

In contrast, naval officers Julian Wheeler and Glen Howell had been living it up as the passenger liner they were riding docked at Constantinople. The two were coming from naval duty in the Philippines and had traveled via the Indian Ocean and Suez Canal. From Port Said their vessel docked briefly at Athens and Smyrna before steaming up the ancient Hellespont. With their uniforms packed at the bottom of their trunks, the two were posing as rich world travelers and having great fun with the girls they met along the way.

Both officers were heading home. Wheeler intended but a brief visit to Constantinople, but upon making a courtesy call on the admiral, Wheeler was persuaded to take a six-month stint on the admiral's staff. He ended up staying three years.[9]

Not every traveler reached his destination. At the armistice, Constantine Brown was working in Europe as a journalist for an American paper and could not quickly maneuver his way up the long waiting lists for passage home. Offered a four-month newspaper assignment to Turkey and the Balkans, he got a place on the old French steamer *Chaonia*. He boarded it in Marseilles along with several hundred other passengers, most of them Catholic priests or nuns returning to their war-interrupted work as teachers or missionaries in Syria and Lebanon. Brown shared his cabin with a just-retired British colonel who was on his way to represent a London syndicate in the Levant. Though it was winter, the weather was calm as the ship entered the Straits of Messina. The two men began flirting with a young Romanian woman, suggesting they could show her the sights in Athens if she could ditch her husband for a few hours.

Suddenly there was a loud report, which frightened everybody except the colonel. He announced that the ship had just hit a mine, and he calmly helped Brown into a life jacket before heading below to get a whiskey flask. "It will be a good half hour before this old tub goes down," he predicted. Before the colonel could return, though, the ship had begun to founder, the Romanian woman had jumped screaming over the stern, and Brown found himself stepping into the sea. The young journalist frantically swam from the suction of the ship, looked fearfully for sharks, worried about the well-being of his wife and baby, and thought conscientiously of his tailor in London, for he had not yet paid for the suit he was wearing, nor for two other suits in his luggage. Then he blacked out. He came to among several inert forms on the deck of a British collier, one of them the headless corpse of the Romanian woman, apparently decapitated by the ship's screw. Brown and eighteen others were all the passengers (of five hundred or so) who had been rescued alive, although the ship's captain and crew had saved themselves by abandoning the passengers, jumping into lifeboats, and rowing away.

Once they reached port, through the intercession of an Italian admiral, Brown got passage on the royal Italian yacht *Trinacria*, sailing from Taranto. It reached Constantinople without further incident. Brown would be a strong supporter of Admiral Bristol over the next several years.[10]

―◆◆◆―

Almost all the Americans received their first impression of Constantinople in the "famous approach from the sea."[11] As writer George Young romantically pointed out, the typical liner route from Athens northeast between various Greek islands into and through the Homeric Dardanelles, and then across the Sea of Marmara, was "the high road to the Golden City. Along this road you approach her, as an Empress of the East should be approached, by the front gate and step by step through each successive court until you come to where she sits enthroned."[12]

The Dardanelles, or Hellespont, was renowned both from ancient legend and from very recent history, as almost all travelers remarked on it in letters home. When approaching Cape Helles from the south, to starboard was the low-lying Troad. Fewer than fifty years before, archaeologist Heinrich Schliemann had excavated many layers of Troy's citadel, which lay just three miles from the coast, and he had publicized his excavations and theories in several books. Of course, even from their schoolwork, children and sailors in those days knew the Trojan story. The supposed tombs of Achilles and Ajax were pointed out to Near East Relief recruit Stanley Kerr as his steamer ran by.[13] And the famed river once known as Scamander (flowing down from the storied slopes of Mount Ida) could be seen entering the Dardanelles from within the strait itself, even if it did remind naval officer Robbie Dunn of a salmon stream rather than a site of heroic contest (or so he would write, tongue in cheek).[14]

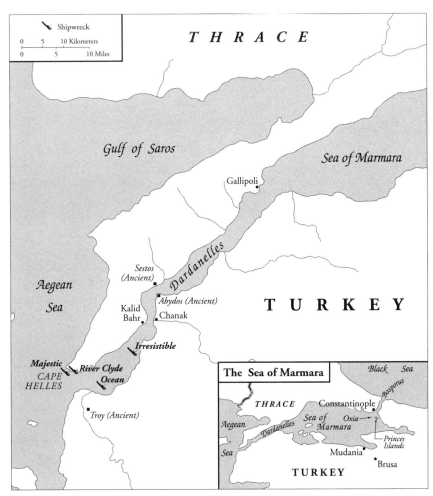

Map 1. The Dardanelles, or Hellespont

On the port side as vessels entered the Dardanelles lay the Gallipoli Peninsula, in 1915 the site of a disastrous Allied campaign that had provided the burial grounds for thousands of Allied and Turkish troops and the proving ground for a certain Turkish infantry colonel who began, just after World War I, to begin a revolution that would ultimately result in a new Turkish state. But to enter the strait a vessel first had to find it. Junior officer Olsen was chagrined that his cruiser's captain mistook the unlighted entrance just before dark and *St. Louis* almost went aground. Even at daybreak, the navigation watch mistook two sets of wrecks as marking the two sides of the channel, and *St. Louis* almost found itself on the beach once again.[15]

Vessels had other worries, too—those pesky mines, again. During the war, the Turks had laid vast sets of minefields across the throat of the strait (with devastating effect on several Allied ships), and for a time after the war a small British vessel was stationed to warn approaching ships of continuing danger. The captain of the Italian tramp steamer in which journalist Alexander Powell was traveling tried to reassure the writer by showing him the charts. All sorts of little red arrows pointed the way between the minefields' diagonal shadings, but to Powell those channels seemed "as narrow and devious as a forest trail." To Powell's distress, even though the captain had never navigated the strait before, he refused to take on an expensive pilot. The journalist translated for the Italian captain a British officer's angry insistence that *Padova* lay up till the morning. As the anchor rumbled down off Cape Helles, the relieved Powell noticed what seemed to be a patch of driven snow up on the hillside. Looking through glasses, he saw instead a field "planted thickly with small white wooden crosses, standing row on row." He recalled that it was here, at the foot of these steep bluffs, that Allied troops had landed and soaked the land with blood.

The next morning *Padova* crept warily through the minefield.[16] In their letters and journals, many Americans mentioned the "thrills" of seeing the shores of Gallipoli and nearby waters, which included the visible remains of many sunken wrecks, "the bleak masts and spars protruding from the water at grotesque angles."[17] After passing Cape Helles on the cruiser *Pittsburgh*, Ens. Dan Gallery would comment in his diary, "Saw the English hulks sunk in 1915 and the place where the landing party was mowed down. When you look at the place just passing casually as we were it seems like nothing but sheer folly to have tried to force a place like that." The whole Allied campaign had been "magnificent but futile," naval officer Dolly Fitzgerald would later reflect; he had first steamed by Gallipoli on the destroyer *McCormick* in 1922.[18]

Within the famous strait, the landscape was also impressive. As George Young remarked, "The great water-gate of the Dardanelles and the towering heights of Gallipoli put even a Transatlantic liner in its place."[19] At the narrows opposite Chanak, travelers could gaze up on the left at Kalid Bahr, the strategic heights the Allies had held only briefly. All along the strait, Lieutenant Olsen noted gun emplacements.[20] Not only wrecked forts from 1915, shell holes and Turkish trenches,[21] but even ruins from earlier days were visible, including piles of stone cannon balls.[22] At Chanak itself, the slopes were white with British tents, because, while the Gallipoli campaign had been unsuccessful, the Allies had eventually won the war, and in 1918 the British had occupied strategic points throughout Turkey.[23]

From the Dardanelles, one sailed further east through the very blue Sea of Marmara, about half the size of Lake Erie. Travel through this body of water was usually uneventful, but not for writer Charles Woods. He took passage to Constantinople from Mudania, the port of Brusa on the sea's southeast shore. A storm that forced his vessel to shelter in a small bay compelled Woods to spend sixty hours among a hundred "sprawling, screaming, sea-sick people, who behaved as if their last hour had come." They were also a very dirty and smelly lot, Woods discovered unhappily. The storm eventually subsided, and Woods was among the hungry and thirsty passengers very glad to feel their ship get under way again.[24]

Soon that vessel steamed by a small group of islands on the starboard side, among them one named Prinkipo (Princes Island), now a resort for the city, but once famous as a place of exile for Byzantine princes. Before long it would be a place of exile again, as Russian revolutionist Leon Trotsky took asylum there in the early 1930s.

Near Prinkipo and also sometimes visible from the decks of vessels as they neared Constantinople was the tiny island of Oxia, a frequent source of traveler conversation. Some years before the war, the Young Turk government in Constantinople had dealt with a messy civic problem in a curious way. Great packs of scavenger dogs were notorious in Constantinople; indeed, they had plagued the city since the sixteenth century.[25] In 1910 the Young Turks determined to deal with them. However, as the rulers interpreted their Muslim religion, they could not directly harm the animals. So the government transported the dogs in barges to Oxia and other barren rocks and offloaded them there. The dogs first set up terrible howls, which were heard for days in Constantinople fifteen miles away. Then they fiercely turned on each other; eventually the survivors starved to death.[26] Ensign Gallery and his mates (and no doubt many others) discussed the propriety of this Turkish action while en route to Turkey, for it had been widely reported.[27]

—◆◆◆—

Map 2. Constantinople

As a ship approached Constantinople, passengers and seamen alike anticipated their first views of the city by rising early and thronging the decks. What first caught most travelers' eyes were the minarets, those slender pillars "set about everywhere like the little ivory men on a cribbage board," as novelist and journalist John Dos Passos described them in 1921.[28] The best Constantinople guidebook waxed romantic about these same architectural features: "When on a clear summer night the sun sinks into the sea of Marmora . . . then the minarets of [this] city of a thousand towers look like so many immense purple needles directing human thoughts and wishes, human longings and endeavours, to the Throne of God."[29]

On his visit to the city upon the Smyrna and Chanak crises in late 1922, journalist Ernest Hemingway was considerably less impressed, regarding the minarets as "dirty, white candles sticking up,"[30] but being both physically sick and assigned to report on some of the sicker sides of human nature, Hemingway wasn't thrilled by any aspect of the city. More typical was tourist Frank Carpenter's description of "hundreds of minarets cutting the sky and standing out like so many white pins on a huge cushion of green."[31] Lt. Julian Wheeler had a unique first view of Constantinople in which these slender towers figured prominently. His Italian steamer had anchored right off the suburb of Scutari near the little island called the Maiden's Tower, or Leander's Tower,

Three American sailors and a chief stand in front of the great Byzantine church named Sancta Sophia, or "Holy Wisdom." (It was now a mosque.) *From a photo/postcard produced in June 1920, author's personal collection*

during the night. When he looked out the porthole at first light, "Nothing was visible except the tops of the minarets of the hundreds of mosques which dot the area, as the surface of the city, the Bosporus, and the Golden Horn were covered with a thick blanket of fog."[32]

Most travelers regarded the whole view as one of "unique magnificence,"[33] as one description put it. According to another, this confluence of the Sea of Marmara with the Bosporus was a "meeting-place the picturesqueness of which is unsurpassed throughout the world." In an oral history about his naval career, retired admiral Dolly Fitzgerald was to term the vista "Fairyland."[34] As a ship churned nearer and turned up into the Bosporus Strait, the great skyline unfolded before one's eyes. To the left lay the ancient city of Stamboul, with its huge Roman walls near the water and its great religious buildings on the hills up above. First came the Sultan Ahmed mosque, with its six minarets; then followed the wonderful Byzantine church originally named Sancta Sophia, or Hagia Sophia, the Church of Holy Wisdom, "her great dome gleaming in the sunlight."[35] (Now it was also a mosque.) Closer down were Topkapi Palace (the historic palace of the Ottomans) and then Seraglio Point. with its "black pins of cypresses."[36] Just beyond Stamboul and to the left as one came abeam the Maiden's Tower was the famous harbor called the Golden Horn, with its thick forest of masts.[37] This narrow harbor was spanned by the fascinating Galata Bridge, a movable structure made entirely of boats, which was usually thronged by a colorful crowd of pedestrians and a variety of vehicles.

Directly ahead as one's ship continued up the strait beyond the Golden Horn lay Dolmabagtche Palace, a huge rectangular edifice standing right at the water's edge. This palace was variously described by American naval visitors as a "dazzling white" palace or as a "wedding cake gone moldy."[38] The European suburbs of Galata and Pera rose up to the left and behind this extensive building, and American destroyers usually anchored to the buoys just in front of it. Dolmabagtche Landing, the main landing for those U.S. naval vessels, lay at the palace's southwestern tip.

On taking over as the American port officer in the city, Lt. Cdr. Webb Trammell's first duty was to respond to a unique request. The sultan's wives who lived in this palace complained that the USS *Trinity* was moored so close as to allow its crew to peer into the sultan's harem, which meant the sultan's wives could not look out of the palace windows. Trammell ordered the offending ship to shift to a buoy further off.[39] Earlier, just after the Great War, the new sultan had been so offended by all the Allied warships, especially a Greek naval vessel that impudently moored right outboard this great palace,[40] that, leaving those wives behind, he moved permanently to Yildiz Kiosk, a smaller palace up the hill.

From Dolmabagtche, the Bosporus Strait trended away toward the north-east, its hillsides studded with kiosks and castles and a few modern buildings. High on the left some four or five miles up the strait were those two American college campuses (Constantinople Women's College first, and then a bit further north, the more prestigious, older, and larger Robert College for men), insti-tutions unique both in their character and in their stunning hillside settings. Robert College's modern buildings were situated just next to and above the medieval Turkish castle Rumeli Hissar, the ramparts of which were climbed by many a naval officer among other college visitors.

On the other side of the strait, to the starboard or generally east throughout a ship's transit upstream, the sun (or "Extraordinarily swollen moons red as ward-rums") rose out of Asia, behind the Asiatic section of the city known as Scutari.[41] A major feature of the latter suburb, quite imposing from the water, was the huge Selimieh Barracks. This barracks, which lay right at the entrance to the Bosporus, had been made famous by celebrated English nurse Florence Nightingale as a hospital for British and French soldiers during the Crimean War.

In 1920 journalist Powell remarked that even though he had seen it many times and in better days, he was still very much moved by the whole scene. In 1922, Ensign Gallery was similarly affected. Having come on deck just as his cruiser was passing St. Sophia and seeing in turn "The mosques, built in some cases by the Roman emperors, the walls, the Golden Horn, and the Bosphorus," he confessed he simply "stood there almost with my mouth open looking at the famous city."[42]

Nevertheless, there were major flaws with this idyllic portrait. Although merchantmen of every description could be seen throughout the panorama and some were quite picturesque, from 1919 to 1923 an armada of Allied war-ships interrupted the view. When Fireman Berthelsen arrived in 1920 aboard his destroyer, for instance, he identified the French battleships *Provence* and *Lorraine* along with the British battleships *Revenge*, *Royal Oak*, *Royal Sovereign*, *Resolution*, and another dreadnought, the name of which he could not make out. Accompanying these huge vessels were all manner of cruisers and destroyers and gunboats, some of them American, Italian, and even Greek, though most of them British and French ships.[43] (No wonder the sultan had moved up the hill.)

To add to the darker tones of the picture, visible on hillsides above the har-bor were scars from hundreds of acres of fires that in recent years had inciner-ated as much as a fourth of the city.[44] Within one week in the summer of 1918, for example, two great fires had destroyed over 20,000 houses. With "vast areas of tinder-box houses built one against another" and an absurdly inefficient Turkish fire control system, such conflagrations were still occurring.[45] Beyond that, much of the city could seem very dirty even seen from a distance, for most buildings were unpainted and weather stained.[46] As for the odors, reeking as they did from a city with little acquaintance with modern sanitation and detectable on an approaching ship's decks (as Berthelsen pointed out),[47] they were unwelcome in the extreme.

Hence, opposed to the wide admiration of the mosques and minarets was an equally striking unanimity of a different nature. As the 1922 *National Geographic* noted, while admiring the approaching skyline, a liner traveler "becomes suddenly disenchanted, as if a once beautiful woman had dropped her veil and revealed the ravages of time."[48] A 1921 issue of *Travel* asserted that "one never can forget the magnificence of its distant view, nor . . . the sordid terribleness of a nearer inspection."[49] Few writers went so far as to "execrate" the city, as had Mark Twain half a century earlier, but most agreed with Twain about the terrible contrast between the "noble picture" they had seen from a mile away and the literal monstrosities they found underfoot. As a wide-traveled British journalist averred, of all the world's great cities, this was "the most beautiful in the mass and the most squalid in detail."[50]

—◆◆◆—

The ugliness was multifaceted. To mention just one example, although Peking was renowned for its raucousness, the Chinese metropolis was said to be a "deaf-and-dumb asylum" alongside Constantinople.[51] Rather than any romantic sensation, it was primarily this frightful clamor that afflicted Americans who journeyed to Constantinople by train. In contrast to the magnificent sea approach, a visitor's approach by rail to Sirkedji station in Stamboul was "about the most ghastly experience possible," according to a contemporary guidebook.[52] Most Americans who traveled by the "Simplon Orient Express," the expensive trans-European train already made famous by the novels of British writer E. Phillips Oppenheim (Agatha Christie's *Murder on the Orient Express* didn't come out until 1934) suffered this experience.

For instance, writer Constantine Brown had gone home after a few weeks in Constantinople in 1919, but he returned on the Orient Express in 1920, having been hired by the *Chicago Daily News* to replace another reporter who had run afoul of Admiral Bristol. At the station he and his wife, Ethel, were greeted by "a mob of native ruffians, who at once began screaming and fighting over our luggage while the Turkish police looked on impassively." A dragoman from the Pera Palace Hotel strode into the mob and began to lay about him with a heavy metal-tipped walking stick in order to rescue the pair. He told them they had been waylaid by "hamals," or members of the city's ancient guild of porters, fighting for business. Most other startled train travelers met the same assault.[53]

Although the train approach to Constantinople was unimpressive, up to this point most passengers had been relatively comfortable. To be sure, on the four-day trip from Paris, you had to pay for your meal in a great variety of currencies, and sometimes your trip was interrupted by customs agents searching for interlopers, or by some national upheaval. Cdr. Harry Pence's train from Marseilles was delayed for six hours when it ran over three Bulgarians sleeping on the track.[54] Other travelers complained that their "wagon lits" (sleeping cars) were "already inhabited" with bedbugs, or that their cars had boards nailed up in place of windows.[55] But this was not the common experience, especially as the deprivations of the Great War receded. Although Capt. Bill Leahy (on his way in late May of 1921 to take command of the cruiser *St. Louis*, then stationed at Constantinople) regarded the train as slow and "lacking in creature comforts" by American standards,[56] in general travelers reported satisfaction, and even found deep interest in the journey.

Allen and Clover Dulles had just gotten married before sailing to Europe on the liner *Olympic* in late 1920; they visited with diplomatic officials in the capitals of Western Europe before entraining for Constantinople (Allen was taking a diplomatic post under Admiral Bristol). Allen wrote his mother that he and Clover had spent five very leisurely days on the train, which "ambled" through Switzerland and northern Italy and then "crawled" through Serbia and Bulgaria before arriving at its destination.[57] Supplied with books and a private compartment beautifully upholstered in deep blue brocade, they enjoyed watching the varied people and the interesting countryside, even if they did have to peer through unwashed windows. The meals were usually good, although Clover mentioned in her letters having to drown with wine the "illusive slavic flavor" she detected in the food once the French diner had been left behind.[58] Since Allen was taking that diplomatic position, the two were met at Sirkedji station with a Cadillac at two in the morning driven by the American foreign secretary F. L. Belin, who knew how to avoid the onslaught of Turkish porters.[59]

So that Allen could confer with embassy officials, the Dulleses had spent about a week each in London, Berlin, and Paris before boarding. A year and a half later, Lt. Cdr. Thomas Kinkaid and his wife, Helen, also saw a bit of Europe on their way to Turkey, where Kinkaid was to be Admiral Bristol's assistant chief of staff. After a ten-day Atlantic crossing on an army transport, they got a quick tour of Antwerp and then took a train to Paris for ten days of leave. In the French capital, "their dollars went a long way. During their stay they took sightseeing trips; visited Navy and civilian friends; took in the Follies Bergere; ate in the best restaurants; visited the Louvre, the Pantheon de la Guerre, and the races at Auteil; and had tea daily with new or old friends, often at the Hotel

Ritz." Finally, they boarded the Orient Express for Constantinople and had a quick trip of three days.[60]

We will have occasion as we go to describe a bit more of the perennial sweat and clamor of Constantinople's streets, the stinking beggars and vendors who assaulted every visitor, the hopeless refugees in the gutters, and of course all the bars and prostitutes and drunks, for there was a great deal to offend the eyes and turn one's stomach. However, to many Americans (including many Navy people), much more important offenses were the enormous assaults upon the human spirit, those almost unimaginably infamous assaults that, under the cover of war, had been inflicted on tens of thousands of helpless human beings. The latter offenses included the attacks, massacres, and death marches since become known to history as the "Armenian Genocide" that had taken place in Turkey during the Great War (though there had been similar events before the war, and, as we will see, American destroyer captains would report the recurrence of such activities on a large scale during the first years of the postwar period). In addition to these terrible events in Turkey, huge continuing armed conflicts and follow-on humanitarian crises in Russia that had begun with the Russian Revolution would also impose themselves upon the collective American conscience, and on America's pocketbook.

Accordingly, before we can consider in detail the special parts that the American Navy was to play in this area right after the war, we must consider in detail what had happened to draw so much American interest, money, and personal dedication to so remote and unfamiliar a region. We'll do that in the second chapter, and, necessarily, we must discuss those events at some length because of their complexity and also because of continuing modern controversies surrounding them. However, before turning to that historical survey, let's conclude our account of the typical postwar arrival of American naval personnel to this ancient city by recounting briefly the advent of senior naval captain Pratt Mannix.

—◆◆◆—

Hearing of troubles in the Near East and seeing the opportunity for an interesting assignment, Mannix got the Navy's Bureau of Personnel to agree to give him command of the large destroyer tender *Denebola*.[61] In late 1922 this vessel would be sent to Turkey to help support the twelve American destroyers that were being sent to Admiral Bristol to join the eight destroyers already serving in Turkish waters. *Denebola* raised the Azores on November 12, and once those islands dropped astern, the large repair ship rounded the southern end of

Portugal, entered the Mediterranean, and stopped briefly at Gibraltar. The next morning *Denebola* sailed for Constantinople, a trip of a little over a week, given this ship's relatively slow cruising speed of ten knots.

Mannix had been told that a British navy tanker had been fired on by a French battery two weeks before as that tanker was passing through the Dardanelles at night (the French had thought the tanker was a Turkish ship), and so he determined to enter the famous strait in full daylight and to have *Denebola* fly its large American battle flag. While en route he had also heard a rumor that the Turks had captured the strait and were forbidding all foreign passage. This moved the captain to make small arms ready topside (the ship's only weapons), and to order that fire hoses be charged with maximum pressure from the fire main and be laid out near all the gangways so as to help the crew oppose any party that might attempt to board.

As *Denebola* entered the strait itself, Mannix noticed all those wrecks of ships from the Gallipoli campaign and, further on, saw some ruins up on the hillside. "Among them, perched on top of a hill, was the fort of an old Turkish corsair. From this vantage point the pirate could see approaching ships a long distance away and decide which ones he wanted to plunder. It was hard to believe that here in the twentieth century we were making preparations to repel boarders much as other vessels had done since time out of mind."[62] The American ship suffered neither signal challenges nor any other martial interference as it proceeded. Shortly, though, just as *Denebola* was approaching the narrowest part of the strait at Chanak, where several British battleships, cruisers, and merchant ships were anchored, a gale blew up and it started to snow. Complicating matters further, after the ship left the Hellespont and entered the Sea of Marmara, evening approached, and with the darkness and the bad weather, navigation became very uncertain.

Neither Mannix nor his navigator had ever been to Turkey. Moreover, for some reason, few of the charted lights that the navigation team looked for were burning, so the best specific course to take from the Sea of Marmara into the Bosporus (and thereby into the port of Constantinople itself) became a matter of debate on the ship's bridge. As *Denebola* neared the glowing city, the ship's navigator identified three dark blotches looming right ahead as three anchored ships, and he also cited the twenty-fathom sounding that the navigation team had just taken as evidence that the ship was well within the channel. He advised that *Denebola* continue right on, following a course close by those three anchored ships. The ship's captain demurred, however, and ordered that they lay up till morning. Sure enough, "When the sun rose, we found that we were cozily nestling against three rocky little islands," Mannix would comment later.

What Mannix said to the navigator that morning is not recorded. But the captain saw to it that those rocks were given a wide berth as he ordered the ship under way to enter the Bosporus.[63]

Upon rounding Stamboul and turning into the latter great strait, *Denebola* would exchange bugle salutes with four British battleships, two French cruisers, a Spanish cruiser, several Italian warships, and a flotilla of British destroyers. (All of them were apparently moored just within the Bosporus, right off the city.) Then it sighted five American destroyers moored at a buoy. Upon identifying the destroyer tender, the American naval vessels started signaling about expected spare parts, and so on—and *Denebola*'s year of naval service in Constantinople had begun.

However, before getting even that far, Mannix himself (like so many before him) found himself gazing with admiration at the fabulous display. The weather had cleared up, and so they were entering the strait with the city's "mass of towers, mosques, and minarets brilliantly colored and all sparkling in the sun." This was like something out of a dream, Mannix found himself thinking, or rather like an image out of the *Arabian Nights*. Although the captain had traveled the world in his nearly three decades of naval service, he considered that this city was like nothing in Europe, or America, or anywhere else he had been.

Indeed, Captain Mannix concluded that the city of Constantinople was the most beautiful sight he had ever seen.[64]

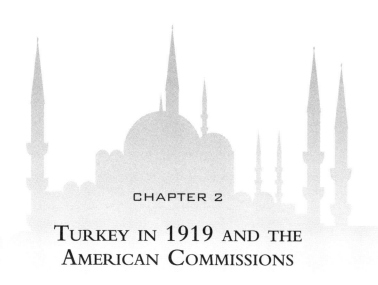

CHAPTER 2

TURKEY IN 1919 AND THE
AMERICAN COMMISSIONS

An American mandate is the solution which I urged three years ago.
President Hibben then asked me what is the solution if America does not
take part. I replied, there is no solution.

—Caleb Frank Gates, in 1922

America, as it happens, had held more than a passing interest in Turkey since the early nineteenth century. By the time the Navy and diplomatic people began to arrive in 1919, Americans had become passionately concerned with what was going on in these strange regions halfway around the world.

To explain this, and to provide context for understanding the naval and the diplomatic situation (Adm. Mark Bristol being both America's naval and diplomatic head in these large regions for the four years right after World War I), we must describe the historical background at some length—perhaps unusual length, for a naval history. Partly this is so simply because that background is very complex, and partly it results from the fact that aspects of it (including whether there actually was an Armenian genocide at all, for instance) remain very much contested issues even to this day. An ability to understand Admiral Bristol's point of view, those of his ship captains, and those of native Turks of several ethnicities and differing politics with which American officials (including destroyer captains) regularly had to deal requires an in-depth understanding of the historical situation.

I point this out ahead of time, lest readers be perplexed as to why they do not encounter much that is specifically naval until the USS *Arizona* comes on the scene briefly toward the very end of this chapter. To be sure, an important figure from the American *Army* does have a prominent role in the journeys of the American commissions that are briefly chronicled here. Maj. Gen. James Harbord had been Gen. John Pershing's chief of staff in Europe in 1917 and later commanded the 4th Marine Brigade during the Battles of Chateau Thierry and Belleau Wood and the 2nd U.S. Infantry Division during the Second Battle of the Marne. As we will see, this very capable officer headed the American Military Commission to Armenia, traveled adventurously with his team through the entire subcontinent of Turkey, and met personally with Mustapha Kemal (Atatürk) within a few months of the latter's landing in northern Anatolia intent on organizing a revolution in Turkey. On all of the fundamental issues, Harbord's assessment is important, as are the insights of several other Americans who traveled through the region and attempted to comprehend and report back on what was actually taking place there.

————◆◆◆————

America's original dealings with the Ottomans had involved several famous naval officers. For example, when Captain William Bainbridge took the 24-gun *George Washington* to Constantinople in 1800 (falling under the guns of Algerian forts, he had been coerced by the dey of Algiers to transport the dey's annual tribute to the sultan), he found he was received kindly enough, but that the Turkish officials had never heard of the United States. They would hear a bit more shortly, during the "War of the Barbary Pirates" that America waged successfully with Tripoli, an Ottoman vassal state.[1]

In the 1830s Commo. David Porter would be appointed the first American diplomatic representative to the "Sublime Porte" (the name traditionally used for the Ottoman empire's foreign ministry, located in Stamboul). Porter would stay on until his death in 1843, and so deeply interested would he become in the place that he would eventually publish a two-volume collection of letters describing Constantinople and the surrounding territory.[2] Later yet, in the late 1860s, Adm. David Farragut visited the city with America's European Squadron. Cyrus Hamlin, the founder of America's locally famous Robert College, would give Farragut credit for interceding with the Turkish government to allow Robert College to be built.[3]

Over this same century, America would begin doing business with Anatolian merchants (buying tobacco and licorice and selling oil and sewing machines), while travelers like Mark Twain and Herman Melville would call at Constantinople and memorably describe the place.[4] Nevertheless, myths of harems and camels and nightingales and princesses and tales from the *Arabian Nights* typically imposed themselves much more powerfully on the American imagination than did contemporary travelogues, opportunities for American business, the sultan's political intrigues, Turkey's halting military campaigns, European countries' regular interference with Ottoman affairs, and the oppressive circumstances suffered by many of the peoples of the Near East.

In the 1890s, however, Americans started to pay particular notice to events transpiring in Asia Minor (Turkey and its environs). Specifically, they began to hear of and greatly to deplore the phenomenon of the massacre of Christian minorities by what was widely known as the "unspeakable Turk." Typically Americans saw these events through the eyes of American missionaries.

Protestant missionaries from the United States had begun carrying the word to Turkey in the early nineteenth century. American Presbyterians having decided to focus on Syria and Persia, they ceded the Turkish field to the Congregationalists, as organized under that denomination's "American Board of Foreign Missions."[5] Over decades, this group not only sent missionaries of a variety of Protestant denominations to Turkey (not just Congregationalists), but began recruiting educators and doctors as well. With generous donations from its churchgoers, it built many schools and hospitals alongside its mission churches and storehouses. By 1914 the American Board had established a larger mission field in Turkey than anywhere in the world, one that included over twenty substantial mission stations in the subcontinent known as Anatolia (also known as "Asia Minor"), and many substations. In that year, American mission schools throughout Turkey enrolled 25,000 students.[6]

Originally, the Americans had hoped to convert Muslims and Jews throughout the region. However, when they discovered that it was a capital offence to convert a Muslim (or sometimes to be converted *from* Islam), they decided to focus their evangelizing on the *Armenian* citizens of the Ottoman Empire. Most of the Armenians were already Christian—they were Armenian Orthodox—but the American Protestants typically did not think much of that faith. The American missionaries considered that since the Armenians were locals, once the Armenians saw the light of protestant Christianity, they might more easily convert the Turks.[7]

That was a very unlikely prospect, however. In the 1894–96 period, partly to make sure the native Christians knew their place (as subordinate both to Islam and to the Ottoman government), Sultan Abdul Hamid II ordered the massacres of tens of thousands of Armenians in Turkey. Many American missionaries went through great ordeals alongside their flocks, and afterward, at the risk of their lives, helped to provide relief to the massacre survivors. Of course, the Americans also wrote home about their experiences, and their accounts were read by churchgoers and got into the American press.

The sultan's generally despotic rule and, just as important, his lack of success in keeping European powers from interfering with Ottoman affairs, offended many ethnic Turks as well as the minorities, with the result that many Turks began to seek independence from the Ottoman yoke. Eventually, a political party grew up in Turkey that opposed the sultan, the "Committee of Union and Progress." In 1908 these "Young Turks" forced the sultan to install a parliamentary system. After the sultan attempted a counterrevolution in 1909, the party deposed him. Stories spread worldwide about the great rejoicing in the Near East and the democratic hopes that these events provoked among Turkish citizens of all ethnic groups.

However, after unsuccessful experiments with a liberal Ottomanism (under which the Christian, ethnic minorities in Turkey might still have been acknowledged a place), and upon Turkey's suffering devastating defeats in the Bulgarian and Balkan revolts of 1908 and 1912, the Turkish revolutionary party gravitated toward a narrow Turkish nationalism.[8] Under the control of three Young Turk officials, or pashas, named Enver, Djemal, and Talaat, this nationalistic emphasis was to have fateful implications.

For a couple of years after the overthrow of the sultan, the Turkish Christian minorities in Constantinople had breathed the air of freedom, establishing clubs, joining unions, exploring their ethnic literatures, and embracing their novel right to send members to a Turkish parliament. There were warning signs, however. Some 15,000 to 20,000 Armenians (including two American missionaries and twenty evangelical Armenian pastors) were massacred at Adana in 1909.[9] Most ominously for the Turkish minorities, and actually for the ethnic Turkish majority, too, at the outbreak of the Great War in 1914, the Young Turk leaders were drawn by various unfortunate events and by their imperialist, pan-Turkish ambitions to align Turkey on the side of the Germans and against the Russians.[10]

Two great events in Turkey succeeded early in World War I that became widely known in the Western world. One of them, already mentioned, was the defeat of a large Allied force by the Turkish army at Gallipoli in 1915 under the leadership of the German general Liman von Sanders. A Turkish colonel also played a vital part in the Gallipoli defense: indeed, Mustapha Kemal became the Turkish hero of the war.[11]

Although this great Turkish victory effectively denied the Allies use of the Dardanelles, unfortunately for Turkey, the wartime leadership at the very *top* of the government (that is, in contrast to the leadership of the military colonel Kemal) was neither effective nor heroic. Among other things, the Young Turk government and its military establishment allowed an estimated one and one-half to three million *ethnic Turks* to die of nonmilitary casualties during the war, mainly of diseases and malnutrition.[12] Moreover, in 1915 the Turkish leaders initiated another campaign against that same, allegedly seditious Turkish

minority population that American missionaries had long befriended—
the Armenians.

—◆◆◆—

The Armenians were a historically cohesive Middle Eastern people who
claimed to having been the first nation to become Christian, way back at the
beginning of the fourth century. As a people they had stubbornly maintained
their cultural and religious identity despite invasions and conquests and persecution ever since.[13] Under Ottoman rule they had regularly been much
oppressed. Like other minorities, they were subjected to heavy taxes; referred
to regularly as giaours, or infidel dogs; treated as inferiors in courts of law; forbidden the possession of arms; and usually forbidden to participate in military
service. Yes, Turkish Armenians and Greeks were usually allowed religious freedom and might sometimes be treated relatively well—"so long as they behaved
as slaves," as Admiral Bristol would once explain.[14] Formally, it was under the
"millet" system, a kind of nonterritorial, ecclesiastical structure that allowed
ethnic minorities some independent religious and community organization,
that the Armenians and the Greeks were, to a degree, tolerated.[15]

Despite their subject status, since the Armenians and the ethnic Greeks living in Turkey were generally more industrious and commercially adept than the
Turks (particularly outside of Constantinople, many ethnic Turks were notori-
ously indolent), the minorities even could be said to have prospered up to a
point. This particularly was so in the nineteenth century, when the Armenian
millet, in particular (and ethnic Greeks in Turkey, too, although that's a somewhat different story), participated in a general cultural renaissance. This period
saw the establishment of hundreds of schools, a flowering of Armenian literature, an enhanced success at commerce, and a new political assertiveness.[16]
Through the formation of three Armenian nationalist parties, some Armenians
began to think about fighting back against oppression and to seek some degree
of political autonomy.

All of this enhanced the Armenians' ethnic consciousness, but it also had less
fortuitous consequences. Like the sultan before them, the Young Turk leadership became increasingly envious of the growing success of what they regarded
as a pariah or outcast population broadly sown throughout Anatolia. Influenced
by a nationalistic ideology called "Turkey for the Turks" and also motivated
by the dream of a new, all-Turkish empire stretching from Turkey into Asia,
Young Turk leaders, or pashas, Enver and Talaat found the Armenians increasingly inconvenient. Two of the Armenian nationalist parties had supported the
Committee on Union and Progress in its overthrow of the sultan, and the great

majority of Armenians remained loyal to the Ottomans. Nevertheless, the continuing activities of the Armenian nationalist parties (sometimes under leadership from outside Turkey), those parties' support by interfering Europeans, and some Armenians' military cooperation with the Russians in the far eastern part of Turkey and southern Russia created a paranoia in the minds of many Turks toward this supposedly disloyal segment of the population.

In April of 1915, at the city of Van in eastern Turkey, after direct Turkish provocation later testified to by American missionaries (Turkish officials had invited Armenian leaders to a "peace conference" but had murdered them instead), some fifteen hundred Armenian fighters, armed with a few hundred rifles, a few ancient flintlocks, and many pistols, banded together to protect 30,000 Armenians. For several weeks the Armenians in Van defended themselves from Turkish siege and bombardment. This successful defense against great odds, which partially stymied a planned massacre of all the Armenians in the province (a massacre that had been planned by the province head, Jevdet Bey, Enver Pasha's brother-in-law, and that took a terrible toll outside Van itself), enraged the Young Turk leadership. The bare fact of Armenian resistance to a Turkish majority provided a convenient propaganda tool. The Turkish leaders were further enabled in their propaganda by the fact that, when the Turks in that province were eventually put to rout by czarist armed forces, Armenians burned and looted and murdered Turks in retaliation.[17] With such opposition as evidence, Armenians throughout Turkey were said by Turkish leaders (and still are said by some) to have provoked the Turks.[18] Provided cover by the world war, the Young Turk leaders in Constantinople proceeded with their plans to rid Turkey of the Armenians entirely.

——◆◆◆——

From various sources, Europeans and Americans would learn a great deal about what happened next.[19] For one thing, in 1916 a long-time proponent of the Armenians, Britain's James Bryce, published, with the help of his young assistant (and later famous historian) Arnold Toynbee, a 684-page compilation of witness testimony called *The Treatment of Armenians in the Ottoman Empire, 1915–16*.[20] Excerpts from the Bryce report would fill three pages of the *New York Times* on October 8, 1916, and before long the book itself would not only find its way into the hands of the U.S. president, but to the desk of every American congressman.[21] This tome indicated that, beginning in 1915, on orders from Constantinople, a campaign against the whole Armenian people had begun. First, in cities throughout Turkey, Armenian men were disarmed, imprisoned, and then killed. Afterward, the remaining older men and virtually all the Armenian women and children were sent to the east and south, the latter treks euphemistically termed "deportations to the interior," but actually death marches through mountains and plains toward southern deserts.

Herded along with little or no food or water, periodically robbed of all remaining money and goods, the women often raped and then sometimes murdered, too (or if young and good looking, carried off as slaves or concubines), hundreds of thousands of deportees suffered unspeakably. The numbers affected have long been disputed. However, counting those massacred initially and those who died along the way, over a million Armenians probably died, as well as tens or even hundreds of thousands of ethnic Greeks.[22] All this occurred despite objections by principled Turks and efforts to support the minorities by Americans and other foreigners in Turkey, especially by the American missionaries.

Rather than the Bryce report, though, or another significant documentary written by the German pastor Johannes Lepsius,[23] probably the primary source for ordinary Americans' understanding of what had gone on in Turkey was a book by Henry Morgenthau, who had been the American ambassador in Turkey from late 1913 to early 1916. In five chapters of a memoir about his experience in Turkey, the ambassador described the horrible suffering encountered by the Armenians throughout the country. He also attempted to demonstrate, in detailed accounts of his interviews with Turkish leaders Enver and Talaat, that these atrocities were the product of conscious decision at the very top of the government. *Ambassador Morgenthau's Story* was not only widely read at home when it was published in 1918 (it was also serialized in the magazine *The World's Work* and in several newspapers), but it also was often read on the boat by Americans on their way to Constantinople, including some naval officers.[24]

Not too long ago, a scholar noted significant differences between the diaries Morgenthau wrote while he was ambassador and the portrait found in Morgenthau's memoir. From these discrepancies and other circumstances, Heath Lowry charged that many details of those conversations with Turkish leaders were invented out of thin air and that Morgenthau's book is mostly wartime propaganda.[25] Although one might argue that not every detail one recalls with accuracy will necessarily be recorded in a diary,[26] a careful weighing of Lowry's challenge to the authenticity of Morgenthau's account indicates there probably was some exaggeration in the ambassador's book.

However, quotations from Morgenthau's own wartime diary (on which Lowry depends heavily) indicate that the ambassador was enormously concerned about the Armenians and met with Talaat about those wretched people again and again. It also shows that both Talaat and Enver *did* admit to

Morgenthau (as Enver also reportedly admitted to Johannes Lepsius) that they had already "disposed of three-fourths" of the Armenians, and that they intended to complete the job.[27] Lowry argues that as late as September of 1915, the ambassador had not firmly concluded the Young Turk leadership was out to exterminate the Armenians. However, one can judge the date and degree of Morgenthau's concern from the ambassador's own cables to the State Department. Take this one, for example, from *June* of that same year:

> Persecution of Armenians assuming unprecedented proportions. Reports from widely scattered districts indicate systematic attempt to uproot peaceful Armenian populations and through arbitrary arrests, terrible tortures, wholesale expulsions and deportations from one end of the Empire to the other accompanied by frequent instances of rape, pillage, and murder, turning into massacre, to bring destruction and destitution on them. These measures are not in response to popular or fanatical demand, but are purely arbitrary and directed from Constantinople in the name of military necessity, often in districts where no military operations are likely to take place.[28]

Where was Morgenthau getting his information? Of the ambassador's many sources, especially devastating were accounts from American consuls or consular agents throughout Turkey.

As just one example among dozens, consular agent W. Peter at the Turkish Black Sea port city of Samsun reported in August of 1915 that great numbers of Armenians had been sent inland from that Black Sea port city. Of these, most of the men had been murdered somewhere beyond Amasia, while many women and children had been taken to Malatia and ultimately thrown into the Euphrates. Forced conversion of Christian minorities to Islam (regularly attempted) did not always save the Armenians from deportation, the official reported, nor did lack of transportation. Specifically, Consular Agent Peter regarded the situation of women and children who had been put into carts and sent to a probable death from hunger, thirst, and despair as a "horrible slaughter" reminiscent of the time the dogs of Constantinople had been gathered up and sent off to die on that island in the Sea of Marmara.[29]

Such reports came not only from Peter in Samsun and Consul Oscar Heizer in Trebizond but also from consuls at Aleppo, Mersina, and Beirut in the south and from American officials at interior cities. Some officials who could not get material to the embassy in Constantinople at the time and who were later forced to destroy their records when America entered the war would eventually write summary reports of their experiences. A treatise of the latter kind was written by Leslie Davis, who had been the American consul in the city of Harput, deep in the interior of Anatolia. In this document, he reported that in 1915 thousands of Armenians had been herded through his city. Such mass deportations, with associated starvation, abuse, robbery, and rape, had resulted in widespread emaciation, disease, nakedness, brutalization, and much death.

Davis was moved to hide dozens of Armenians in the attic and the garden of his large consulate, but meantime he saw the results of carnage on an even more terrible scale. For his only real recreation, Davis had taken horseback rides outside Harput, sometimes accompanied by an American missionary named Atkinson. One day in the fall of 1915, Davis rode further than usual from the city to the beautiful Lake Goeljuk. There, on the shores, in the water, and in nearby valleys, Davis came across the remains of what he carefully and conservatively estimated to be ten thousand Armenian dead. Most of these people had been slaughtered not with guns, but by bludgeon, knife, or bayonet. Davis visited the lake again a few weeks later, and then a year after that, and in his 1918 report he described the scene in awful detail. As a result of such experiences, Davis would come to term the Turkish province in which he had worked the "Slaughterhouse Province."[30]

Although Morgenthau could not have seen this particular document (it was written long after the ambassador left Turkey), the reports he did see were just as damning. He was not just reading, of course, but also listening, to American, Canadian, and even German missionaries, for example, who would sit in his office in Constantinople with tears streaming down their faces as they recollected the horrors through which they had passed.[31] From all he heard and read, the ambassador decided that the world was seeing something unique.

So, at the same time he and others were attempting, unsuccessfully, to get the Turkish leaders to change their policies, in September of 1915 Morgenthau cabled Secretary of State Robert Lansing to request that his friend, philanthropist Cleveland H. Dodge, and others begin to raise funds to help relieve the great suffering. On its organizational meeting, Dodge's committee received pledges of $50,000. By the time America entered the war in 1917, they had raised over $2 million. This same group, incorporated shortly after the war ended as an official government agency and eventually titled the "Near East Relief" (the name we'll know it by here), would raise more than a hundred million dollars over the next fifteen years.[32]

— ◆◆◆ —

Such astonishingly successful fund-raising was made possible by a huge publicity campaign throughout America. It was, in fact, as a modern scholar has pointed out, "a twentieth century public awareness bureaucracy."[33] Everybody helped, from the organizers of the Harvard-Yale football game of 1916, who sent the game's proceeds to the relief committee, down to thousands of ordinary citizens, these helped along by influential groups like the Rockefeller Foundation and the American Red Cross.[34]

To aid in publicity, not only did the State Department open its files to the relief committee (which thus could make use of all those consular reports), but sometimes the State Department also sent information to the relief and missionary leadership by cable. Hence the relief committee could get material in prominent American newspapers within days. On their part, American newspapers often donated space.[35]

Consequently, before long not only ordinary book-reading adults but virtually every God-fearing schoolchild in the United States knew of the Armenians' woeful circumstances. Children heard sermons on the Armenians' plight, they were urged by their parents to eat their suppers because the "starving Armenians" could not, they stared at photographs and watched heartrending films in schools and churches (even in movie theaters) they acted out the Armenians' prostration under the "Terrible Turk" in school and church dramas, and they and their parents contributed their pennies for help.

This great relief campaign, amounting almost to a "national crusade,"[36] naturally led to a somewhat simplistic view of the situation, especially as it pertained to the far eastern provinces of Turkey. Those areas had long a seen a rising Armenian ethnic consciousness, successive massacres of Armenians, the flight of many Armenians to Russia, Armenians volunteering for duty in Russian armies, and military campaigns between Russia and Turkey surging back and forth, which were accompanied by atrocities on both sides. The PR plot being good versus evil, underdog versus oppressor, and innocent Christian saints versus barbaric Muslim villains,[37] American investigators would be surprised when they encountered greed and vice among the victims, as they very frequently did. Surprise grew to bewilderment when Americans found that where Armenians had gained power, they had sometimes been guilty of retaliatory massacres and scorched-earth policies equal in ferocity to that of their oppressors.[38]

Yet even if the portrait was simplistic in some respects and propagandistic in others, the great need was obvious.[39] The American outpouring was correspondingly great. Because of Morgenthau's foresight and the immediate response of influential American citizens, upon the war's end the Near East Relief was poised to help.

— ◆ —

So much, then, for a brief and incomplete survey of what had happened in Turkey before the end of the Great War to attract enormous American interest and compassion. In the first six or eight months following the armistice, several

American commissions were sent to investigate conditions in the Near East, so as to recommend what the United States should do about various aspects of the Turkish situation.

One set of commissioners was a Near East Relief team composed of prominent lawyer Walter George Smith and business leader Howard Heinz, who in April of 1919 traveled to Batoum on the converted private yacht USS *Noma* (supplied by Admiral Bristol) and traveled via Tiflis, Georgia, into Armenia to assess the relief problems there. These men had wondered if there had not been much exaggeration in the terrible reports of Armenian death, disease, and suffering they had read and heard of. Upon their return, a shaken Heinz announced that published tales of suffering had, if anything, *underestimated* the problem: "Merciful God," he was quoted. "It's all true! Nobody has ever told the whole truth! Nobody could!"[40] Smith and Heinz returned to Constantinople and then to Paris and elsewhere in Europe and proceeded to do all they could to ensure grain and medical help were expedited to Armenia from the United States.

Another group traveling to and beyond Turkey was the King-Crane Commission. It was headed by the president of Oberlin College, Henry King, along with a wealthy industrialist named Charles Crane, and was charged with investigating some of the *political* problems of the Near East. In July these men would travel to parts of southern Turkey and then head further south into Syria, Lebanon, and Palestine, transported part of the way down and back by an American destroyer. Yet a third team, which was also to look into political issues, got under way a bit later. It was called the "American Military Mission to Armenia" and was headed by Maj. Gen. James Harbord. As mentioned above, Harbord had served as Pershing's chief of staff in Europe (and commanded troops in very important battles of the Great War). He was also an amateur student of history.

Both of the latter groups were very late in being commissioned, included only Americans, and perhaps were being used by politicians as a cloak for their own delay. Indeed, these two American commissions would later be criticized famously by Winston Churchill as composing "a roving progress in search of truth through all the powder magazines of the Middle East with a notebook in one hand and a lighted cigarette in another."[41] No doubt, by inquiring as rigorously as they did into all local parties' conditions, attitudes, and requests, the commissioners raised hopes that never could have been realized. Still, most commission members were responsible men trying to assess difficult situations.

For our purposes, it makes sense to follow General Harbord's group most closely through the remainder of this chapter. Not only did his group travel from one end of Turkey to the other, even into that part of eastern Turkey

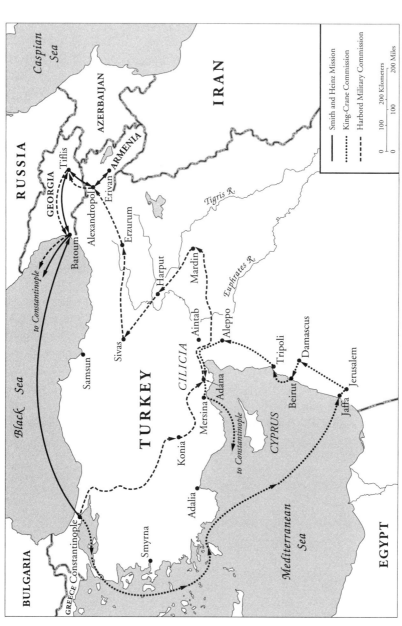

Map 3. Journeys of the Major American Commissions

known as Armenia, but it also was, in many ways, the most adventurous and probing of the American commissions. For example, both Harbord's team and the King-Crane Commission used automobiles (offloaded from the train, which took them part way), but Harbord's party, in addition, was lightly armed and thoroughly equipped for a trek across desolate and hostile country. Harbord's men donned military uniforms rather than the business suits those of the King-Crane Commission usually wore, and they carried fuel, water, and other provisions with them. Following cart paths and sheep trails as they traveled east through half a subcontinent, they often had to haul their Fords across rivers or up mountain slopes, or build the roads ahead of them. Rather than check into tourist hotels, they camped by clear-running streams "under the full splendor of an Eastern moon," and were occasionally disturbed by passing caravans. Twice they faced the muskets of local brigands, some of whom ran off with a couple of cars at one point, but then decided better of it. A King-Crane commissioner delighted to dabble a hand in the Jordan River, but Harbord one day invited his men to swim with him in the remote, icy headwaters of the Euphrates.[42]

The two commissions, of course, interviewed many of the same people and considered some of the same problems. Among the main issues the political commissions were charged with were, first, what to do with "suffering Armenia" (in whatever way "Armenia" was to be defined geographically, a greatly vexed issue), and second, whether to recommend that America take on a "mandate" or not: that is, whether the United States should commit, for a considerable period, to govern the affairs of Armenia, or Turkey, or both. Most Americans in Turkey (including Admiral Bristol) thought America should take on a mandate of some sort, and friends of the Armenians thought the country should take on a mandate for Armenia only. One important pronouncement to the contrary was made by Robert College president, Caleb Frank Gates.

—◆◆◆—

Gates made his own relief investigation into southern Turkey by train, traveling along with James Barton, head of the organization that would become known as the Near East Relief, and Gates' son, Moore. On his return to Constantinople, Gates dismayed many friends by saying that the Armenians were asking too much. Referring to a pamphlet that included demands for an independent Armenia made up of no less than half of Asiatic Turkey, Gates argued that the Armenians not only risked not getting their own nation, but also invited further depredations, especially since there was insufficient Allied power to protect them. Instead of America taking a mandate for Armenia, he thought the country should take a mandate for all of Anatolia, Constantinople and Armenia included.[43]

Gates considered that to create an Armenia out of a part of Turkey and leave in existence a Turkey governed just like the one that had gone before would be catastrophic. The idea that Turks would become subject to armed Armenians, already suggested by talk of an independent Armenia and by the French bringing some Armenian legionnaires into Cilicia, was creating defiance. Gates argued further that "a malefactor who is afraid for his life, is always the most dangerous kind of criminal." Hence, if the Armenians were to be given rule of Turks in any provinces where the Armenians were in the minority (which, especially after 1915, was virtually everywhere in Turkey), the Turks could and probably would "butcher the Armenians" yet again.[44]

Gates possessed great credibility, partly because of his long experience in Turkey and his dedication to Turkish people of all ethnicities, and hence his opinion was considered seriously. King and Crane had spoken to Gates at Paris before embarking on their journey. Although Gates had left for America before Harbord's group was organized, the general would have heard Gates' position cited at every hand, and no doubt had read the educator's statements as well. However, in contrast to Gates' call for a universal mandate, at least one voice of equally great credibility cried for a sharp separation of the Armenians from the Turks. Like Walter George Smith before them,[45] both the King-Crane and Harbord commissions were most impressed by Mary Louise Graffam, the indomitable American missionary who had remained at Sivas throughout the war (deep in Turkey's interior), who not only had witnessed 25,000 Armenians "walk over the bridge" at Sivas in deportation, but who also had accompanied her beloved students for over a hundred miles of their journey until forcibly turned back by Turkish authorities. Then she insisted on staying in Sivas despite Turkish threats on her life and the deaths of three of her companions from typhus.[46] Eventually, she earned even the local Turks' great respect.

Graffam had earlier declared to Smith that the Turks should be allowed no political domination, or the massacres would recur.[47] She was just as frank in her comments to the King-Crane Commission, for which she briefly recounted her own experience: "I went out with a party of three thousand. After one day the men were all gathered out, shut into a stable for the night, and killed the next morning. The despair and horrors were hard to imagine. The younger boys were massacred later. Women were stripped and searched for money, practically all disappeared." Now maybe some 10,000 or 20,000 Armenians out of an original 80,000 through the entire Sivas region had drifted back.

Graffam acknowledged some arguments on the side of keeping Turkey together, but she was most fervent that the Armenians had suffered too much at the hands of the Turks for this to be a solution. The prospect of having a nation of their own was offering the Armenians some fragile hope; without that, she feared the Armenians would lose their faith. Graffam quickly dismissed the facile arguments being put out, some of them apparently being made by the American admiral: "Admiral Bristol speaks of [the] establishment of justice. How can you have this? An Armenian comes back, his women are in one Turkish house, his rugs are in another, and the Turks hold his lands. Give them some kind of an Armenia and *then* say let bygones be bygones. Otherwise the Armenians will drift into brigandage *and I will too*. It is *past human imagination* to leave them together."[48]

Such statements were striking. However, General Harbord preferred to test character and assertions by personal observation, and this was made possible to an extent by his mission's penetration into the heart of eastern Turkey and Armenia. Harbord said later that many documents he had read were so lurid that "in another cause [they] might have been classed as propaganda," but he found the witnesses unimpeachable when he met them "on the ground."[49] The character of the American missionaries (like Graffam) he had met particularly impressed him, especially those who had endured the great Armenian trials: "Their experiences and devotion in the massacres of 1915 and those that periodically preceded them, are quite beyond any words of mine. There is nothing in my knowledge of history that quite corresponds to them."[50]

Not only the heroism of the recent past but also the daring of the present caught his eye, such as that of the young Near East Relief worker he personally noticed "up in the hills, away from every Occidental sign . . . a laconic American youth maneuvering an unwieldy truck over roads built only for camels and donkeys." Similarly, when he came across two Smith College graduates in Malatia, miles from any foreigners, running an orphanage for seven hundred children despite not speaking Turkish, he marveled to see the young women's confidence and unconcern.[51]

Of course, the general also formed his own opinions of the condition of the distraught locals he met and talked with in camps and in "rescue homes for women" (which had been set up by the British in many cities when they occupied Anatolia) and later of the actual "starving Armenians" he witnessed lying by the roadside in Armenia, too weak even to stand. Members of the King-Crane Commission had visited Armenian refugees in a camp in Aleppo—"an unpromising lot of seed corn for the future Armenian nation," Albert Lybyer reported, "ugly, stupid, diseased, lazy, ragged and wretched—many of these qualities are not their fault—but at the best the outlook is discouraging."[52] Harbord, however, was able to make a comprehensive judgment as to the Armenian character and the impression it made upon others.

The general admired the achievements their history manifested: "They were translators, bankers, scholars, artisans, artists, and traders," and he marveled at the willing martyrdom of many whom a conversion to Islam would have spared. Despite the fact that, as a race, under the Ottomans they had been "forbidden military service, taxed to poverty, their property confiscated at pleasure, and their women forced into the harems of the conqueror," they nevertheless had preserved their religion, language, and even their racial purity. Persecution had brought cohesion rather than disintegration.[53]

Yet he recognized that the race did not always endear itself to others. Even American missionaries, he noted, did not personally like the industrious Armenians as much as they did the "the more genial but indolent and pleasure-loving Turk."[54] And although most American missionaries loved the people they worked with, it is simply true that derogatory comments about the Armenians (and Greeks) can be found in many an American diary or missive. As Russian relief worker Anna Mitchell commented in a letter home, "I do think the Turks are savages, in their treatment of minority populations and perhaps as bad rulers as one can find, but one cannot help being continually impressed by what *unat-tractive* people they massacre!"[55] Harbord himself remained unsure whether the Armenians were ready for self-governance, especially since so many of the best of the race had perished.[56]

Besides that, there was also blood on Armenian hands. "Where Armenians advanced and retired with the Russians, their retaliatory cruelties unquestionably rivaled the Turks in their inhumanity."[57] Harbord had not just talked to Armenians. "Kurds appealed to this Mission with tears in their eyes to protect them from Armenians who had driven them from their villages,"[58] and the Turkish general Kiazim Karabekir pointed out to Harbord the rubble of two houses in Erzerum in which he said Armenians had burned a thousand Turks during the Russian occupation.[59]

Whatever he thought of the truth of the latter claims, in Harbord's eyes the basic fact of the horrendous Armenian massacres and deportations certainly remained unaltered. As the general put it, "Mutilation, violation, torture and death have left their haunting memories in a hundred beautiful Armenian valleys; and the traveler in that region is seldom free from the evidence of this most colossal crime of all the ages."[60] Harbord had personally passed through some of those valleys and obviously had been moved by the terrible things he recognized must have happened, based on what he saw and heard. Yet when one was recommending policy, one had to view the entire situation as realistically as possible.

In yet one other way Harbord's method enabled him to go deeper than the other commission's investigators (to be fair, the King-Crane group had a larger tasking and a much smaller staff). In Constantinople, King and Crane listened to several representative Greek, Armenian, and Turkish groups, including a deputation from the Turkish Nationalists. Most of the Turks spoken with were Westernized ex-government officials, journalists, or professors.[61] On his interior journey, Harbord tended to visit with the leaders themselves: Armenian politicians, Kurdish chieftains, Turkish generals. Most important, at Sivas for two and a half hours Harbord interviewed the man soon to become the most important Turkish leader of the century.

When he met Harbord on September 20, 1919, Mustapha Kemal (later, Atatürk) had more potential than actual power. Still, Harbord, as a military man, was most interested in meeting the man, in part because of the personal example Kemal had set in battle at Gallipoli by his notorious disregard of danger.[62] Here is the gist of Harbord's description: "Mustapha Kemal Pasha is a slight, erect, soldierly looking young man of thirty-eight, with cropped brown mustache, cold gray eyes, light brown hair brushed straight back. . . . His marshaling of his facts through the interpreter was orderly and logical. . . . His personality easily dominated his associates of the committee."[63] Kemal discussed the origin of his movement, his respect for the sultan, but also his insistence on the integrity of the Ottoman empire. The possibility of an American mandate over Turkey being brought up, Kemal said the Nationalists liked the idea of a "disinterested great power, preferably America" taking a mandate. However, Harbord rightly discerned what some later historians also recognize, that Kemal had no interest in any real foreign supervision, no matter whose: "Their idea of a mandate differs from ours, however, in that they conceive it as advice and assistance from a big brother, with such slight exercise of authority as not to interfere with their interior government or their foreign relations."[64] Harbord replied by saying no self-respecting government would take a mandate without complete authority.

Then the general raised the Armenian issue. When Kemal replied that people of other nations also had committed crimes, Harbord said pointedly that "no nation but the Turks stood accused of the murder of eight hundred thousand of its own citizens."[65] So confronted, Kemal countered by discussing the very recent Hellenic Greek occupation of Smyrna.

Back in May 1919, when Walter George Smith and Howard Heinz had just returned to Constantinople from Armenia and before King and Crane had even set out, an event was taking place in the city of Smyrna on the Ionian Sea, Turkey's largest Anatolian city and a major Near Eastern center of commercial

The Nationalist leader Mustapha Kemal. He would become known as Atatürk, or "Father of the Turks." *Thomas Kinkaid collection, The Naval History and Heritage Command*

activity. This action would have historic results far out of proportion to the actual events.

Italian troops had landed in Adalia and were advancing west and north around the Mediterranean coast of Anatolia, apparently bent on occupying areas that they had been promised during the war but had not yet been allotted by the Allies. And so the bosses in Paris, including Britain's prime minister, David Lloyd George; France's prime minister, Georges Clemenceau; and the U.S. president, Woodrow Wilson, decided to ask the *Greeks* (who were nearby with a military force, and whose premier, Eleutherios Venizelos, was quite willing) to occupy the city and adjacent region for them, thereby forestalling the Italians. When informed of the decision, British field marshal Sir Henry Wilson asked Lloyd George "if he realized that this was starting another war"—but Lloyd George brushed him off.[66] Even at the last minute, the captain of the USS *Arizona*—which, along with major vessels from other Allied nations, had been sent to Smyrna as a show of force to help deal with the Italian-provoked crisis—asked the British general on the spot at least to allow a combined American, British, French, and Italian force to do the *initial* occupation before turning Smyrna over to the Greeks. However, the British admiral Somerset Calthorpe insisted on the original plans.[67]

The Greeks occupied Smyrna and the surrounding regions beginning on May 15. It was a huge mistake, not only because the historic antagonism between Ottoman Turk and Hellenic Greek would make this action an enormous insult to virtually all ethnic Turks,[68] but also because the action would abet Greek designs to build a greater Greece stretching into the ethnically Greek populations in Ionia (western Anatolia). It would allow the Greeks a foot into the door of their imperial ambition, so to speak.

In the landing itself, things got out of hand, so that several dozen Turks were killed by Greeks near the docks, and things escalated from there. Capt. J. H. Dayton of the *Arizona* personally noted "promiscuous firing" on the part of the Greek troops, and later reported the ransacking of large quantities of paper money, gold coins, jewels, and watches by Greek soldiers and civilians alike.[69] Things got worse the further you got into the city. Scholars have since estimated that somewhere between two hundred and three hundred Turks were killed both in and right outside Smyrna, along with maybe a hundred Greeks. Many more were killed in outlying regions, some by ethnic Greek civilians, particularly in locations where Turkish oppression had been very brutal.[70] Though the Greek authorities within a couple of weeks exacted harsh punishments upon soldiers convicted of killing or of committing brutalities, news of the Greek occupation and associated bloodshed spread like wildfire throughout

Turkey, being fanned by newspapers, nationalist speakers, even clerics,[71] with associated huge inflation in the number of casualties.[72]

Hence, the recent event enabled Kemal to present Harbord a ready rhetorical response to his posing of the Armenian issue. As Harbord put it, Kemal "deprecated the Armenian massacres but was inclined to balance against them the murders and other atrocities committed by the Greeks at Smyrna."[73]

Of course the notion that there really was any balance between the several hundred Turks who were killed in the brief chaos in and around Smyrna and the many hundreds of thousands of Armenians who had died in the wartime months of organized deportations and massacres through all of Turkey would have been ludicrous. (Nor was there a balance between the respective numbers of guilty, either, the deportations having been "a gigantic plundering scheme" as well as a method of race extinction, as Consul Jesse B. Jackson of Aleppo, Syria, had once written Morgenthau, and hence directly involving a significant segment of the population.[74]) However, in his article describing this interview, rather than point out the disparity of Kemal's rhetoric, Harbord chose instead to comment on how the occupation of Smyrna by the Greeks had awakened the Turks and made for great potential danger. As Harbord put it, the Smyrna occupation had "cheapened every Christian life in the Turkish Empire."[75] In this, the general was unquestionably correct.

Harbord walked away from the interview recognizing some bluff in the Nationalists but also perceiving "a sincere patriotism" in its leader and certainly a power to be reckoned with. He warned specifically that Mustapha Kemal was "no cheap political adventurer."[76] On his part, Kemal would remember General Harbord with respect. Harbord's was the first official interview of the Nationalist leader by an American since Kemal began to make noises in Anatolia,[77] and the general could offer this valuable glimpse of a key personality precisely because he had put himself physically so deeply into Anatolia.

⎯◆⎯

Once the American commissions had heard the depositions, taken all the statements, and finished their interviews, they drafted their reports. In the end, though the specifics and reasonings differed (King-Crane endorsed a separate Armenia), both of these political commissions recommended that America take a mandate. However, Harbord's way of listing fourteen reasons *for* a mandate versus thirteen *against*—the thirteenth negative point being an estimate of the anticipated monetary cost, *some $756 million* over five years, hardly small change[78]—confused many readers as to what Harbord was actually recommending.[79] From one point of view it doesn't matter much, as both reports were shelved (partly because of President Wilson's sudden illness), and Harbord's was brought out again only when there was little chance of the mandate's passing.

However, particularly in view of twenty-first-century adventures of America into the Middle East, it is important to know what Harbord was actually about. Reading his conclusion carefully and his articles as well, there's no question Harbord was recommending a mandate, but the general also wanted to make sure the American people knew the costs, including the moral ones. He pointed out that there was one great "faith" in the Near East, which only someone who had been there could fully appreciate. The faith "held alike by Christian and Moslem, by Jew and Gentile, by prince and peasant in the Near East" was faith in and respect for the United States.[80]

It was true. In contrast to the "ugly American" image so widespread half a century later (which dogs America even to this day, especially in the Middle East), almost every visitor from the States after World War I was struck by the admiration shown widely by Turkish and other Near Eastern people for Americans. No doubt this partly resulted from the work of the missionaries and relief workers, including (especially) the evenhanded relief they offered during famine and other catastrophes. Harbord thought this admiration was very gratifying. But should America take a mandate, the general pointed out, the burden "would have to be carried for not less than a generation under circumstances so trying that we might easily forfeit the faith of the world."[81] In other words, taking up the mandate would mean a major commitment, and a commitment of the heart.

Despite this warning, Harbord's unopposed fourteenth point is the critical one, and the fact that his fourteen points *for* the mandate correlated to President Wilson's fourteen points is seldom remarked. That last point reads like this: "Here is a man's job that the world says can be better done by America than by any other. America can afford the money; she has the men; no duty to her own people would suffer; her traditional policy of isolation did not keep her from successful participation in the Great War. Shall it be said that our country lacks the courage to take up new and difficult duties?"[82] From another perspective, the general thought the key issue was very simple. His thirteenth point *for* the mandate was the question of Cain, which the Christian Harbord (no doubt like many a missionary) thought was the major question to be asked: "Am I my brother's keeper?"[83]

Thus, the general's principled idealism, though balanced against a frank assessment of costs, resembled the idealism and Christian charity of Smith and Heinz, Gates, and the young relief worker with his truck on that mountain; of the two Smith College girls off alone with their orphans; and of Dr. Charles

King, too, the principal author of the other report. It was also characteristic of the Americans who had just won the war; who were a generally moral and relatively religious but also grandly optimistic people; who, like the world, were under the great influence of Woodrow Wilson; and who were all filled with hope that a new era was beginning. This committed idealism was not fated to be realized in Turkey or anywhere else in the Near East. And no doubt, like the views of American authorities in our time recommending (indeed, *successfully* recommending!) American incursions into the always-simmering powder keg of the Middle East, the American idealism of that day was in many respects naïve.

But as the Armenian genocide of 1915–16 had shown already, and as similar terrible events of the postwar period chronicled later in this book will also indicate, if any region on earth needed a far-seeing and committed tutelage in justice and love, or merely in basic humanity, it was the Turkey of 1919.

CHAPTER 3

THE ADMIRAL, THE EMBASSY, AND THE CRISIS IN CILICIA

I am holding no brief for any race in the Near East. I believe that if the Turk, the Greek, the Armenian, the Syrian, etc., were shaken up in a bag you would not know which one would come out first, but probably the Turk is the best one of the lot.

—Mark Bristol

Prior to assuming his post at Constantinople, Admiral Mark L. Bristol's background on the Near East (what we generally call the Middle East) seems to have consisted mainly of three things: a quick meeting with naval authorities in Paris, a hurried reading of Ambassador Morgenthau's book while en route to the city,[1] and a conversation he had at some point with a former American missionary. The missionary had been convinced that none of the Near Eastern races knew the difference between right and wrong, a conclusion Bristol was to trumpet with conviction again and again. In other words, Admiral Bristol had been assigned his post not because he knew anything about the Near East, but simply because he was a well-regarded naval officer of the proper high rank.[2]

Just over fifty when he received his orders, Bristol had already spent over thirty years in the Navy, twenty-one of them at sea. Besides taking one of the last Navy cruises under sail round Cape Horn, he had served on every class of battleship, done tours on all principal American naval stations, and performed substantial gunnery and torpedo work. He was aboard *Texas* at the Battle of Santiago, and served as executive officer of *Connecticut* during the cruise of the Great White Fleet.[3] Though the cruiser he thereafter commanded in 1911 went aground near the South China coast, he survived this possible career ender, apparently on the intervention of high-placed friends.[4] Just before

American's entry into World War I, Bristol had served energetically as director of naval aeronautics, this in naval aviation's earliest days. He consistently played down the theoretical capabilities of aircraft carriers in favor of his beloved battleships,[5] but he wasn't alone at *that* mistake. During World War I, Bristol commanded a cruiser and finally, for several months, a battleship.

The admiral had a reputation for industry and forcefulness. When American civilians met him in Constantinople, they were impressed with the tremendous determination seen in the set of his jaw and the immensely broad shoulders of this short, barrel-chested man. Some American diplomats liked him for his "square, bluff, straight-forward" manner, but one of them also noted that he did not seem to know when to stop talking.[6] A young officer reporting to the Turkish station in 1922 was impressed by the admiral's general affability, despite the "aggressive scowl" that he noticed the admiral could instantly assume. Consul George Horton of Smyrna pointed to "the sheer magnetism of his genial and engaging character," which typically created a school of admirers and disciples.[7] Not surprisingly for a naval flag officer, the admiral was quite at home with the social dimensions of a diplomat's life.

Bristol hoisted his flag on the embassy station ship USS *Scorpion* in late January of 1919. However, finding this yacht's quarters inconvenient either for work or entertainment, he soon moved into the U.S. embassy in Pera, a building complete with "marble galleries and naked ceiling nymphs." Soon he would place a radio station in the embassy that would afford him regular and confidential communications both with his ships throughout the region and with Washington. From the embassy he fought hard with superiors to secure a battleship. After all, the British, French and Italians all had battleships in the straits—why shouldn't the United States? Among other things, one of these great vessels would also provide a good place to show movies, and thereby help distract his sailors from the notorious local vice districts.[8]

He never got a battleship, although for a couple of years a cruiser was routinely assigned to him. More than a flagship, though, Bristol desperately needed destroyers. After all, he had charge of all American naval activities in the Aegean, the Black Sea, and the eastern Mediterranean—a very large area of operations—and all he had initially (besides the *Scorpion*) were two converted yachts and some subchasers. Within a couple of months, Bristol got a few of these fast and quite versatile small combatants, and the number of destroyers assigned him increased somewhat as time went on. Moreover, over the first year and a half or so of his duty in Constantinople, no fewer than forty-five American naval vessels called briefly at the city, two of them battleships.[9]

Bristol saw to naval logistics, worked to get an effective staff, visited the panoply of Allied, Turkish, and Levantine officials in this great city, and regularly kept

In early 1919 Admiral Mark L. Bristol was named commander of a small detachment of American naval forces being sent to Turkey; shortly thereafter he was put in charge of the American diplomatic staff at Constantinople, as well. *U.S. Naval Institute Photo Archive*

the State Department informed about conditions throughout the region. He disposed his ships so as best to aid all the Americans who, after the war, were now scattering throughout the Middle East and the Caucasus (particularly relief workers and missionaries), and soon he was also providing a destroyer to an American admiral acting as an observer with the beleaguered White Russian Army in southern Russia. Since it was sometimes difficult to communicate to the rest of Europe directly from Constantinople, Bristol regularly stationed a destroyer at a port in Romania or Bulgaria as a radio relay ship. In Constantinople itself, Bristol succeeded in getting American organizations such as the Near East Relief and the Red Cross to cooperate, and thereby to conserve efforts.[10]

He also helped such organizations in other ways. For instance, commercial wire services were expensive and open to foreign scrutiny, so the admiral opened Navy circuits to many American groups. At one period the Navy was said to have handled two thousand messages a day.[11] This service could be a bit problematic to the sender, to be sure. Anna V. S. Mitchell, who worked with Russian relief, discovered that although the admiral would let the Red Cross send cables on Navy circuits, he proved "anxious to get in his own special point of view." On some occasions, the Red Cross chose to bear the commercial expense rather than the admiral's agenda.[12]

Meanwhile, friction developed between Bristol and the leading American diplomatic holdovers from before the war, that is, Commissioner Lewis Heck and Consul General G. Bie Ravndal. Their respective lines of authority were ill defined, and Bristol wanted complete control. Moreover, Bristol regarded his unimpressive initial title "Senior Naval Officer Present" as a hindrance in dealing with the Allied "High Commissioners" at Constantinople. Eventually, by force of personality, he imposed his will on Commissioner Heck, several years his junior and very ill at the time, and also persuaded prominent Americans in the city to write letters to the State Department on his behalf. Friends in Washington also intervened. After six months, Bristol was appointed America's "High Commissioner" to Turkey.

Although a State Department official then refused to make Bristol "the big chief of our Consuls" in the area, nevertheless the admiral could now settle into his assignment (before this, he had talked of resigning), for he had become both the senior American naval officer in waters east of Greece and the senior American diplomatic official in this same region and was provided with two separate organizations (naval and diplomatic) to assist him.[13] To be sure, his new title and his commensurate responsibilities did not ensure either equivalency with the Allies or cooperation. At Paris the United States was a full partner with the Allies; here Bristol was left out. Americans neither provided members of the city's police force (as the Allies did), nor had any part in giving the sultan his orders. Of course Americans had also played no part in the disarming of Turkey, something done by the occupying British army (all this, again, because America had never declared war on Turkey).

Nor, later, did the United States have any role in the sudden imprisonment of a hundred Nationalist leaders and the Allied occupation of the Turkish ministries, post office, and telephone and telegraph offices, actions that would take place simultaneously on March 16, 1920.[14] By arresting Nationalist Turkish agents and formally imposing martial law, the Allies hoped to thwart growing Nationalist power. Concurrently, thousands of British, French, and Italians troops moved into Constantinople itself and the nearby straits, each of these powers overseeing a special zone of the city. In contrast, American military forces in the area never exceeded the small number of Navy men manning the American naval ships actually in port—no more than about half of which were available for landing forces, at best a few hundred in all.

Finding himself uninvited to the Allies' deliberations and frequently complaining he was uninformed about Allied actions,[15] Bristol retaliated both by symbol and by action. For example, he ordered his ships' crews not to render the traditional honors to the yachts of the Allied high commissioners (manning the rails and saluting),[16] and he refused to be bound by Allied decisions. In such ways Bristol offended the British, who sometimes responded in kind. On one July 4th, the British admiral Sir John de Robeck was said to have sailed his whole fleet down into the Sea of Marmara rather than be forced to honor America's independence by dressing ship.[17]

More important, the British early on developed a very dim view of Bristol's personality. During the period in which he served in Constantinople, British diplomat Neville Henderson found the "pugnacious" Bristol "the greatest thorn" in the British high commission's side.[18] The British high commissioner, Sir Horace Rumbold, once wrote the British foreign minister that Bristol possessed "limited intelligence and outlook." From London, Lord Curzon agreed. "We have had abundant proof for nearly 2 years that he is suspicious, anti-British, stupid, and at times malignant. You must be careful with him, for he reports everything in an unfavourable spirit." The British also thought Bristol flattered the Turks,[19] but if so, he was just returning the favor. In a travel book about his journey through Europe in 1919, American journalist Alexander Powell remembered the amusement of the European colony in Constantinople as they observed the Turks "rushing" the rear admiral as fraternity members would rush a desirable freshman. On his own part, Powell expressed wonderment at the "dogmatic opinions" spoken by certain Americans "on subjects of which most of them were in abysmal ignorance prior to the Armistice," that is, only a few months before. For Bristol, this description was a perfect fit.[20]

—◆◆◆—

However, although certainly dogmatic and also chronically suspicious of British actions,[21] Bristol was not unintelligent. He simply had a different agenda than the British and an opposing one, or rather, two related agendas.

First, he was determined to fight Allied monopolization of commercial opportunities. Vice Admiral William Sims had directed Bristol to safeguard American interests,[22] and Bristol thought the most important American interests were commercial rather than humanitarian, educational, or religious, even though support of the missionaries had traditionally played a controlling part in American foreign policy toward Turkey. By favoring business, of course, Bristol was also supporting what was known as the "Open Door" policy, an agenda intended to give American firms a fair opportunity to compete for overseas markets. "Helping trade was the admiral's pride," Bristol's aide, Robbie Dunn, later wrote,[23] and it was simply true. The pages of Bristol's war diaries, long daily summaries of each of his afternoon conversations, bristle with records of the admiral's conversations with businessmen of all kinds, particularly Standard Oil people, but also bank representatives, shipping agents, tobacco company men, and various salesmen bent on opening new markets. In 1921 America had a steamship line, two trading companies, and two banks doing business in Turkey, and another fifteen to twenty firms had representatives there, most of them unknown before the war. Much of this was a result of Admiral Bristol's efforts.[24]

Bristol also regularly wrote to business acquaintances back in the States, and he frequently wrote the State Department on commercial topics,[25] always with the same themes: the United States needed overseas markets; Allied barriers to American trade in Turkey and elsewhere should be torn down; American firms must employ Americans only; American banks, shipping firms, and merchants of all sorts should come to Constantinople. Bristol spoke to local businessmen at the American Chamber of Commerce for the Levant and at the embassy itself. He was always available to offer salesmen tips, or to provide general pep talks on trade, that is, on his support of American business interests "first, last, and always." In fact, Bristol promoted "the gospel of American trade" at every opportunity.[26]

Beyond this, Bristol offered businessmen very specific help in pushing the level of trade reached in 1920 to over ten times the level that had obtained in 1913 (from $3.5 million to $42 million). He successfully fought the sultan's new taxes on importation of whiskey to Constantinople, important for U.S. interests because, despite Prohibition, America provided over 90 percent of the city's liquor imports after the war. Bristol also staved off new consumption taxes on sugar, coffee, petroleum, and tea, most of which also came from the States. And he cooperated with businessmen like retired admiral Colby M. Chester and his son, who for years had been negotiating massively with the sultan (and later would bargain with the Nationalists) for valuable oil concessions to the east.[27]

Individually, Bristol helped American drummers in several ways, some of them unique. Not only did he allow commercial messages on his Navy cables, but he also allowed businessmen access to local information on "crops, minerals, manufacturing, port facilities, trade opportunities, [and] weather data" that he had his officers gather.[28] And he also encouraged salesmen and managers to hop his destroyers virtually to anywhere his ships steamed, by no means the normal naval practice. True, he would offer passage to other Americans, too, particularly relief workers. Some missionaries, a few professors, and a number of journalists also took rides on what became known informally either as "Bristol's Ferry Boats," "The Black Sea Express," or "The Black Sea Express and Mail."[29] Although it was against regulations, American women even rode the destroyers at times. Naval and embassy wives took short pleasure trips (once on *Scorpion*, they steamed even so far as Yalta), while female missionaries and relief workers sometimes were given rides from Constantinople to and from Samsun, Batoum, and other hard-to-reach Black Sea ports.[30]

Still, American businessmen were welcome almost anywhere the "tin-cans" went, and at almost any time. A glance at various documents finds several Standard Oil officials riding *McFarland* from Constantinople to Constanza, Romania; a salesman catching an overnight ride from Beirut to Mersina, a trip that otherwise would have taken him a week; two American tobacco men riding from their business in Samsun to Constantinople and back; and an occasional transport of gold bullion from Constantinople to Smyrna, this to pay for tobacco exported to the United States.[31] If the ship were going to the same port anyway, a businessman could simply pile his suitcase on a junior officer's bunk and his samples on the ship's fantail, and no one would be inconvenienced (except the junior officer). However, on one occasion at least, the captain of *Overton* was told to "take orders from Mr. St. Phelle" of the Baldwin Locomotive Works, a situation in which the ship's support of commercial trade had obviously become a primary, not an incidental duty.[32]

St. Phelle, in turn, wrote home that he could only visit certain regions because he knew Bristol would evacuate him, if need be.[33] Bristol was well aware that business could not thrive in unstable environments, which knowledge was of importance in the development of Bristol's second agenda, a program that offended the British and many of his own countrymen. From almost the beginning of his assignment, the admiral went out of his way to befriend the Turks, both government officials and private individuals in Constantinople, and increasingly the Turkish Nationalists on the mainland of Asia Minor and their confederates within the city. Bristol seems to have concluded early on that a Nationalist takeover would offer the country its best chance to develop the stability it needed to prosper, and to provide a stable market for American goods. If Armenian and Greek businessmen suffered in the process (they often provided tough commercial competition for the Americans), that would not be all that bad a thing.[34]

In all of this, Bristol's motives were not purely commercial. He was idealistic in his way. There is no doubt that the admiral came to "believe" in Turkish nationalism, as did many Americans at one time or another, including not a few missionaries who had suffered under the sultan's despotic rule and from the greed, tyranny, and incompetence of local Turkish officials. In a letter to a friend written as early as December 14, 1919, Bristol commented that the Nationalist movement "is the best thing that has taken place since I have been out here."[35]

Contributing to the admiral's education along these lines were the people he was talking to. Regularly calling on the admiral, for example, was the president of Constantinople Women's College, Mary Mills Patrick. Decidedly pro-Turk herself (as everybody noticed), Patrick also introduced the admiral to Halide Edib, the first Turkish woman to receive a BA from that American college and already highly influential by 1919 as a Turkish writer and speaker.[36] Halide became Bristol's frequent confidant, both in person while she remained in the city, and later by letters and more discreet communication when she fled Constantinople (lest she be interned at Malta by the British along with many other Turks having Nationalist leanings) to join the Nationalist government in Angora (the name of Ankara before 1930). An increasingly liberated Turkish woman of intelligence with strong American connections, Halide was one of the admiral's most trusted inside sources and strongest influences.

Another personal influence working on Bristol was his intelligence officer, Lt. Robert (Robbie) Dunn. Dunn was an interesting character, an "inferior precursor of Richard Halliburton," as Bristol's biographer Peter Buzanski put it.[37] Having once worked as a newspaper correspondent under famous journalist and editor Lincoln Steffens, Dunn very much preferred firsthand reporting, or journalism "in the heat," as it were. He had reported on mountain climbing expeditions from Alaska to Martinique, had ridden with General Pershing in Mexico, had explored the Kamchatka River in Siberia, and during the early days of World War I, with John Reed (later to become infamous as the only American to be buried in Red Square in Moscow; Reed's career was popularized by Warren Beatty's 1981 movie *Reds*), Dunn had jumped in the German trenches to report on the beginnings of the Great War.

Something of a drifter, Dunn "lit out for the territory" more than once. He had grown up in Newport among various naval personalities and had accompanied the world tour of the Great White Fleet as a correspondent, supposedly at Teddy Roosevelt's specific invitation. Hence when America was about to enter the war in Europe in early 1917 and Dunn heard of some destroyers heading for Ireland, he attempted to enlist. Though he was just shy of forty, the Navy let him in. Dunn claimed he had great fun in standing lookout in the North Atlantic (!), and, as a yeoman, in changing "commences" to "begins" every time the first word occurred in several months' worth of engineering logs. His boss, a friend of Dunn's, caught him doing it. "'Commences' is a vulgar latinism, sir," Dunn primly replied. "Well, you put it back on every damned page," said the officer, characteristically valuing naval tradition above beauty.[38]

Then somebody recognized that Dunn was "officer material"—well, he was hardly that, but he did have some useful writing ability. Admiral Sims was said to have admired a story Dunn wrote, and the former reporter suddenly found himself commissioned and transferred to archival work. Stultified, he requested a transfer, and although he did not get that, before long he was working for Sims in naval intelligence. At the Armistice, Lieutenant Dunn took the advice of a friend to ask to accompany Adm. Mark Bristol to Turkey.[39]

In Constantinople Dunn was Bristol's first lieutenant by name, but really was his intelligence officer. Dunn delighted in learning the spy trade while snooping around in the dives of Constantinople, a city with enough tricks, secrets, and vice to satisfy the most ravenous appetite. But Bristol also sent this one-time mountaineer out and about, allowing him to use his own judgment as to what he did and, often, where he went. Hence, in the summer of 1919, upon the admiral's direction, the adventurous Dunn traveled from the Caucasus through Armenia to the north coast of Turkey and back to Constantinople, almost entirely without escort. Dunn found the countryside aflame with Turkish anger at the recent occupation of Smyrna. He also heard of the revolutionary Nationalist Congress of Erzurum, soon to assemble. Although he did not then meet Mustapha Kemal (or any leading nationalists), early on Dunn formed a most favorable opinion of the Nationalist leader and his cohorts.[40]

Back home, Dunn waited while the admiral read his report. Bristol's response is recorded in Dunn's memoir *World Alive*, most of the Turkish parts of which were probably written only a year or two after the events. "Do you think, Dunn, that this Turkish national movement is an honest thing?" Dunn reports the admiral asking: "How sincere?" When Dunn replied, "Damn yes, I do," the admiral looked out the window. "I've been wondering quite a while. . . . You know, I think this man Kemal is *right*."[41]

In Dunn's description, it is certainly possible to see some sincerity on Bristol's part. The American naval professional finds himself offended at constant abuse of the local (Turkish) officials by arrogant Europeans. He notes also the incursion of a Hellenic Greek army onto the mainland, and, remembering his own country's revolutionary origins and its democratic principles, responds warmly to native patriotism.

Sincerity, however, is not necessarily wisdom. Local British officials typically regarded reactions of the kind described here as terribly naive, as being conditioned by a lack of knowledge of the nature of the prewar and wartime Turkish Committee on Union and Progress (colloquially known as the "Young Turks"), for example, and of the general political history of Turkey's last ten or fifteen years. British High Commissioner de Robeck, for instance, thought the Americans in particular were "'green', easy for the Nationalists to spoon-feed, and ready to rise to such catchwords as independence and self-determination."[42] He was no doubt referring primarily to Bristol and his naval aides, and perhaps diplomatic staff members like Allen Dulles, too.

Surely most Turks were genuinely upset with the prospect of Greeks ruling over Turks, which seemed to be the implication of Smyrna. The prospect of vengeful rule by the previously abject and gravely injured Armenians also bedeviled them. Unquestionably, Nationalist leaders were determined to prevent any such reversal of roles. Such an intention, however, would say nothing about the character of the people, or the character of the Nationalist movement itself, which was still very much in the making, anyway. In America at about this same time, many Southern whites would have gotten enormously upset if they thought blacks were getting the upper hand, but the Ku Klux Klan hardly rates a positive assessment. That the Turk of the day was a "Near Eastern Ku Klux Klan," by the way, was a contemporaneous assessment of the Harvard professor Albert Bushnell Hart.[43]

To his credit, Bristol did recognize the importance of Kemal's movement long before the Allies did.[44] However, such an early taking of the cudgels for the Nationalists with so little to go on would not only have been premature, but would have been very dangerous. Whatever the basic character of Mustapha Kemal himself, for instance, he was in those early days, and actually for a considerable time, at least the companion and perhaps partly the creature of many cutthroats. As just one example, Kemal's bodyguard beginning in late 1920 and apparently extending as far as early 1923 would be provided by Osman Agha, or "Lame Osman," a notorious leader of irregulars who, according to Kemal's recent Turkish biographer, was "a sadistic ethnic cleanser of Armenians and

Greeks," a description that documents in the Bristol papers amply confirm. It would take three years before some of Kemal's associates would murder Osman on Kemal's behalf (though perhaps without his knowledge), and thus rid the Nationalist leader of an increasingly inconvenient association.[45]

In any case, Bristol's approval of the Nationalist movement was sometimes manifested in very dramatic fashion. We've noted above how Bristol shared his musings with Dunn; he then had the deeply pro-Turkish lieutenant draft many of his memos to the State Department. Sometime later, the admiral spoke memorably of Mustapha Kemal to the whole naval staff. Naval officer Webb Trammell was one of Bristol's destroyer captains, but also at one point he became his aide at the embassy. Trammell told the following story to his son: "One day Bristol came downstairs. . . . He announced to the staff that he had had a dream. In the dream the Turks had won the war of independence, and would become an independent country (and more), and 'Gentlemen, it will be our work to see that this comes true.'"[46] Whenever this dream occurred (if it wasn't simply a strategic fiction on the admiral's part), it probably grew out of the admiral's nightly ruminations about the Turkish situation.

We need not depend only on anecdote, of course. The fact that Bristol was pro-Turk in matters having to do with the Christian minorities in Turkey (these were ethnic Armenians and Greeks, for the most part), though sometimes contested by scholars desiring to present the admiral as an objective witness of events,[47] can be further illustrated both by testimony and the admiral's own conversations.

As for testimony, consider just a few of many possible citations from both American and Turkish sources. In diaries jotted down in mid-1919 while serving with the King-Crane Commission, Albert Lybyer noted that the admiral was "very sympathetic" with the Turks as opposed to the Greeks, and that, conversely, Bristol disliked both the Armenians and the British. In time for the 1922 publication of his book *Speaking of the Turks*, the Turkish author and propagandist Mufty-Zade Zia Bey pointed out that the American high commissioner and his assistants were "more liked" by the Turks "than any other foreigner in Turkey"; in contrast, Zia Bey thought, it would be better to rid Turkey of many of the American missionaries. Edgar Fisher, professor of history at Robert College, had "gained sidelights" of Bristol's views before, but when in April of 1922 he heard for the first time Bristol's "thoroughgoing exposition of the Turkish situation as he saw it," Fisher was "astonished and amazed" at the extent and depth of Bristol's pro-Turkish views. Although Joseph Grew liked

Bristol when he met him at the Lausanne Conference in January of 1923, he noted that he found Bristol "very pro-Turk."

Finally, the Turkish journalist Ahmed Emin Yalman ran the Turkish paper *Vakit* in Istanbul from 1917 to March of 1920, at which point he was imprisoned by the British for his Nationalist sympathies. He later reported he had turned down the car Bristol had offered him to aid his escape, lest it embarrass the admiral that Bristol appear so supportive of the Nationalists. In his memoir, this University of Columbia-educated journalist (reportedly the first Turkish citizen to receive a PhD in the United States) concluded that Bristol's "activities from the beginning to the end of our struggle for independent national existence amounted, in effect, to almost an informal alliance between Turkey and the United States."[48]

As for Bristol's own statements, most revealing is his favorite analogy, his comparison of relations between the Christian minorities and the Turks to those of a small boy stirring up a hornet's nest. Typical of such conversations is his discussion with an Armenian delegation from Cilicia that came to the American embassy in October of 1920 with complaints about a recent French agreement that would force many of the Armenians out of Turkey entirely. Bristol attempted to demonstrate to this group that the contemporaneous circumstances were primarily the Armenians' and the Europeans' fault:

> I informed them that the present conditions in Turkey, which were more or less the same all over the country, were, in my opinion, like a hornets' nest that had been stirred up by a small boy who could not defend himself against the hornets and was calling upon his father to come save him. At the same time this same boy had been warned by his father of the dangers of stirring up a hornets' nest and, in addition to that, had seen people that had been stung before by the hornets and yet he persisted in stirring up the hornets' nest. The hornets' nest, in this case, is Turkey with the Moslems as hornets, and the small boy is composed of the Christian races and the Allies, together with the [Hellenic] Greeks. . . . Therefore, it seemed to me that this small boy should be treated in much the same way that the father treated his son and that is, the father spanked the son for disobeying his orders and also for showing such little common sense.

The admiral made this analogy again and again in his conversations and correspondence, although sometimes the Turks with their "brutal instincts and fanatical ideas" became a ferocious bull, or a pack of mad dogs. The point, of course, was that by claiming independence, or by bearing weapons, or by listening to the Allies' encouragement, or indeed by asserting themselves in virtually any way at all, the Armenians and Greeks were responsible for the suffering that they themselves had endured (though usually in Bristol's pronouncements the European Allies bore responsibility, too—as surely they did).[49]

No doubt, from one standpoint, Bristol had a case. If, as we will shortly see, the French were not to commit enough troops to Cilicia (south-central Turkey) in attempting to take over that region, and the Armenians there had no force of their own, any actions that either group was to take in defying the Turks in that area could well be regarded as imprudent—indeed, as suicidal. However, there being no good assurance (and about a million bad assurances) that bowing passively to the Turks in early 1920 would have saved the Armenians in the various cities of Cilicia, one could argue that at least this time the Armenians would have *gone down fighting*. (Americans like Consul Leslie Davis of Harput not only blamed the Armenians for their general baseness, but also for their general lack of "heroism" in 1915.)[50] James Barton once commented that Bristol seemed to blame the Armenians for their *not trusting the Turks*. Bristol was absolutely right about that: they didn't. However, they had no good reason for such trust. Eventually, when the French made an agreement with the Nationalists and completely withdrew into Syria, virtually all Armenians remaining in Cilicia, absolutely panic-stricken, left the country too—*tens of thousands* of them. (Those who didn't leave were unsubtly encouraged to go.)[51]

However, not only was Bristol always blaming the Armenians for bringing upon themselves their massacres and deportations—as an American teacher at Constantinople Women's College once put it[52]—but by his typical analogies, he was, of course, also excusing the Turks. Notice that the primary focus the admiral's analogy is on the *boy's* actions, and not on those of the hornets. The ferocious bulls or mad dogs or angry hornets all being amoral creatures, such analogies conveniently leave the Turks out of the moral equation. Obviously, it is one thing to blame somebody for dealing foolishly with hardened criminals—for arousing their fierce instincts without providing protection—and quite another to obscure the criminals' much greater responsibility.

Yes, in his conversations and letters Bristol would customarily begin or end by saying, "I hold no brief for the Turk," and he would also state that he was quite knowledgeable about the Turks' brutal and fanatical instincts, for example, that the "Moslem Turks" would "rob, pillage, deport and murder Christians whenever the opportunity is favorable from their point of view." Then he would often add that he pitied the poor Armenians (or Greeks), or indeed, that "there was no one that sympathized more with them more than I do."[53] Despite such assertions, sometimes very strongly put, the admiral's passion obviously lies in his contentions about Armenian or Allied imprudence rather than in any pity for the victims or horror at the crime, or revulsion at the criminal either. In fact, Bristol continued regularly to treat with the Turks in Constantinople and, increasingly, the Turkish Nationalists in Angora, in very friendly fashion.

—◆◆◆—

Bristol did not behave in this way, however, because he had never seen evidence that the Armenian deportations and massacres had actually occurred. Although Bristol on his arrival in Turkey had not made anything like the tour of mainland Turkey that Barton or Gates did, let alone the arduous junket that General Harbord and his party had taken, he had personally investigated conditions in one location. In March of 1919, two months after he arrived in Constantinople, Bristol rode the converted yacht *Nahma* to Samsun, the major port city on the north coast of Turkey, and filed a report about conditions there. In his report he states that there had been about seven to eight thousand Armenians in Samsun; now there were seven or eight hundred.

Moreover, in the region near Samsun that Bristol visited (he reported making two twenty-mile trips into the country on different days), the Greek and Armenian villages had been "practically wiped out and the villagers driven into the interior. The houses were burned and leveled to the ground." Only 10 percent of these villagers had returned, the admiral wrote, and even those few had "no houses to go to, no oxen or farm implements and practically nothing with which to go to work in the fields." Of all the cattle in the hands of the Turks, probably a great number had been stolen from the Greeks and Armenians. Moreover, reports indicated that Armenian women had been forced to marry Turks and were living in Turkish homes.

Finally, Bristol stated that although some refugee women and children were returning to Samsun itself, "no great influx is expected because the people deported were *taken too far inland*" (italics added).[54] This statement might seem to indicate Bristol thought the deportees were just living elsewhere, perhaps in a more hospitable region (as some Turkish propagandists claimed). However, Bristol certainly knew of the horrors the minorities had suffered. For example, from Samsun he wrote his wife a description of how, at one spot nearby, "Greek women and children were first put in the Turkish bath in mid winter [and] then driven into the country only half alive." These people died "by the wayside of hunger and cold. This was the so-called 'white death.'"[55]

Though Bristol's visit to Samsun took place after the war and at the beginning and not at the end of the deportation trail (down in Aleppo, Syria, American consul Jesse B. Jackson could have shown Bristol in fearful detail what happened when people were "taken too far inland"), the horrific nature of the past events was clear enough to the admiral at the time. Yet the very end of the admiral's letter to his wife, Helen, indicates Bristol might have had some reservations about what his subsequent stance should be: "These massacres were terrible beyond description and yet the Greeks and Armenians are most unattractive and in some ways have irritated the Turks." A year later he made a similar comment: "The Armenians have for centuries suffered under Turkish rule and in recent years have been subjected to massacre, deportations, and many cruelties, but it is useless for any one to disguise to himself the personal characteristics of the Armenians."[56] Massacres terrible beyond description, *and yet.* . . . Massacre, deportations and cruelties, *but.* . . . Clearly the admiral is hedging. A kind of "realpolitik" has begun to take root. "The Armenians are unattractive, and some are provocative. Moreover, there are few of them, compared to so many million Turks. The Kemalists, increasingly powerful, are also 'sincere' . . . and the Turks all seem such good fellows. They trust us Americans, surely they will listen to us and stop any objectionable behavior. . . . Can't we just let 'bygones be bygones'?"

Some such pragmatic naiveté led the admiral to play down the significance of the prewar inhumanities, and of their extensions during the admiral's early tenure to Marash, Aintab, and other cities in the region known as Cilicia.

━━◆◆◆━━

Cilicia is an area of south-central Anatolian Turkey that once had been known as "Lesser Armenia," and had traditionally maintained a large Armenian minority. On November 1, 1919, the British began to hand over Cilicia to the French, because the French had been promised it by secret treaties during the Great War. In this region, the wartime deportations had been severe; in Marash, for instance, of an original population of 30,000 inhabitants before World War I, some 24,000 had been deported.[57] Nevertheless, persuaded by the Allied victory (and Allied and American encouragement), thousands of deportation survivors from Syria and elsewhere had recently returned to Marash and other Cilician cities, several of which were now in the process of being occupied by French armed forces. In Marash, the three thousand-plus troops of the occupying French army had among them hundreds of Armenian legionnaires (some of whom had been recruited at Musa Dagh, the site of a heroic stand of Armenians against Turks during World War I), that inclusion apparently being a thoughtless blunder on the part of the French that inflamed Turkish feelings and provoked several incidents.[58]

With the additional emotional inflammation already being provided by the Greek occupation of Smyrna, not only were feelings running high, but the fledgling Turkish Nationalists were also determined not to accept a French occupation of one part of Turkey any more than they were going to accept a Greek or Armenian occupation of another. Here in Cilicia, Mustapha Kemal would send a trusted colleague, the Nationalist officer, Kuluj Ali (a Kurd), to organize a revolt. Even before he arrived, some Turks in the Marash region had begun organizing against the French in November of 1919. The attack on Marash was to be spearheaded by thousands of *chette* forces (irregulars, or bandit groups, pronounced "che-tah") as well as Turks from within Marash and local villages, rather than by "regular" Nationalist forces (such as they were at this point),[59] most of which would have their hands full elsewhere.[60] Nevertheless, with this Cilician attack, the Nationalist movement was to initiate a major revolution that, over three years, would first crush the army of the fledgling Armenian state far to the east and then eventually succeed in defeating the large invading Hellenic Greek army in the west of Anatolia—these things in addition to eventually bringing about the negotiated departure of the French from the south of that same subcontinent, here in Cilicia.

Not counting the outlying villages, the population of Armenian civilians in Marash (including a variety of Cilicians who had returned after the war from deportation to Syria and settled in this city) was roughly 24,000. A few of these civilians had been organized by the French army to help in a defense of the city. However, only a couple of hundred Armenians actually had been given guns, and the multitude of Armenian civilians in the city were unarmed and unprotected.[61] Besides the Armenians and many thousand ethnic Turkish civilians, also in Marash were some twenty Americans—doctors, relief workers, or missionaries. These Americans went through the entire siege (some also endured the terrible evacuation that followed), and several of them would later write about it. Although, like all other Americans in Anatolia, the American men and women in Marash were under Bristol's orders to be neutral, they were doing most of their medical and relief work under the French umbrella. French guns were set up at the American hospital, for instance, and hence once hostilities opened, the hospital and the Americans inside immediately drew the Turkish fire.[62]

The Nationalist forces began their surprise attack on January 21, 1920. Near midday, rifle fire broke out all over the city, with coordinated fire immediately directed at street intersections and at any French troops who happened to be out and about, after which large sections of the city were put to the torch by Turkish units attempting to get at the buildings occupied by the French. The French responded with a destructive bombardment of Turkish positions.[63] An intense battle went on for twenty-one days, which destroyed much of the city.

Normally very careful not to take part in the battle themselves (except perhaps accidentally to expose themselves while rescuing wounded Armenians), the Americans witnessed or heard of terrible events from every side, including much slaughter of helpless Armenian civilians. Finally, on February 8, an approaching French army relief column made contact with French forces in the city. The Americans and Armenians began rejoicing, and the Turkish forces were about to withdraw when, unaccountably, the French leader decided to withdraw all the French forces, this just at the moment when a victory had apparently been achieved! Emotions quickly reversed themselves. The Turks were ecstatic, while the Armenians (and some of the Americans) were possessed with dread. Maybe three thousand desperate Armenians decided to accompany the French army on its evacuation (a few Americans accompanied them), but a terrible blizzard over that three-day trek would pave the way to the railroad head at Islahiye' with a thousand skeletons.[64]

Meanwhile, the victorious Turkish *chette* continued to slaughter the Armenian civilians whose homes or other places of refuge they overwhelmed, as they had done throughout the conflict. (This was testified to by the Americans in the city.[65]) Upon his announcing the French departure to some Turkish officers, the American missionary James Lyman made a personal plea to Kuluj Ali—that the Turks "stop slaughtering the Christians." The Turkish leader agreed and issued orders to this effect, which helped save the three thousand Armenians in the Franciscan Monastery at Marash, all of them civilians who, upon the French deserting them, were expecting death.[66]

In 1973 Stanley Kerr, a Near East Relief worker who had gone through the siege, published a very thoroughly researched account of the battle he had personally endured over forty years before, naming it *The Lions of Marash* and basing it on all the written accounts he could find, and on many interviews. Overall, Kerr estimated that some eight or nine thousand Armenians within the city itself had died, many of them having been slaughtered or burned in homes or in churches where they had sought protection.[67] Hundreds of French troops and thousands of Turks had died in the battle as well. Moreover, stretching over a couple of months, many Armenians outside Marash also lost their lives. For instance, Kerr interviewed in 1968 a man who had been among nineteen villagers from the village of Don-Kale' who happened to be visiting a market in Marash on January 6. On that day the rest of the four hundred Armenians in their village had been massacred.[68] Overall, among the great ironies of the outcome as noted by Kerr was that many thousands of the Armenians who died at or around Marash had returned to the Cilician city as survivors of the Armenian deportation only a year or so earlier.

Since the Nationalist campaign was regional, other cities in Cilicia witnessed similar events. The small and remote city of Hadjin, for instance, held out against a Turkish siege for several months despite having no French help at all, only to finally fall; ultimately, virtually all of the roughly seven thousand Armenians who had gathered there after the deportations and had dared to resist the attacking Turks were massacred.[69]

At a city called Aintab, though, things were different. For one thing, by April 1, when Kuluj Ali and others (including some of the Nationalists who had fought at Marash) began their assault on Aintab,[70] the events of Marash were well known. For another, in Aintab were found a few Armenians with military experience, including two who had been officers in the English army, and one former lieutenant from the U.S. Army Corps of Engineers. Under the leadership of these and others, the Armenians began to build defensive redoubts on the quiet and to supplement the few guns they had. In this city, the Armenian quarter lay between the Turks and the French, so that the way to attack the French was through the Armenians. But when the Turks attacked this minority quarter, hoping for surprise and planning to catch the Armenians scattered and unwary and "slaughter them wholesale," quickly the Armenians withdrew to their homes, stone barricades descended into position, and gunfire raked key approaches. The attack was stymied; the Turks could not penetrate the Armenian quarter and so could not approach the French.

At the end of May, after seventy days of fighting and the Armenians having foiled repeated Turkish attacks upon them, a temporary armistice was arranged between the Turks and the French. The French agreed to leave the city and its Armenian inhabitants to Turkish control, while the Turks agreed not to bother the Armenians, and—what was almost unheard of—to leave the Armenians *in possession of their arms.* In late July the Turks started fighting again—but now they directed their attention solely to the French, while the Armenians carefully maintained a position of armed neutrality.[71]

Eventually, in February of 1921, the Turks at Aintab surrendered to an investing French force of some 15,000 troops. The heroism shown by the Turkish troops in this battle, part of a campaign that eventually resulted in the complete withdrawal of the French from Cilicia,[72] was later recognized by the Nationalists by their renaming the city "Gazi-Aintab"—Aintab of the Father (the "father" being Mustapha Kemal). The prior and arguably even greater heroism of the Armenians against the Turks was, of course, almost entirely forgotten.

—◆—

Jesse B. Jackson, the American consul at Aleppo, wrote Admiral Bristol and the State Department after the June armistice at Aintab was concluded to applaud the Armenian courage there. He argued that the Armenians had protected not only themselves but also the Americans who had been at Aintab. Admiral Bristol responded with an astonishing statement: "I was very glad to hear the reports of the fight the Armenians put up in Aintab and I think they undoubtedly prevented a massacre or a wholesale killing at that time, but this may only be laying up trouble for themselves in the future. . . . Sometimes discretion is the better part of valor." The absurd notion that the Armenians perhaps shouldn't have tried to defend themselves for it would "make trouble later," despite the decades of past experience as to what happened when Armenians had had no arms, *and in the face of the evident prevention of massacres even on the present occasion*, manifests the deep contradictions of Bristol's policy. In the same letter, the admiral admitted, "The Turks, undoubtedly, want to get rid of the Armenians and will probably exterminate them if they cannot find another means." He resisted the obvious conclusion proposed at the time by Jackson and later vehemently argued by Dr. Marion Wilson (who had been the relief director at Marash), that the Armenians should be allowed to leave the country.[73] Bristol would resist this conclusion again and again,[74] and would be irate when the relief workers and missionaries ultimately (in late 1921) took some part of the situation in their own hands despite Bristol's advice and spirited all their remaining orphans out of Cilicia.[75]

In his reaction to the events at Marash, too, the admiral's correspondence shows a grand disconnect between his preconceptions and the actual events. Originally he argued that there probably had been no massacre at all: "when we get the true facts we will find that the killing of Turks by the French and of French and Armenians by the Turks has been about equal and it was really a fight and not a massacre."[76] The same day in which he wrote that in a letter, he cabled Washington, "It is believed refugees are made up of all classes and races. Armenians are not being massacred by the Turks."[77]

That confused the State Department (which had received reports of massacres from other American sources "closer to the events"),[78] and he had to backtrack. By the middle of March Bristol seems no longer fully able to argue in this case what he consistently said in general, that both sides killed each other equally and indiscriminately. So he fell back on an oft-asserted position, although with reluctance and qualifications. Yes, there had been a massacre of some ten thousand Armenians (but thousands of Turks had been killed, too) and yes, women and children had been killed (but Turkish women and children had been killed too); however, whatever had happened, *the Turks had first been provoked*: "the Turks, during the fighting, had their usual brutal instincts aroused and resorted to massacres of Armenians." He ended this message by inveighing against "exaggerated reports of massacres" and with a plea that "The Turks are human beings however vile their character might be."[79] A year later, despite having by then received damning eyewitness reports from Americans Kerr, Wilson, and others, Bristol had overcome any scruples at all about staying close to the facts, and had reverted to his earlier position: "The so-called massacres of Marash and Hadjin were really indiscriminate killing of each other."[80]

Finally, briefly consider Bristol's response to Americans' witness of events in yet one more Cilician city, in Urfa. In April of 1920, after eight weeks of resistance, nearly five hundred French soldiers and their officers had marched out of Urfa *under Turkish safe conduct*—only to be attacked and massacred in a narrow defile.[81] In August American classicist Francis Kelsey (who was traveling through the Near East on a search for ancient manuscripts, sometimes being transported on Bristol's destroyers) sent the admiral an extract from a letter he had been shown, a letter that had been written by Mary Caroline Holmes, who was in charge of American relief at Urfa.

The morning after the French had made their agreement with the Turks and departed the city, several Turkish officials, including the Mutesarrif (the local governor), had gathered at the orphanage with Holmes and spoken to her about their great vision for a Nationalist future. In the new Turkish republic, they predicted, all Christians and Muslims would be treated alike. As these men were leaving the orphanage, though, Holmes suddenly realized that the Kurdish leader was missing. She took alarm, which increased when she saw loot begin streaming into the city. Urgently she wrote to Lt. Charles Weeden, an American relief worker she called "Sonny," who was elsewhere in Urfa at the time:

> Sonny,
>
> Please come right back at once. The French have been attacked, and the head of one of them is being displayed in the street. Some say that it is that of the Commander, others that it is our dear Marcerou. In coming, go to the Mutesarif, with this letter from me, in which I beg of him to disprove what we have heard, as well as to say a word for yourself. While they were here with all the fine talk, *this awful thing was known to them*. The panic of fear is spreading. Come at once.[82]

What was Bristol's response to Urfa? Three refrains: There are two sides to every story (a frequent Bristol argument); "the Turks did just what one would expect them to do"; and, once more, the French had been the small boy playing with the hornet's nest.[83]

Apparently Bristol had convinced himself that virtually everyone who spoke for the minorities now was exaggerating their past injuries, or that the afflictions they in fact had incurred, no matter however severe, were comparatively unimportant. Surely, the admiral would often argue, although the Turks may sometimes have been just as bad as described, the Christians were not as good as has been made out, and they would be equally bad if opportunity offered.

—◆◆◆—

And of course there were genuine complexities to the Turkish situation. Few Armenians were saints, and there had been bloodshed on both sides. On Lt. Robbie Dunn's first trip through Armenia and into Turkey, while he had heard rumors of Armenian killings of Turks (and vice versa), he only actually witnessed two Tartars assassinate an Armenian peasant.[84] He made no attempt to identify the bones he saw everywhere. On a second trip to Armenia in the Caucasus, however, he had a different experience.

Dunn accompanied an Armenian leader named General Dro and his irregulars during an attack on a Tartar village of some eight hundred residents in the south of "Russian" Armenia, deep in the province of Zangesour, near Persia. There he witnessed these Armenian troops literally massacre the village's inhabitants. Before the attack, Dunn noted that Dro's final appeal to his fighters was neither patriotism nor Christianity but instead "primordial greed." The American was left on the hillside during the onslaught itself, but afterward he was led through the village to see the carnage inflicted on those who had not gotten away. Dunn was understandably sickened by the sights of bayoneted children, the slashed genitals of a slain old man, and Armenian villagers plundering happily. For Dunn this firsthand experience with butchery was a terribly revolting sight, for which General Dro's excuse, "We must keep the Moslems in terror that our cruelty beats theirs," was hardly sufficient. Dunn thought, or hoped, that some of the general's comments and laughs really covered for a sense of guilt. "For somehow, despite my boast of irreligion, Christians massacring 'infidels' was more horrible than the reverse would have been."[85]

Dunn had here had been caught in a terrible feud between Tartars and Armenians that General Harbord had mentioned in his articles, and about which the general had commented, "The Tartars of Azarbaijan . . . are hereditary enemies of the Armenians wherever found, whom they massacre, and who retaliate in kind when possible," an assessment that seems to have been an understatement, if anything.[86] As we have seen that the Armenians had also shed blood and were involved in "the outstanding feature of the political situation in Trans-Caucasia . . . the intensity of racial hatreds" was a qualifying circumstance for Harbord, one which tempered his conclusions about the 1915 Armenian deportations and massacres and subsequent Turkish abuses, but hardly reversed them.[87] He knew that, in Anatolia (as opposed to the Caucasus), with the exception of the short period of wartime Russian advances, very few Armenians ever had significant power to harm the Turks. Over centuries since their original ascendancy, it had been the Ottoman policy to keep the minorities disarmed, and they still were, for the most part. Harbord's personal observation upon his trip through Turkey proper was that "the Armenian, unarmed at the time of the deportations and massacres . . . is still unarmed in a land where every man but himself carries a rifle."[88]

In contrast to Harbord's balanced assessment, Dunn's witness of the raid seems to have substantially jaundiced his viewpoint, perhaps being a major reason he puts quotation marks in his book around reported "massacres" and "rape" of the minorities, and otherwise regularly depreciates Armenian and Greek suffering. "After Zangesour," he writes, "I was callous to the plight of the Christian refugees,"[89] a remark that suggests, of course, that he really knew better. In a passage prefatory to his Zangesour narrative, Dunn spoke about Enver Pasha and certain other Young Turks as having gone into hiding, being under death sentence for murdering Armenians. In his book, which was published posthumously in 1956, Dunn has the harshest possible words for these men. He calls Enver and the others "forerunners of the Nazis convicted of genocide." Unless one thinks Dunn would deny the holocaust, this statement would seem to manifest the writer's recognition of the real nature of the 1915 events, on which an understanding of all later events (and all relations between the Turks and the minorities) must depend. Yet other statements of the author belie this assessment, and his presentation is conflicted.[90]

Anyhow, knowing that the admiral has heard tales like Dunn's account of Zangesour, one sympathizes somewhat with Bristol's frustration when visiting dignitaries would come through Constantinople, having taken a quick trip that seemed only to confirm their original impressions, their perspective having been formed by the slick and extensive public relations campaign on behalf of the Armenians back in the States. Bristol regularly complained about the disproportionate stories being broadcast at home concerning the Armenians, and his complaints were not without foundation here, either.

Although James Barton did not agree that Near East Relief publicity was of this kind, he acknowledged to Bristol that both Greek and Armenian "publicity bureaus" were active in America, and that the one operated by a brilliant but unscrupulous young Armenian named Cardashian was especially troublesome, "constantly reporting atrocities which never occurred, and giving [out] endless misinformation."[91] Thus, some Stateside reports gave a false picture just as the admiral insisted (and there were very few stories put out by anybody about atrocities *done against Turks*). Still, Bristol himself seldom commented on the ludicrous tendencies of *Turkish* propaganda circulated everywhere by billboards, by Turkish newspapers, and in the case of Marash, by the Turkish foreign minister and by Bristol's Turkish confidant, Halide Edib.

About Marash after the French evacuated the city, for instance, the Turkish foreign minister told the Associated Press, "the Armenians there enjoy the protection of the very persons they attacked with such hatred," thus confusing the victims with the aggressors in that episode.[92] Halide's account, sent to the admiral a few days earlier, was in the same vein: "not only [are the Americans] safe [but] the armed and fighting Armenians who have ruined the city, killed Turkish children, violated Turkish women are safe," she reported.[93] In fact, of course, not only had the Armenians there been mostly unarmed, but at Marash months before the battle, civilian Turks had been required by Nationalist leaders to swear to kill their Armenian neighbors.[94] Yet instead of castigating such Turkish propaganda, in his Marash correspondence Bristol consistently weighed in against the credibility of "native sources," that is, reports from Armenians or Greeks.[95]

In sum, besides being biased in favor of the Turks, Bristol was at once vain and naïve. He thought that he had been responsible for the end of the massacres in Marash, for he was coordinating with the Nationalists via Halide Edib about that.[96] (Actually, if any American had helped stop the slaughter, it was the missionary James Lyman, who had successfully pleaded with the Turks on the spot.) And Bristol considered things throughout Turkey could also be ameliorated by similar moral suasion, if only the traditional hatreds (for which all races were equally guilty) could be suppressed, and Kemal could take power, democratic reforms could take root, education develop, favoritism toward Christians diminish, Turkish authorities mellow out, and, especially, if business could get started, American men would lead the way.[97]

<hr>

Anyway, Bristol was certainly putting out his share of effort along these lines. Rising to be at his desk by nine, he dealt with his correspondence before noon.[98] Besides official reports, messages, weekly summaries, advisories to consuls, and letters to naval superiors, he frequently wrote five, six, even ten-page single-spaced letters to a variety of people back in the states, industrialists, businessmen, and college presidents among them. Robbie Dunn expressed amazement at the load of correspondence his idol handled,[99] but Bristol never complained; he was pressing his agenda at every opportunity.

Just before lunch, Bristol put out instructions to his naval staff. In the afternoon, he took an average of five callers and preached his word to them, too. Either later in the afternoon or the next morning he always found time to dictate his war diaries. These diaries indicate that for sightseers or traveling businessmen who stopped in on courtesy calls, besides offering solutions to local problems and offering pointers, the admiral provided a kind of personal publicity bureau on political and social issues. As for VIPs, Bristol would deal with them argumentatively, hearing their experiences and viewpoints and then arguing his agenda in response. (The admiral inevitably becomes the hero of these war diary narratives.) Bristol was not only partisan, of course; indeed, among other things, the admiral should be given credit for aiding dozens of humanitarian causes over the years.

Bristol sent his war diaries back to the State Department every other week, and he required his ship captains to write up their own daily war diaries and weekly intelligence reports about the ports they visited; a selection of these he also sent back to Washington. Through such detailed reports from ports throughout the Near East; by his conversations with American relief people and missionaries and other Americans scattered throughout Turkey, southern Russia, and the Caucasus who often visited with the admiral upon their return; through discussions with American businessmen and representatives of the YMCA and Red Cross; through conversations with ethnic leaders and foreign representatives in Constantinople itself; and through diplomatic and covert contacts, Bristol became one of the most knowledgeable officials in the entire region.

Then, in the evening and on weekends, Bristol and his wife, Helen, set about an extensive social life, including banquets and concerts and tea dances and dinners and the like. No doubt, here too he was learning a great deal, though sometimes indirectly. When Captain Bill Leahy arrived in Constantinople in mid-1921 to take command of the cruiser *St. Louis*, he attended all the receptions, teas, dinners, and dances put on by diplomatic or military officials that he could. Why? He found them vital to his education. Gossip and misinformation about "the game of acquiring from Turkey" was broadcast at such informal sessions like it was nowhere else.[100]

The small diplomatic dinners put on by Clover and her diplomat husband, Allen Dulles, seem to have been comparatively more genteel. Clover's guests were mainly American and British, along with an occasional French couple. For a table of twelve, she spent considerable effort orchestrating the seating to enhance the guests' conversation. Still, Clover seemed to regard the hosting as more necessity than pleasure. She held dinners even in Allen's temporary absence in Paris, but her letters home were much warmer in discussing her charity work.[101] On his part, Allen complained in letters that "Constantinople is rather gay to suit us," pointing out that, in the current season, a Jewish charity ball was followed by an Armenian one, and then by balls put on by each of the various navies, the occupying armies, and so on. "We dodge as many balls as we can but are lucky if we get off with less than two a week."[102]

It was difficult to get away from society too much, though, for the American embassy itself was ever hosting events. Helen Bristol once wrote home that on successive days the embassy was putting on a tea dance for the Russians, a dinner party, a picnic for the YMCA secretaries, and a tea for a Turkish prince.[103]

The American embassy was, in fact, the "height of society," although perhaps a somewhat snobbish society, "made up mostly of navy men who have no manners," Helen Ogden once complained. This YWCA worker was embarrassed to have only one dress to wear for two coming dances at the embassy and one at the women's college, all three in the same week.[104] From another local point of view, American embassy parties might have been considered very *lowbrow*, for Bristol regularly invited Turks to the embassy and made them feel quite comfortable. According to one source, the American embassy was the "first place where Turkish women have ever danced with men."[105] The middle-aged bachelor Cdr. Harry Pence was delighted with that, for he found some of the Turkish girls very beautiful, and quite good dancers, too.[106] The British were scandalized by such fraternization.[107] Robbie Dunn contended that American embassy parties were quite gay precisely "because you saw there people the British barred on grounds of morals, the last thing the rest of Constantinople fussed about."[108] The British, of course, were favoring the Greeks and Armenians as well as the Turks in the sultan's favor rather than the Nationalists.

The admiral's staff members were invited to follow the admiral's lead, and many made good friends among the Turkish elite in Constantinople. At the same time, of course, much of the staff's time was spent escorting prominent American tourists (congressmen, oil barons, and so on) around the city. The staff officers acted as tour guides and sometimes were given special assignments. Lt. John Williams, for example, was tasked to keep liquor away from the artist Chandler Christie, a great lush.[109] Nevertheless, staff members still had plenty of time to enjoy themselves. As a patriotic duty, the bachelors among the young officers sometimes attended parties every night of the week.[110] However hard they partied, though, it was difficult to keep up with the pace of the admiral, who was as "indefatigable" at his social duties as he was at working his political and business agenda. As an admirer pointed out, "The Admiral can dance or play bridge all night, and be at the breakfast table at eight, go through the daily papers, have a French lesson, and be at his desk at nine. And his aides are expected to do the same."[111]

Bristol's naval aides were strongly influenced by their boss in every possible way. Naval officers typically take their lead from their superiors anyway (especially on foreign stations), and career wise it was often dangerous to speak another point of view even if you happened to form one. Hence Bristol's chiefs of staff, first Lyman Cotten and then A. J. (Japy) Hepburn, and other aides like Robbie Dunn, Julian Wheeler, Thomas Kinkaid, and Tip Merrill (most of whom would have big naval roles to play later, between the wars and in World War II) almost always ended up siding with Bristol. An officer reporting to Turkey in 1922 noted that most officers in the command were pro-Turkish and that their opinions caused pain to several American missionaries and relief workers. At Smyrna during the 1922 fire, American consul George Horton was concerned to discover that American naval officers (even high-ranking ones) freely identified themselves as pro-Turkish, even though they were under Bristol's own orders to remain neutral.[112]

Not many such naval officers were serious students of political science or history, of course, and their tours were usually too short for them to develop any depth of local knowledge. Most had been picked not for their diplomatic expertise but for their technical aptitude or administrative talent—or perhaps for their social ability. While serving aboard the destroyer *McCormick*, Lt. Dolly Fitzgerald was rudely informed one morning by an unhappy captain that Fitzgerald had just been temporarily transferred to the *Scorpion*. Fitzgerald then remembered that, a night or two before, Mrs. Bristol had particularly appreciated his ability to play a good hand of bridge. (Bridge was Helen Bristol's great passion.)[113]

The several diplomatic secretaries who reported to work at the embassy—Allen Dulles, Ferdinand Lamot Belin, Howland Shaw, Pierrepont Moffat, and Frederick Dolbeare among them—also usually ended up adopting the admiral's views. The admiral regarded Allen Dulles as a kind of Bristol staffer even when he departed Constantinople in 1922 to head up the Near East Division at the State Department, so closely did their views coincide.[114] In contrast, some American officials did *not* regularly find themselves in agreement with the American high commissioner. Consuls George Horton in Smyrna and Jesse B. Jackson in Aleppo, Syria, frequently had sharp exchanges with Bristol by correspondence. These men were much more sympathetic with the Christian minorities than Bristol was, partly from their decades of experience in the Near East, and Jackson from his specific witness of the wartime deportations. Both their relatively independent status as consuls and their geographical separation from the mesmerizing old Ottoman capital also helped make them less readily persuadable.

Even in Constantinople, some Americans on Bristol's staff or in the wider American community could disagree with him. William Peet was the Constantinople secretary of the missionary board and had long been in charge of the American missionaries scattered throughout Anatolian Turkey. Protection of these missionaries being an important part of Bristol's mission, of necessity Peet and Bristol regularly conferred. Although Bristol's war diaries seem to indicate a general rapport between the two men, in fact they often disagreed. Peet was no doubt very diplomatic in expressing his views, although the older man may also have been cowed somewhat by Bristol's domineering personality. Privately Peet sometimes defied Bristol's policies. In one case, he was so moved

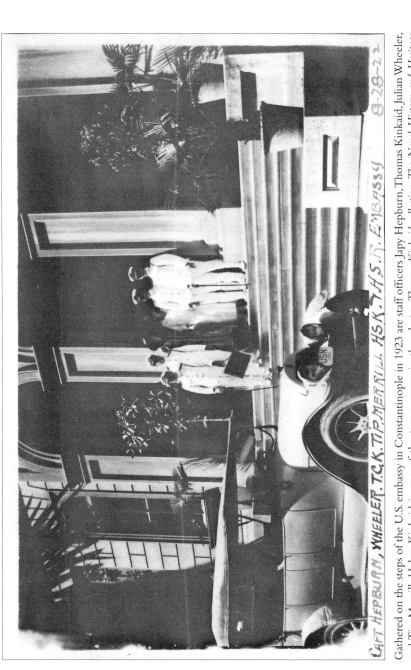

CAPT HEPBURN, WHEELER, T.C.K. TIP. MERRILL, H.S.K., H.S.K. EMBASSY
8-28-22

Gathered on the steps of the U.S. embassy in Constantinople in 1923 are staff officers Japy Hepburn, Thomas Kinkaid, Julian Wheeler, and Tip Merrill. Helen Kinkaid is one of the two women in the photo. *Thomas Kinkaid collection, The Naval History and Heritage Command* by the admiral's lack of support of the minorities and the Americans in the field that, with others, he covertly attempted to have Bristol removed.[115]

Within the Navy and the embassy staff, however, the admiral's power and will were critically formulative, especially buttressed as they were by suave Turkish officials. As Edward Hale Bierstadt was to point out in 1924, "the Turks with whom our naval officers naturally come in contact are, as a rule, men of considerable polish and charm. They believe thoroughly in their cause and are convincing in the presentation of their point of view. Good diplomats, they set out deliberately to please, and they succeed in doing so."[116] Most easily influenced were naval officers who lived right in the embassy and, except for sightseeing tours, almost never got out of Constantinople.

Oral histories narrated toward the end of one's life are often less reliable than contemporaneous letters or diaries about a person's actual experience. It nevertheless remains telling, I think, that, in his oral history, Adm. Julian Wheeler would make the following astonishing assessment about his three years' experience (1921 to 1924) on the American embassy staff: "Throughout my entire period in Turkey I never saw any evidence whatsoever of the so-called terrible Turk. They were an educated, thoroughly charming, delightful, and friendly people."[117]

Wheeler had obviously not heard about that French head on that Turkish pole at Urfa, or if he had read that account, he didn't believe it or the countless similar reports in the embassy files. Wheeler's statement, in fact, speaks volumes about the insularity that tended to infect anybody working in the early 1920s at the American embassy in Constantinople.

CHAPTER 4

THE WHITE RUSSIAN INVASION

Everywhere is brightness, but underneath is the tragedy of a great nation.
Death on his pale horse is ever present on the streets of Constantinople.

—Elizabeth Cotten

In early 1920 the Nationalists seemed to threaten Allied suzerainty in Constantinople and Anatolia in so many ways that the Supreme Council in Paris repeatedly felt called upon to respond. As mentioned above, in March of 1920 the Allies had been so worried about a possible takeover of the Turkish government in Constantinople that they had thousands of British, French, and Italian troops occupy the Turkish capital and concurrently imprisoned many prominent Turks who manifested Nationalist sympathies. About the same time, not only had the Turks attacked the French throughout Cilicia, but in May, Kemal's forces also had the temerity to attack British forces at Ismid, right near Constantinople itself. As a result of the latter affront, the Allies' Supreme Council once again called on the Greek premier, Eleutherios Venizelos, to ask whether the Greek army might intervene in northeast Anatolia. Venizelos promised that his troops could quickly take control of the threatened area, and he ordered them to do so. Greek troops swiftly moved north from the Smyrna region, and (to everyone's surprise) quickly routed Kemal's forces, which retreated east.

That fall, when the two forces met again, once more the Turks were defeated decisively, and the Greeks moved their lines even further east toward Angora. In the late fall of 1920, however, back in Athens, Premier Venizelos failed a plebiscite, and King Constantine took power. By the winter of that year, the Allied support for the Greek army had begun to slacken; indeed, eventually it would become clear that the French and Italians were secretly assisting the Nationalists. Yet, instead of withdrawing his army from Anatolia, King Constantine maintained the offensive after replacing the army's officers with officers of his own. Originally the Greek army had been the tool of the Allies. Although Britain's Lloyd George persisted in supporting the Greeks, increasingly the war had become one between the growing forces of the Turkish Nationalists and the 200,000-man army of the Hellenic Greeks.

Meanwhile, in November of 1920, a crisis occurred in Constantinople itself that for a time drew attention away from events in mainland (Anatolian) Turkey. Virtually overnight, the residents of the city awoke to find over a hundred and twenty Russian, French, and American ships steaming into the straits and anchoring near the city. Nearly 146,000 White Russian refugees were aboard these vessels.[1]

Refugees on some ships were standing, packed so tightly that they could not move. "You realized with a shock, as the morning light grew clearer, that what had appeared at first to be piled-up superstructure was in reality a solid mass of men,"[2] commented an American reporter. Many of these wretched people were half crazy with thirst, having received no food and little water for several days; most had to defecate in place. Americans who boarded the ships reported that the crowding and filth were indescribable.[3] Drawn to these wretches like carrion birds, Levantine boatmen extorted wedding rings, watches, and fur coats in exchange for bottles of water or loaves of bread.[4] Eventually, most would be tended to briefly by the Allies and the Americans (particularly the American Navy), but their numbers would overwhelm a city already occupied by tens of thousands of refugees.

—◆◆◆—

The evacuation from the Crimea that produced these fugitives in late 1920 was one of the last pages of a horrific story, for as it convulsed Russia and inundated Europe, the Russian Revolution also sent successive waves of terrified refugees down the Bosporus.

A few Russians had fled to Constantinople immediately after the fall of the Aleksandr Kerensky government in late 1917. Then, in the spring of 1919, as successive evacuations of Odessa by French and Russian troops had pushed thousands of refugees into the Crimea, some vessels had steamed further south.[5] In April of that year, before traveling on to Hadjin, relief worker Alice Clark had written home about seeing ships carrying thousands of Russians in Constantinople's harbor. Many of these Russians were newly impoverished aristocrats.[6]

For some time afterward, White Russian forces headed by General Anton Denikin fought back against the Reds, but a series of disasters broke Denikin's army. In February of 1920, the wing of the White army under General Schilling fell back on Odessa again and began evacuating its troops on ships steaming toward Constantinople, resulting in yet another panic.[7] In the harbor at Odessa were the American destroyer *Talbot* and later the *Biddle*, one of which was carrying Admiral Bristol's representative, Lt. Cdr. Hamilton Bryan.[8] Bryan watched as snipers fired at the crowds on the docks from nearby houses and then as mobs rushed the Russian transports. Seamen aboard one of these Russian vessels, itself already filled to the gunwales, used machine guns to drive off additional maddened hundreds.[9]

Moved by the people's desperation and incensed at seeing a Greek destroyer hoist a piano aboard instead of evacuees, Bryan commandeered the American merchant ship *Navahoe*, which happened to be in port, and filled it with hundreds of Russians, one of whom was future Broadway composer Vernon Duke, then known as Vladimir Dukelsky.[10] Bryan had all these people taken down to Constantinople. The commander's action earned the admiral's ire, for Bryan had no authority to take control of the merchant vessel,[11] and Bristol would talk of taking the costs out of Bryan's pay.[12] Eventually, however, the admiral got the Red Cross to underwrite *Navahoe*'s expenses, and he settled for dressing Bryan down.

According to Duke's memoir, the scene at the port of Odessa had been worthy of Hogarth or Doré': "Literally thousands of frenzied citizens pushed and kicked madly, all codes of decency abandoned, with men fighting women, lost children howling in a maze of luggage, bundles, and even furniture."[13] When the ships began to steam out of Odessa's harbor, the crowds left behind went down on their knees in their great distress.[14] It was to no avail: thousands were left behind. These ships eventually deposited some ten thousand refugees in Constantinople, though en route they first had to weather a terrific blizzard in the Black Sea.[15] Of one such evacuation, American naval officer John Waller told his son, "It was heart-breaking. We bodily had to throw them off the ship; they were hanging on the lifelines. We would have lost them during high seas."[16]

The White Russian army fought on. Serving with that army as an observer was the American admiral Newton McCully. McCully had served two significant naval tours in Russia, first as a mid-grade officer observing the Russo-Japanese War in 1904, and later in 1914, when he was assigned as naval attaché at St. Petersburg. By 1916 he could speak Russian and had become a perceptive observer of events. He informed the State Department that food shortages, corruption of officials, and general disintegration of morale might soon force Russia out of the war. In 1917 he witnessed the beginnings of the Russian Revolution. Shortly after this, he was sent back to sea duty in the Atlantic, but just before the war's end, McCully was put in charge of some American sailors serving under a British admiral in Murmansk, when the British and Americans were helping to support Allied intervention there.[17]

Such work was discouraging, for the Russians did not seem to want the Allies. McCully also recognized that the Russian forces they were working with were not dealing successfully with the land distribution problem. The suffering of the Russians at every hand greatly moved the American officer (before this, McCully had been troubled by the plight of the Poles), and he recommended to his superiors that America send grain to these starving people. That recommendation was turned down. McCully later made a plea that America provide asylum in Alaska for the tens of thousands of Russians who faced likely reprisals from the Bolsheviks. Although approved by naval superiors, this request was rejected by the State Department.[18]

The American contingent in which McCully served was withdrawn from northern Russia in July of 1919. Admiral Bristol then suggested that his friend and Naval Academy classmate, McCully, be given orders to travel with Denikin's White Russian army as an observer. Wanting eyes in Russia's interior, the State Department agreed. So McCully took passage to the Black Sea via Constantinople in January of 1920. While traveling with Denikin, McCully and his assistant, Cdr. Hugo Koehler (also fluent in Russian[19]), kept close touch with Bristol by letter and occasional visit, for Bristol was providing successive destroyers as base, and McCully once or twice rode a destroyer down to Constantinople to confer with Bristol and others.

As McCully grew pessimistic about the growing problems of the politically inept Denikin, he continued to feel for the Russian refugees. Admiral McCully now recommended the United States grant asylum to the Russians massing in Black Sea ports, but the State Department once again said no.[20] Although McCully and Bristol were friends, the contrast in their outlooks was sharp. Bristol made clear to McCully that he would not tolerate yet another unauthorized shipload of Russians on his hands like the one Bryan had saddled him with: in the event of yet another evacuation, McCully should bring no more than two hundred and fifty refugees down the straits.[21]

In March of 1920 an evacuation of over 80,000 troops and refugees from Novorossisk became imminent. Following Bristol's instructions to the letter, McCully selected about two hundred upper-class women and children, some of them wives and children of Denikin's staff officers, and had them shipped to the Island of Proti in the Sea of Marmara. The cruiser *Galveston* and destroyer *Smith Thompson* took part in this evacuation. On the destroyer, finding only one of their twenty-nine Russian passengers spoke anything but Russian, officers detailed two of their ship's crew as translators; both the sailors spoke excellent

Russian.[22] McCully also used American ships to transport a thousand refugees from Novorossisk to the Crimea, where the White army was preparing a last stand, thinking that was the least that America could do in the circumstances.[23] Meanwhile, besides the troops and refugees pouring into the Crimea, some 50,000 more Russians steamed down the Bosporus on Russian ships. Although a majority of this group would travel on to other countries, maybe 20,000 of these refugees remained in the city, this on top of many thousands of Russians already there.[24]

The tidal wave of refugees was still to come. The Russian general Denikin was replaced by the more politically astute General Peter Wrangel in April of 1920, and Wrangel tried to rally White Russian forces in the Crimea. McCully admired this man, although he knew that Wrangel faced nearly impossible odds.[25] For a while, things augured better for the White Russians, and the Bolsheviks were locally held to a stalemate. Over several months, besides travel, liaison, and reporting, McCully began visiting orphanages. He had become so frustrated by America's refusal to help the suffering Russians that he was considering a relief project of his own. McCully started writing Bristol and his diary of his notion of personally adopting maybe half a dozen Russian waifs.[26]

Back in February McCully had discovered a lice-covered eleven-year-old boy living in the water closet of an abandoned railroad car in Sebastopol, and after placing him in a hospital and visiting him regularly for three weeks (the child had developed typhus), the admiral had him taken to a refugee camp on one of the Princes Islands in the Sea of Marmara.[27] Now he began befriending other children who he found living in ghastly conditions in the Russian orphanages.[28] Soon he would have a couple of young Russian girls taken down to that same refugee camp. Eventually, recognizing that his requests to adopt children through regular channels would likely be snarled in red tape, he decided to engage a nineteen-year-old Russian governess, take seven children home with him, and present the matter to the State Department as a fait accompli. He anticipated receiving some disparagement here and there, but he was an admiral, and Navy gossips could safely be ignored.[29]

Occasionally, the American Navy ships would get a glimpse of the Russian conflict. In early June, Admiral McCully had *Smith Thompson* carry him and Commander Koehler from Sebastopol toward the Sea of Azov; McCully had heard of a White Russian landing to be carried out in Eastern Russia from within that body of water. So the American destroyer entered the Kerch Strait on June 6, keeping to the port side away from the Bolshevik batteries to starboard. They were taken under fire, and the first shot came very close. The ship came up to twenty-five knots, turned even further to port, and hugged the western side of the strait. Despite a brief fusillade, *Smith Thompson* made it through unharmed and eventually joined the Russian ships supporting the troop landing.

McCully and Koehler left the destroyer and joined the Volunteer Army to observe the battle. After several hours, McCully returned with ten badly wounded Russians, and *Smith Thompson* took them on board. That night the destroyer exited the Kerch Strait at darken ship, this time without being noticed by the Bolshevik batteries. On the ship's arrival in Sebastopol, a boat from the British ship *Ajax* took the wounded Russians aboard. Apparently McCully stayed in the city, while the *Smith Thompson* steamed on.[30]

In late October, the slight prospects of Wrangel's small army completely dissolved. General Wrangel had counted on the tidal marshes at the neck of the Crimea to hold out the Bolsheviks, but when in November a series of extremely low tides drained many of the marshes and a violent cold snap froze the rest, the Bolsheviks suddenly poured across the frozen marshes and sent Wrangel's army into full retreat.[31] That the end was near was very clear now; everybody had to go.

McCully cabled a request that the United States be allowed to aid in the evacuation but did not wait for the State Department's response. He ordered Cdr. Alexander Sharp of the destroyer *John D. Edwards* to gather a group of refugees and then steam to Constantinople to present a letter to Bristol asking for more ships. Sharp collected five hundred and fifty Cossacks and other Russians off the Sebastopol dock. As the destroyer sped south, these men, women, and children spread all over his ship and hungrily wolfed down as much food as his cooks could dish up. The ship moored in the city, and the destroyer's captain reported personally to the admiral. According to Sharp, on reading McCully's letter Bristol ordered up all the ships he could find.[32] *John D. Edwards* offloaded its passengers at the Russian summer embassy and soon headed back north. In its wake were four other destroyers, the American merchant ship *Faraby*, and the cruiser *St. Louis*. The destroyer *Overton* (already at Sebastopol) also took part in the evacuation.[33]

Although most of this final rescue operation was carried out by French and Russian vessels, the American vessels took human cargo too. Besides evacuating all the American citizens in the vicinity (consuls, relief workers, Red Cross and YMCA workers, and more), over several days the American ships loaded some thirteen or fourteen hundred refugees from Sebastopol and Yalta. Seven hundred refugees piled on *Faraby*, five hundred boarded *Humphreys*, a few dozen boarded other destroyers, while *St. Louis* took seventy-eight.[34]

When the latter vessel had initially arrived in Sebastopol, Charles Olsen had been astonished to see the people on all the ships there all packed in, "Nothing to eat and all exposed to the cold." Apparently most refugees had already gotten away there, so the next day the cruiser loaded some upper-class passengers at Yalta. The young Russian women who came aboard told of their parents having been killed, of their money inflating to nothing, of having no food at all, of only possessing the clothes on their backs. One woman had been parted from her mother, sister, and baby on the docks, and Olsen took her back to look for them without success. The last boat brought out the sister and the baby, but the missing mother had not been found when *St. Louis* put to sea.

Though Olsen was angry that some officers quartered a group of pretty Russian women near the wardroom and ignored the rest, he himself talked with many of the White Russian refugees, and *St. Louis*'s crew fed and helped them in every way they could. On an evening en route to Constantinople, the wardroom showed movies, after which a Russian girl danced, her husband played the piano, and the two sang a number of Russian songs. It was a pleasant evening.[35]

Much less pleasant was the ship's encounter with a big Russian steamer named *Rion*. Although many other refugee ships that *St. Louis* passed had neither food nor medical supplies, they did have fuel enough to reach port. *Rion*, however, was adrift when the cruiser ran across it in the midst of the Black Sea, having run out of coal. *St. Louis* sent a party to investigate, under the direction of one Lt. A. C. Hoyt. Hoyt reported that the six thousand men, women, and children on the ship, packed like "sardines in a box," had had nothing to eat for days, and for drink had only been able to scoop a little rain from the ship's waterways. The cruiser sent over some bread and water in a motor sailor and ordered a destroyer alongside the transport to transfer a thousand gallons of water, but heavy swells forced the destroyer to desist. Fortunately, the weather was relatively calm; had it not been, not only *Rion* but many of the Russian ships would have foundered, being little better than derelicts. As *St. Louis* officers estimated they were only forty-eight miles from port, they took *Rion* in tow at three knots.[36]

When the cruiser reached the Bosporus, a tug took over their tow. *St. Louis* offloaded its own refugees on the evening of November 16, and then Hoyt returned from *Rion*. He reported the continuing distress of its passengers: "two suicides, two insane, and one childbirth" in the short time he had ridden the ship, with conditions aboard ripening toward an epidemic. Sailors and officers passed a hat and collected several hundred dollars. On taking provisions aboard *Rion*, Olsen was astonished at the Russians' civility: the men stood aside to ensure that women, children, and the wounded all ate first.[37] As the Navy relief party left, it was given three cheers, and a letter of thanks from the Russian women on *Rion* followed soon after.[38]

Still, Olsen knew that many Russians were in even worse shape, and indeed, two days later, McCully was to count fifty-four vessels in the Russian refugee fleet at Buyukdere Bay, most of them still loaded with an average of a thousand refugees apiece.[39] Prospects for all these Russian people were very grim. There was little work to be gotten in Constantinople, and about the only thing the women among the refugees would be able to do, Olsen thought, was to turn to the streets. That trade, however, was already very much overpopulated.[40]

Admiral McCully left Yalta with *Overton*, the last American ship to leave Russia; another destroyer had brought McCully's own remaining orphans down a bit earlier. When he arrived in Constantinople, the admiral discovered that the State Department had at last officially authorized the Navy to help with the Crimean evacuation. While recognizing that had he known of this order earlier, he could have saved even more, McCully was pleased that the Americans had accomplished what they had.

During the next several weeks, the admiral again attempted to get America to offer some Russians asylum; once again he was unsuccessful. Hearing that the Near East Relief had filled a hospital with three hundred children from *Rion*, he found himself wishing he could take a dozen more children home.[41] However, he already had quite enough to manage. At the end of November, with his small charges and their governess, Adm. Newton McCully took passage home in the Navy tanker *Ramapo*, noting in his diary, "We are off on the biggest adventure I ever undertook—an old bachelor with seven children."[42] Though the immigration officials initially balked and kept the children at Ellis Island, McCully's "fait accompli" eventually worked. It also ended his bachelorship. Before long, he had married the governess.

———◆———

Meanwhile, other Americans were expending great effort to help cope with the enormous relief problem that the city had suddenly been saddled with. Admiral Bristol set up an American disaster relief committee to coordinate all the American efforts (not just the Navy's and the embassy's), and this committee would continue operation for many months. With an American doctor, many members of *St. Louis*'s crew reported to the Isle of Proti to help disembark and clean the Russian ships. While some of the sailors washed down and fumigated the vessels, others tended the refugees ashore. They recorded the refugees' names, inquired if they had any support, helped them clean themselves up, and gave them a run on a beach. Most important, they provided them with two square meals apiece (corned beef and canned milk). The idea was to put them back aboard their ships with another twenty-four-hours' ration and then send the ships off to some other port. However, although Serbia took many, few other nations would accept refugees without a great deal of negotiation, so usually the passengers ended up in a nearby refugee camp or spilled onto Constantinople's streets.[43]

Other *St. Louis* sailors worked for a week with Admiral Bristol's wife, Helen, and a committee of American women who set up a soup kitchen in a train yard near Sirkedji train station in Stamboul. They fed daily about four thousand refugees who were being offloaded into makeshift camps. Admiral Bristol was to write that most of these Russians were people "like ourselves, brought up in comfortable homes: doctors, lawyers, editors and writers, musicians and artists, ladies of birth and title, officers of the army and navy."[44] Now they were starved, exhausted, soiled, and penniless. Many children were part of the mix. In "drizzling rain and mud ankle deep," Mrs. Bristol's team doled out great quantities of hot chocolate, tea, and bread and kept the canteen operating from early morning till as late as two at night. The Americans also set up a restroom and dressing station for the women and continued the whole operation until some 22,000 Russians under the Americans' care had been put up in makeshift quarters somewhere about the city. Meanwhile, the much larger contingents of British and French in Constantinople were also furiously at work.[45]

Some of the refugees stayed in the camps or hospitals; others stole away to join the thousands on the streets or sometimes in places of business, for many Russians who had come earlier had made a place for themselves. As journalist and novelist-to-be Kenneth Roberts reported on his visit to Constantinople in early 1921, "There are Russian restaurants, Russian newspapers, Russian tea shops, Russian gambling houses, Russian dance halls and Russian shops of every description. Some shops drive a thriving trade in good Russian vodka."[46] As for the vodka, Vladimir Smirnoff (whose grandfather had been a vodka-taster for the czar) set up a vodka factory in Constantinople, and also opened a high-class nightclub called the Parizyen (often visited by Americans). Eventually Smirnoff left Constantinople for Paris, where he continued producing the famous Russian liquor. For him Constantinople was a jumping-off point.[47] Other Russians opened restaurants like Le Grand Cercle Moscovite (or simply the Muscovite), the Petrograd Patisserie, and the Black Rose.[48] But the vast majority of refugees owned no shops or restaurants or nightclubs, and after they sold their furs and diamonds, or fans and snuffboxes, or traded their rifles and swords for pieces of bread,[49] they scrambled to get any work at all.

"Scrambled" is a polite word for it. Male Russians worked as carpenters, bricklayers, stonemasons, chauffeurs, gardeners, fishermen, deckhands, or mechanics.[50] But these were the lucky ones; compared to the numbers, there were few who could find such work to do. Women washed, cooked, and darned socks; they also made dresses or hats, manicured nails, and dressed hair, if they were lucky or particularly good at such work. Others hawked flowers, kewpie dolls, cakes, trinkets, shoelaces, and jumping jacks.[51] Some handsome Russian women (often former aristocrats) became waitresses in Constantinople's restaurants. Others took to the streets. And, as we'll see later, many fine Russian musicians made a rather decent living playing or singing in the restaurants and nightclubs. For music, Constantinople had never had it so good.

Some refugees were quite ingenious. The June 1922 *National Geographic* mentioned one enterprising refugee who installed electric lights in the Basilica Cistern with its three hundred pillars and charged half a Turkish pound to row visitors around the beautiful, dim spaces.[52] Red Cross worker Eugenia Bumgardner spoke to a Russian officer who had earned enough money to buy a ticket to Paris; he had made a small fortune in the Turkish morgue by washing dead bodies that had been fished out of the Bosporus or that had been found murdered in the streets. (The decedents' relatives paid him handsomely.) She also found a former financier who had "cornered the market" on scented toothpicks and sold them at an 80 percent markup to local restaurants. Perhaps strangest was the fellow she ran into who was earning a "living" (twenty-five cents a day) working with the boiled heads of sheep. He was making them more attractive to customers by cleaning their teeth.[53]

Especially poignant was the juxtaposition of the trivial or low kind of work being done with the upper-class status of many of the refugees. "You found titled ladies trading jewels and caviar for American flour and pork and beans; defunct czarist courtiers hawking papers on the street, while former premier dancers of the Petrograd and Moscow ballets were singing jazz songs and teaching the fox-trot in the restaurants," reported Isaac F. Marcosson in the *Saturday Evening Post*.[54] Clover Dulles spoke of the Russian officers who peddled sausages at one's door, and of the former millionaires' sons on ladders around her house, washing the upper windows: "If it weren't such a tragedy it could be looked at first as a wonderful romance—such a turning up-side down of things."[55] Ens. James Clay accompanied a distinguished Russian on a train out into the marshes. This former aristocrat had once used a shotgun for sport, and Clay noted with admiration that even now he never missed a shot. He was making a little cash by shooting ducks and supplying them to several restaurants.[56] Kenneth Roberts was shown a Russian who had set up operations in a vacant lot in Pera. Wealthy before the revolution, he had earned some minor fame as an amateur astronomer. Now he had begged enough cash from someone at the American embassy to buy a telescope and was selling views of the stars for five piasters, or about five cents apiece.[57]

Not all the money earned was spent prudently, of course, nor was everybody diligent. Helen Ogden was amused that princesses, generals' wives, and countesses (or whatever they called themselves) were mending shoes, running laundries, making furniture, and peddling, yet would buy violets or rouge or powder with their last cents, going hungry as a result.[58] The young naval officer Ash Pleasants met a man selling pistachio nuts who had been one of the czar's ambassadors. This man spent all of his sparse earnings once a month at a famous local restaurant so that, for at least a few hours, he might live the life to which he had once been accustomed.[59] Warm overcoats given out to the needy found their way into the pawnshops at lightning speed, merely so the recipient could go on a spree. And more than one individual was given the passage money to America or elsewhere only to hold a farewell dinner at the Muscovite the night before he was scheduled to leave, and spend all his passage money on a specially good champagne.[60]

Some Russians refused to work, while thousands had no employment at all, or simply gave up. It was common to find people sleeping on stone doorsteps in the street across from the Red Light district in Pera.[61] At the YMCA shelter, then-journalist Roberts witnessed a young woman go mad and choke her child.[62] Roberts also pointed out that you might be walking behind a Russian man in an overcoat, and suddenly realize that underneath he had nothing on but underwear.[63] All these were the ones you saw. The many you did not see, naked, starving, diseased (or caring for those who were), were often the very worst off.

And it was all these destitute who the Americans (again, their work coordinated by the embassy committee), along with some Turkish institutions like the Red Crescent, many Allied organizations, and dozens of Russian self-help groups, did their very best over many months to get on their feet, or, better yet, to get on to a more hopeful spot. (Getting the Russians off to other countries in Europe was the major preoccupation, which took great patience and negotiation and soaked up much of the cash.) Of all the American institutions other than the embassy, the American Red Cross no doubt did the most good. In April of 1921, it was feeding six thousand a day in the city proper and was in the process of giving out ten thousand men's suits, countless outfits for women and children, and all the clothing for the city's many orphanages.[64] With the YMCA, the Red Cross helped to operate schools in subjects ranging from carpentry to chauffeuring. Before pulling out most of its resources in October of 1921 (to the consternation of most of the city), the American Red Cross had also aided countless individuals with loans or small grants.[65]

The two American colleges gave some of the refugees employment, and admitted many Russian students, whose academic preparation was often superior to those students who had grown up in the Near East. In 1921 twenty young Russian women were admitted free of charge to the women's college.[66] The author interviewed Tatiana Boyadjian Erkmen in Istanbul in May of 2001. She reported that her father, fearing the Bolsheviks, had traveled to Constantinople in 1920 to talk to Dr. Patrick. Boasting of his daughter's talent for languages, he got her admitted. He then rushed back to his summer house in Georgia and had Tatiana shipped off to Constantinople, while he and his wife made plans to follow. After landing in the city, Tatiana went up to the college with several Armenian girls and addressed Dr. Patrick with great trepidation. She was not yet twelve. Dr. Patrick embraced her, kissed her, and responded, "You're *our* daughter now, Tanya. Now go to your bed and relax." For months the Boyadjians failed to come, and when on a blessed day they finally did arrive, they were virtually penniless (they had been imprisoned by the Bolsheviks and robbed of all they had). The college kept Tatiana anyway. Like all the Russian students, Tatiana was enormously grateful to the college, and she performed some domestic work to help pay the costs.[67]

Robert College had as many as sixty Russian students at one point. A few Russians even became teachers there. Beyond that, the college's kitchen became "a colony of White Russian cooks, scullions, and waiters," according to President Gates, and two White Russians experienced in the restaurant business became the school's concessionaires. At the women's college, a Russian choir performed on "Charter Day." This group was composed of all the young Russian women students and many older Russian men who were employed as groundskeepers, "some of them men of great culture and education." According to Dr. Patrick, the gratitude shown by all these Russians was "a wonderful thing."[68]

Other American organizations also pitched in. The American embassy itself sponsored tea dances and benefit concerts for Russian musicians, while the admiral and his chief of staff and both of their wives posed for portraits by the Russian artist Nicholas Becker, then down on his luck, but very, very good at his work; Becker's beautiful painting of Captain Hepburn's wife, Louise, is still in the family.[69] Several Navy people hired Russians to teach them French, including officers, officers' wives or sisters, and even some enlisted men. The admiral saw to it that groups of Russian refugees (rather than Turks) were hired to scrape the bottoms of his ships in dry dock and to unload American cargo ships.[70] More than once so many Russians rushed to the docks at the naval base for the latter purpose that hoses had to be turned on them.[71]

American businesses in the city gave cash and contributed in other ways. The head of an American steamship company happened one day to speak to the company's night watchman down at the docks. This man, as it happened, had had a splendid record in the Russian navy; he had reached the rank of admiral. Among other things he had commanded the cruiser *Admiral Makaroff* at the time of the earthquake at Messina, in Italy. This ship had reached that disaster scene before all other warships and had rushed a thousand Italians off to safety at Naples, though the captain had contracted typhoid in the process. Hearing this account, the American official sent a message to the Italian government, with the result that the admiral, with his family, was soon provided free transportation to Messina, where he was given a house and a piece of land for himself and his descendants. That house was back near the site of the earthquakes, to be sure, but it was far from the human cataclysm that was Constantinople.[72]

The Red Cross financed a maternity clinic for Russian women, the YMCA ran an employment agency and several schools for the Russians as well as a club called the Russian Lighthouse,[73] while the YWCA provided lodgings for young women. Helen Ogden ran one of the YWCA houses. Since she had nothing to offer beyond the lodging, she was greatly distressed when two Russian women came to her, one who had eaten only bread and water for three days and was nursing a sick husband, and the other attempting to care for six of her brother's children. Helen had to send them on to somebody else. But the lodging she was able to provide was a priceless commodity. Among those to whom she offered a room was a pretty Cossack woman of about eighteen, originally dressed in a big black sheepskin hat, a soldier's coat, and big Russian boots. This girl had served several months in the White Russian army, right in the battle-lines. Her first husband (an army officer) had been killed, and her current officer husband (who she had rescued when wounded in battle) was now living somewhere on the streets of Constantinople, suffering from tuberculosis.

Moved by the girl's predicament, Helen gave her board and room and a small salary to act as their maid, although she insisted that the girl wear a skirt. Then Helen was progressively shocked, first when the girl brought her husband into the house for a marital visit (the other women scattering off), and later to find that rather than offer some of her earnings to her destitute husband, she was paying a doctor to treat her for venereal disease. Soon enough the girl left the house, and Helen was frankly relieved.[74]

A couple of months later two young lodgers further stretched Helen's patience by attempting suicide while in the house. Helen thought it was remarkable more refugees didn't try it. Her other girls were in a nervous state over the affair, but Helen seems to have taken the trouble in stride.[75] Tending for the distressed Russians was said to have taken its toll on some Americans, however, who were overwhelmed by the great need, and who became depressed at the impossibility of meeting it.[76]

One member of the American diplomatic community made particularly distinctive contributions to the Russian relief work. Before marrying Allen Dulles, Clover Todd had done volunteer work as a "canteen girl" for the YWCA in France during the Great War, where she once had dressed in rags as a mendicant and strolled the streets of Paris to feel what it was like to beg for bread.[77] She arrived in Constantinople with diplomat husband Allen a month after General Wrangel's defeat and found the Grande Rue jammed with "ragged and tragic" Russians. While Allen worked at the embassy, Clover took off on her own to help.

She began by visiting a little village on the Sea of Marmara that featured one of the worst of the Russian soldier camps. Some invalids there were forced to stay in bed for lack of clothes to wear. (The Red Cross had apparently not yet reached them.) On her visits to these desperate people she typically brought along cigarettes and Russian newspapers, remarking the pathetic happiness she provoked among the refugee news sellers by buying their papers for a few cents apiece. Clover began to visit eight of these men regularly to teach them English. "The men seem tremendously interested and learn very fast." Another Russian that Clover was introduced to was a brilliant, though desperate, lad who had learned to speak English in ten days from a book, hoping to get employment with an American. Clover was trying to invent some work for him. She also told her parents of her delight in getting a Princess Gortchakoff "launched on Therapia high life"; the princess was superb at sketching pencil portraits.[78]

In her journeys about town Clover eschewed the official car and chauffer that anxious embassy officers urged her to take, preferring more immediacy with the refugees' predicament. Sometimes she was accompanied by General Wrangel's wife, Olga, a saintly woman doing everything she could for her fellow Russians. General Wrangel himself would decorate Clover for her refugee work, which she kept up until, after a year, she became pregnant and had to return home. At about the same time, Allen was transferred to the Near East branch of the State Department.[79]

Anna V. S. Mitchell, a relief worker with the Russians who had come to Constantinople in December 1921, happened on a superb manner of fundraising. At one of Admiral Bristol's "disaster relief" meetings, somebody suggested selling refugee products on visiting liners. So, over a period of about twenty days, Mitchell boarded five successive vessels with a little group of Russians who would either sell what they had made themselves, or peddle some of their former possessions, including laces, jewelry, furs, and old silver. "I often heard people say to one another what beautiful things we had. It seems sad to think of selling them but one lost this feeling when one saw the owner's feverish desire to do so, and their joy when they had the money which meant actual food, for so many days to come." Mitchell oversaw the currency exchange on the liners' decks. Over those three weeks, her small group made several thousand dollars, and until the competition ratcheted up, they held the sales whenever passenger ships were scheduled in.

Their success resulted, in part, from Mitchell's great energy. She had to get all the permits to board the vessels beforehand, organize her Russian group, do liaison on the spot with the ships' officers and the Allied police, and (particularly challenging) fend off each ship's outraged tour guide, who regarded the local doings of the ship's passengers as his own prerogative. Indispensable to Mitchell's enterprise, by the way, was the strong backing of the U.S. embassy. This included key phone calls from Mrs. Bristol and the supporting presence of the admiral's aide, Lt. Julian Wheeler.[80]

Still, Mitchell's most reliable way to raise money was to write letter after letter, filled with descriptions like these:

> I am supporting a baby, with its father, whose mother . . . has tuberculosis, and was nursing the baby. I am feeding up, temporarily, a very nice Doctor, who after supporting himself here for the past year, was lying ill in a little attic room from which his Greek landlady was about to turn him out as he had no money for rent. There is a very sweet looking woman who supports herself, six children, a husband, and an old father by making cakes and selling them at different houses. She has had bad luck lately and I have given her a bag of sugar bought at relief prices. A man who has eked out his and his family's livelihood by selling chocolate on a little tray was burned out. . . . I have set him up again in business. . . . I am giving some [qui]nine and pillows to the most horrible looking hospital I have ever seen. I only saw it the other day.[81]

These descriptions go on for page after page, but after the letters circulated back home, the money would keep coming in too.

However, the most influential individual in all this work was probably Helen Bristol, in part because she was the "first lady" of the embassy, but also from her deeply generous nature. The canteen she set up was just the beginning of her great exertions. With her husband's encouragement, the admiral's wife was constantly arranging benefit dances and dinners and auctions, attending others' benefits, listening to concerts, and writing notes of introductions to employers and institutions, which ran into the hundreds. She raised funds by speaking to tourists from liners, and as the admiral's wife, she had implicit credibility here; donations from a single ship sometimes reached four or five thousand dollars. She also visited orphanages, refugee homes, and hospitals.

Moreover, like Anna Mitchell, Helen was also penning descriptive letters. She was writing a Mrs. Jaspar Whiting, who, after visiting Constantinople and seeing the terrible plight of the refugees, began running a large fund-raising operation in Boston.[82] Ironically, the letters from the admiral's wife about the suffering of the White Russian refugees closely resembled another kind of "propaganda" to which the admiral furiously objected. The publicity office of the Near East Relief in New York frequently asked American relief workers like Elsie Kimball (then in the Caucasus) to send stories about the Armenian massacres. They wanted to hear firsthand accounts from Armenians, for this was the most effective technique to stir sympathy, and thereby to help raise more money.[83] Helen Bristol was doing the very same kind of thing to help the Russians.

To be sure, virtually no American was out there asking for stories from *Turkish* refugees, of whom there were a great many, thousands (or at times maybe even *tens* of thousands) in Constantinople itself.[84] Given the historical circumstances and all the Armenian-Greek publicity, such lack of effort for the Turks on the part of the Americans was not surprising, but the Turkish refugees' suffering could be terrible too.

Anyway, for years Helen Bristol would continue to use her position to help the Russians. For instance, to guests at the embassy she would tout a store where refugees were selling handicrafts and pleasantly bully her guests to buy.[85] The episode described below took place long after the other events narrated here, but it was characteristic of her actions.

In 1925 a group of Russian refugees was stranded somewhere on the side of the Bosporus, after their voyage from the Black Sea had ended in shipwreck. They had almost drowned, and now they were starving, too. The English sculptor Clare Sheridan (then living in Constantinople with her children) had pleaded to the Russian embassy on their behalf, but she had had no success—perhaps not surprising, for the Russian embassy by then was being run by Bolsheviks. So Sheridan went to Helen Bristol:

> Mrs. Bristol was in the throes of organizing a ball supper for that very night. I hesitated to intrude my story at so inopportune a moment. Mrs. Bristol urged me. I blurted it out hurriedly. Her advice was: "Come to-night—there will be people whom you can talk to who might help!" I said I couldn't; "Not at a ball—people don't want to hear about the starving." I didn't go, but the next morning she telephoned to me triumphantly. She had in the midst of dancing collected enough to save them for a month.[86]

It is worth noting that Russians did not stop fleeing the Bolsheviks in 1920; they kept dribbling out in smaller numbers for years after that. It wasn't fast enough. Although a bureau operated that kept trying to locate missing relatives and pass along word about those left behind, the vast majority were never heard from. As the French writer Paul Morand aptly put it in a short story, out of the "abyss" of Red Russia came "nothing but cries, gunshots, whipcracks, never any news of one's relatives, shut in there, hopeless." This lack of contact

Like other Americans, sailors on the destroyers sympathized with the Russian refugees. Here sailor Dyson of the destroyer *Barker* stands with young Russian friends (probably orphans) in Batoum, in 1921. *Author's personal collection*

with family was yet another aspect of the tragedy of the Russians who had fled their homeland.[87]

American Navy and embassy people, in particular, kept helping Russians for years, even after they returned to the United States upon the completion of their tours of duty. In late 1923 Commander Hamilton and Margaret Bryan put up Olga Wrangel (the sainted wife of the Russian general) for at least a month while she was raising funds in the States for her compatriots. Olga was just one of many Russians the Bryans hosted, and Margaret had also brought her own White Russian maid with her to America.[88] During their tour in Constantinople, Capt. Japy Hepburn and his wife had engaged the Prince and Princess Gagarine to manage the summer cottage they had rented on the Russian embassy grounds near Therapia. The Hepburns treated the Gagarines like friends of the family. For years they continued to help this Russian couple, particularly when the Gagarines immigrated to the United States.[89]

Most enlisted men could give no more than temporary help, but for one Russian boy of fifteen, the men of the destroyer *Litchfield* did much more than that. Having found the boy in Varna, Bulgaria; learned the tragic story of his family; and noted how bright the lad was (he quickly learned to read and write English), they named him "Pete" and put him in first division. When the admiral inevitably ordered all such foreign nationals put ashore, *Litchfield*'s crew held a tarpaulin muster and raised enough funds to send Pete to New York. Then they practically adopted the boy when the ship returned to its home port. When last heard from, Pete was serving as a radioman in the U.S. Coast Guard and was married to a "little Irish girl in Flatbush."[90]

But the vast majority of those who owed their evacuation, feeding, support, or relocation to the Americans lived out their lives in Europe. In May of 1923, the United States agreed to take in nineteen hundred selected refugees,[91] a pitiful number, really, although by hook or by crook at least a few hundred others had gotten in before that. Some (like Vernon Duke) would become celebrities in their new homeland. Most, however, soon disappeared into the fabric of American society. Occasionally they would briefly surface, as the following anecdote, narrated to the author in the year 2000, will indicate.

As a young naval officer, John Waller had served his time in Bristol's small navy. Over the next twenty years he continued to pursue his naval career and pretty much forgot those early days. During World War II, having reached the rank of captain, Waller became skipper of *Tuscaloosa*, a heavy cruiser. In 1943 *Tuscaloosa* escorted Winston Churchill and his staff on *Queen Mary* from England most of the way to New York. Then the cruiser entered drydock in Brooklyn.

Waller seized this rare wartime interlude to invite his wife to stay with him at the famous hotel called the Sherry-Netherlands; it was a kind of second honeymoon. The two had dinner one night at the hotel. When Waller asked for the check, the waiter indicated another table and said, "That gentleman has paid the bill." Intrigued, Waller walked over and spoke to the man, who was either the hotel's owner or its manager. (Waller could never remember which.) The man related that as a young Russian boy, he had been evacuated from Yalta to Constantinople in 1920 by USS *Whipple*. He remembered Waller from that evacuation.[92]

Indeed, it was true. In 1920, during all the Russian chaos in which the American Navy had participated, Waller had been *Whipple*'s executive officer.

CHAPTER 5

DEATH IN THE PONTUS

The heaviest winter weather, when a howling blizzard was raging during a blinding snowfall, was the favorite time chosen by the Turks to drive the Greeks on. Thousands perished in the snow. The road from Harput to Bitlis was lined with bodies.

—Emily Thompson

A few months after the White Russians descended on Constantinople, Admiral Mark Bristol was taking a break from the various Russian difficulties and was attending a party arranged by the embassy at the resort island of Prinkipo. In the early afternoon, an American destroyer let down the hook off the island after a high-speed run from Samsun, and the destroyer's captain sought the admiral with an urgent message. Bristol's ships had already told the admiral of the reported destruction of dozens of Greek villages in and near Samsun.[1] Now, with the arrival of a leading cutthroat band at that city, a massacre of the whole Greek population of the city itself seemed imminent. The captain thought that the admiral ought to know.[2]

———◆———

From Roman times, the northern coast of Asia Minor has been known as the Pontus. Like the Aegean coast of Turkey, the Pontus historically had included a very substantial Christian population, predominantly ethnic Greeks but with a number of Armenians mixed in. As was the case in most of Anatolia, the Turkish majority ruled, but almost all the commerce was in Greek and Armenian hands. Usually the Christians were either forbidden military service in the Turkish army or were forced into labor battalions rather than combat units. So it had been in the Great War, with some additional complications in the Black Sea region.

For one thing, during that war, virtually all the Armenians in this area had been deported or killed outright, along with many Greeks. According to a certain point of view, some military reasons existed for corralling dissidents on the Pontus, especially in Trebizond, because Russian forces had occupied that city during their incursion into eastern Anatolia in 1916, and some Armenians had been fighting with that Russian army. Then, too, the presence of armed Greek guerillas in the hills around Samsun and elsewhere made some measures to control the population justifiable from a military standpoint. Still, most of the 1915 and 1917 deportations in the Pontus had involved slaughter, rape, brutality, and robbery that reached far beyond any justification, military or otherwise.

As just one example, in 1919 Oscar Heizer reported that, when he had been the American consul at Trebizond in 1915, the adult Armenian population there had been entirely deported, "mostly massacred." Afterward, a group

Map 4. The Pontus and Central Turkey

of three thousand orphans (girls under fifteen and boys under ten) had been collected by a kind Turkish governor general with the help of a Greek archbishop and placed in a group of empty houses, to be cared for and educated. Then a representative of the Committee of Union and Progress took over, advertised the children as free for the taking, and fastened on ten of the better-looking girls for himself. Most of the others he had loaded on boats, taken out into the Black Sea, and tossed overboard.

Back in 1915 Heizer had looked into this story personally, and after the war he hoped that this Turkish "monster" would be condemned by the anticipated allied tribunal.[3] Heizer's 1915 reports had outlined the whole sequence of Trebizond deportations and the utter despair of those affected.[4] As we have noted, Admiral Bristol himself looked into reports of the killings of Armenians in the territory around the Pontic port of Samsun in 1919 and found the reports horrifying. The admiral sent officers to all the Pontic ports where he did not go himself, and they authored similar chilling accounts. To be sure, one of those who spent eight days in Trebizond in September of 1919 (he traveled there on the cruiser *Olympia*) thought some reports of violence in the Pontus should be discounted because he had come across exaggerations, and he also pointed out that several Turkish officials had attempted to ignore the deportation orders. Still, even this officer acknowledged the great persecutions, massacres, and displacements that the Greeks and Armenians had suffered. He pointed out that the Armenians had suffered more than the Greeks because they were further from the coast and therefore more fully under Ottoman control.[5]

Of some five thousand ethnic Armenians originally living in Samsun (the most important port on the Black Sea between Constantinople and Batoum), there were fewer than 1,000 left, and about 10,000 ethnic Greeks remained of an original 15,000. During the war, many Greeks had escaped the deportations, massacres, and military draft by becoming bandits in the hills, while ethnic Turks avoiding the draft also formed bandit groups.[6] Though some of the Greeks came down from the hills upon the Allied victory, others did not, and in any case, many Greeks kept their arms. Hence, under subsequent oppression or threat, hundreds of Greek males and some of their families took to the hills again, in part to commit raids or reprisals, and in part simply to try to survive.[7]

Meanwhile, those Greeks who returned home to the Pontic cities after the war naturally objected when they found Turks occupying their former homes who refused to get out, which often happened.[8] Hence, resentment simmered among the Christian ethnic groups. This resentment was exacerbated both by Hellenic Greeks like Premier Eleutherios Venizelos, who before being deposed had dreamed of an empire stretching from Greece into Asia Minor (and therefore had willingly offered his army to the Allies at Smyrna), and by some local

Greeks who promoted an independent "Republic of the Pontus." Greek organizations outside of Turkey also promoted the latter, and much more openly
than anybody in Turkey itself did.

Turks in the Pontus region were nervous anyway because of a population
living among them that often did not speak their language and that excelled in
business and trade when most of them did not.[9] Especially anxious were those
Turkish officials and civilians who had helped carry out the original deportations or had profited by them, and who were now watching their backs. Upon
the Hellenic Greek army's occupation of Smyrna and nearby regions, and with
that army's subsequent heavy reinforcement and advance eastward, fears grew
among ethnic Turks of a rumored "Pontus plot" that might attempt to overthrow Turkish rule.

To what degree the Greek army or others actually coordinated efforts with
local Greek officials with the specific aim of a revolt is contested, though there
certainly was some machination toward this end.[10] However, that fear and
rumor *by themselves* could have enormous effects can be demonstrated by nar-
rating how they destroyed a longstanding American institution in the Pontus
region, the American mission college at the city of Marsovan, one of the first
of several significant events observed by Americans in the Pontus in the years
1921–22. These events would eventually become the subject of great conten-
tion between Admiral Bristol in Constantinople and the American relief workers and missionaries who had witnessed them. As we will see, Bristol would
attempt to hush up the renewed death marches and massacres that the Turkish
Nationalists had begun to carry out, despite having received admonitions from
some of his own destroyer captains as to the hideousness of what was going on.

—◆◆◆—

Marsovan, which lies fifty miles southwest of Samsun, had hosted "Anatolia
College" since 1886. By the beginning of the Great War, the college had grad-
uated over two thousand students.[11] In 1915 the Turks began deporting the
Armenians, who composed almost half of the city's population of 30,000, and
as a further sign of their intentions, they plowed the Armenian cemetery there
and sowed it with seed. Although for a while the mission at Marsovan was
unaffected, on August 19, 1915, the college gates were forced open and Turkish
officials demanded that all Armenian students, teachers, and families climb into
some sixty oxcarts and come with them. Although President George White
argued with the officials, he failed to change their plans, and after he conducted
a brief prayer service, the Armenians were taken off, the men to be shot nearby
and the women sent on east, never to return.[12]

Two days later, sixty-three women students in a distant college building who had apparently been overlooked were carried out in another group of oxcarts. However, in one of the legends of the Anatolian mission, two veteran American teachers there did not just pray with these students, but also took action. Charlotte Willard and Frances Gage cabled urgently to Ambassador Henry Morgenthau, who sent back a message demanding these students' release. Armed with this document, the two teachers chased after the students on horseback. Willard and Gage had little success in pleading with the Turkish officials along the track, but they did better when they turned to Turkish women. By enlisting the help of one official's sympathetic wife and another's kind daughter, the teachers not only got official approval to pursue their students, but once they found the girls, got permission to take them home.

Although the young students had had to fight off filthy men trying to seize them, had seen bodies pushed under bushes and bridges, had recognized with horror the unkempt wives of their murdered professors trudging along hopelessly, and had withstood pressure to convert to Islam, the two college teachers got to Sivas before most of the girls had actually been harmed. A few days later the teachers were able to escort forty-eight of sixty-three young women back through the college gates at Marsovan, to great rejoicing.[13]

In 1916 the college was closed by the Turkish government. It reopened in October of 1919 with about two hundred students, mainly Greeks (and many very young). Thirty Turkish students were now enrolled, more than ever before. A "baby house" for rescued Armenian girls and their babies was also set up on campus (such houses were being established throughout Anatolia), as were facilities for six hundred Greek and Armenian war orphans. Things began to settle into old patterns. However, the peace conferees in Paris dithered, the Greeks were invited into Smyrna, and eventually, in February 1921, the college's one Turkish professor (newly hired) was beaten to death just outside the campus. Turks accused the Greek students, but the Americans thought the professor was murdered because of his friendship with the Christians.[14] A few days later, a disgruntled laundry worker who had been dismissed from the college told officials that "bombs" were being made in a college basement. She had heard strange noises there. Turkish search parties looked through the whole campus for munitions without finding anything. The college president, George White, took a Turkish investigator to a basement and demonstrated what happened when the generator started up. A strange sound indeed.[15]

Parenthetically, about this same time, Americans in the Anatolian missions of Talas and Caesarea (far inland) were being accused of manufacturing munitions and of rousing native feeling against the government. Those American compounds were repeatedly searched, and many suspicious items indeed had to be confiscated—bullet-shaped window springs, an electric door bell, apparatuses for physics experiments, and an expensive set of taps and dies, among them. The Americans there were eventually exonerated, and it might all have been laughable, except that coincidentally many native workers at those missions were imprisoned and beaten. One was blinded, and others died from their mistreatment.[16]

In Marsovan, the Turkish investigator pursued his task single-mindedly despite the American explanations, and in the president's office found some incriminating maps inscribed with the word "Pontus"—maps printed in Chicago to indicate the Roman provinces (including Pontus) that existed in the time of St. Paul.[17] Despite White's protests, not only were these maps taken as evidence but so was the seal of a student group that before the war had been known as the Pontus Society. This was a literary, debating, musical, and athletic society for Greek students. Sometime prior to the Turkish search, White had convinced a Turkish official who inquired that this was a completely innocent student group. Now, the investigator reported discovering some Greek flags and a few student essays about Pontus autonomy and concluded that the campus group harbored revolutionaries. One of White's letters was also reportedly found to be incriminating, both because it expressed hope for eventual conversion of Turks and Kurds and because it indicated that larger funds had been spent on relief for Armenians and Greeks than on Turks.[18]

Whatever the cause, the officials connected with the student organization— three teachers, an alum, and two student leaders, all of them ethnic Greeks— were arrested "just for questioning." They never came back. Before long they were all executed, as were at least five hundred other Pontic Greeks, similarly condemned of sedition before a kangaroo court.[19] As a Turkish scholar familiar with Turkish sources put it recently, "It seems that many of those sentenced in Samsun were leaders or assumed leaders of Greek or Armenian irregulars. . . ." It *seems . . . many* of those . . . *leaders or assumed leaders.* Andrew Mango's qualifications are actually rather spectacular.[20] In other words, of those executed, *a few* might, *in fact*, have been revolutionaries.

At any rate, within a month of their investigation, officials told White that his college was now closed. White and other officials had to leave within a few days and students were required to return home. Only two young teachers could stay, not to teach, but to feed the orphans.[21] Carl Compton with his wife, Ruth, and Donald Hosford remained at the college. In late March, President White and some of his staff arrived in Constantinople from Marsovan and complained to Bristol, who in his diaries and correspondence blamed White for the imprudence of having a Greek "debating society" *at all*, especially one headed up by a Greek who, of course, "being a native . . . could not be trusted."[22]

The college having been closed because of its reputed connection with the Pontus plot, Hosford later explained to Bristol in person that he knew the students and their leaders and had attended some of the society's meetings and found them all innocuous. Nevertheless, to Hosford's considerable frustration, despite having "absolutely no proof," Bristol stubbornly insisted that revolutionary activity had indeed been taking place at the American college.[23] To the secretary of state, however, the admiral was a bit more circumspect, admitting that while Emin Bey had promised to show embassy officials the relevant documents, Bristol had never received evidence to substantiate the Nationalist claim.[24]

From the later testimony of all the principal Americans on the scene, it appears that the whole episode was the effect of one Turkish official's personal spite against the Americans, this along with general ignorance and widespread hysteria. As Lt. Robbie Dunn put it, "the Turks are now spy and sedition mad."[25] Nevertheless, not only did Turkish propaganda at the time credit Anatolia College for centrally directing all revolutionary activities in the Pontus region,[26] but as late as the summer of 2001, the Marsovan incident also was cited to the author by a Turkish scholar in Istanbul as evidence of *the existence of a Pontus plot.*

Two American relief workers who had been sent out of Marsovan, nurse Sara Corning and relief worker Gertrude Anthony (the latter a niece of women's rights champion Susan B. Anthony), decided to stay in Samsun at a Near Eastern Relief (NER) orphanage while seeking permission to return to Marsovan. Several events were then transpiring in the coastal region. For one thing, Greek warships bombarded Pontic cities on several occasions, starting with a shelling of Inebolu on June 9, 1921.[27] Such foolish actions on the part of the Hellenic Greeks (which had little military effect) no doubt played a part in furthering deportations by the Turks. Six months even before the shelling began, however, back in December of 1920, a brutal Turkish general named Noureddin Pasha had been sent to the Pontus to clamp down on any revolutionary activity along this supposedly vulnerable homefront.[28]

Clamp down he certainly did, acting chiefly by means of local Turkish bandit groups. As early as March of 1921, American missionaries in the Pontus and naval officers on destroyers visiting Trebizond and Samsun began to hear reports of Greek villages up and down Turkey's northern coast being destroyed and their inhabitants massacred. An influx of Greek children at the American orphanages seemed to verify these stories.[29] Such reports continued for months. About the last week of May, Osman Agha's "Laz" bandits swarmed into Samsun itself. Although not allowed out of Samsun, Americans like Gertrude Anthony observed the nearby village of KadiKeuy being systematically looted, while its residents and those from other villages fled to Samsun for refuge. Before long, most of these frantic people were forcibly sent back out (deported) by the Turks. According to Anthony, no one in Samsun doubted they were being sent to their deaths.[30]

Later, from seeing one of Osman's men with impunity commit murder on the city streets and from watching other bandits carefully case the Christian residences, Anthony became convinced that much more was in store, in fact, the ravaging of Samsun itself. She pleaded with Cdr. C. S. Joyce of the *Fox* to inform Admiral Bristol of the apparent Turkish plans.[31] With Joyce in command, the *Fox* immediately steamed to Constantinople and then further to Prinkipo, where the commander interrupted the admiral at the luncheon party mentioned above. Joyce passed on to the admiral the widespread reports of perhaps a hundred Greek villages destroyed, the inhabitants killed, the priests crucified. Small Greek children, most from outlying villages, were flooding the NER orphanage at Samsun, some ninety within the past few days, the ship's captain reported. Anthony had listened to one child's story. Soldiers had come to her house and had been friendly at first, but then they had killed the men and begun struggling with the women. Not knowing what to do, this child had crawled into the oven, and thereby escaped. Then she made her way to the American orphanage at Samsun. Joyce concluded his report (all of it found in his ship's war diary) by stating that a large number of Greek women had been warned by Turkish friends that they were in imminent danger.[32]

Admiral Bristol immediately wrote a protest to the Turkish officials at Samsun and handed it to Joyce to be carried back to the city—but later, for unknown reasons, ordered the two destroyer captains there not to deliver it. (They had already done so.)[33] At about the same time, Lieutenant Dunn drafted a message to the secretary of state informing him of the reported destruction of villages and this threatened "extermination." However, he also partly excused these actions: "If this occurs it will have some explanation according to [the] well known custom of this country." Dunn cited as possible justification some recent atrocities by Greeks against Turks in Marmara regions under Greek control, for which the Samsun actions might have been viewed as reprisals.[34]

But Dunn failed to tell the whole story of the latter events. Significant Greek atrocities toward Muslims certainly had occurred recently at Guemlek and Yalova, cities near the Sea of Marmara, not far from Constantinople. Massacres of Turks had reportedly taken place there (Dunn put the figure at two thousand killed), along with much looting, systematic burning of many Muslim villages, and general uprooting of the Muslim population. Greek army commanders responsible for the region seem to have countenanced or even encouraged the depredations of Greek, Armenian, and Circassian bands, and some regular Greek troops may also have participated. Whether for the military purpose of protecting the Greek army's flanks, or for simple revenge, a "systematic plan" for getting rid of the Muslim population there seemed to be in the process of execution.

Arnold Toynbee personally witnessed Greek soldiers fire a village during a troop evacuation at Ismid, watched Muslim corpses being unearthed from freshly dug large graves there, and interviewed many Turkish survivors throughout the area. "For about the first time in history the Turk is quite undoubtedly the injured party," he would write Admiral Bristol.[35]

Terrible as such actions were, however, there was much more to the story of Greek atrocities in the Gulf of Ismid region than either Toynbee's letter or Dunn's draft message suggested. Not only had the 1915 deportations of Armenians and Greeks been very severe in the Marmara region, with associated great brutality, suffering, and loss of life, but Dunn also had to know what the report of the official Allied investigation pointed out repeatedly, that Greek actions like those noted above were not only reprisals for general Turkish oppression in the past, but specifically were payback for atrocities committed just the year before, that is, in 1920, when many Greek villages had been burned at the hands of Turkish irregulars and reportedly thousands of Greeks had been massacred. Even now, as Turks were lamenting Greek attacks upon Turks, thousands of Greek refugees were complaining of massive recent attacks by Turkish bands at nearby Ismid, including 12,000 Greeks massacred and thirty Greek villages destroyed, the latter facts being accepted as "fundamentally true" by Allied investigators, "not-withstanding a certain amount of exaggeration in the figures."

Indeed, at one port where a party of Allied investigators put in, they found a group of Greek refugees "raving with anger." A guide to the Allied commission was a leading Turkish figure from a neighboring village. On his debarking, several Greek refugees denounced him as having been responsible for several massacres in the neighborhood. It was all the commissioners could do to distract the refugees, push the Turk on a boat, and beat a quick retreat, the boat being "pursued by a howling crowd" that rushed into the water after it.[36]

Admiral Bristol loved to argue that every atrocity in Turkey was just a reprisal following another reprisal ad infinitum (all races being equally atrocious), and certainly there was much mutual racial hatred in Turkey—some of it being evident in the Greek actions near the Sea of Marmara. However, in Dunn's draft of the particular message mentioned above (the gist of which the admiral soon signed and sent off), he conveniently failed to mention any reasons that the Marmara Greeks might have had to be upset at the local Turks in the first place.[37]

——◆◆◆——

About this time (in July of 1921), the young writer John Dos Passos visited Constantinople on a tour of the Near East and made a call on the admiral. When the writer informed Bristol that he represented the *New York Tribune* and *Metropolitan Magazine* (Dos Passos would send off a few articles during his trip), Bristol invited him to join some other correspondents on a visit one of his destroyers was about to make. At some nearby ports, the admiral said, desperate Greek peasants were fleeing the Turks (who had burned their villages), but at others, Turkish villagers were said to be frantic to get away from raping and murdering Greeks. The admiral said he was hoping to get the truth about the Near East situation published in American newspapers, so somebody might stop the senseless war being waged on the mainland between Nationalist Turks and Hellenic Greeks.[38]

Dos Passos accepted the admiral's invitation. When the destroyer arrived at the small ports the admiral had spoken of (which lay near Ismid), the correspondents found the Turkish and Greek refugees hard to tell apart but equally pathetic and desperate. All of them begged to be taken aboard. However, while the destroyer could have accommodated several hundred on its weather decks, once the correspondents returned from their interviews, the ship quickly took in its brow and sped right back to the old Ottoman capital.[39] Dos Passos does not say so, but it appears the admiral was more intent on furthering his own views than on helping to solve the actual problems of the refugees. Indeed, when Dos Passos met with Bristol, the admiral had explicitly fed the writer his storyline: "I suggested that he might then write one story bringing out the savagery of both the Greeks and Turks against each other."[40]

Just before Dos Passos' visit, Lieutenant Dunn had left Constantinople for Angora (later renamed Ankara) to interview the Nationalist leaders there. On his way through Samsun, the American naval officer listened to some Greek women in the city talking about purchasing poisons like strychnine or corrosive sublimate, saying they were determined not to leave themselves at the mercy of the Turks. (In the Pontus in 1915, many women had purchased poison for the same purpose.)[41] After listening a while, Dunn pointed out that corrosive sublimate was a bad thing to take, for it worked so slowly that the Turks would be able to accomplish their purpose on the young ladies before it became effective. An American destroyer captain was standing by, and it is clear from his report that he found Dunn's comment hilarious.[42]

When he got to Angora, Dunn talked twice with the Nationalist foreign minister, Youssouf Kemal, and once with Mustapha Kemal himself. Among a large number of topics (one should remember that the Turkish Nationalists were fighting a war and had many things on their minds; indeed, they were about to be sent reeling by another Greek offensive), Dunn brought up the deportations from Samsun that had begun to take place, including the threatened deportation of innocent women and children there, and also the deportations of the Greek tobacco sorters who were working for the American tobacco in or near that city. Didn't the Turkish leaders understand the need for American business? In response, Youssouf argued that there had been no deportations until the Greeks had bombarded Inebolu, an action that had taken place on June 9. He also brought up the alleged Pontus sedition and some reported burnings of Turkish villages on the Pontus by Greek bandits. Youssouf claimed that the local Turkish officials who had threatened the deportations of the Greek women at Samsun were now under a tribunal for doing so.

Although Youssouf further admitted that, both in principle and in detail (as to the character, ages of deportees, and so on), all deportation orders were issued from Angora, he also claimed "it had never been and was not now, the intention of the Angora government to deport any women—only men between the ages of 18 and 50."[43] Dunn left Angora convinced that local officials rather than the Nationalist government were responsible for any excesses, and that any atrocities were pretty much confined to the Samsun region.[44]

As Dunn was interviewing the Nationalists, a Near East Relief official named McDowell brought permission from Angora for relief workers Anthony and Corning to return to Marsovan. In Samsun, McDowell called on many influential Turks to try to convince them that the Nationalist government had not issued any deportation orders. The town became quieter as an apparent consequence, but shortly afterward, two hundred more men were deported to join the thousands that had been sent before them. In her November report, after noting this timeline, Anthony pointed out two other discrepancies. The local head of the Near East Relief had gotten the local Mutasarriff (governor) to agree that no NER employees would be taken, and the American tobacco officials had convinced him to promise the same concerning their employees. Yet, said Anthony, "Neither promise was kept."[45]

Anthony and Corning would soon travel on to Marsovan, but in later weeks the threats to the Greeks in Samsun grew worse. Cdr. G. L. Bristol of the *Overton* (no relation to the admiral) had served more than one stint of duty at Samsun and, unlike some destroyer skippers fresh from the States, knew something about Turkish officialdom. On July 18 he was moved to write yet one additional plea to the admiral and send it by another fast ship. The night before he had heard of an order for the deportation of all remaining local Greeks (mostly old men, women, and children), something that he reported was "naturally regarded as the end by everybody." The next morning, along with Capt. Victor Stuart Houston of the *Brooks*, he went to visit the Samsun Mutasarriff.

The Mutasarriff said the order was indeed in effect, and that all the Greeks had been notified. They soon would be sent out. He admitted that many of the Greek men who had been deported earlier had, in fact, been killed, though he claimed the government had tried to protect them, with the fortunate result that at least half of them had reached their destinations. (He blamed local Greek and Turkish brigands for the killings.) Commander Bristol asked how one was to consider this new action, pointing out that the Mutasarriff's assurances to him regarding the past deportation had not been adhered to in any particulars.

When the Mutasarriff responded that women and children would be sent out in small, well-guarded parties and all in conveyances—no one would have to walk—Bristol answered that they both knew this was impossible. Bristol went on to say that "he knew as well as I" that large numbers of the deportees would not survive. Commander Bristol then protested in the name of humanity as strongly as he felt he could, but (being the pretty low-ranking figure he was) he was convinced it wasn't strong enough, and later a Turkish official who had been present at the meeting privately confirmed that it was, in fact, too weak. The Mutasarriff had been expecting Bristol to say, "*You must stop it.*" The Mutasarriff's answer was that he would proceed anyway, that his orders had originated from Angora, and that they were quite positive.

After describing all this, Commander Bristol wrote the admiral of his conviction that the deportations would be carried out quickly, and that the death of large numbers of deportees would be the natural consequence. To his hand-penned missive, he added this conclusion:

> American prestige is now at a low ebb here. We have the only war vessels present in the harbor, and whether true or not are being put in the position of passively standing by and watching what everyone, including Turks[,] considers a massacre. The officials representing the Government know that we don't believe what they say to us and they also know that we are fully convinced that few deportees will reach [their] destination alive. If this goes through it will at later date . . . be classed with the Armenian affair, and we will occupy in the public mind very much the position of the Germans. Time will impute to us not only doing little to prevent it but actually the attitude of complacency if not concurrence.
>
> There is a feeling among all (Turks included) that concrete action by the allies or strong action by America can stop it. This must be communicated to Angora. The local Turk will not feel when you are dealing only with him that you are serious in your intentions.[46]

Note the perceptions here, startling in their clear contrast not only to the regular evasions by Turkish officials in Angora but also to the regular excuses of the American admiral in Constantinople: Turkish officials *never mean* what they say; *we all know* they don't mean it; most deportees are *likely to die*; the orders come from Angora . . . *we're ourselves responsible.* The letter is all the more remarkable for its being originated by a commander whose career rides on his relationship with his superiors, in this case a superior who does not want to hear *any* of what Commander Bristol has to say.

Commander Houston of *Brooks* (for some reason, both *Overton* and *Brooks* were present simultaneously at Samsun) carried Commander Bristol's message to Constantinople and urgently asked to speak to the admiral—but the chief of staff (it would have been Capt. Lyman Cotten) would not let him in. The admiral was busy, he said. A careful reading of an episode in Dos Passos' 1927 travel book *Orient Express*, along with study of related documents, tells us what happened next.

In his book, the writer describes an extraordinary meeting in the Pera Palace Salon that took place between an American naval officer, the Greek Orthodox archbishop, an elaborately dressed Greek lady, a couple of other locals, and "a journalist," obviously Dos Passos himself. Over coffee the group discussed the recent Turkish order to deport the remaining thousands of Greek women and children from the major Turkish Black Sea port of Samsun.

"Of course that means . . ."
"*Massacre,*" someone whispered.

The American officer reported that the Greek men had already been sent inland and that the Greek women were openly weeping in the city's streets. The archbishop proposed sending a telegram to the American president.[47]

How Dos Passos got invited to this meeting is unknown (perhaps he just seemed a sympathetic writer), and anyway it is a much less important question than who the naval officer was, and what he thought he was doing meeting the Greek patriarch. From archival sources, it is clear that the American pictured as speaking out in the meeting was Commander Houston.[48] In his travel book, Dos Passos does not notice that by this ship's captain reporting what he and his crew had seen going on in Samsun to a major non-American authority (a Greek dignitary for whom, by the way, Admiral Bristol cared very little) and to other individuals not at all connected with his military mission, Commander Houston was not only most likely violating naval protocol, but was also circumventing his admiral's certain wishes.

Missionary L. P. Chambers would later complain in a letter that Admiral Bristol had sent home destroyer commanders who had been stationed at Samsun because of derogatory opinions they had expressed toward the Turks.[49] Did Admiral Bristol learn of, and then take offense at Captain Houston's outspokenness? And had the admiral in fact sent the offending officer home? Even more important, had Captain Houston carefully measured the possible personal consequences of his attending an uncleared meeting with a local "chief of state," as it were? (In several respects, the Greek archbishop or "primate" acted as the head of all ethnic Greeks in Turkey.) That is, had this experienced American naval officer in frustration decided to brave any possible damage to his own career so as to trumpet the word of the impending massacres to *somebody* who might help?

Apparently he had. Bristol's war diaries and other documents indicate that the Greek archbishop used Commander Houston's name (with Houston's permission) in pleading with Admiral Bristol for his fellow ethnic Greeks on the Pontus, and that the admiral took great offense at Houston's having let the archbishop know what was going on in Samsun. Navy personnel files contain the original copy of the letter that Bristol appended to the commander's next fitness report. In that letter, the admiral pointed to Houston's violation of Bristol's policy of neutrality between local contending forces, the commander's certain knowledge of what that policy involved, and the overall lack of discretion in the commander's actions.

In Houston's required response to this decidedly "adverse" letter (which would have ended any chance of Houston's being promoted to captain), rather than apologize or otherwise attempt to blunt the letter's impact, to the admiral's wonderment the ship's captain dared to defend his actions. By implication, he was also putting Bristol down.

Houston explained that he had found his original report to headquarters about the Turkish orders to deport 15,000 Greek women and children from Samsun was not being taken seriously back at the American embassy, this despite the death of "thousands upon thousands of Armenian women and children" during the war by similar methods (in what we now call the Armenian genocide). He went on to remind Bristol (the "Detachment Commander") that although he had asked to see the admiral personally, he had been turned down, and was informed that the admiral was too busy to talk to him. Houston's letter displayed a sardonic tone: "I am aware that the Detachment Commander is more than busy. I am aware that my personal feelings are not to be considered; but in such a matter, affecting the lives of fifteen thousand odd women and children, not yet killed, the personal touch which a word from the Detachment

Commander could have given, would have gone a long way toward relieving the tension of the situation as it appeared to me."

Houston also suggested that, even though he had not been allowed to speak to the admiral, it was possibly because of the very vehemence of his pleas to the naval chief of staff that Bristol subsequently decided to send a protest to Mustapha Kemal. Commander Houston concluded his unrepentant missive by arguing that if he had erred and violated policy, "it was through zeal for the cause of humanity."[50]

Maybe, despite appearances, Admiral Bristol had, in fact, been moved by Commander Bristol's letter and by Commander Houston's personal appeal to the chief of staff—or perhaps the admiral had become leery lest there be some fallout for him resulting from the two ship captains' pleas, and particularly from Commander Houston's apparent willingness to fall on his sword for the Samsun Greeks. Whatever the reason, the admiral again protested the deportations, this time to the Nationalist government at Angora.[51] A day or two later, the *Overton* commander signaled from Samsun that he believed the order for deportations had been rescinded. Moreover, Osman Agha had suddenly left the city. (Reportedly he had been ordered to Angora.)[52]

On July 23 Youssouf Kemal wrote Mark Bristol that the word of transportation of old men, women, and children from Samsun to the interior was completely in error. Only the inhabitants of some villages implicated in the Pontus Society had been so treated, and then only from military necessity.[53] No less prominent a figure than the American secretary of state would later credit Admiral Bristol with averting a Greek deportation from Samsun.[54]

However, all this business about saving the Samsun Greeks was largely smokescreen, for whatever was happening in Samsun proper, the whole countryside was still being devastated. Village by village, Greeks everywhere in the Pontus were either being massacred or deported south. A few Americans would witness this. On the very same day that Youssouf Kemal penned his response to Bristol, Osman Agha's men arrived at Marsovan.

———◆◆◆———

From mid-June on, many desperate deportees from nearby villages had come to Marsovan with terrible tales, and some were admitted into the college compound.[55] With the arrival of Osman's brigands, things became very uncertain. In the Comptons' house at the mission, things more or less continued as before. After dinner on July 24, some of the older orphans, their Armenian supervisors, and the American teachers listened to the Victrola. Then they said a prayer and retired for the evening. They omitted the ordinary Sunday-night sing for fear of attracting attention. Shortly afterward they were awakened by glass shatter-ing, doors crashing open, and screams piercing the night. Compton ran to the gate, and a crowd of crying women and children rushed in. After slamming the gate shut and slipping out a side door, he informed approaching Turkish sol-diers that this was American property. Astonishingly, they responded that they had orders to stay out of American property and left.[56]

For the Americans, the next four days and nights—especially the nights—were ones of "constant fear."[57] More than fear, however, confronted the city's Greek and Armenian residents. Although, as at Samsun, some care had appar-ently been taken to inhibit Americans from making firsthand observations,[58] the facts were clear enough. On Sunday night, the mission leaders heard the crying and screaming, watched houses being sacked, and accepted refugees over the walls. Monday night the screaming was less prolonged, but there was some gunfire, and those who came in over the compound wall reported "much kill-ing with knives." On later nights, stories of rape (indeed, multiple rape) were added to the mix.[59] During these terrifying nights, groups of Armenian and Greek men and older boys were sometimes marched up the hill past the col-lege, after which shots rang out. These people were never seen again. On such occasions, Compton opened the gate, hoping some prisoners might be able to slip inside, but those who did were seen by their guards and were quickly forced back up the hill.[60]

The five American men and women organized a "big boy patrol" of orphans around the inside of the compound wall day and night, and spaced themselves between the boys. They got little sleep. Many refugee women and children climbed the walls into the compound, along with a few men. Turks sometimes followed them, but when informed they were on American soil, they invariably left.[61] The Americans and their native helpers did what they could to comfort the hundreds of orphans in their midst. Steve Stephanides and another Armenian boy slept at the Comptons at night. Years later Stephanides recalled Ruth Compton coming into their room, pulling down the shades, and reading them stories, this to divert their attention from the terrible scream-ing[62]—and from the fires.

During Wednesday fires had broken out simultaneously at several places in the Christian part of the city, which lay just outside the campus. The fires burned all night and destroyed some four hundred houses.[63] Ruth and Carl Compton sat on the steps of the girl's dormitory with the mission's meager fire-fighting equipment and watched the houses collapsing, one by one. Could this really be happening? Fortunately, the fires did not leap the compound wall.[64] Outside, though, terror and chaos ruled. Refugees reported several dead bodies and some live ones being tossed into the fire and people being shot as they tried to escape.[65] A young Turkish officer, a former student at the college, discovered that thirty Christian women had been driven into a school building in the city, where they remained huddled. The building had just caught fire and the women had begun singing hymns. Recognizing that the women were giving up to the inevitable, the officer became furious, and the surrounding Turkish crowd gave way to his wrath. However, when he shouted to the women, insisting they all come out, they at first hesitated. Would it only prolong their agony? When he promised to lead to them to the college, though, they plucked up their courage and rushed out in a group, just before the building's floors collapsed. Compton would find a place for all these women in one of the college buildings.[66]

Toward the end of the week, the Turks began carrying out cartloads of dead to the Christian cemetery, to five large freshly dug pits in view of the Americans. Through binoculars, Gertrude Anthony sometimes watched the bodies being stripped before being dumped off the wagons and discovered that some were not yet dead. She estimated a thousand (or maybe half the postwar Christian population of Marsovan) might have been killed, though she admitted it was impossible to say. About the same time, for over a week "the roads were alive with villagers carrying off loot. Stoves, pots, windows, doors, tiles, and masses of bundles were carried by donkeys, carts, and men, women, and children. Cartload after cartload, for days, went up the hill past our house." The Armenian women with whom she talked said the Turkish residents of the city had done more looting and killing than even the *chettes* themselves.[67]

By the end of that fateful week, hundreds of refugees, mostly women and children, thronged the buildings of the American compound. Some Christian families escaped into the hills, passing the college on their way. In the mornings, outside the walls, the Americans would gather the babies who had been left there in blankets. Eventually they would collect twenty-five of them.[68] Though the Greek women remaining in the city were all deported,[69] some of the city's remaining Armenians were allowed to take shelter at the college. Most of those already in the compound were Greeks who had come in not by the main gate, but surreptitiously. Sixty years later, a woman wrote Carl Compton from Canada after hearing of the death of Compton's wife, Ruth. Compton's name was treasured by the family, she said, because in those days, her mother, sister, aunt, and seven cousins had been taken over the college walls at night, and Compton had hidden them all until the trouble was over.[70]

Knowing the Americans sheltered many refugees, Turkish authorities eventually insisted that Compton list the Greek and Armenian men who were sheltered there (apparently about two dozen). Compton gathered them together, and most agreed to be listed, but some decided to attempt to escape instead.

Carl and some helpers provided a Greek and his two sons (the boys had been college students) with a blanket each and a little food and money, and then boosted them over a remote part of the wall. Many years later, one of them walked into Compton's office in Thessaloniki. Somehow they had all survived and gotten out of Turkey; this man was living in Greece.[71]

The Americans were forced to send out some men and women, of whom some were killed. Even more might have died, except that there were more refugees in the compound than Carl Compton knew. Efthimios Couzinos was a student of twenty-two who Compton had kept to interpret for him after the college was closed, and as Turkish officials began to look at the campus for possible escapees, Couzinos began getting worried, particularly since he had been closely associated with the Greek student group. He was apprehensive that his name might be on a rumored list of subversives, as indeed it was. The college head nurse happened to be his sister, and she suggested he should hide in a small crevice under the kitchen floor in the infirmary, actually, under the vegetable box. So, without telling Compton, one day Couzinos simply disappeared. Resembling Jews who would hide away from the SS in cupboards, shelves, and tiny cellars through much of World War II, this young man would spend the next seventeen months in that hole in the floor, only arising in the middle of the night to stretch his legs.[72]

At least one other person was also hidden away. Ruth Compton was searching through some supplies in an empty faculty house one day when she heard a door open upstairs followed by some quiet footsteps. Frightened, she kept absolutely still. Stealthily, a bearded face peered around the corner at the top of the stairs, then vanished. In that moment Ruth had recognized an Armenian teacher who had left the college when it had been closed in March. Upon conferring with Sara Corning, Ruth learned that this man had escaped a Turkish labor battalion into which he had been drafted, and then had returned to the campus. Sara had hidden him. They decided it was better that Carl Compton did not know.[73]

Eventually, with the departure of Osman's *chettes* and the infamous Osman himself (the Americans agreed to give him a ride toward Angora, as a way to get him out of town), with the glutting of the appetites of the local population, and perhaps also because of some pressure from the American high commissioner, the storm mostly blew over. The trades of the Christians were now more badly needed than ever in Marsovan itself. With some assurances from Turkish friends, the refugees on the campus petitioned Compton to let them move back to their homes, or to what was left of them. And so he did. The Comptons and the other Americans, the orphans, some native helpers, and the hidden ones remained.

After Marsovan and their many other such "victories," Osman and his one to three thousand cutthroats were acclaimed in all the cities through which they passed. Osman himself would be called a patriot or hero in the Turkish press of Angora and Constantinople.[74] Observing the group in Angora, where they were received with great ceremony,[75] one of Bristol's representatives there, Florence Billings, happened to remark upon the picturesque quality of Osman's men as they marched through the streets. Halide Edib responded that it was a pity to be compelled to use them, although they might have to continue doing so. Since they were "not amenable to discipline," she said, the use of such "irregular forces . . . would make the situation worse regarding reprisals." If Billings reported Halide's statement correctly, Halide would seem to have meant that one massacre was likely to beget another—"but nevertheless, massacre we must."[76] A year later Osman was featured on one of the new Nationalist stamps, and he is still occasionally memorialized in Turkey by statue and in travel literature today.[77]

In contrast to Osman's triumphal procession through cities of Anatolia, Donald Hosford's reception in the American embassy at Constantinople in December of that year (1921, still) was less than satisfactory. Not only did Bristol arrive late and terminate their interview early, but despite Hosford's protests, he stood by his conviction that the Marsovan Greeks were part of a seditious organization. Bristol also stated his current soapbox opinion that missionary work should be carried on with no religious tone whatsoever. Hosford forwarded the State Department an account of this interview.[78] He then immediately wrote up a further memo that called for the admiral's replacement, arguing that Bristol was "so strongly pro-Turk" that he was not only unfair to the Christian minorities, but failed to give Americans in Anatolia the sympathy, support, and protection they warranted.[79]

Hosford was not the only person to seek Admiral Bristol's replacement, by the way. About this same time, no less dignified a trio than William Peet (the missionary head in Constantinople), James Barton (the national secretary of the American Board), and Charles Vickery (national secretary of the Near East Relief) sought to have Bristol removed from Constantinople. However, the admiral's position was never seriously threatened.[80]

In the detailed report Gertrude Anthony submitted at about the same time Hosford did, she did not criticize Bristol. Indeed, she partly credited one of the admiral's protests with preventing a massacre at Samsun.[81] Bristol, in turn, voiced some respect for this "level headed" woman, and on one occasion in 1922 he spent considerable time explaining to her the "complete picture of Turkey," that is, what the Armenians and Greeks had done that had drawn down the Turkish wrath. Right after the Marsovan events, when former Marsovan physician Jesse Marden had called on him, Bristol had also explained the "causes that produce the effect" to him. The underlying causes Bristol named to this man were the policies of the Allies and of Greece.

Bristol's complaint about both Anthony and Marden was their insularity, that they did not see beyond the local conditions, but were being governed solely by their knowledge of the small locality they knew.[82] In this connection, when Carl Compton called on Bristol in Constantinople in July of 1922 (he and Ruth had stayed with their orphans for a whole year), he was astonished to find that, despite hearing from both Hosford and Anthony, Bristol was skeptical that there had been a massacre at all: "Did you, with your own eyes, see anyone being killed?" Here (as elsewhere, with Bristol) it seems that screams, gunshots, crying, despair, disappearances, mass looting, tales of rape and killing, multiple fires, and sights of wagonloads of hundreds of bodies (dead or alive) being dumped in mass graves counted for virtually nothing.

Bristol was no doubt right to beware of exaggeration, of course (he had certainly heard plenty of it in his three years in Turkey), but he seemed chronically unable or unwilling to recognize the real thing. In a memoir written sixty years later, Carl Compton pointed out dryly, "The High Commissioner and some other Americans who had never been outside Constantinople or Smyrna had great sympathy for the Turks."[83] Compton thereby implied that it was Bristol in his comfortable diplomatic and pleasant social life on the beautiful Bosporus, rather than the relief workers and missionaries daily facing the terror and tragedy of emergent Anatolia, who suffered from insularity.

From September of 1921 on, Admiral Bristol had to confront many even more ominous reports, especially from his destroyer captains at Samsun. In early September, a destroyer commander reported in his war diary that fifteen hundred women and children who were from nearby Greek villages and had recently been living in the city were now being deported. He also said that he had heard reports (which he believed) from the American tobacco men that deportation of some six thousand women and children from the Baffra district was well under way. To be sure, at about the same time, a Greek band of nearly a hundred had attacked a Turkish village eight miles away, killed some villagers, and burned their houses. A similar Greek raid seems to have taken place in early October.[84]

U.S. Naval Institute Photo Archive

At one point, Admiral Bristol sent the cruiser *St. Louis* to Samsun, apparently as a show of concern for the Black Sea Greeks. In command was Captain Bill Leahy, later a famous admiral. *The Naval History and Heritage Command*

A couple of weeks later, Bristol sent Capt. Bill Leahy and the cruiser *St. Louis* to the Pontic coast, perhaps as a brief show of American concern. (It was very unusual for Bristol's one assigned cruiser to leave Constantinople.) Leahy reported that the ethnic Greek males from the Samsun tobacco warehouses were all gone, that their wives and daughters were in constant terror of being sent out too, and that the foreigners there believed the Turks intended to eliminate the Greeks entirely. At the end of his paragraph, Leahy commented, "I could take and hold the city indefinitely with the force and guns available on the *St. Louis.*" As an exception worth noting (particularly in light of the terrible events in Smyrna later, but also in reference to the events that had occurred over months in Samsun and elsewhere in the Pontus) here was one senior American officer willing to contemplate military action to set things right.[85]

In mid-November, Cdr. Webb Trammell of the destroyer *Fox* (he had recently relieved Commander Joyce as the ship's captain) told Bristol that seven hundred women and children who had earlier fled to the hills had just returned to the city (from fear of the approaching winter). Now they were being fed by the Near East Relief before their own deportation. The NER head asked the Turkish governor to let them keep the two to three hundred children among the seven hundred, but he refused. After this group was sent out, Trammell found that five hundred more ethnic minorities were being held in prison prior to being deported, too. Their crime? Some member of each of their families had escaped a deportation convoy.[86]

Fox then spent considerable time in Russian waters, but when his ship returned to the Pontus in April 1922, Trammell reported yet another thirteen hundred Greeks being sent out from Samsun, mostly women and children, but also a few old men. The Near East Relief issued these people rations for the road. Some of these deportees were "so weak they could not walk out to the truck for their bread." Somebody found some carts, and they were sent out, too, except for twenty-seven orphans that the NER took in.[87] And so on. (In May, Harry Pence, captaining *McFarland*, found deportations of fifty males occurring from Trebizond twice a week; only five hundred minority males were left there. No women and children had been deported so far.[88])

As for events anywhere inland, even American authorities did not always have immediate, firsthand knowledge. Back on November 7, 1921, the State Department had to ask other agencies what they knew about the reported massacres in Marsovan, over three months after the events themselves. Though he knew nothing of Marsovan, Near East Relief foreign secretary Charles Fowle passed on to Allen Dulles several reports about the Samsun atrocities, including one from transportation worker Stanley Hopkins, who three times from September to October had traveled the several hundred miles between

Harput and Samsun by automobile. (Hopkins had been on relief or mission work.) On the first trip he had seen an estimated 12,000 deportees on the road, consisting (it appeared) of entire families and villages; the people were regularly being robbed and mistreated, he reported, and moving so slowly they would probably not reach safe harbor before the winter snows. On the second trip he passed groups of feeble old men from Samsun being pressed to march thirty miles a day. Many corpses of both sexes were lying on the roadside.

On the third journey Hopkins passed several other groups, one of them composed of women alone, most of them shoeless, many carrying babies. "A driving cold rain was falling . . . they had no protection whatsoever and their only place to sleep was the wet ground." He estimated that on this last trip he had passed ten thousand Greek deportees and pointed out that the deportation was a general one, and was not limited to the Black Sea coast. Also in Hopkins' report and in another attachment to Fowle's letter were reports of earlier massacres of Greek males near Kavak, a village just inland from Samsun. An American destroyer captain reported 550 Greek men had been shot near there on June 26. (Some had escaped.) Hopkins had also heard a report of thirteen hundred Greeks near that village on August 15th having been "shot down by fire of Turkish troops."[89]

And, in fact, despite some limitations to his knowledge, Admiral Bristol was able to draw very strong conclusions. In January 1922 he wrote Henry King (the former cohead of the King-Crane Commission) that the Turks had "killed people indiscriminately" and generally persecuted the Christians throughout the Pontus. "I don't think there is any doubt that the Greeks have been pretty well cleared out of the whole region and deported to the interior and the villages wiped out." He cited as justifying causes the Pontus society, the many Greek bands in the area, and (again) various Greek atrocities for which these Turkish actions could be understood as reprisals.

However, in this letter to King (as seldom elsewhere) he did admit that "horrible massacres" were being committed throughout Turkey.[90] In other letters, however, Bristol showed himself very much *out* of touch. For instance, he informed relief worker Stanley Kerr there was some measure of military justification for the deportations (possibly true), "especially if they are carried out without committing atrocities or submitting the deportees to unnecessary hardships"[91]—as if there were no precedents indicating what habitually happened when Christian minorities were "sent into the interior" in Turkey. Bristol here was also belying his own oft-repeated statements about the "well-known character of the Turks," that is, how "the Turks will rob, pillage, deport and murder Christians whenever the opportunity is favorable," or about the "horrible atrocities committed by the Turks," a picture of which "is as horrible as you desire it painted,"[92] and so on and on. Like many others, the admiral had originally thought an American mandate was the answer. After those hopes evaporated, Bristol constantly preached that Americans (such as himself) should attempt to influence Turkish (and Christian minority) behavior by moral suasion. Thereby he manifested a great naiveté of his own.

And at the same time he was writing King about the "horrible massacres," the admiral was sending his commercial attaché to Angora, seeking various concessions. On separate occasions, Bristol and Commercial Attaché Julian Gillespie told the Nationalist foreign minister that they knew that subordinate officials sometimes failed to carry out wishes of the local government, or that troops simply got out of control.[93] Thus, by attributing excesses to the actions of subordinates, the American officials essentially gave the responsible authorities in Angora a free pass.

Over the winter, few Americans traveled far in interior Anatolia, limited as much by Nationalist travel prohibitions as by the weather itself. Sometimes they heard little from Americans there. Moreover, Bristol and the State Department—and the Near East Relief, too—had a policy of keeping private any embarrassing or damaging reports they did receive. That any adverse publicity might offend the Nationalists and interfere with future diplomatic and especially commercial relations was no doubt one motive. On their part, relief authorities worried that such negative publicity might incline Turkish officials to interfere with their relief operations.

What kinds of things were being hushed up? At the personnel house in Trebizond, relief director J. H. Crutcher heard a terrifying report from two Greek women who were begging food. Turkish officers and soldiers had entered the village where these women lived, packed up all their belongings, and marched them to the central village of Jevislik.[94] The men and boys from eleven up were then marched off and were not heard from again. However, the women personally witnessed seventeen men decapitated, and their heads strung on a long stick. Three children about ten were also killed before their eyes, and four young girls were taken to be raped and eventually put to death. This story was corroborated by other refugee accounts, and Crutcher had heard other similar stories from the surrounding villages.[95]

The Jevislik incident had occurred around February of 1922, but Crutcher did not pass this information on to Constantinople (via Commander Trammell) until July, and even then he asked that it be treated "confidentially." (Bristol of course would make sure it never saw the light of day.) Meanwhile, in May, on the occasion of an American writer visiting the area and threatening to report what he knew, Crutcher reassured local Turkish authorities that "conditions were excellent and there was not the slightest ground for any articles being written on Turkish atrocities."[96] And so the cover-up—and complicity—proceeded.

In late March F. D. Yowell and physician Mark Ward, the directors of Near East Relief at Harput (in the deep interior of Anatolia) reached Beirut, having been expelled from Harput under police guard. In a brief report, they explained to Consul Jesse B. Jackson at Aleppo that they had been in the center of the deportation miseries and had seen terrible things. Some twenty thousand Greeks had come through Harput, they said, two thirds of whom were women and children. Yowell and Ward had carefully estimated that some 14,000 people had died somewhere along the deportation routes, primarily from starvation, exposure, typhus, or dysentery. Of course, these poor people had also suffered many atrocities en route. Turkish authorities in Harput had been frank about their intention to have all the Greeks die. Consequently, they not only failed to supply any food or clothing themselves, but strongly opposed (though they did not always prohibit) the Near East Relief's attempts to feed and shelter the suffering.[97] From reports that reached him from elsewhere in Anatolia, Ward would later conservatively estimate that a hundred thousand Greeks had been driven out of their villages toward the south or east.[98]

When Ward and Yowell traveled on to Constantinople in early May of 1922, they met with Admiral Bristol and let him know they intended to speak out about what they had seen. Back in mid-1921, Arnold Toynbee had visited the Yalova district and then come to Admiral Bristol to tell him how "wrought up" he had been over the Greek persecution of Turks that was happening there. The admiral had assured the British writer he would have the American press representatives in Constantinople contact him to make sure his information was made public.[99] Now, however, Bristol advised the Americans, Ward and Yowell, against their publishing anything. Not only would their information just be used as "propaganda," but in his opinion such reports were the cause of the Christian subjugation in Turkey in the first place. Yowell responded that he felt himself under a necessity to state the facts just as he saw them, and to make them widely known.[100]

Actually, the day before Yowell's meeting with Bristol, an extraordinary action had already occurred among some of the Americans in the city. As has been noted, the Constantinople office of the Near East Relief had thus far kept such stories under wraps, for otherwise (it was feared) Turkish authorities might interfere with their orphanage work. However, the information provided by Ward and Yowell made it clear that "conditions have existed in Harput which are similar to the conditions that existed in the interior in 1915"—in modern terms, we would say that what the admiral and others were hushing up was, in fact, genocide. Having come to some such opinion (though not using that term), Harold C. Jaquith, the Constantinople NER director, decided not only to allow Ward and Yowell to place their reports in government files (giving copies to Bristol and the State Department), but he also officially consented to the publication of "such news material as may possibly awaken the conscience of the American people." After all, he seems to have thought, what was the Near East Relief trying to do but to aid the suffering . . . but if the suffering were mostly dying by Turkish design or (in the case of the men, especially) being killed outright, what was the point?

By whatever logic he came to his decision, on May 2 Jaquith convened a meeting of the local NER administrative committee (which included Professor George Huntingdon of Robert College, a Mr. MacCallum who I believe was a local relief worker, William Peet, and the regional relief official, E. A. Yarrow, just in from the Caucasus) and found they were all in agreement on such publicity. Jaquith wrote his NER boss, Charles Vickery, in New York that by the time Vickery received his letter, the Ward and Yowell articles would probably already be published (by British papers). Jaquith told Vickery that he was destroying all reference to his letter in the Constantinople Near East Relief files and was also scrubbing the minutes there.[101]

Ward and Yowell might have published their reports anyway, but this endorsement by Jaquith and the other chief NER authorities in Constantinople was strong support indeed, and a courageous divergence from the obvious wishes of the dominating, often scowling American high commissioner. The reason the two NER workers went to the British to get publicity was Bristol's cover-up policy that he announced to them on May 3; Ward said as much to Bristol a few weeks later.[102] A report of Yowell's story was printed in the *London Times* on May 6, 1922. This publication provoked alarm and dismay in both America and Britain.

Furious, Bristol branded it all variously as propaganda or old news or the fruit of personal spite,[103] and he had lots of sychophantic help. *Chicago Tribune* reporter Larry Rue (working in Constantinople) assured Bristol he had already resisted pressure to get the Yowell reports in print and instead would do what he could to get the "true facts" in the papers at home. Constantine Brown of the *Chicago Daily News* assured his eminent friend that, if called for, he would argue that the *London Times* material was propaganda, and he would also make sure to send his own paper the "news" coming out of Angora (that is, one guesses, the Nationalist propaganda).[104] Meanwhile, in Angora Turkish papers eagerly cited the refusal of these two reporters to take the stories (and another reported refusal of the Associated Press representative in Constantinople) as evidence that the material was wholly without foundation. The Turks had other help, too, or at least said they did. They quoted Bristol's commercial attaché

Julian Gillespie as saying that Yowell's statement was "nothing but a repetition of old lies," and they also cited Florence Billings, relief representative in Angora, who chipped in her bit. Billings telegraphed Bristol on May 22 that there were no massacres in Harput, this despite the fact that no massacres per se had been alleged in the Ward and Yowell reports.[105]

The Nationalist minister of the interior did even better in terms of propaganda than representatives of the American press. Along with several other absurdities, he contended that while, of necessity, some Christians had been sent into the interior, it had all been done in a very orderly way and the Christians had been set free there. Indeed, the sick and feeble among the deportees had been taken care of by the government and were even now sending money to their families.[106]

Despite such denials, and notwithstanding the kindred success of the U.S. State Department in keeping Yowell's statements mostly out of the American press (their statements did eventually get into the *Christian Science Monitor*), Ward and Yowell's accusations were painstakingly accurate.[107] Ward's diaries listed the numbers in each group that came through Mezerah (neighboring Harput) from May through December of 1921, along with their origin and destination and the treatment each group received. In all, there had been over twenty thousand refugees who came through the city, in groups of hundreds or a few thousand, spoken of in diary entries like this one:

Dec. 13.

Fourteen hundred deportees arrived today. They originally came from Ordou, Kirasoon, Amalia, Sparta, Mordour, and Endenish. . . . They were more than 2500 when they left Cesarea but many died on the way from starvation and cold. They were all robbed on the journey so they were in terrible condition.

Later: In spite of their condition they were sent on three days later in the midst of a heavy snow storm.[108]

Ward's diary reported that some refugees were in relatively good condition for a while, but most were "half dead" or "very poor and needy" or "pitiable" before they were forced over the next mountain. The reliefers at Harput or Mezerah were sometimes allowed to give bread to refugee groups that would last as much as a day or two days, or even three or four (the Turks never gave them anything). But the refugees were usually *weeks* on the road.

Such pictures as Ward and Yowell painted were so fully corroborated by the Americans who had been in or near Harput, or Sivas, or Malatia, or Arabkir, and who chose to speak out (usually to government officials, less often to reporters) that it would be possible to compose a long descriptive litany of this "road to Calvary" of the Pontic Greeks, composed of reports from relief workers or missionaries such as the following from Bessie Murdoch and Edith Wood. Bessie Murdoch, writing of a group of a thousand near Arabkir in the late fall, 1921, who she saw being herded toward Harput: "It was a sight that one can never forget to see middle-aged and old women and men, to say nothing of the younger women and children, carrying on their backs large loads of bedding, food and fagots, and in their hands pots and kettles and perched upon their load a child . . . the storm which was brewing in the early morning on the mountains, soon developed into a blizzard . . . the roads were left strewn with their dead bodies the next day."[109] Or the following from Edith Wood, on the road from Samsun to Harput: "It took me fourteen days' constant travel to get from Malatia to Samsun. . . . Bodies lay along the roadside and in the fields everywhere. There was no hope for the Greeks from Malatia to Samsun, and the most fortunate were those who perished at the start."[110]

Some of these same missionaries or relief workers got ill with typhus themselves, as they dressed frozen hands or handed out bread to the deportees.

Several relief workers went out of their way to visit Allen Dulles or other officials at the State Department when they came to the United States. Gertrude Anthony, for example, handed her highly specific, fifteen-page report about the massacres at Marsovan directly to officials at State in case Admiral Bristol had not forwarded it, and the admiral apparently had not.[111] As a result, Dulles got a strong sense of the real state of things. As he wrote Bristol,

> If we could state that the stories of Turkish atrocities were unfounded or even grossly exaggerated, it would make our position easier, but unfortunately the evidence, even though it be from prejudiced witnesses, has not been refuted, and I am afraid it cannot be. It is not a satisfactory answer to the Christians in this country that the Greeks and Armenians have also been guilty. They ask whether the Christians can be blamed after what they have suffered at the hands of the Turks. I write you this so that you can fully appreciate our position here.[112]

Still, the State Department followed Bristol's lead in resisting any formal investigation, and, in fact, though the various foreign powers negotiated about an investigation for some time, none ever took place.

Not every American reporter toed the Bristol line, and some news did get printed in the United States. Just after the Yowell story was published, Henry Gibbons, visiting Trebizond reportedly on his way to visit Yowell in Tiflis,[113] apparently got news about that terrible refugee cauldron at the village named Jevislik from the aged Trebizond missionary, Mrs. Crawford. Mrs. Crawford had become particularly distraught, for not only had thousands of Greek adult males been "deported" from the city (probably all shot), but authorities had just rounded up the boys from eleven to fourteen. Included was a Greek lad who had been in her household since childhood. To Mrs. Crawford, Gibbons seemed a heaven-sent messenger.

The local NER director (and longtime American missionary) Crutcher failed to convince Gibbons to drop his story. (Crutcher complained that it would cause complications with the local Turks.) Gibbons, who had written a book on the 1915 deportations, had already heard far too much, and he was out of anyone's control. On return to Constantinople he also was to bypass Bristol and file his story through the British. In that story, he not only told of the thousands of Greek men being sent forever into the "Moloch jaws" of Jevislik, but also spoke of several Turks protesting this inhuman action. One Turkish hodja, for example, was reportedly so moved by the plight of the Greek boys that he went to the director of the area's schools, suggesting that, as he knew Greek, he could open a school for these boys. According to Gibbons, the director became furious: "What, when we are working to destroy these people, would you keep them alive?"[114]

This story appeared in the *Christian Science Monitor* on May 31, 1922. Sometime later Gibbons met nurse Edith Wood and filed her story, too. Wood had been in Malatia, where the Americans had been allowed to take in and care for the Greek orphans over the winter (something she said had not been authorized in Harput). The children came to Edith in the very last stages of exposure and starvation, however. Even of those who passed the simple test for admission—to be able to stand food and washing—from four to seven children died each day. "The children would often be gone before I had taken their names," Wood reported. Dozens of Greek women passed away each day, as well. Meanwhile, according to Wood, the Turks were doing nothing at all for the deportees. In Malatia, bodies lay all about in the streets and fields, and no attempt was made to bury them. "And they receive us coldly in Constantinople when we want to tell what we know . . . and let it appear very clearly that my story is unwelcome and that I am a hysterical woman, exaggerating or falsifying—that is the way it is."[115]

Finally, reporter John Clayton (representing the *Chicago Tribune*) would take a different tack. He would attempt to prove Yowell right or wrong by traveling into the interior himself. In early summer of 1922, Clayton traveled from Samsun toward Harput, and as he traveled via American missions like the one at Malatia, he heard tales of terrible cruelty. As it was summer, though, he found himself "almost persuaded that this smiling country with its wonderful views and broad vistas cannot be wicked." However, with Harput almost in sight, Clayton glimpsed a large trench that had not been dug deeply enough to obscure the stench of decomposed flesh.

At Harput, the American relief workers he visited could not speak freely, apparently coerced by local threat. Too, like other reliefers, they had signed an agreement to say nothing of the deportations until out of service with the Near East Relief. By chance, however, Clayton discovered the location of a diary of a relief worker named Applegate, who had been in charge of food distribution at this mission. One night Clayton surreptitiously copied the diary, a catalogue of fifty-three refugee groups that had traveled through Harput from June 1921 to late May 1922. The diary fully verified the Ward-Yowell summations. (Indeed, the numbers of the different groups closely match extracts from Mark Ward's diary, which Clayton apparently had not seen. Applegate's diary did differ in that it continued on for the three months after Ward and Yowell had been expelled, for the deportations continued for months after the two men left.)[116]

Clayton then traveled on to Diarbekir. Somehow not under the restraint of Harput, the relief workers there freely described the terrible conditions of the camps in their area, details of which the reporter found absolutely unprintable. These Americans also praised their vali, or local governor, however, the "one humane figure" of all this story, said Clayton. According to a report that one of these Americans wrote, when the vali of Diarbekir saw the pitiable condition of the deportees, not only did he refuse to allow them to be herded further, but he called on the Americans to help. Even the Turkish gendarmes were subject to the Near East Relief in Diarbekir. When they were guilty of cruelty or extortion (as several were), a mere word to the vali caused their removal. Moreover, when Yowell had arrived from Harput, ignominiously under police escort, the vali immediately had him released and asked him to consider himself a guest of the city. Indeed, the vali went so far as to request (unsuccessfully) that Angora give Yowell an audience.[117]

When Clayton's report reached Constantinople, although Admiral Bristol would argue (predictably) that the events could only be understood by those acquainted with the complicated background of the Near East, even he acknowledged the report's accuracy. Besides the transcription of Applegate's diary, Clayton's report included poignant descriptions of the suffering of the refugees and of their captors' inhumanity (apparently drawn from interviews), an excoriation of those responsible, and some estimates of the numbers of the dead. As just one indication of the terrible toll, Clayton found that only 10,000 refugees reached Diarbekir from the 17,000 that were driven on from Harput. (And of course many thousands of refugees had never got so far as Harput.) A reading of both diaries also indicates, by the way, that it was not just from the Pontus that the death marches had proceeded, but that they had also come from many other areas also under Turkish control.[118]

Clayton's report also failed of publication, probably not so much because of Bristol's predictable complaints, but because it was swallowed up in subsequent events. Worth noting, though, is Clayton's assertion of an enormous irony. He pointed out that the Pontic Greeks had not suffered and died in the famine-afflicted areas of Russia. Instead, these refugees had starved and frozen to death not far from "the mythical location of the garden of Eden."

CHAPTER 6

AFTER DARK IN PERA AND GALATA

Oh! things are humming,
Night time coming
Drinking and eating,
Lying and cheating . . .

Sometimes a sailor just from sea
Imbibes his dusico too free,
Or an officer haughty
Gets a wee bit naughty
In Constantinople town.

—Capt. Lyman Cotten,
Admiral Bristol's chief of staff

L eaders have always understood that those same people you have to send into battle or depend on during high seas have nonnautical interests that can greatly affect their performance of duty. Particularly on deployments involving enticing shore leave, a leader would be remiss not to recognize all the pressures by which a sailor might be affected. Similarly, it would seem shortsighted for the naval chronicler of a period to omit portraying in some detail sailors' after-hours' experiences, particularly in such an entrancing city as this one. Taking this view, I'll proceed in my portrait of Constantinople by describing the nightlife, and then I'll show several examples of how American Navy men were affected by it.

From 1919 to as late as 1923, one of the first things that American visitors noted about Constantinople's nighttime atmosphere (particularly that of the European quarters of Pera and Galata) was the music. Some of it was played or sung by Europeans and Americans, but most of the performers were Russians. Among the Russian refugees who fled to Constantinople after the Revolution were many fine musicians, and it would appear that most of them ended up playing at the city's restaurants and nightclubs.

Many Russian refugees first tried to earn their bread by offering lessons, to be sure, while others gave concerts. With the exception of full-scale grand opera, performances of almost every possible kind were given in Constantinople from 1920 to 1923.[1] Outward appearances notwithstanding, benefit concerts could be of superb quality. The Nouveau Theatre, for example, was a "tawdry, tinsel theatre built out of an old skating rink," but once a week you could hear an excellent symphony there.[2] At the Petits Champs, two concerts per day were offered by Boutnikoff's symphony orchestra,[3] while pianist Paul Lounitch played almost a hundred recitals throughout the city between 1920 and 1921.[4]

Naval and civilian Americans alike embraced these artists. Robert College invited the pianist Serge Bortkiewicz to its chapel to perform, for example. Then the social secretary for the American Sailors' Club arranged for the same pianist to play for Adm. A. P. Niblack, the visiting admiral in charge of all American naval forces in Europe. (The admiral was embarked in the battleship *Utah*, then visiting the city.) An official of the club (a former sailor) decided the admiral would not appreciate a classical pianist and told the secretary to uninvite the Russian; after all, he was only a refugee. The social secretary quietly ignored the man's direction. The evening arrived, and the secretary brought the pianist in, introduced him to the admiral, and then placed him at an instrument. Bortkiewicz's mazurka brought down the house. After seeing the audience clamor for encore after encore, the club official confessed himself enlightened about the musical tastes of American admirals and their guests.[5]

Several American men's organizations also hosted the Russians. At one time or another all the YMCA clubs in the city featured Russian musicians,[6] while the larger Navy ships sometimes invited artists aboard to sing or play. However, the American embassy led in sponsoring benefit performances. As just one example, Jeanette Edwards (visiting her brother in the city, who was an American naval officer) was especially taken with the singer Alexander Vertinsky, who had once performed before the czar: "He sang at a dinner at our Embassy the other night, and I could see the Cossacks marching—going away—away—faint in the distance, never, never to march again. Everybody cried." Jeanette added that Vertinsky was a drug fiend and would no doubt soon die; but he could really sing.[7]

Russians also danced throughout the city. At least one full-scale ballet, *Scheherazade*, was put on, complete with scenery, costumes, and a very large troop. Some said the production was on a par with those of New York and Paris; others were not so impressed.[8] In any case, it hardly made expenses, and usually smaller productions held the stage. The talent could be very good, whatever the scale. Vernon Duke created the ballet *Tale of a Syrian Night* for a premier at the Theatre des Petits-Champs in 1921. This production featured sets by Pavlik Tchelitchev, who would move on to design sets for the Berlin Opera House, while the dancers were the Russian Viktor Zimin and the Italian ballerina Bianca Fosca. Navy people were capable of admiring this kind of art, too. Late in 1922, Navy captain Rufus Zogbaum enjoyed sitting at small tables at that same garden, "sipping champagne and watching the excellent Ballet Russe." Such nightclub ballets had to compete with the bustle of service and the popping of corks, of course, but many were quite charming, nevertheless.[9]

Probably more popular than the ballet among Navy people and other Americans was Cossack dancing. You could find it throughout Constantinople, and not only in places like Maxim's, where the dancers "shouted and stamped and did particularly wonderful things with their swords."[10] In looking to buy some rugs at a Russian house somewhere in the city (he had heard about them from an Englishman), naval officer Charles Olsen came across Cossacks putting on dances for some American Red Cross girls. Sitting in a circle with a chair for a drum, the soldiers sang. After several drinks, they began to dance, and very gracefully too, Charles thought. Every so often they gulped a shot of vodka. These Russians could not understand why Charles himself would not drink. After all, the American women did, and somehow they "got away with it," as Lieutenant Olsen wrote his young wife.[11]

Occasionally Americans tried out their own feet. Hearing some Cossack music deep in the Caucasus east of Batoum, the executive officer of an American destroyer (I'm not sure which one) jumped into a ring and danced well enough to be showered with money by appreciative bystanders. "Nothing like this had ever hit dear old Adzharistan. A U.S. officer in uniform, crossing gold armstripes, squatting and kicking out in rhythm!" The American officer had probably been taught by Russian officers back at Constan.[12] Even very senior Russians could dance, by the way, and dance well. At a stag dinner to which the Russian commanding general was invited, General Wrangel performed a Cossack sword dance.[13]

A good deal of the Russians' dancing and music was spontaneous. After the Muscovite's large orchestra retired late in the evening, gypsy songs with guitar often enraptured both its late diners and its own Russian staff. "More than all else this Gypsy music brought back Russia to them, their lost Russia. What was happening in Russia? Millions were dying of starvation, so the relief agencies reported, and letters sometimes came through—it was quite true that human flesh was being eaten. What was the fate of the old mother, the little child, the sister, the friends left behind? Eyes swam with tears, but they were resolutely held back; lips smiled on."[14] After all, the Russians had to eat, too, and it was in the restaurants, the nightclubs, and the small cafés that the artists typically earned their living.

The music at the hotels and at the best restaurants was of high caliber. A chamber music orchestra was employed by the Pera Palace Hotel, for example, and the Tokatlian also had its orchestra.[15] Groups performed outdoors, as well. Not only did an orchestra sometimes play at the Petit Champs, for example, but Taxim Garden employed an operatic group.[16] Nightclubs more commonly had smaller groups or soloists, but they could be first rate as well. Ivan Ontchik, a former first violinist at several Russian symphony orchestras, played at the nightclub Rose-Noire, for instance.[17] At that same club, Ens. Dan Gallery heard a violinist he called "Gurlesque" (probably Jan Gilesko) perform *Etude, Humoresque, Minuette*, and *Ave Maria*: "He made that fiddle weep & sing as if it were human."[18]

American fox-trots and other pieces were part of the mix. A Russian pianist at the Muscovite got considerable attention by picking up any song that an American might whistle to him and quickly putting it in parts for the orchestra. "One is apt to hear anything from 'Home, Sweet Home' to the latest rag, which ends in the middle because the ensign who whistled it to the pianist couldn't remember how the last half of it went," wrote journalist Kenneth Roberts.[19] Some Americans were themselves musicians. The larger Navy ships like *St. Louis* and *Alameda* had bands or orchestras, and even the destroyer *McCormick* had a jazz orchestra, which frequently did gigs ashore.[20] As an enlisted radioman in the city, "in the days of my pious youth," Arthur Godfrey had played banjo in his destroyer's band.[21] American blacks also performed. Right near Taxim Garden was the popular nightclub called Maxim's, and an American jazz orchestra played there. Not only were the members of this orchestra often black,[22] by the way, but so was the club's proprietor. He was an imposing though polite American black named Thomas, or, as he is usually referred to by Istanbul's historically knowledgeable, "Black Thomas."

In the early 1890s, Thomas had apparently been living somewhere in Virginia (or Mississippi or Georgia—the accounts do not agree) and attracted the attention of a Russian prince traveling through the American South, who engaged him as his valet and took him back to Russia. Thomas, who somewhere along the line acquired the Russian name "Feodor Feodorovich Tomas,"[23] became butler in his employer's household. Then he worked as a waiter in a

St. Petersburg restaurant, and eventually from there he is said to have become the owner of a jazz hall called Maxim's in Moscow, or a Moscow amusement complex called the Aquarium.[24] When the Revolution occurred, his first wife was killed, after which Thomas married his children's nurse. But according to Lieutenant Dunn (who once interviewed Thomas at the American embassy), Thomas had trouble with this woman. One day he found her in bed in his own flat with a Bolshevik commissar. He divorced the woman, but she ran off with the children.[25]

Thomas himself fled south and ended up in Constantinople. He had some money, and so he started a cabaret called Stella's, a sort of "improvised box under the trees," as Captain Lyman Cotten's wife, Elizabeth, would put it.[26] It was said to be the first dancing establishment in Constantinople and seems to have introduced the Charleston and the fox-trot to the city. Before long, Thomas was running Maxim's, near Constantinople's Grande Rue, "a [wild] place, but everyone goes," according to Jeanette Edwards.[27] By this time, Thomas had married again to a "titled" Russian wife, a woman who was also a fairly good dancer.[28] Like the Muscovite restaurant, which employed over a hundred Russians and fed two hundred more, Thomas's place hired Russians as cooks and helpers of various kinds. Captain Mannix watched Thomas one day go to the help of a Russian busboy. This Russian had dared return the blow of a drunken British patron. On Thomas' mild inquiry, the British man's friend shook his fist in the proprietor's face and screamed in outrage, "He struck an ENGLISHMAN." Thomas replied, "You shake your fist in my face again and I'll strike another." Taken aback, the Englishmen both left the place.[29]

Maxim's, like everybody else, also employed Russians as waitresses, a great attraction throughout Constantinople. The young Russian women who got jobs at premier restaurants like the Muscovite, the Hermitage, or Maxim's were typically very beautiful. Some had aristocratic backgrounds; others had once been very rich. The Muscovite, Cleveland Edwards' sister Jeannette wrote home, "was the famous Russian restaurant where a general checks your coat and helps you on with your rubbers; and a princess, very likely, brings your soup."[30] In a short story, French writer Paul Morand described the situation in this way: "Waitresses sat about at the tables. They fetched the food, gave orders, took them with a gentle distinction; here and there the ease, the fine word, the elegance of some gesture ordinarily servile betrayed their former condition."[31] At the Muscovite it was not uncommon to see a party of guests get up from their table and kiss the hand of the waitress who came to take their order.[32]

One night at this restaurant (the most popular and fashionable in the city), journalist Roberts found himself being waited on by a granddaughter of one of Russia's former prime ministers. At an adjoining table, five American naval officers were being served by Madame Shmeman, whose husband had once been many times a millionaire. Roberts admired these handsome and cultivated women, for they seemed completely without air or haughtiness. They also proved excellent dinner companions, for at leisure moments they would sit at the tables, eat, and talk. After midnight, once the full orchestra had packed up, these waitresses would often waltz to the accompaniment of a pianist and a few strings and with American or British officers as partners.[33]

Young naval officer Dan Gallery, with date, in a ship's hatch, probably that of the cruiser *Pittsburgh. Courtesy of the Special Collections and Archives Division, Nimitz Library, United States Naval Academy*

In his six months in the city while attached to the cruiser *Pittsburgh* (when he was not visiting Anthie Angelides, the Greek girl he dated regularly for several weeks), Ens. Dan Gallery would usually begin his evenings at the Muscovite, admiring both the waitresses (with whom he would sometimes dance), and the music, too, "not more than a month behind New York," he noted. By midnight he and his friends would typically find themselves at Maxim's. Before heading back to the ship (typically committing some kind of petty vandalism on the way), these high-spirited young officers would dance with all the girls at this place. In his diary, Gallery described the waitresses' attractions: "Most of them sling a fragrant sock, speak English well, and would pass for respectable girls. As a matter of fact I think over half of them are but of course some of them would be except for one bad habit."[34] And indeed there was another side to the romantic portraiture of the Russian waitresses drawn by magazine writers, an aspect that journalists sometimes left out.

Red Cross worker Eugenia Bumgardner described the very difficult situation facing the young women who worked even at the very best restaurants. They were not well paid, but they still had to look very good every evening, and hair treatments, manicures, clothes, and shoes could be expensive, Bumgardner wrote. As meals were not a part of their wage, they might be hungry even as they served dinner. Given their precarious economic status, they could be quite vulnerable, especially when offered large tips or invitations to dine, which were the surest approaches to them. "There was nothing so crude in the management of the restaurants as an understanding that the waitresses were employed for any other purpose; but if one of them refused the proposals of a wealthy client, and he reported his disappointment, the management simply dispensed with her services. . . . The cards were stacked, and it was inevitable that she must sometimes play a losing game."[35] Some of the Russian women (like Madame Shmeman) supported relatives or families or husbands, and those husbands, often diseased or wounded or unable to find work, could be tortured with jealousy. Yet the women could not let any anxiety show. Hence the atmosphere of these restaurants was so charming that casual visitors often did not notice the dark underside of the business, the "tears behind the smile, the nightly traffic in souls and bodies."[36]

—◆◆◆—

Actually, most of the vice in Constantinople—again, it predominated in so-called Christian (actually, European) districts as it always had—was quite unabashed. In his 1922 book, Turkish writer Zia Bey described an evening when he and his young American wife were shown the sights of Pera by a friend, an ethnic Greek. They noted prostitutes strolling arm-in-arm everywhere on the Grande Rue of Pera, including some girls of fourteen and fifteen, and prostitutes of the male sex as well. Their host invited them to a show, "the rage of the moment," so lurid that attendees were given masks to let them hide their identity. His wife was so shocked at the idea that they went to *Scheherazade* instead. It dragged a bit, so they adjourned to Stella's, noted its black proprietor and the Negro jazz band, and also witnessed the surreptitious glances their Greek host exchanged with a Russian waitress beauty. The Greek obviously being bent on getting into the action, Zia Bey and his wife soon excused themselves and left the "sinister noises" of Galata for their home in Stamboul, which was, he wrote, sleeping "the sleep of the just."[37]

Zia Bey was, of course, part propagandist. At one point Admiral Bristol felt he had to warn the Turkish writer to "avoid writing propaganda articles"; instead, he should write articles in such a way "that they would appear impartial."[38] Still, much of Zia Bey's description here, at least, rings true. Not everyone was interested in the more lurid activities of Pera and Galata, of course, but other than the fellow who came to lecture the British military on the nobility of sex, almost nobody *did* much about the situation. Well, the French did inspect a few whorehouses and issue those specific addresses to their troops (separate addresses for officers and men, by the way), and they also attempted to standardize the prices.[39] Some of the more shabby and disease-ridden houses were put out of bounds for the Allied militaries, and of course venereal disease was treated after the fact.

Western writers did sometimes comment upon the rampant immorality. Comparing Constantinople's vice to that of other port cities he had visited, William T. Ellis argued that Constantinople's vice was "far and away the most immoral on earth." He not only cited an American naval officer's dismayed reaction to the spectacle—"It makes you feel as if there is no God"—but also reported the instincts of a veteran American missionary. She confessed longing for the good old days of Sultan Abdul Hamid (known widely as "Abdul the Damned"), when the city had been so much less immoral a place![40]

Anyway, contemporaneous descriptions of the prostitutes plying their trade ranged from naval officers' comic verse to dry academic prose. After considerable observation of Constantinople, for instance, Bristol's chief of staff, Capt. Lyman Cotten, composed rude lines like these for the amusement of the admiral and his staff:

> In Constantinople Town,
> Lovely ladies can be found. . . .
> Tall and short and young and old,
> Fat ones, thin ones, gay and bold. . . .
> Oh! they are perfect ladies, quite,
> Except they swear so when they're tight.[41]

Contrasted to this doggerel was the matter-of-fact prose of a contemporaneous sociological survey of Constantinople that was conducted by the American colleges. It discussed prostitution under the heading of "Adult Delinquency": "In the registered houses, the girls are usually paid one-half the fee received, and are given board and room. The fees run all the way from 15 piasters ($.12) a visit in some of the lower houses in Galata to 5 liras ($4) in what is called the

Yankee House in Pera and one other. In one of the private houses at Shisli, patronized by rich Moslems, the price is from 5 to 10 liras ($4 to $8) a visit."[42] The survey also reported fourteen hundred beer halls throughout the metropolitan area: "Most of them are rather disreputable places, where there is low dancing and where prostitutes solicit trade."[43] Bumgardner, by the way, seems doubtful about the usefulness of this "queer American Survey" of employment, industry, wages, recreation, and education. Indeed, given the terrible suffering existing at the very time the survey was being conducted (mid-1920 to mid-1921), the great effort expended would probably have been more fruitfully dedicated to relief work, as Admiral Bristol argued.[44]

Still, in retrospect, the survey helps paint a picture. For example, although it was very difficult to find out what was going on in Turkish houses run by Muslim women in Scutari and KadiKeuy, the survey reported almost two hundred registered "houses of ill repute" in Pera, these owned primarily by Greeks, Jews, and Armenians. Over four thousand prostitutes were estimated to work in the city, some of them registered (that is, monitored and treated for venereal disease) but most of them not. Greek women predominated, but a quarter of the prostitutes in Galata were Russian, the survey stated, and their number was growing. Interestingly, one American woman was listed among the registered prostitutes.[45]

The young Vernon Duke was turned off by the "terrifying fat whores in Galata,"[46] but such revulsion was atypical. Most young American men found Pera quite a place. Naval officer Robbie Dunn described the scene in this way:

> At Petit Champs you could watch Cossack dancers, see clean, U.S. tincan sailors pile out of arabas [carriages] into the stew of tarts cadging for champagne, one on stage singing "Madelon." There I met Blanche, a pallid-plump, clever Rumanian Jewess who had the junior staff [Royal Navy] paymaster in tow. Blanche was my first Pera friend.
>
> Across at Bertha's bar, the madam was out of a Lancashire music hall, blondined, loud, and handsome. The house girls she'd named 'Frying Pan,' 'Square Arse,' 'Mother's Ruin,' 'Fornicating Fannie'; she herself lived alone off over Tophani Landing and virginally locked the door on whoever took her home. She was, of course, a top limey spy.

Loving the atmosphere of intrigue as he did, Dunn avoided the embassy social circuit and made lots of prostitute friends. At one point he got sick with typhoid and spent six weeks in a British hospital. Although everybody from the American embassy came to see him, his Pera friend, Blanche, came by most often. Her visits scandalized the British nurses there.[47]

Not all Navy people liked the nightly entertainment. After helping with the Crimean evacuation in October of 1920, *St. Louis* mostly stayed anchored in the Bosporus for the next year or so. The young officer Charles Olsen, serving in this ship, frequently wrote his wife and often commented disparagingly on the drunkenness, the fights, and the vice. On Christmas Eve of 1920, for instance, he had the midwatch. His relief had come aboard drunk and would not get up even when Olsen dumped a pitcher of water over him, stuck him with his sword, then threw him out of his bunk to the deck. Olsen gave it up when two other drunken officers came aboard and engaged his relief in a fight.[48] On this occasion virtually all the officers returned to the ship drunk, but more typical were problems with the enlisted men, especially after payday. Twice a month they "drank the town dry," and sometimes as they came aboard, three men had to wrestle one to the deck till a doctor's needle put him to sleep.

According to Olsen, the men were usually okay when they ran out of money[49]—unless they had brought liquor aboard. A couple of nights before New Year's, at midnight, a chief petty officer came on the quarterdeck with a bulge in his pocket. Officer of the Deck Olsen had the man searched and found a bottle. The chief immediately sobered, but Olsen still put him on report.[50] Four days later, at morning quarters, Olsen was embarrassed to find that overnight one of his own men had returned drunk from shore patrol with liquor in his possession. This sailor had also been drinking on duty. Olsen was totally exasperated, for now three men in his own division faced General Court Martials. Drinking on duty was a major offence: "It is a G.C.M. every time and they all know it," Olsen lamented. The penalty was five to ten years in prison. At this time, by the way, *St. Louis* had eighteen G.C.M. prisoners aboard (from several Navy ships), all apparently having been awarded five to ten years' sentence.[51]

In late January, even one of Olsen's own Annapolis classmates (a young naval officer) was undergoing a G.C.M., this for climbing up and into the second-story window of a house in Constantinople and raising hell in somebody's home.[52]

Of course, there were also frequent fights ashore, and many murders. In early January 9, 1921, a sailor from *Scorpion* shot an Italian; around January 15 another American sailor shot a Japanese man. That same night seven Greeks and three Frenchmen were killed, this during the celebration of the Greek New Year. A few nights after that, while Olsen was on shore patrol, several English and Italian nationals were killed while fighting: "The rumpus started near the dock yard gate at Tophany and ended up in the wops *throwing hand grenades*." (Normally the Italians, as in *Romeo and Juliet*, just fought with knives, which was certainly bad enough). In the letter to Edna describing the latest incident, Charles concluded that Constantinople was at the same time interesting, dirty, and terrible.[53]

The wickedness was sometimes ridiculous. One night Charles found a Russian kid trying to pimp two streetwalkers for him and the sergeant of marines, even while Olsen and the marine were on shore patrol. Later he saw something else: "Just imagine darling, a man, painted and powdered up with rouge, penciled eye brows and painted lips, dressed to kill, with short trousers with cuff and cloth top shoes and silk socks. An overcoat with narrow waist and it all walking past so dainty and delicate, wiggling her sterns. Oh my. . . . They tell me that this is a common sight."[54] All this time, although Edna wanted to join him, Charles was writing her not to come to the place.

Of course, the great interest both officers and men took in the available women also bothered Olsen. When *St. Louis*'s executive officer (a commander) was not gambling, for instance, he was chasing women and coming back at five or so in the morning. One night the exec had a girl aboard ship to sing. Fine, but at the end of the evening the exec had given the girl eight of Olsen's favorite piano pieces, his very latest and best. Olsen was furious: "He would give anything away to a pretty face. 'Japanese Sandman,' 'Irene,' 'Just Like a Rose,' etc., all gone. Damn his soul anyhow." Because he was so junior, Olsen feared to confront the exec. On another occasion Olsen told Edna that a Russian girl had come aboard. She had demanded the captain marry her to a sailor who had lived with her for two months and gotten her pregnant. Of course the sailor called her a slut, and two other crewmen came forward to say they had also slept with the girl. The captain resisted forcing the marriage on the sailor lest it make a precedent for all the Russian women in Constantinople.[55]

Then there was the affair of one of Olsen's friends with a Russian ballet dancer. A fellow officer named John began befriending this decent woman. (Though her looks were unremarkable, she had some artistic talent, Olsen thought.) John brought her aboard to dance and to teach the officers some basic ballet steps. He started spending all his spare time ashore with her. Not surprisingly, she fell for John, and John eventually also for her. John, however, was already married. Eventually, he told the Russian girl of his marital status, and she made plans to leave for Vienna. But then she put it off to stay with John, and at last report John was reading the Russian girl his wife's letters. Charles was disgusted with the whole business.[56] Meanwhile, in the junior officer staterooms the conversation was always turning to the cafés and to the women. That disgusted Charles too.[57] (Well, he *was* in the Navy; what did he expect?)

After months and months, Charles caved in and invited his wife to come to Constantinople. (At some point he would transfer to become the commanding officer of a subchaser, apparently so as to stay longer in the city, while *St. Louis* returned home.) He made sure Edna knew what she was in for: "Constantinople has [neither] the luxuries of the States nor are the houses new

After a year in Constantinople on board the *St. Louis*, Lt. (jg) Charles Olsen took command of the subchaser shown to his left. His friend, Lt. (jg) Oran Maser, commander of another subchaser, stands behind Olsen. *Courtesy Lawrence Olsen*

or modern. They are old weather beaten shacks for the most part. . . . The local-
ities of apartments are horrible, the places are on side alleys in the midst of the
slum. There [are] no nice sections of the town. The streets are crooked and cob-
blestone, narrow and dirty, and hilly. The people, well dear, there are many nice
people and also bad. They all live together in this town. Your next door neigh-
bor might be a ———. Especially if she is a Russian girl, of which this town
is full." He also warned Edna that there wasn't much to do: dinners at cafés,
movies, sightseeing, dancing at the embassy, YMCA, and the Near East Relief.
That was it. He wasn't fond of any of it.[58] When she arrived, Edna wrote home,
exclaiming that American women dared not go out after sunset without a man,
lest the girls find a group of men at their heels. All unaccompanied girls were
assumed to be prostitutes. Once Navy wives went home, she later reported,
their officer husbands seemed always to be chasing women, getting drunk, and
worse.[59]

It could work the other way, too. In late 1922, when another dozen destroyers came and several officers brought their wives, complaints were heard about
the wives' regular flirtations with married officers other than their husbands.
One explanation for the behavior of these married women might have been
the competition they faced. As Bumgardner pointed out, "Wives were always a
bit de trop [in the way] in restaurants of Constantinople. The Russian waitresses,
quite unconsciously apparently, dimmed the charm of other women."[60] At any
rate, the young naval officer Orin Haskell said it was typically the younger
women who behaved like this: "This bunch of newlyweds try to outdo the
Russians on their own soil while their husbands sit back and try to watch their
smoke. I could stand such a life just about a week and then I should be tempted
to try a little smoke myself."[61] Edna Olsen was not that kind of woman. To be
sure, she did like the swimming and picnics, the dinners and teas and nightlife quite a bit more than her husband did. Although she had originally been
shocked about the circumstances she encountered, her letters home indicate
that before long she had gotten quite used to the place: "Well it's a rather hard
step to take to leave U.S.A. for wicked old Constantinople but after one lives
here six months all the weird and awful sights pass by unnoticed."[62]

In contrast, Jeannette Edwards was not just enthusiastic about the city—she
was breathless: "It's a delirious life for a British or American girl. *Thousands* of
British officers (the most handsome creatures on earth—so slim and straight,
and just poured into their uniforms); fiery Italians and French; the mad, impul-
sive, pathetic Russians; all lonely for women of their own class to talk to, all
new and strange and exciting." For Jeannette, every meal was a party; almost
every evening a dance. There were lunches at famous restaurants, teas on the
ships, tea dances at the embassy and at the restaurants, dinners (with dancing)

at apartments. If Jeannette did occasionally hear screams or gunshots or see fires when coming home at night, it only added to the fascination of the place.[63]

Jeannette was not the only young American woman interested in men and marriage. Although, according to Edwards, American naval officers took only a brotherly interest in the American women (the American men were all entranced by the beautiful Russians), the Near East Relief girls were said to be marrying the British at an "alarming" rate. It was true. By June 1922, Admiral Bristol had given away six American girls to British officers.[64] To be sure, some of the American women had a few special attractions of their own. A Russian author spoke of what typically happened, say, at the Hotel Splendid on Prinkipo Island. The American girls there danced in such close proximity to their partners, and wore "an expression of such ecstasy," that an Englishman, after dancing an entire evening with one of them, asked his friends if it were not his duty, as an honorable man, to marry the girl.[65]

Marriage was an interest of both men and women in this astonishing city, and for a great variety of reasons. The women sometimes were quite forthright about it. An enlisted man on the *St. Louis* asked Olsen's advice about marrying a Russian girl in Stamboul, and Olsen convinced him not to, as her only desire seemed to be to marry somebody who would take her to America. The man took Olsen's advice.[66] Naval officer Ash Pleasants later told his son that a Greek lady at a social function had once offered him 15,000 drachma to marry her beautiful daughter, but Ash had turned her down. "Dad often said, between chuckles, that the daughter wasn't bad, but that he didn't much care for the look of the mother."[67] Conversely, when Baroness Wrangel complained to Captain Bill Leahy that, in their association with men, many Russian women in Constantinople didn't seem to care whose husbands they might be, the captain replied that the Russian women he had met "were not hard to look at, but that none of them had seemed to show any interest in me." Yet a Turkish official's wife did once offer to marry Leahy, in order, she said, that she might get to America. When Leahy politely informed her that this would not be possible because American men only married one woman at a time, she went on to offer herself in turn to each of the *St. Louis*'s officers. However, she had no success.[68]

Some Americans did marry foreign women in Constantinople during this period. One reporter talked to a sailor who was about to marry a French girl from the city and bring her back to New York before he entered flight training.[69] Another writer told of an American sailor who asked his officer not only for authorization to marry a local girl, but also to have the use of a naval car to take his bride to the wedding. The officer gave his consent, but then happened to ask about the nationality of the girl. Grinning, the sailor replied, "She says

Commander Harry Pence and Captain Daniel P. Mannix, III, with friends on Mannix's nonregulation captain's gig. Day or night, this was the best way to cruise the Bosporus, especially with someone beside you. *Mandeville Collection, University of San Diego*

she's a Hellene, but confidentially I think she is a blooming Greek."[70] Robbie
Dunn's yeoman married a Russian "princess," and officers married Russian
girls too. A Navy chaplain married a young Russian woman named Elaine to
Lt. Edgar Winckler while he was serving in *Scorpion*, for instance.[71] And during
the time that *Gilmer* saw duty in Russia, Lt. Edward Jones met a young Russian
woman in Yalta named Thais Jarochev.

Thais and her mother had fled from the Bolsheviks, her father being a
White Russian officer. Later, Edward and Thais met again in Trieste and got
married there. They honeymooned in Venice. Some months after that, Edward
shocked his staid, aristocratic family back in Virginia by sending home on a
Greek steamer a beautiful and young but also quite Russian and newly pregnant wife.[72]

Despite the other enticements, and no matter what their age, many
Americans would remain romantic rather than merely venereal even in this
apparently godforsaken place. Alice Clark, Anna Mitchell, and Cdr. Harry
Pence (the latter with the Russian waitress Tania from the Muscovite beside
him) on different occasions all were moved by the wonderful sunsets or the
beautiful moonlit nights, as they took Navy boats south through the Bosporus
back to the city from a day of recreation further north.[73] And in a half dozen
American ships out in that harbor would be another hundred hearts with their
minds on something other than their nightly duty. Some, like Charles Olsen in
the months before Edna joined him, might be reminded of nights on the water
back home in Waukegan by hearing a porpoise splash. Through the still, cool
night he would hear the shouts or noise of the city, while all about the ship he
could see the lights of the other vessels and the glow of the city beyond. The
scene would remind him of the girl he had left behind. "Oh darling, my heart
longs so for you."[74] Conversely, the beautiful nights and exotic location would
make many other officers and sailors yearn for the restaurants and streets of
Pera, and the Greek, Armenian, and especially the young Russian women who
they planned to visit the very next night.

CHAPTER 7

THE GREAT RUSSIAN FAMINE

The Odessa opera is now open and there is a performance nearly every evening. A member of the American Relief Administration who attended last evening said it was very good, but that the effect was rather spoiled when he stumbled over a corpse lying on the sidewalk just outside.

—Webb Trammell, commanding officer, USS *Fox*

In July of 1921, while sailors, naval officers, and many other Americans were delighting in the astonishing Russian music suddenly available in Constantinople, and were also becoming more and more enchanted with the beautiful Russian women, Russian author Maxim Gorky made an emergency appeal to the world for his homeland. Back in what was now Bolshevik Russia, millions had begun suffering from a massive famine. Could anyone help?

Admiral Bristol heard of the Russian's appeals and wrote the State Department of his willingness to cooperate in relief measures, but Commerce Secretary Herbert Hoover had already promised food for a million children, some medical supplies—and further investigation.[1] Hence, before long, American teams set off on yet additional investigatory journeys, this time to southeastern Russia.

———◆◆◆———

Traveling with a five-man Near East Relief Commission in August of 1921 was the American relief head in the Caucasus, E. A. Yarrow. Yarrow had been doing extensive Armenian relief and orphanage work, but on this journey he would encounter conditions at least as frightful as any he had witnessed in Armenia. In late August, his commission began sending preliminary reports to Hoover and others by a series of long telegrams.

One message pointed out that this was the second year of the famine and that the peasants were now living on bread made of millet and chalk, or grass mixed with earth. Over the winter, many farmers had sold their household goods to maintain life, hoping to pull through till the next harvest. It was not to be: "This summer whole southeast Russia upburned by drought Stop Army grasshoppers ten miles wide swept from Novorossisk through grainbelt destroying what little rye left Stop Population forced eat draught animals when harvest failed now have nothing."[2] A great wave of emigration resulted. Whole towns and farming districts were fleeing by train to neighboring regions. Ironically, peasants were piling into trains traveling *in both directions*, as nobody knew where food was actually to be had.[3] On reaching the cities, the peasants sometimes became struggling mobs. Usually, though, they just lay lifeless about the railway stations.

Members of the commission walked through these camps and came on dying children at every turn. Mothers with shrunken, empty breasts were attempting to nurse their babies on a diet of watermelons. Many of the suffering were emaciated; others featured grotesquely swollen abdomens and limbs. Hence, as the commission reported, these "acres" of helpless humanity were ripe for "death's sickle" at the moment winter set on.[4]

An American newspaper writer who visited the train stations toward the end of 1921 found the sickle in full swing: "The people died while they waited—died not by the one, but by the dozen and by the hundred. The children died like flies. They died in the trains, they died around the stations. The women crawled out into the streets and sank dead on the ground. Death became so commonplace that you scarcely noticed it."[5] Having observed trainloads of refugees being forcibly evacuated by a Bolshevik committee, Dr. Henry Beeuwkes would find the situation appalling in the extreme. "I saw one echelon arrive in Moscow from Kazan, where all children in several cars were found frozen to death upon arrival."[6] Hoover's initial plan to feed a million children (already proposed and agreed to by Bolshevik authorities in July) was obviously insufficient. Somebody had to provide grain for literally millions of starving peasants, along with medical help prodigious enough to stave off mammoth epidemics. Moreover, the grain had to be transported deep into the interior of Russia, all the way to local villages, so the peasants would be on hand to plant corn the next year. Otherwise, not only would millions soon die and more millions in years to come, but aimless refugees (it was thought) would spread social disorder throughout the continent.

Some American politicians wanted the Bolsheviks to fry in their own grease. They argued that by prohibiting trade and private enterprise and by confiscating peasants' foodstocks—even by confiscating the seed corn for the next crop!—the Bolsheviks had helped to bring about the famine in the first place.[7] The Reds should be left to deal with it. Others disagreed. In urging that the relief be approved, many Americans were actuated purely by humanitarian motives. Some (like Herbert Hoover) were largely altruistic but also hoped that ending hunger and starvation would enable the Russian people to gain the physical and moral strength to throw off the Bolsheviks.

In any case, in January of 1922 Congress appropriated $19 million for grain—mainly yellow corn, new to Russia. Additional millions' worth of medical supplies were to come from the War Department and the American Red Cross. Private contributions and aid from religious charities would greatly swell the total.[8] Plans were quickly drawn up. Under the American Relief Administration (ARA), with headquarters in Moscow, some two or three hundred Americans were already locating warehouses and setting up food kitchens for the child-feeding program. Now, in addition, they were to help organize distribution of the huge shipments of corn and assist the American medical teams that were coming.

To what ports should the corn be sent? In September of 1921, Admiral Bristol ordered the destroyer *Gilmer* with its commander, Mike Robertson, and Bristol's aide, Lt. Robbie Dunn, to southern Russia to investigate. The Soviet officials there were full of threat and bluff.

—◆◆◆—

When *Gilmer* docked at the port city of Novorossisk, port authorities announced as they boarded that Russian guards would have to be placed on the American Navy ships, lest the Americans land contraband through offshore portals. Robertson responded that the guards could only stand on the dock. The Bolshevik officials then stipulated that the ship must be quarantined because of "cholera in Constantinople," at which the Americans just laughed. "But of course you'll have to shut down your wireless." Again Robertson refused, and went on to tell the communists that if they insisted on such absurd conditions, they could forget about any food. When the Russian commissar pushed the point, demanding surrender of the radio key, the tough Navy CO gave orders to get his ship under way—whereupon the Russians backed off. Of course the American Navy ship should stay; everyone would cooperate.[9]

Over the next several months, the Navy's stiff resolve in the face of Bolshevik blustering was to become typical. Even now, despite their newfound cooperation, some Russians officials boasted, "We live under dictatorship, yet it is one more just and human than the capitalist tyranny." To this, Robertson argued that the Russian system had created a greater famine than the czar ever

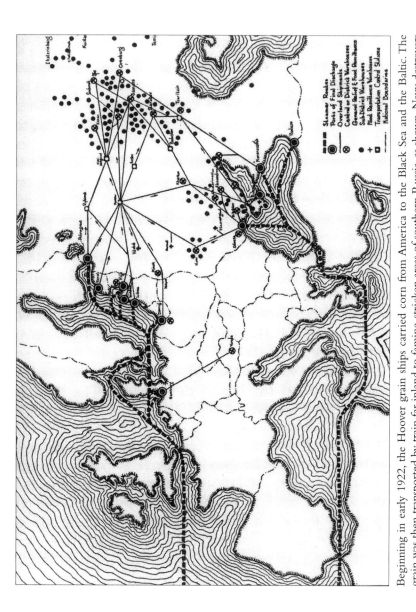

Beginning in early 1922, the Hoover grain ships carried corn from America to the Black Sea and the Baltic. The grain was then transported by train far inland to famine-stricken areas of southern Russia, as shown. Navy destroyers coordinated the ships' movements. *Reproduced from H. H. Fisher, The Famine in Soviet Russia, 1919–1923 (Stanford, CA: Stanford University Press, 1927).*

had. Actually, only a few officials spouted propaganda, usually the higher-ups. Even on *Gilmer's* initial visit, the Russian pilot and the Greek translator whispered to the Americans that nothing would make *them* Bolsheviks. With good meals on the mess decks, loafs of bread as they left the ship and offers of rare cigarettes, even the surly dock guards soon warmed up. The Greek interpreter privately informed Robertson and Dunn that the 90,000 people in the city had no work, lived three to a room, and from fear mostly stayed off the street. "We starve, but lots of food and plunder are stored away," he averred. Walking through a bedraggled black market, Dunn witnessed one frail old lady trade her fine ermine stole for a paper spill of salt.[10]

On returning to Constantinople, the American officers reported that the Bolsheviks were in complete control of the city, and though there were few true believers, the people were utterly demoralized. There would be no chance of a revolt. American food would be welcomed by all, though, and, with some repairs, facilities at Novorossisk would be good enough.[11]

Over the winter the grain operation got rolling, with ships being loaded in the United States and then sailing direct to Baltic and Black Sea ports. From these ports a vast grid of rail lines would transport the grain an average of a thousand miles inland per trip. Over that winter, most of the Baltic froze up. For several months, transport in the north came virtually to a halt. Moreover, everywhere there was a shortage of locomotives and railcars. (Rail stock had been vandalized and allowed to rust during and since the Revolution.) At Black Sea ports, fewer than 60 of a promised 240 cars per day actually materialized.[12] Despite these and other problems, including deteriorated warehouses, warped and spread rails, rotted ties, and so forth, in late January of 1922 supplies of American grain began shipping through Novorossisk and, to a lesser extent, through Theodosia and Odessa.[13] In his memoir, Robbie Dunn reported that the grain mainly went through Baltic ports,[14] not the only time Dunn got his facts exactly backward: most of the grain actually shipped through the Black Sea. Several Baltic facilities were used, though. Beginning in the spring of 1922, after the freeze, grain also began shipping in the north.

The main contribution of Americans from Constantinople and Turkey was naval liaison, and even this was kept low key lest the naval presence suggest recognition of the Bolsheviks.[15] Nevertheless, the relief of the starving in Russia constituted yet another significant part of the American naval service in the region. Admiral Bristol assigned a permanent rotation of destroyers to the northern Black Sea, so at least one destroyer was in Novorossisk at all times, and another at Odessa. The destroyer captains on the Russian stations were kept busy making arrangements with port authorities for the grain ship entry, meeting incoming vessels, relaying communications, and handling unforeseen difficulties.

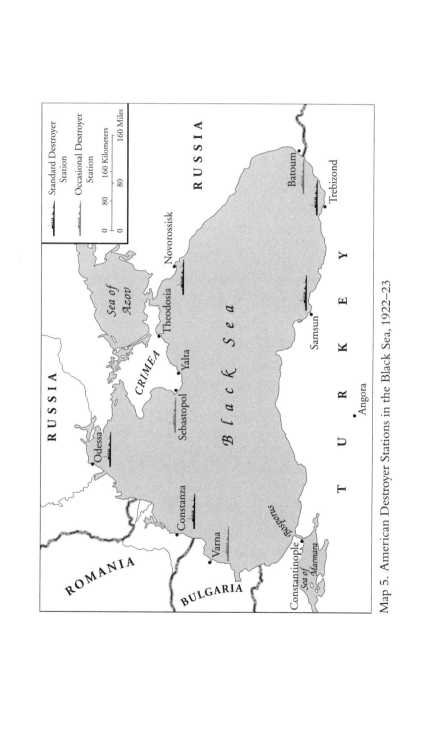

Map 5. American Destroyer Stations in the Black Sea, 1922–23

Lt. Cdr. Webb Trammell, commanding officer of *Fox*, was sent by Admiral Bristol to coordinate the initial grain shipments. On January 19, 1922, *Fox* reported to Novorossisk after a day's steaming from Constantinople, and over the next several days, Trammell dealt with the local police and other key Bolsheviks. He also visited with ARA officials, who were already in the city preparing for the grain shipments. Trammell reported some of his conversations by message back to the admiral.[16] On January 29, *Fox* made a day's visit to Theodosia to offload some ARA passengers, and Trammell visited with many officials there, too. Among other things, he learned that *Fox* was the first foreign vessel to visit Theodosia since the Russian Revolution. Trammell suggested that Bristol consider offloading some of the grain ships in Theodosia, too, for the positive effect it might have on Russian morale.[17]

Fox returned to Novorossisk, and while awaiting the first grain ships, Trammell visited a nearby Greek refugee camp. The five or six thousand ethnic Greeks in the camp had sometime earlier fled to Russia from the Black Sea coast of Turkey. They were having to beg for what little food they could get—which wasn't much, for they only could beg from already destitute Russians! Hence five Greeks were dying daily, and the Greek leaders told Trammell they were all hoping one way or another somehow to get on to Greece.[18]

On February 6, *Fox* went to sea to meet SS *Winnebago*, the first American relief ship to arrive in Russia. *Fox* transferred a Russian pilot to this grain ship and then led the way back into Novorossisk.

Two days later, Trammell handed the Novorossisk diary he had begun to Capt. Robert Ghormley of *Sands* and steamed southeast toward Batoum (en route, the destroyer battled heavy winds and seas).[19] He spent a few days there, then steamed west to Constantinople for another week, and then traveled back north, this time to coordinate the initial arrival of grain ships at Odessa. Reaching Sebastopol on February 21, *Fox*'s captain relayed to Bolshevik officials the requests of the SS *Effna* and SS *Deepwater* for pilots and for permission to enter port at Odessa. *Fox* then got under way to meet and accompany the latter two grain ships to berths in that city, which they reached on February 26, and the ship and its officers would also coordinate the arrival of SS *Ward* at Odessa a few days later. On March 2, *Fox* transferred two American correspondents and an ARA official to another destroyer steaming back to Constantinople. (The correspondents had apparently been reporting on the grain delivery.) A few days later, SS *Duquesne* also arrived at Odessa with grain, and on March 14, Trammell arranged for lighters and a tug to aid SS *Western Glen*, which had gone aground near Sebastapol. Eventually, *Duquesne* and *Ward* began offloading grain in Odessa, after which, on March 23, the destroyer *Sturtevant* arrived to relieve Trammell's ship.[20]

A succession of destroyers continued this coordination work for over a year. Two destroyer captains kept complete files of their war diaries for this period in their private papers,[21] noting the overall conditions in Russia, the specific difficulties they were encountering, their strategies for dealing with the Bolsheviks, and general impressions. A few other captains' periodic reports can be found in various archives. Hence one can describe the situation from the American naval point of view in some detail.

For example, consider Webb Trammell's war diary description of the terrible conditions he or his men encountered at the formerly beautiful city of Odessa. A Russian priest complained in an American's hearing that the government refused to bury the 600 bodies that had just been piled in front of his cemetery, and that dogs and vultures were devouring the dead. Trammell's war diary mentions that Americans themselves regularly came across bodies left in the streets, including one right in front of the ARA building.[22]

Further, a doctor from a local hospital told Trammell that there were 6.000 cases of typhus in Odessa, 150 of whom were dying daily, this in addition to deaths caused by starvation. A couple of months later in this same city, the commanding officer of *Williamson* would find 800 corpses in the basement of a hospital; outside, carts stood idle in the street, piled with dead bodies. "Were I to try for hours I could not paint a picture as gruesome as I saw conditions this morning," he would write. Cdr. Harry Pence of *McFarland* heard that forty doctors had died in Odessa over the winter, mainly from typhus.[23]

The great desperation of the Russian people was visibly manifest when *Effna* and *Deepwater* started discharging their grain. Trammell described the scene when wheat was spilled inadvertently: "Thousands of people gather on and near the piers to collect the scattered grains of corn. They crawl on hands and knees and pick up the grains one at a time, women leaving their babies lying on the ground nearby [in order to do so]. In the meantime, the soldiers endeavor to keep them off the piers. The rifles are used as clubs as well as being continually discharged to frighten them. The fusillade continues day and night, women and children driven back at the point of the bayonet, crying. This is not an occasional happening, but a continuous performance." Daily theft by workmen, who carried the grain in pockets or in bags under their shirts, was so bad that each man had to be searched on leaving the piers, a procedure "similar to the diamond mines," Trammell thought. When a sympathetic sailor from *Fox* carried a pan full of scraps out onto the dock, it created such a riot that a special guard had to be called out.[24]

Throughout their coordination work, the American naval officers reported that the Bolshevik military exercised a very harsh discipline—some of it no doubt necessary, but much of it not. In April an American relief administrator named Clement told Commander Pence that when a man had attempted to steal a mere handful of grain, a nearby sentry immediately had mashed his face to the bone with the butt of his rifle, and then hit him again and again. Clement had also seen a man and boy shot dead for stealing a little grain, the sentry who fired those shots afterward not giving the bodies a second glance. In May nearly all hands on Pence's ship saw a small boy shot and killed nearby for stealing food.[25]

All the destroyermen felt sympathy with the suffering, and many tried to help in one way or another—by saving scraps from their meals to send to the local hospital, for instance, or again by feeding those on the pier. Sooner or later almost every destroyer tried the latter tactic. Seeing "a motley crowd of waifs and others" one day waiting expectantly with buckets from early morning to late evening, *McFarland* fed soup to 250. After all had been served, the chief Russian Cheka informed the officer of the deck that they could not continue the feeding; it would attract too many starving people.[26] The sailors of another ship learned to slip by the guard gate with loaves of bread under their jackets, having found that the Russians ashore would swap almost anything for a few slices of bread, or for cigarettes. Moreover, before the practice was stopped, several destroyers even gave some Russians menial jobs aboard ship, a measure for which there was ready precedent: in America's China Fleet of that day it was common practice to employ coolies aboard ship, even when under way.[27] Ens. Dolly Fitzgerald recalled in an informal oral history that *McCormick*'s sailors made mess cooks of some of the local Russians while his ship was at Odessa. One of these mess cooks had been an officer in the Russian navy; in the ship's laundry they had a prince.[28]

And at one point, small boys began to swim out to *McCormick* to collect food left for them on the deck. After wrapping it for their families, they would swim back ashore. But if a Russian guard spotted a swimmer, the American sailors could only grimace and hope that the guard's shots would go wide.[29] Word of American generosity traveled quickly. The commander of a Soviet destroyer told Trammell that when his ship stopped in Yalta, a number of children had rowed out in small boats and asked for loaves of bread, certain that the ship was American. It was all he could do to persuade them otherwise.[30]

——◆◆◆——

Russian officials sometimes had political reasons for objecting to the Americans' charity. Cdr. Robert Ghormley, then commanding *Sands*, found that his sailors' feeding of the Russians outraged the local Bolsheviks, for it gave the lie to all their propaganda about the hated "Capitalists."[31] Indeed, the very presence of the Americans was hard for the communist officials to accept. "Without saying a word, the men [go] among the populace, smiling, well-fed, clean and warmly clothed, generously spending their money. They are a walking advertisement for America and an undisputable argument against Bolshevism."[32] At first, the Bolsheviks tried to convert the Americans. Sometimes they wined and dined the naval officers. The officers, however, noted that the officials themselves always had plenty to eat and drink despite the famine. Also, the Americans learned that for furnishings, the communist officials could easily draw on great quantities of furniture, rugs, and other articles that had been recently "nationalized" and placed in warehouses.[33]

The communists addressed the naval proletariat more often than officers, though. For instance, the "International Seaman's Club" in Odessa regularly gave a concert or a dinner for American sailors. With the "results of Communism so plainly written on everything in these cities,"[34] Commander Trammell thought he had little to fear of his men being contaminated, and so he sent twenty of them to a concert. The political propaganda began at a supper afterward. "The general trend of the speeches was to the effect that Russia is the working man's paradise, that when American sailors can call the Captain down off the bridge and take charge of the ship they can call themselves a free people." Unaffected by such barely veiled suggestions, the men reported the whole episode to their CO.[35]

Back home in the States, the Bolsheviks' message would have gone over even worse. A letter found in the Bristol files was written by a Russian who somehow had gotten to America at about the same time the destroyers were visiting Odessa. This dressmaker was urging a fellow Russian dressmaker in Constantinople to follow him to the States.

> Sell everything and come. There are lots of Russians here and as much work as one likes to have. Life is cheap, and the bolsheviks will not have the pleasure of seeing revolution started here in [the] near future: the workman is able to eat and to drink and to dress same as a millionaire. I am not exaggerating. . . .
>
> Why are you afraid of coming? We should have so nice a time. Dressmakers are greatly asked for, we should rent a flat, open a shop. No evacuations, no scandals, neither Turks, nor Soviets.
>
> . . . I give everyone the [same] advice: Sell anything you've got, throw away what cannot be sold, and come to America.[36]

Lieutenant Holmes of *McFarland* attended another Odessa propaganda session. An excellent musical program, including selections from Kreisler and from the opera *Rigoletto* (performed by hungry singers), was followed by a long and fiery speech from an Italian Bolshevik. The American sailors were invited to return. However, even though Holmes counted twenty-six bottles of wine on the sailors' table (the party had reportedly cost over a billion rubles, or, allowing for the great inflation, about $350), when he stopped by the next day, he found that none of *McFarland*'s crew had come back. Holmes did find a black seaman from SS *Gaffney* being lectured by two English-speaking communists. The American seaman offered his hand to the American naval officer, but Holmes refused to shake it, thereby no doubt giving the communists a talking point.[37]

On at least one occasion, two merchant sailors *did* jump ship because of the Bolshevik propaganda. A day or two later they showed up at the duty destroyer, looking for something to eat and a place to lay their heads. However, Webb Trammell turned them away, saying he did not recognize them. He accused them of being Bolsheviks. Each day they would come back "more hungry and more disgusted" than before. Finally, when they were reduced to the state of *begging* to be recognized, asserting they had had enough of Bolshevism and were now completely cured, Trammell put the desperate seamen aboard another merchant vessel so they could finally get out of the wretched place.[38]

Otherwise, there wasn't much doing ashore to interest the Navy men. Though the merchant seamen were drawn to the vice of the city, the Navy sailors do not seem to have been much attracted. After all, their home port was the inimitable Constantinople, and they hardly needed to slum it for vice in Odessa. Well, several of *McFarland*'s sailors did jump ship one night. Captain Harry Pence was much surprised and chagrined, and immediately awarded several summary court-martials and bad conduct discharges.[39]

A specific form of local entertainment did attract widely. Sailors and officers from virtually every ship attended the Odessa opera at least once.

Sometimes they used the box that the American Relief Association had rented for the season, at the cost of a few cents. Pence found the performance unworthy of the good artists, who deserved a better fate. The orchestra was weak, the house was poorly lighted, and the odor from the audience was nauseating. He stayed for less than an act.[40] Ens. Dolly Fitzgerald liked the opera better (he also saw a ballet), but he was bemused to note that the people who attended were very raucous. Someone had taken fiendish delight in putting the most obnoxious fellows in the czar's box, he thought.[41] Commander Trammell wrote in his war diary that the members of the opera troupe were paid one hundred thousand rubles per month, the current price of a loaf of bread.[42] As members of the former bourgeois, they apparently had the alternative of singing for this ration, or being imprisoned, or shot. Not surprisingly, a couple of months after Trammell's visit, Cdr. Harry Pence recorded that five of this same company had died of starvation.[43]

No doubt manifesting their own bourgeois taste, the American officers were especially interested in the visual arts. At Sebastopol, Trammell visited the famous *Panorama*, which depicted the siege of Sebastopol during the Crimean War. He regarded this cylindrical work of art as the most interesting painting he had ever seen.[44] Harry Pence met the widow of the famous Russian sea painter Ivan Ivasovsky at the Ivasovsky Art Museum at Theodosia. She invited him to take what he liked, for otherwise the communists would just shred the paintings. Pence bought some, which remain in the family to this day.[45] Cdr. Carlos Bailey of *Sturtevant* also met the painter's widow, who he found living in the museum's basement with her granddaughter: "That evening two or three of the ship's officers and I took them some food—bread and other delicacies. They brought out some wine and ate ravenously, after which we danced half the night to the music of the ship's Gramophone." The Russian women were excellent dancers, though their dancing was so vigorous that they almost swept the men off their feet.[46]

◄ ◆◆◆ ►

As various episodes show, tragedy lay at every turn. Indeed, in many parts of Russia, cannibalism was taking place. In May of 1922, Commander Pence was told by relief worker E. P. Murphy in Theodosia that two girls of eighteen had been boiled and eaten there just the other day; several other children had also been stolen and killed for food.[47] Writer F. A. Mackenzie saw photographs that haunted his memory, and from American relief workers he heard many terrible accounts. Although some of their stories were said to be "unspeakably gruesome"—and they were—in his 1923 book *Russia before Dawn,* the author described them in detail anyway.[48] Americans doing publicity for the Russians back in Constantinople found their fund-raising adversely affected. The starvation that afflicted the White Russians in the city (about which they were writing home) was simply "too colorless, compared to cannibalism in Russia itself."[49]

Few if any Navy people actually saw evidence of cannibalism, but they were much disturbed by seeing the dying on the streets and the dead "stacked like cordwood" in Novorossisk and Odessa,[50] and seldom quickly interred.

Lt. Matt Gardner and another officer of the destroyer *Biddle* were assigned to locate the bodies and arrange the burial of two American merchant sailors who had died at Odessa during a flu epidemic. Gardner and his friend were worried about this assignment, because there was no vaccination available to protect *them*. After talking it over, the officers improvised with a few drinks of cognac. Then they proceeded to the city morgue.

This proved to be a vast charnel house with bodies stacked upon bodies, all still wearing the clothes in which they had died. The attendant led the Americans through row upon row, turning over the stiff, frozen bodies to check identification tags by lantern light. After examining seemingly every single corpse in the place, they finally found the seamen's bodies in a small adjacent building, a place set apart strictly for victims of the flu. The Americans arranged the burial details and quickly beat a quick retreat for more cognac.[51]

Webb Trammell had no such fortification when he visited a Princess Soumbatoff on a brief stop at Sebastopol, an experience quite disturbing in its own way. Despite her advanced age, this former aristocrat was continually persecuted by the Bolsheviks. Nevertheless, she willingly risked even further maltreatment by requesting a meeting with Trammell, the representative (as she put it) of "a sympathetic and fearless nation." Soumbatoff desperately wanted Trammell to see the true conditions in the city, normally kept hidden. When Trammell replied that he could not investigate further because his ship was leaving within two hours, the princess broke down and wept bitterly.

She lamented not for herself, she said (old servants, friends, and people she had once assisted now helped her out, and a single bowl of gruel daily was all she needed) but instead for the Russian people. Before the Revolution she had been criticized for giving the simple folk so much attention. Now it hurt her terribly to see these beloved people "not only dying, but becoming such brutes; that these once gentle and loving people are actually turning into animals." She took one of Trammell's hands in hers and begged that he would do everything in his power at least to save the orphan children. And Trammell found himself promising, though he thought he could do very little about it all. Afterward the commander was startled to realize that despite the woman's weakened condition, the interview had lasted for over an hour. It was "one of the worst hours I've ever spent, but one that I would not have missed and shall never forget."[52]

Rather than aristocrats, the Americans were more commonly accosted by people caught in the country unexpectedly and now wanting out of it—a Russian merchant marine officer, for instance, who had worked many years in the United States. This man had been educated as an electrical engineer at the University of California. Afterward, while taking out citizenship papers, he had taken a job as a commercial representative for the International Harvester Company. Then he got caught up in the Great War and ended up serving as a Russian naval officer. Later, as a captain of a merchant ship in the Mediterranean, he had left his ship at Constantinople to fetch his wife and child from Odessa, only to be stranded by the Wrangel collapse. Now he had a job as a port pilot with the American Relief Administration—for a few months.[53]

In that same city a bit later on, the bachelor Trammell had a somewhat more welcome experience: "Today a woman asked me to marry her. I didn't have enough presence of mind to make the customary remarks about 'This is so sudden,' etc. I told her that I was already married—that being the best excuse I could think of. She said that made no difference, that she was too." The woman's husband was in France and she wanted to join him. The marriage would be fictitious, and she realized the procedure would be irregular—but not nearly as irregular as present-day life in Russia. She knew of a German who would marry her, but she wouldn't marry a German even fictitiously. Trammell told the woman that if he found somebody suitable he would certainly let her know. "She seemed to be very nice, was quite good looking, and I think has good taste."[54] Harry Pence later recollected that girls in Russia would marry any American at all in order to get out of the country.[55] Several American relief workers, including the district supervisor in Odessa, did marry Russian women (some of whom worked for the ARA) and took them back home with them. In fact, one ARA official wrote at the time that there was "an epidemic of marriages" among the relief workers; he was skeptical that these marriages would work.[56]

Not everybody wanted out of Russia. Some wanted in—if they could profit by it. American trade commissioner Gillespie forwarded a message from the destroyer *Overton* to E. St. J. Greble of Baldwin Locomotives, then in Bucharest trying to sell locomotives to the Romanians. The message stated that a Russian general named "Ships" was enthusiastic over the idea of an influential American commercial representative coming to Novorossisk. On receiving this message, Greble and two associates traveled to Constantinople, where Bristol put them on *Sturtevant*, which immediately steamed off to the Russian port.[57] Trammell, there in his destroyer, expressed amusement upon hearing of Greble's hopes, for the commander knew General Shtip, and could accurately estimate the general's likely knowledge of Russian railway transportation. Greble was irritated by Trammell's attitude, but, as Trammell recorded in his war diary, it took about thirty minutes to get telephone connection to the general's office, ten minutes to explain the purpose of Greble's visit, two minutes for the general to say he knew nothing of Russian rail transportation in general or of buying locomotives in particular, and another two minutes for Greble to decide to return to Bucharest via Constantinople.[58]

However, in Greble's opinion the journey was not a waste. He insisted to Trammell he was "sowing the seeds of great commercial concessions in Russia."[59] Greble was the archtypical salesman, always on the lookout. En route to Novorossisk, *Sturtevant* had visited the czar's palaces and wine cellars near Yalta. The five glasses of wine Greble tasted there had not only given him warm feelings about Yalta, but had also aroused his commercial enthusiasm. Greble was struck by the fact that the wine cellars' seven tunnels contained a collection of over ten thousand casks plus two and a half million bottles of aged wine from throughout the world. It had cost the czar a fortune. Greble conceived the idea of trading for the wine, that is, "to take the wine we saw in exchange for coal, locomotives, and cars and some wheat maybe for the inhabitants." Yes, some wheat for the starving . . . what a happy last thought. The Greek interpreter thought Greble's idea excellent, but whether anybody in Moscow also did is not recorded.[60]

After the abortive trip to Novorossisk, Greble rode *Fox* back to Constantinople, stopping first at the Turkish port of Trebizond. There Greble tried to sell the Turkish governor some locomotives, only to discover there was no railroad in or near Trebizond (there once had been). Undeterred, Greble tried to interest the Turks in building one. Well, maybe after the war, the Turkish governor replied, and of course he hoped the Americans would build it.[61] Back in Constantinople, Greble wrote a ten-page letter to the admiral justifying his recent efforts.

━━◆◆◆━━

What did the Americans achieve with their Russian relief work? To the naval officers success sometimes seemed hollow. Dolly Fitzgerald had looked on with futility while professors from the university at Odessa who were dressed in rags loaded bricks into wheelbarrows under the close watch of Red guards. Unaccustomed to labor, many intellectuals in Russia died of such treatment.[62] In addition, the communists were sometimes obstructive, and they frequently allowed widespread graft. The army and outlaw bands often took grain for themselves, while at one location a local despot prevented the American feeding for two or three weeks by putting guards around the warehouses, inhibiting the relief distribution, and calling a general strike.[63] At Black Sea ports, when dock and railway workers saw relief supplies pile up without themselves getting much, they tried capitalist tactics and struck for higher wages. Some workers began to seize the food by carload lot.[64]

American reliefers occasionally got depressed. On a day in September of 1922, Anna Mitchell and a relief official named Ringland and his wife drove from Constantinople up to the summer resort of Therapia, where they found two relief men just down from Russia. A third man, expected the next day by boat, was said to have very "ill nerves" and tuberculosis, and Mitchell was told that breakdowns among the relief workers were not uncommon, especially on remote sites. Mitchell gathered that the work was terribly trying. The reliefers were always fighting impossible obstacles, not only from incompetence, but too often from deliberate obstruction. The Americans might be able to make soup for the starving if they had fuel and a pot, for instance, but they often couldn't get them—and people would die as a result, sometimes right in front of the Americans. One of the relief men at Therapia, reportedly a mild and unemotional person, said that during the war he had specialized in machine guns. Now "he sometimes had a pleasant dream of putting all the Bolshiviki authorities up in front of one of them."[65]

Both at the time and for decades to come, the Soviet government would greatly depreciate America's help, making Herbert Hoover (who had spearheaded the relief work) a kind of villain guilty of the murder of many Russian people, in one of the most extreme examples.[66] In fact, this was the opposite of the truth. Overall, the American effort, including the required naval coordination, was magnificent. While it could take many weeks for the food to get to the interior even after it reached the Russian ports, it eventually did get there.[67] Estimates of the number kept alive are difficult, but at the peak of its effort the American Relief Administration was feeding maybe 10.5 million hungry Russian people, at an overall cost of tens of millions of dollars.[68] Also, millions of people were inoculated against cholera, typhoid, and paratyphoid fevers or vaccinated against smallpox, while thousands of hospitals, dispensaries, and children's homes had been given medical help.[69] Perhaps most important, the Americans provided the peasants ample seed for planting. As a result, good harvests in 1922 and 1923 would quickly end the need for American help.

The gratitude of those helped by the Americans was sometimes profoundly expressed. At a small village along a railroad line, peasants from the surrounding region received their share of corn even as the Easter bells were ringing. Before beginning their long march home, one group of these men and women sought out the American supervisor. They told him that they and their neighbors would always associate the ringing of Easter bells with the yellow American corn, which had come at that season to rescue them from death.[70] Some Soviet officials at the time also expressed a deep gratitude, and Maxim Gorky (in a letter to Hoover) gave tribute to the American generosity as "unique in human history."[71]

As for the American Navy people, while they objected to much that was going on in southern Russia (this included the execution of many returning Deniken and Wrangel soldiers, despite Bolshevik promises of immunity[72]), from their firsthand point of view of the grain being offloaded and entrained and of desperate thousands being fed, they often could see in context the specific importance of their own country's generosity.

Like most American commanders (including Admiral Bristol himself at one point, with his staff and their wives[73]), Commander Pence had visited the czar's wine cellars at Yalta, being made welcome there by a Mrs. Vedel, an Englishwoman who was the wife of one of the managers. Her husband had been imprisoned for eight months and sentenced to be shot, but had finally been liberated. A son, an officer in the Imperial Army, was not so lucky: he had been killed by the Bolsheviks at Yalta.

When Pence spoke with Mrs. Vedel, she was doing her best to make a happy home for her family and hoped to send her remaining children to the American schools in Constantinople. But things had gotten very tense before Pence met her. Hearing of the American relief, this woman had once taken some wine on her back and walked the fifteen miles of mountainous territory to Novorossisk to exchange it for forty pounds of American flour—and then walked back. The flour had helped her keep her remaining children alive.[74]

Thanks to American generosity and the efficiency of the American relief workers, the doctors, the merchant seaman and the officers and men of the American destroyers sent from Constantinople, and because of the arrangements of Admiral Bristol and his staff as well, from January 1922 into 1923 episodes of this kind had occurred all over the famine-stricken heartland of Bolshevik Russia.

CHAPTER 8

SWIMMING THE HELLESPONT AND OTHER NAVAL RECREATION

Took the ball squad ashore again today and played to a gaping crowd of about 700 Arabs. They were a dumb lot and persisted in crowding right up to the base lines and around the catcher. One of them got knocked out by a foul tip.

—Ens. Dan Gallery of *Pittsburgh*, in Alexandria

As a reported five hundred to a thousand Russians died daily of starvation in Odessa in May of 1922, American sailors from *McFarland* (whose officers were helping to coordinate the delivery of grain) played pickup games of football or indoor baseball right on the dock. About the same time, while American officials at Trebizond debated whether local Greek males being "deported to the interior" was a serious issue or not, crew members of the same destroyer played baseball and held boxing matches.[1] Wherever an American naval vessel docked, in fact, and whatever the local circumstances, sports were always a great interest of its crew.

———◆◆◆———

Those who watched the Americans often wondered at the variety and strangeness of their sports, especially on American holidays. In Varna, Bulgaria, perplexed locals wondered at the mad American sailors from the destroyer *Goff* running back and forth carrying potatoes in spoons, eating pie and whistling with their hands tied behind them, climbing greased poles, and running races with their legs in flour sacks. It was Washington's birthday, 1923. In 1920, in Samsun, the crew of the destroyer *Whipple* had celebrated July 4th by challenging HMS *Dianthus* to swimming races, this followed by competition at diving and racing with punts. A few days before, several divisions of *Whipple* had played practice baseball games against one another on a newly constructed diamond, and *Whipple* and *Barker* had played a match game. After the turkey dinner on the 4th itself, the Navy crews watched the locals compete at soccer matches and horseracing, which featured fine Arabian thoroughbreds.[2]

In comparison, cut off in Urfa in March of 1921 and hearing of the election of President Warren Harding, the small circle of American missionaries in that city, mainly women, celebrated by inviting the Turkish officials to eat with them on the day of the inauguration. At dinner they drank toasts (in lemonade) to the new president, and until midnight they played parlor games like Up Jenkins, the latter proving especially popular among the Turks. Ens. Dan Gallery's extensive personal diary of this same period indicates that he typically scoffed at such "parlor stunts." However, when among young American women, he sometimes participated in them.[3]

Back in Constantinople, the Navy occasionally celebrated holidays in "crossing the line" fashion. On New Year's Day, 1921, *Scorpion* signaled *St. Louis* to prepare to receive the admiral and his staff. Soon Charles Olsen saw a motor sailer painted up like a warship and filled with pirates come alongside the cruiser. "It was a lot of gobs [sailors] dressed as pirates in all descriptions of dress, The Admiral, King Neptune, his wife and baby. It was a scream. We gave them regular side honors as they came over the gangway. . . . Then they held a courtmartial on Commander Linden, calling him Commander England, sentencing him to whitewash the ship with something or other. The baby, a big fat man dressed in a pair of ladies pajamas cried out, 'Papa, I want to go to the head.' The aide took her off. I nearly split laughing." Charles wrote Edna that whaleboat races were supposed to follow, but the officers who should have been in charge had gotten in at six or eight in the morning (one of them so drunk he had to crawl back to the ship on his hands and knees), and nobody was in shape for further celebration.[4]

Nevertheless, whaleboat crews from American ships often did race one another, as many as eight at once, and often with great enthusiasm.[5] Despite the many other attractions of Constantinople, when their ships were moored there, the crews kept competing, particularly at baseball. Working recreational schedules around ships' movements, the "Far Seas League" organized games between crews of homeported and visiting naval ships alike from 1920 to 1923.[6] Other sports usually took a backseat at the old Ottoman capital. (The drinking, the music, and the astonishing Russian women there had so captured sailors' and officers' interest.) However, occasionally Navy people played basketball at the Robert College gym or at one of the YMCA centers in the city. Indeed, sometimes Navy fives played against native teams there.

The *Pittsburgh*'s baseball team (captained by Ens. Dan Gallery, fifth from left) played frequently at Constantinople in the Far Seas League. *Courtesy of the Special Collections and Archives Division, Nimitz Library, United States Naval Academy*

On occasion, crew members even took part in international competition. A couple of excellent American boxers fought the White Russian Kirpichev (Kirpit), for instance—but he beat them. By the way, the Allied navies with their huge contingents (which always dwarfed the American numbers) also had regular athletic contests. Many fine athletes were on hand to compete in a sort of mini-Olympics that was held at Taxim Stadium in June of 1922, for instance. Organized by the YMCA, this contest featured track and field most prominently, but also included many other sports.[7]

—◆◆◆—

The YMCA in Constantinople at that time was wholly under American leadership. With six college-trained physical directors on its staff in 1921 and with five well-equipped centers, the YMCA could offer sports ranging from basketball and volleyball to boxing and fencing to young men of all ethnic groups. The centers featured many other kinds of recreation too, among them music, dramatics, nature study, pool, and billiards. Reading rooms with libraries, clubrooms, lounges that doubled as movie theaters, and small restaurants could also be found at these centers. Educational and religious classes were an important part of the mix.[8]

A special YMCA "American Sailor's Club," located on the Grande Rue de Pera, sponsored activities similar to those of the other clubs. However, it had been created with the American sailor in mind and was in essence an early USO (United Service Organization). In a letter home from this club's reading room, Charles Olsen described the club: "Several empty writing places on each side of me. In the other room are several sailors playing pool on the only table. On the floor below a piano is being played and the chairs all set for a movie show. . . . The Y is the only American place here in Constantinople, and every night it has the better behaved boys gather for some entertainment or chow. On the first floor is a restaurant and a Russian string orchestra. Something new. . . . I had for dinner Roast Chicken, Mashed potatoes, peas, Bread, Coffee, Ice Cream and Cake for 67¢. Can you beat that!"[9] The cheap American food made the sailors' Y very popular both among sailors and American civilians: in April of 1921, it served twelve thousand meals. Another of its attractions: it let sailors sign chits for their meals and pay later. In 1923 writer Bill Ellis witnessed sailors, officers, and civilians all gathering to dine and play in fellowship at this, "the most popular and most American place of resort in the city." He regarded the sailor's Y as a brilliant success.[10]

Of course, few American males visited only the Y. Many had lower tastes, while others were more particular. Mentioned in officers' letters and diaries more often than the Y was the Club de Constantinople (or simply The Club), which was also located in the heart of Pera. Many an American diplomat, naval officer and businessman anted up the membership fee required to eat, drink, read, play tennis, play cards, gamble, or simply socialize at this institution. In contrast, few Americans joined the several British athletic clubs in Constantinople or at nearby Prinkipo, though these clubs offered rowing, yachting, squash, swimming, tennis, and other such "officer sports."

Several American residents did take advantage of the American-founded Bosporus Golf Club, the links of which lay near the American colleges above Arnaoutkeuy. Admiral Bristol, many embassy staff members, several American businessmen, and some professors played here. One of the hazards of the game at this site was the practice of small Greek boys to lie in wait and then swoop down and carry a ball away.[11]

There was also a good British club at Therapia, a swanky suburb several miles up the Bosporus, near which virtually every European country had a summer embassy. Occasionally Americans (naval and civilian) would visit this club. During his trip through the region, writer John Dos Passos sat on the terrace with the green Bosporus flowing in front of him, watching Englishmen who were wearing white flannels play tennis, this on a hot, stagnant afternoon. Then he walked to the bar. "A British major with a face like the harvest moon was shaking up Alexanders. A man in a frock coat was trying to catch in his mouth olives that an American relief worker was tossing in the air. The talk in the bar was English, Oxford drawl, Chicago burr, Yankee twang, English and American as spoken by Greeks, Armenians, Frenchmen, Italians. Only the soberer people in the corners spoke French."[12]

A bit further up the strait from Therapia, at a village called Buyukdere (the large bay in the Bosporus here was named Buyukdere Bay), was a large field that the British used for horseracing, cricket, and polo. Many Americans enjoyed these spectator sports, mingling with great crowds of fans over the weekends. Of course there was a good bar near the race track, and here Lt. Robbie Dunn of the embassy staff once met some Arabs who spoke English and loved whiskey. (He was later to realize they were members of the Hussein family.) During drinks, Dunn said something about his always professing the religion of the country in which he happened to be at the moment. At that, they had him raise his right hand and swear belief in the one God and Mohammed his prophet. "Now you are in Islam. One of the faithful, and no fooling." Just for Dunn, the Arabs waived the mandatory circumcision, and also did not require him to renounce any former religion. Dunn took the name "Mohammed Ali Bey."[13]

Dunn himself was ever bent on having a great time at the "great game" of spying. Whether off alone on horseback in the midst of Asia Minor, shooting the breeze in the race track bar at Buyukdere, traveling on the destroyers across the Black Sea, or conversing with the whores and madams in Constantinople's vice district, he found his work totally captivating. Later he would comment that he "wouldn't have traded with that Lawrence fellow." Hence, his conversion to Islam seems to have been a piece of the good time he was having, a mere joke. (Indeed, given the generally irreverent character he manifests in his memoir, it could hardly have been anything else.)[14] However, rumors of his new allegiance got passed around, and in some quarters it was taken seriously. Eventually, with other unorthodox behavior on his part, this "conversion" would help to do him in.

Near the field at Buyukdere, in 1921 the YMCA and American Navy (with the admiral the chief sponsor) combined to created an American sailor's camp, this at the reputed campsite of the Christian knights on their sack of Constantinople in 1204 during the Fourth Crusade.[15] Relief and YWCA workers Anna Mitchell and Helen Ogden were among the crowd that attended the opening of "Camp Mark Bristol" in May of that year. Anna admired the house that the Americans had taken over, in which some of the meals were served. "It is an old house quite ramshackle but with beautifully sized and lighted Turkish rooms, and delicious touches in them of old Turkish life, and glorious terraces (with pine trees overlooking the Bosphorus) on which they have pitched tents.... The interesting part is that it is open to all Americans as well as sailors, and that for what amounts to seven dollars one can engage a tent for the season, which we instantly did, so we now have a weekend summer resort as well as a town residence." Helen Ogden pointed out that the camp was nearly up to the Black Sea and about a mile and half trek from the landing: "It is in a lovely spot nestled down among the hills. . . . The camp is all of tents, a big tent for eating and another for recreation, that is piano, victrola and writing and reading, and in this tent there is a part reserved for girls who may come up to help or to have a rest or good time, only American girls of course." How did the American sailors celebrate the camp's opening? Naturally, by playing baseball.[16]

In June of that year, Bill Leahy watched boxing matches at this camp between American and British sailors. So did many of the sailors' girlfriends, who were, of course, *not* usually Americans. The event seemed quite a success.

In July Anna Mitchell finally got around to using her tent for a weekend. "We found it perfectly charming. They had pitched it way off by itself as we asked, in a spot with a heavenly view, and it was so nice to lie under pine trees, and feel really 'in the country.'" An American woman who had brought her two babies to Constantinople was offended by the poor quality of what housing her husband could find in the city. She said she was determined to forego housing in Constantinople and instead settle in two tents at Camp Mark Bristol, an announcement that was taken quite seriously. The camp was a rather nice place.[17]

Although the Bristols only visited and did not stay at the sailors' camp, they did spend considerable time up the Bosporus every summer. As mentioned before, unlike other foreign powers, the United States owned no summer embassy, but Bristol does seem to have rented at least part of a "summer palace" at Therapia, a building that is marked the "summer embassy" in the Kinkaid family photographs, while the *Scorpion* is shown anchored right offshore.[18] Even though this yacht was still manned by seventy or so smart bluejackets, by this time it was essentially an excursion boat. Living ashore or on the *Scorpion*, commuting to the city by Navy "barge," and using the local facilities up and down the strait, the admiral was enabled fully to enjoy the summer. He played tennis and swam every afternoon and he played golf twice a week.[19]

Helen Bristol also enjoyed herself, playing tennis and swimming with many an embassy party at various spots up the Bosporus. (Like several other American women, Helen had learned to swim since coming to Turkey.) Few Americans could afford to spend a whole season at such resorts, but Chief of Staff Japy Hepburn with his wife, Louisa, rented a chalet on the grounds of the Russian summer embassy. He traveled each morning to the embassy on the duty Navy launch. Allen and Clover Dulles took a hotel room in Therapia during the summer they spent in Turkey. This allowed them to keep close touch with the European embassies, to get in some tennis and swimming, and to enjoy the regular breezes from the Black Sea.[20]

The Bristols entertained frequently aboard *Scorpion*. Liquor was strictly prohibited aboard naval vessels, but this difficulty was handled (at least for a time) by *Chicago Daily News* correspondent Constantine Brown, though probably the idea came from Bristol's knowledge of the customary practice of the Navy's Yangtze Patrol. Looking for comfortable summer quarters in Therapia and finding only expensive, vermin-infested cottages, Brown bought a sixty-foot lighter in Constantinople's harbor and had it furnished nicely as a houseboat, "the first floating domicile of her sort ever seen in Constantinople," he would claim. He christened his houseboat *Nelly* and had it towed to Therapia for the summer.

Admiral Bristol's barge in front of the American summer embassy at Therapia, several miles up the Bosporus from Constantinople. The naval steam yacht *Scorpion* is back left. *Thomas Kinkaid collection, The Naval History and Heritage Command*

When he learned of the admiral's problem with liquor, he moored the *Nelly* right alongside the *Scorpion*. As a result, "it was an easy matter to place a few planks between the yacht and the houseboat and for the guests to wander back and forth from one to the other. A sailor who had once tended bar in the Palmer House in Chicago would preside at a table stretched along the length of the *Nelly's* fifteen-foot saloon."[21] In such arrangements most partygoers would end up on the lighter, rather than on the *Scorpion*. After the party, some of the Bristols' guests would stay aboard overnight (on the *Scorpion*, one guesses); others would be sent back down the Bosporus in the lovely moonlight by Navy launch.[22]

◄►

Parties and picnics were frequent at Therapia, but residents of Constantinople could visit many other delightful picnic spots. "Every Sunday there's a picnic somewhere," Jeannette Edwards wrote happily. Helen Ogden wrote, "One of the nice things, indeed I can say the nicest thing about Constant. is the getting away from it, for there are lovely trips in every direction, sometimes by water and sometimes by train."[23] For instance, the hillsides overlooking the mouth of the Black Sea, complete with wartime fort and trenches, were quite remarkable, if you or your friend had a yacht to take you there—and some did.[24] The large

Belgrade Forest, which lay between the city and the Black Sea, was another favorite picnic (and hunting) destination. However, the more famous recreation spots were closer to the city.

Near the western end of the Golden Horn, for example, was the small village of Eyoub. Americans were aware that Eyoub's mosque was built over the grave of the Prophet's "standard bearer," which made it the holiest Muslim site in Constantinople.[25] Yet they were more interested in the large cemetery on the nearby hillside, where French novelist Pierre Loti's sweetheart was said to be buried. Many Americans picnicked in this cemetery, usually coming by caique, the Turkish rowboat. The tombstones were in a terrible state of dilapidation. Moreover, as the cemetery was still in use, your picnic might be interrupted by a Turkish burial party looking literally for a few inches of dirt in which to lay their dead.[26] Still, such interruptions were infrequent, and from the hill at Eyoub most of Constantinople and the Golden Horn were spread out before you—a magnificent sight.

Captain Bill Leahy took part in several picnic expeditions organized by the embassy staff, one of which was to Eyoub. While eating supper in the great cemetery, the whole party admired the splendid view of Stamboul with its ancient defensive walls. After the sun went down, he and the Bristols and their other guests all visited a little coffee house in the village before heading home.[27]

Helen Ogden took her friend, Carrie, to this same cemetery late one afternoon, and after picnicking, they rode a caique back to Pera. "Unfortunately there was no moon but the row home was beautiful in the dark with singing here and there as the other small boats passed and the many lights both on shore and on the water. Then just as we were nearing the bridge we heard the priests calling the faithful to prayer. It was indeed a lovely day. We reached home about ten, tired but happy."[28]

You could also go further up the water. The Golden Horn was an industrial harbor, the last thing from a romantic site, particularly in the daytime. However, if you followed on to its end, "past all the bone factories or glue factories of Turkey" (as Ogden put it), you would reach the famous "Sweet Waters of Europe." The banks of this small stream (which trended back northeast) were no longer the tulip-lined pleasure grounds of the eighteenth century, "where the sultan's guests wandered through the gardens and along the marble quays drinking sherbet while candle-bearing tortoises clambered among the flowerbeds, throwing lumbering flickers of light."[29] Still, a casino offered refreshments and music,[30] and a great many people relaxed here, especially Turks.

When Helen saw the crowds both on the water and up on the banks, she considered this must be *the* outing spot of all the Turkish families in Constantinople. As the curfew required many natives to leave early, Helen and her friends were able to find a nice spot for a picnic late in the afternoon. She described the scene and her mixed feelings in a letter home. "There were hundreds of [small boats there,] big and little, some with whole communities in them and some with just twos, many with mandolins and queer sounding pipes and even one with a phonograph horn sticking over the side. The phonographs play the weird Turkish music so they are no better than the other sort and oh! what music it is. They had decorated their boats in greens and with the striped or white tops they use in summer it made it a very gay scene, and one which we were glad to see but won't go to look at again in a hurry. We came back on a rippless water under a small but lovely moon and got home about eleven o'clock."[31]

When Jeannette Edwards visited the Sweet Waters (again, Jeannette was the sister of a naval officer stationed at Constantinople), among all the peaceful Turks on the hillsides she noticed the Japanese high commissioner Baron Uchida peacefully fishing from the bank. Troubled by the Russian tragedy, Jeannette was relieved to see that there were *some* happy people in the city, anyway. Edna and Lt. (jg) Charles Olsen visited this same place one spring. As they drove the winding road into the small valley, they were delighted to find the trees filled with birds and the hillsides blue with forget-me-nots. They gathered great armfuls of flowers to take home.[32]

Another famous pleasure spot somewhat similar to the Sweet Waters of Europe was the Sweet Waters of Asia: this stream emptied into the Bosporus from the Asiatic side of the strait a few miles north of Constantinople. Charles and Edna took a boat up this winding creek the same spring that she had visited the Sweet Waters of Europe. Here, after turning a bend, she suddenly found herself in a "paradise valley." The hillsides were lovely with poppies, she said, while the flowering Judas trees with their deep pink blooms composed the most beautiful sight she had ever seen. The same scenery reminded Anna Mitchell of peaceful American countrysides.[33]

In his 1922 book, the Turk Mufty-Zade Zia Bey was more guarded, though nostalgic. He described an afternoon that he and his American wife had spent here late one fall. "We went in the rowboat up this little stream—a miniature Bosphorus, with old tumbled-down houses by the water, big trees leaning their branches covered with autumnal golden leaves over old walls covered with vines, here and there a ramshackle wooden bridge spanning the stream and giving it the appearance of a Turkish Venice, and then large meadows on both sides, where groups of people were, like us, taking advantage of the last few days of summery sunshine of the year." Although they enjoyed their picnic, Zia Bey reflected that this was no longer the "smartest place to go" on summer

Friday and Sunday afternoons as it once had been. Similarly, the American naval captain Bill Leahy, there on yet another picnic with the Bristols, knew the place had once been fashionable, but he found the valley "brown and poor" in appearance.[34]

Ensign Gallery rowed his Greek girlfriend, Anthie Angelides, a couple of miles up this stream in early 1923 and then walked another mile, only suddenly to run into a sentry from the Nationalist army then threatening Constantinople. "We ran into a Kemalist sentry there with his gun slung over his shoulder and Anthie almost passed out with fright. I wanted to keep going but she wanted to run. The sentry gave us some dirty looks but I was in uniform so he didn't do anything. We finally turned around and walked back. . . . The scenery was very pretty and romantic."[35] These two were not bothered despite being so far out from the capital, but others sometimes were. A couple of years earlier, John Dos Passos overheard this conversation up at the British Club at Therapia: "Did you hear the one about young Stafford was walking with a Red Cross nurse out on the road near the Sweet Waters and bandits held them up? They didn't touch the girl but they stripped him down to the skin. . . . The girl made them give him back his drawers for decency."[36] The latter episode occurred many months prior to the Nationalist army's taking over the whole area.

Helen Bristol (second from left) with other embassy wives and officers after a swimming excursion across to the Asiatic side of the Bosporus. *Thomas Kinkaid collection, The Naval History and Heritage Command*

Other sites on the Asiatic side were also visited. A Standard Oil couple the Bristols knew had a camp over where the Bosporus was clean, apparently right across from Therapia, and on a Sunday morning Russian relief worker Anna Mitchell rode over on the admiral's barge. There she found the swimming "delicious." Afterward she and her friends rode back to the European side on *Scorpion*, "the Bristols showing angel tempers in allowing themselves to be overrun by wet guests." They stayed for Mrs. Bristol's regular Sunday buffet lunch. (These lunches averaged about twenty guests.)

The spectacle on this particular occasion, by the way (in August of 1922), was a long line of British warships steaming down the Bosporus; this naval show of force was intended to help warn off a brief Greek army threat to Constantinople.[37]

On such swimming parties as sponsored by the Bristols, embassy people often let their hair down. A special personality among this group was Margaret Bryan, the lovely young bride of staff naval officer Hamilton Bryan. The two were notorious on Bristol's staff for their heated arguments, and on this day theirs was the worst fight by a married couple that Lt. Julian Wheeler had ever witnessed, or would ever see again. Husband and wife berated each other furiously. Finally, Hamilton said he had had enough: "Now, Margaret, I'm not going to let any woman in the world talk to me like that." After this announcement, though he was fully dressed, Hamilton dove over the ship's side.

The Bosporus current was strong where *Scorpion* was anchored, and concern grew among the staff as the minutes ticked on and Bryan did not reappear. Curiously, though, Margaret did not seem particularly perturbed. After a bit she stood up, walked to the rail and, still irate, called out, "Hamilton, you come up here. I know you're down there sitting on that rudder. . . . I haven't finished with you yet." Hamilton had indeed swum to the ship's stern and was holding on there—but on Margaret calling his bluff, he was reduced to swimming back to the gangway, climbing aboard dripping, and slinking down to somebody's cabin to find some dry clothes.[38]

A year earlier the Bristols had taken a picnic party to Mount Burgurlu, also on the Asiatic side, three or four miles inland behind Scutari. Though more out of the way, this place seemed yet another popular summer rendezvous, as Bill Leahy remarked; it certainly provided a great view of the Bosporus and the Sea of Marmara.[39] However, *the* recreation spot for the city was the group of Princes Islands in the Sea of Marmara itself, located only a couple of hours' boat ride from Constan's quays.

—◆◆◆—

Prinkipo, the largest island, featured shady groves, sports fields, and several cottages and hotels. Cdr. Harry Pence and a friend took a boat out to Prinkipo one afternoon in mid-1919, not long after the war and before the resort's business had built up overmuch. He found it "one of the most enchanting places I have ever visited." Like virtually everybody before and since, the two visitors drove away from the village in a carriage, rode peacefully past old villas and gardens, paced all through and around the island's quiet pine groves, and circled back. The weather, the good breeze, and the surroundings were wonderfully peaceful and invigorating, he thought; he also slept well overnight. The bachelor's only regret was that none of the girls at the small dance the hotel had hosted the evening of his visit had spoken English, so he had not been able to get acquainted.[40]

Bill Leahy also visited Prinkipo one day with shipmates, and his description was succinct: "We found it in the dilapidated condition of repair that seems to be universal in Turkey, took lunch at the Hotel Splendid, enjoyed marvelous views of the sea and shore in crystal clear air, and returned to Constantinople in time for a dinner at the American Embassy."[41] If Robbie Dunn's account is to be believed, not all parties to Prinkipo went according to plan. "Maggie" Bryan had just arrived in Constantinople and was still wide-eyed when, with an embassy party and several guests, she debarked at noon from one of the admiral's subchasers. The whole group traveled to an old estate, to a party sponsored by some local businessmen.

The embassy staff had asked for beer, but instead, cases of brandy lay about everywhere, and there was little else to drink. Some sipped; a few drank deep of the stuff. Meanwhile, Maggie wanted to know who those corpulent Turks were, the ones with red slippers who had lain prone on the subchaser's deck. "Palace eunuchs," one of the naval staff guessed; "full of hashish, too," whispered another. As the party progressed, an old, crocked Turkish admiral briefly astonished the Americans by professing his love for the (male) American vice consul, Kippy Tuck. Then one of the American naval wives (she had been gulping brandy) threw up her lunch over plates and table alike. "Oh, dear. What won't these gossips say about that poor woman!" worried Maggie, in the general scurry away. She complained further to Dunn: "But, Bobby. It's like ancient Rome! In the time of Nero!"[42] And so it seemed, at times.

Embassy people and their guests frequently came to watch the American ships take target practice right near Prinkipo. Junior officer Orin Haskell complained about having "two secretaries from the legation, four other men and one wife" aboard; his ship was having "parties galore" and had become "a regular floating hotel." The guests did not actually ride the destroyers while they fired, but instead boarded other Navy ships so positioned as to give a good view. On an earlier occasion, embassy secretaries F. L. Belin and Allen Dulles and their wives followed a better plan. They boarded a boat to Prinkipo one evening to celebrate Allen's birthday. After staying at a hotel, the next morning they took a donkey ride all over the island and then up to the Monastery of St. George, at the crown of the hill. There they ate their lunch and continued to sit for hours in the sun, watching the sea and enjoying the Navy's target practice down below.[43]

Preparing for these gunnery exercises wasn't an especially recreational occasion for the Navy men who had to do it. As a division officer aboard a cruiser, Charles Olsen had watched the ship's firing rehearsal one morning, and then supervised his men as they stripped ship for action, rebored sights, painted danger circles on the decks, and checked off a myriad of other details. "I hope everything goes right tomorrow. Lord knows I have drilled my men enough for it," he wrote to Edna.

When the firing actually came off, Charles found it quite exciting. Olsen confessed he had never realized how much havoc big guns could wreak upon the firing ship itself:

> The first shot lifted a wooden grating in the waterway, flying over the side. The eight shots fired wrecked the pay office on the boat deck, till it looked like a mass of debris. The wooden bulkheads or sides [of the office] were broken in two, and shelves ripped off, desks knocked down, papers, books, typewriters, everything down. The deck locker had its cover locked down and the concussion broke the latch off, opened the locker and knocked most of the contents overboard. The life preservers stowed by the pay office flew all over. . . . Dr. Tribou after we finished firing stood laughing at the paymaster over his office. Then he went down to his room and oh how mad he was, when he found that his room had been wrecked. You cannot speak to Tribou about his room now because he is so mad. Of course all the lights were broken aft.

Despite the shipboard wreckage, Olsen was delighted. His big guns had scored twenty-four hits out of twenty-four shots, the best score on the ship; it was "the prettiest shooting I have seen yet." Though their time was slow, all his pointers had qualified. His division had won some ships' competitions too—a third and a second prize—which not only meant some modest prize money for his men (five or ten dollars each), but it also provided the kind of boost in morale one gets from successful athletic competition. Even for his sailors, then, the firing exercise had been a kind of recreation.[44]

For Helen Ogden (again, Helen was a YWCA worker regularly befriended by the Bristols), bathing and swimming were tops. On trips to the Standard Oil camp on the Bosporus such as the embassy frequently organized, she found the water a little salty, but easy to swim in and generally delightful. The public beach at Florio was also great fun, even though "the beach slopes out so gradually that it is hard to get out far enough to swim; you just floated around." Indeed, Helen thought, "If it were not for the Bosphorus Constantinople would be unbearable," presumably because you could not get out of the summer heat in any other way. Hence she not only bathed and swam with friends but often took her YWCA girls to the beach with her. There was only one minor difficulty. "Yesterday we went again up the Bosphorus with a mixed lot of girls—very mixed—I had two Russians and the others were Greek, Armenians and Jews. My two girls insisted upon swimming, and finally undressed and dressed in such a public place that I was covered with confusion. . . . None of the other girls seemed much bothered by the Russians' nakedness; they had long since gotten used to such things."[45]

The American men, however, were *not* used to modern Russian habits; hence they were keenly interested when they observed the Russians bathing in the nude. Usually they saw this in Russia, at places like Yalta, or maybe at Batoum rather than near Constantinople. The Yanks would comment on such things in letters or diaries: "Visited bathing beach and saw a beautiful fairy sporting [about] with out a green cap on—figure quite remarkable," recorded the intrigued Admiral McCully, for instance.[46] While Harry Pence assured his diary that only foreigners paid any special attention to the nude swimmers, still he himself could report that the practice was not just a rumor, but a fact. (He had observed it "from a neutral spot.") Sometimes American men would brag in the local bar about the sight: "Last time I was out in Batoum I seen upwards of six hundred women in swimmin' an' not one of 'em had a stitch on." So John Dos Passos reported someone saying, a person, however, who was somewhat under the influence. Others would try to photograph the scene. In Lt. Matthias Gardner's snapshots, for example, there weren't six hundred or even ten naked women, but there was certainly *some* naked female flesh. His photos indicate, by the way, that not only would some men stand nearby to gaze on these large groups of women bathers, but that little boats would often come close inshore to check out the situation.[47]

—◆◆◆—

As for their own bathing habits, in those days by no means was everybody in the Navy even able to swim. About this time a certain assistant secretary of the Navy was troubled to find drownings alarmingly high in the service simply because many sailors were nonswimmers. So Franklin Delano Roosevelt sponsored a fleet swimming trophy, hoping the visibility of this competition would improve the situation.[48] Conversely, in some parts of Asia Minor through which Americans traveled, swimming was an unknown art. Riding with Armenian troops alongside Lake Sevang (deep in Eastern Turkey) on a hot day, the ever-adventurous Lieutenant Dunn stripped and plunged into the water and swam out to some nearby boats. The Armenian soldiers with him drew up their horses and cheered the American, which moved Dunn to perform some aquatic stunts. When he swam back to the shore, they explained their cheers. Before this they had never seen a man swim.[49]

The American officers who swam did so both for exercise and for the opportunity to build morale. In 1914, at age fifty-five and while commanding a battleship, Newton McCully had occasionally put on a suit, dived from his ship's main deck, and then swam all the way around the vessel, this partly to promote the benefits of physical conditioning. When on duty in Russia after the war, he continued his aquatic activity. One day he signaled a destroyer under his command that was anchored out in the harbor that he would be coming aboard shortly. The officer of the deck ordered his lookouts to keep a sharp eye out for a boat. A while later the OOD was startled to hear shouts from the water. McCully and aide Cdr. Hugo Koehler had swum out to the ship in the buff. Later yet, during the dog days of the White Russian collapse, which McCully was helpless to prevent, he would continue swimming just to keep his own morale up. If, in the process, he sometimes shocked a destroyer's captain, he was an admiral, he was in the middle of nowhere, and he couldn't care less.[50]

Not all immersion was voluntary. Winfield Scott Cunningham was then a naval lieutenant stationed aboard *Scorpion*. One evening he and a fellow officer invited two young ladies to dinner aboard the Navy yacht. Afterward, "moved by the magic of the evening," the four took one of *Scorpion's* whaleboats out for a sail. They only overlooked two things: the six-knot current in the strait, and the squadron of five British battleships anchored just downstream. They successfully got under way, but their sail obscured the British ships, and they had failed to post a lookout in the bow. When somebody cried out, it was too late: they were riding down upon the ram of HMS *Royal Sovereign*. After a brief jar they found themselves swiftly carried along the side of this immense ship until the top of their mast hit the battleship's hoisted boat and their sailing craft capsized.

Searchlights pierced the night, the British vessel launched powerboats, and, after having floated a good way further down the Bosporus, the four young people were ignominiously hauled to safety. Cunningham's officer buddy in this episode was senior so that Cunningham did not have to face his captain personally—very fortunately, he thought. What the two young women thought of the whole episode is not recorded, but in general, Cunningham remembered, "The incident was considered something of a blow to American prestige."[51]

Most Americans who purposely entered the strait's famous waters were seeking a challenge. One summer, with a group of friends, embassy aide Lt. Julian Wheeler decided to swim "from Europe to Asia," as he put it. (That phrase does have a certain ring, like General Harbord's telling his U.S. Army troops one day to "Come, take a dip in the Euphrates.") Beginning at the waterfront near the Tokatlian Hotel and accompanied by a boat, the young men swam toward the Standard Oil installation that was on the opposite bank, maybe a mile across. Despite the very swift current, they persevered and reached their goal. A couple of years later, further down the Bosporus at Romeli Hissar, George Young tried swimming across the strait from the same direction but found himself caught up in the "devil current" and swept back to Europe. In sharp contrast was the effort of the British commanding general in Constantinople, Tim Harington, for whom the strong current was not a major obstacle. On one occasion, he not only swam from his house at Therapia across to Yenikali on the Asiatic side, but also then immediately swam back, landing at Roumeli Hissar.[52]

However, the *classic* swim was not across the Bosporus, but instead across the Hellespont. The ancient story, of course, was that Leander had nightly swum the Hellespont to meet his beloved Hero, until one winter night when the nearby beacon went out, and he lost his way. Finding Leander's inert body washed up on the shore, Hero killed herself.

During his far-flung travels, the twenty-two-year-old Lord Byron in 1810 had found his ship becalmed for over a week in the Hellespont. Fascinated by Leander's story (which had been celebrated by poets from Ovid to Marlowe) and finding himself at the legendary site between Sestos and Abydos, Byron decided to duplicate the feat. After one failed attempt (due to a north wind and a rapid tide), he and a friend succeeded in swimming from Asia to Europe, the direction that Leander had swum to visit Hero.[53] Six days later he penned a poem about the exploit, "Written After Swimming from Sestos to Abydos," which has been mildly popular ever since.[54]

Byron was congenitally lame, but a powerful swimmer. Navy Capt. Pratt Mannix was renowned in the Navy for his athletic prowess, particularly in the water. In 1907 at Manila Bay, a typhoon featuring winds of seventy to eighty miles an hour and waves of four to five feet blew up, and a seaman help-ing batten down the anchored *Wilmington* noticed a man swimming along-side *Rainbow*, which was anchored some six hundred yards away. He ran to the officer of the deck to report a man overboard, only to be told, "Oh, that's Mannix at his morning exercise." On a twenty-dollar bet, Mannix had swum from *Rainbow* to *Wilmington*, circled the latter vessel, and then swum back.[55]

As we have seen, the large repair ship *Denebola* that Mannix had maneu-vered to get command of steamed to Constantinople in late 1922. As his ship steamed through the Hellespont, Mannix took note of the famous site of Leander's and Lord Byron's swim and began thinking about trying it himself.

By the time of his ship's return to the States a year or so later, Mannix had read everything of relevance he could find, including tide tables, sailing direc-tions, charts, and encyclopedias (besides famous poems). When *Denebola* was ordered out of Turkey, he arranged with Admiral Bristol to let him anchor for a day in the Dardanelles, thus allowing officers and men to visit Gallipoli, and coincidentally giving himself an opportunity to attempt the ancient feat. Having previously verified the location of ancient Abydos and Sestos, he had only to decide whether to swim with the great current and against the very strong sea and waves, or the reverse. He decided to buck the waves. He entered the strait on the European side and swam toward Asia. A boat from his ship pulled along with him, not just for safety's sake but also to provide witness of the event. Before long the boat was half full of water and the crew had to bail. Despite waves slapping him in the face and some cramping of his legs, Mannix per-severed. "I did all right until I approached the Asiatic shore where I encoun-tered a counter current flowing strongly up toward the Sea of Marmora. When I first put my feet on the bottom they were snatched out from under me by this counter current and I found it impossible to stand up . . . but I finally made it."[56] Mannix had the four enlisted men in the boat sign a certificate that he had actu-ally done the deed,[57] and he also took steps to have the account published in the *Naval Register* of that year. Thus, when adventurer-writer Richard Halliburton circulated a report in 1925 that he had just become the first American to swim the Hellespont (to publicize his stunt, Halliburton reportedly spread rumors that he had died in the attempt), Mannix could produce evidence to papers like the *New York Herald Tribune* that supported his prior claim.[58]

Lord Byron, by the way, had not only swum the Hellespont while his ship waited in the Dardanelles for the wind to turn, but had visited the nearby Troad and also had shot some snipe. Recognizing that, one should not omit to men-tion that in the midst of all their other pastimes, American Navy men during the early twenties in the Middle East took many an opportunity to shoot—at partridge, ducks, quail in season, grail, hawks, eagle, wild boar ("very good," according to a traveler whose hosts fed him this meat at Tarsus[59]), foxes, deer, even an occasional jumping porpoise. They went hunting in the Bosporus, on the Marmara (especially in the Gulf of Ismid), and throughout the coasts of mainland Turkey from Samsun on the Black Sea down to Marash in Cilicia, and south as far as Syria. In Russia, during the famine, Webb Trammell was offered the opportunity to "shoot wolves and other large game."[60] Later yet, in the midst of the human tragedy of mass evacuations throughout the coasts of Turkey, the destroyer *Hatfield* signaled Bristol, "No refugees Knojachesme or Kara Chali. [Yet] we evacuated 36 partridges, six hares one fox. Expect continue operations tomorrow."[61]

And so it went. No matter what their formal naval duty, American Navy people always found ways to play a ball game, to picnic or go for a swim, or in some more creative way to keep their spirits up.

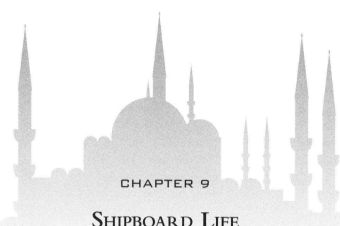

CHAPTER 9

SHIPBOARD LIFE

One January, dispatch orders sent the destroyers McCormick *and* Simpson *on a wild dash to the Black Sea in search of an American merchantman reported lost in a storm. That was the roughest sea trip I have ever made. As we headed into mountainous seas, an especially big one crashed over us and broke the glass ports of the navigation bridge, cutting the men on watch. For several days we searched the waters of the Black Sea and found no trace of the missing vessel.*

—Capt. William A. Maguire, USN, Chaplain's Corps

Yet to be described in this text are the standard in-port routines and underway operations of the American naval vessels that steamed for four years throughout these fabulous but unfamiliar waters. In the foreground of this portrayal will be the "four piper" destroyers that, between 1919 and 1923, were the indispensable workhorses of America's small Black Sea fleet.

—◆◆◆—

Besides the destroyers, other naval vessels played a part on the Turkish station, of course. As we have seen, in early 1919, *Scorpion* had just completed its year of internment, and its crew had to be completely replaced.[1] Nevertheless, with occasional drydocking and repairs, this old steam yacht was fit enough to stay the course in Constantinople until all the American ships were required to leave in late 1923.

While not originally built for naval duty, *Scorpion* had served in the Navy ever since the Spanish American War; the 5-inch guns it had mounted then had long since been taken off.[2] Since 1908, the vessel had served as the yacht for the American ambassador to Turkey in the Bosporus. Naval officers who came aboard in the 1920s found the small ship fitted out with fine rugs and wall hangings quite atypical of naval vessels.[3]

However, *Scorpion* was not merely a pleasure boat. On at least two occasions (once offshore Messina, Italy, and a second time in Turkish waters), the yacht had been employed in rescuing earthquake victims.[4] Even in 1920 Admiral Bristol had trusted the vessel to take him and his guests as far as Yalta in the Crimea. Yes, the main purpose of the latter visit seems to have been sightseeing (visiting the czar's wine cellars, nearby botanical gardens, and a palace), but clearly the old yacht could still go to sea.[5] Featuring a 775-ton displacement and stretching 212 feet fore to aft, *Scorpion* required a complement of ninety sailors to serve it.[6]

Two significantly larger steam yachts that served briefly in Bristol's navy right after World War I had been acquired by the Navy in 1917 from private parties. The *Noma*, of 1,250 tons, had been loaned to the Navy by multimillionaire Vincent Astor. Renamed "USS *Noma*," this vessel had spent the war on patrol and escort both in the Atlantic near Europe and in the Mediterranean and had actually begun its service in July of 1917 by attacking a U-boat. Upon receiving *Noma* in February of 1919, Bristol employed it to help him conduct relief and investigatory operations in the Black Sea. During the same period,

The station ship at Constantinople was the steam yacht USS *Scorpion*, which had served in the navy since the Spanish American War. This photo shows the *Scorpion* at Prinkipo (Princes Island), a famous recreation spot in the Sea of Marmara. *Thomas Kinkaid Collection, The Naval History and Heritage Command*

Bristol sent the converted yacht USS *Nahma* on similar work, but he also once ordered this relatively large ship (its tonnage was twice that of the *Noma*) to take him from Constantinople to Beirut and on to Smyrna and then back again to Constan.[7] During the Great War, *Nahma* had been employed on convoy duty out of Gibraltar.

In May 1919 Bristol was assigned four destroyers, and both *Noma* and *Nahma* were sent home to be decommissioned and returned to their owners.[8] Much smaller vessels that also played a minor but important role in Bristol's small navy were several subchasers. Over four hundred of these craft had been constructed in America during the war (a hundred or so for France); most were fitted out with depth charges aft and a 3-inch gun forward. Perhaps more important for Bristol's purposes, these small craft had some useful deck space, upon which a large variety of supplies could be stowed for local transport.

Subchasers were 110-foot wooden boats that burned gas and had a top theoretical speed of about eighteen knots, with a cruising speed of twelve knots and a theoretical range of 1,000 miles. During the war, each boat was served by its wartime complement of twenty-two enlisted men and two reserve officers.[9] Once the reservists returned home upon the war's end, Bristol borrowed academy-trained officers from ships under his cognizance to command them, and the chasers' manning was reduced to one officer per boat and an enlisted crew of fifteen or so. The admiral employed these vessels locally, employing four of them to start with, and retaining one or two through 1923. They were usually sent no further afield than the Bosporus, the nearby Gulf of Ismid (a major Near East Relief warehouse operation was located near Derindje), and the Sea of Marmara. When all those Russian refugee ships descended upon the city in late 1920, Bristol's subchasers spent eighteen-hour days supplying the refugees.[10] One or two of these craft were still on hand to rescue Greek refugees in the Gulf of Ismid during the Smyrna crisis.

As for large naval vessels, the cruisers *Olympia, Galveston, St. Louis,* and *Pittsburgh* were all sent to Turkey for extended periods, the *Galveston* and *St. Louis* each spending a whole year on the Turkish station. They all featured large guns, relatively good communication facilities, and comparatively large crews. To be sure, the four cruisers differed widely in size, armament, and complement. Nevertheless, the smallest cruiser (*Galveston*) had roughly three times the size and fighting power of a destroyer, and the largest (*Pittsburgh*) had as much tonnage as early battleships.[11]

Arriving fairly early was the *Olympia,* famous for having been Adm. George Dewey's flagship during the Battle of Manila Bay. At Bristol's direction, *Olympia* steamed along the Black Sea coast of Turkey in the fall of 1919, landing naval investigatory parties ashore to study postwar conditions.[12] In July

1919 the cruiser *Galveston* reported to Admiral Bristol for a year of service. Bristol sent *Galveston* to Novorossisk on the Black Sea when the Bolsheviks threatened General Denikin's White Russian army there. As we have seen, Admiral McCully then had sent a couple of hundred Russian refugees down to Constantinople on the American cruiser and a destroyer or two.[13]

Pittsburgh came to Constantinople twice, first very briefly in May of 1920. This old armored cruiser was then steaming in the Black Sea as flagship for Admiral Harry Knapp (Knapp was then commander of U.S. forces in European waters), so the ship was on hand to evacuate some fifty American relief officials from Armenia (via Batoum) when the Bolsheviks began advancing that way.[14] That evacuation complete, *Pittsburgh* soon resumed its show-the-flag cruise throughout the Mediterranean and northern Europe, while *Galveston* stayed at Constan until relieved by *Chattanooga* in July of 1920. *Chattanooga* did not stay long, but in mid-October of that year, Bristol greeted the cruiser *St. Louis*.

As we have seen, *St. Louis* had arrived in good time to help in the last evacuation of the White Russians from the Crimea.[15] Part way through *St. Louis's* stay at Constantinople, Capt. William D. Leahy took command; Leahy's short diary of this period features many entertaining and informing entries about his Turkish experience.[16] When *St. Louis* departed the Bosporus for home (and decommissioning) in September of 1921, the cruiser was not replaced, and hence no American naval vessel larger than a destroyer would be available to speed to Smyrna when trouble erupted there in September of 1922. In November of that year, though, Adm. Andrew Long, having just crossed the Atlantic to Gibraltar on the *Pittsburgh,* was ordered to delay the beginning of his show-the-flag cruise to Mediterranean ports and northern capitals (he was now in charge of Naval Forces, Europe) in order to stand by in Constantinople to evacuate Americans, were any emergency to require that. In the event. *Pittsburgh* remained in the Bosporus for about six months.[17]

Until the Nationalist threat to Constantinople in late 1922, when (as we will see) the stores ship *Bridge* and destroyer tender *Denebola* were sent to support an enhanced destroyer presence, few other large Navy ships spent significant time in the waters of Turkey or Southern Russia. Yes, occasionally supply ships like the colliers *Nereus* and *Mars* and the oilers *Patoka* and *Trinity* visited, but each of the latter seems only to have stopped long enough at Constantinople to transfer fuel, mail, cargo, and passengers. A couple of American battleships did spend a few weeks apiece in the region.[18] Once the *Arizona* had witnessed the Greek occupation of Smyrna in May of 1919, the ship ran up to Constantinople for a brief port visit. Then, in late 1921, *Utah* visited the great city on the Bosporus while it was serving as flagship for the U.S. naval forces in European waters (with Admiral Niblack, commanding).

Overall, though, not only did the two battleships move on quickly, but even the cruisers directly assigned to Bristol steamed hardly at all; most of the time they simply moored in the strait awaiting eventualities. Hence, over the four years that the Navy retained a force in Turkey—for eyes and ears throughout the Black Sea, Aegean, and eastern Mediterranean; for long-range coordination, transport, and mail delivery; for the rescue of refugees and assistance to vessels in distress; to provide an official American voice and presence in a variety of ports; and for a myriad of other purposes—Admiral Bristol depended heavily on his destroyers.

Until late 1922, Bristol typically had only a small number of these versatile ships—typically only four, six, or eight at a time, although for a few months in 1920, he had twelve.[19] However, the Navy continually rotated the destroyers to and from the States so that over the four years that the Navy operated from the Bosporus, at least forty destroyers saw significant duty there.[20]

Destroyers of the day varied slightly in construction, but they all burned oil and most had four boilers and four stacks—hence the prime nickname given to this destroyer type ever since, "four pipers" or "four stackers," though they were also known as "flushdeckers" for their distinctive flush weather decks. These "DDs" were driven by two shafts and two screws, had a normal displacement of about 1,200 tons, measured some 314 feet in length with a 31-foot beam (such a proportion being very narrow or "fine" even for typically long, narrow destroyers), and had a maximum draft of 12 feet. The fastest were rated to steam 35 knots at full horsepower, but 14 knots was their typical cruising speed, at which speed (assuming the propulsion equipment was in good condition and the bottom was clean), a full tank of oil could carry a vessel and its crew somewhere between 4,300 and 5,000 miles, depending on the specific destroyer class.[21] Ship manning varied somewhat, but when *Whipple* joined Bristol's navy in 1920, it had eight officers aboard (including one medical officer), along with twelve chiefs and some one hundred and ten enlisted men.[22]

Externally, the four pipers all had one main mast located just aft of the ship's flying bridge, which was equipped with lines for signal flags, and on most four pipers this mast also supported an elevated lookout mount or crow's nest. An enclosed bridge lay below the flying bridge. A second mast located aft also often carried some flag apparatus and usually another lookout mount. Each destroyer carried a couple of boats amidships and two anchors far forward, housed on either side of the bow. The small single rudder that each four-piper featured made for occasional low-speed maneuvering difficulties.

As for armament, these combatants featured four 4-inch/50 guns (one forward, one aft, and two amidships—one gun each to port and starboard on the top of the galley deckhouse). Each ship also had a 3-inch antiaircraft gun on the fantail and several machine guns. However, their "big punch" was composed of the twelve 21-inch torpedoes that they carried in four triple mounts at the ship's beam, two of these mounts situated on the starboard side, and two on the port.

On the 1919–23 Near Eastern assignment, none of this considerable weaponry seems to have been fired in anger, but no doubt it deterred several attacks.

The destroyers that were assigned serially to Bristol were among the 270 destroyers or so that America had built between 1917 and 1921. Although the submarine threat of World War I had been the occasion of their construction, most of these vessels were completed too late actually to get into that war. In fact, in the early 1920s, some of these new ships were scrapped, and dozens of others, particularly those with lower hull numbers, were decommissioned.[23] (It was fifty mothballed four-pipers that were given to the British in the famous "Destroyers for Bases" deal between America and Great Britain just before America's entry into World War II.) Because of their recent construction, every one of the destroyers Bristol received was pretty new when it reported to Turkey—and most of these ships were pretty reliable, too. According to military historian Donald Kehn, "These ships were nothing if not paradoxes. Small and spartan, yet beloved by almost all U.S. sailors and officers who served in them; equipped with temperamental powerplants, many were quite serviceable well into their third decade. . . . They were obsolete by the mid-1930s (in contrast with Continental and Japanese designs), yet still gave good accounts of themselves in combat,"[24] that is, in World War II.

When American destroyers first arrived at Constantinople, they were typically assigned berths at USN Buoy 1 and USN Buoy 2, mooring buoys located right off Dolmabagtche Palace, just up the Bosporus from the Golden Horn. It was not easy to tie up at these buoys. Richard Field, captain of *Goff* when it served in the Near East, described well for Naval Institute *Proceedings* the fluvial difficulties imposed at this particular location:

> As the current of the Golden Horn joins the Bosphorus it makes a counter current which sets up the northern or European side of the latter toward the Black Sea. The drift of the main current [coming down the Bosporus] is from two to six miles an hour and the average of the counter current [moving back up] is about one mile [an hour]. With these treacherous currents, in a port packed with ships, mariners had to use the greatest care to keep out of grief. In coming into port one was in the main or down current and the mooring buoys assigned to the American Navy were well over on the European side in the counter

current. To get to these buoys one had to thread in and out between the dozens of ships which filled every available berth and, in turning, [make] allowance . . . for the drift of the ship with the current during the turn. There was also to be considered the extraordinary turning moment encountered in passing across the line of demarcation between the up and down currents. I have seen a destroyer jump fully fifteen degrees from her course as she got into this position.[25]

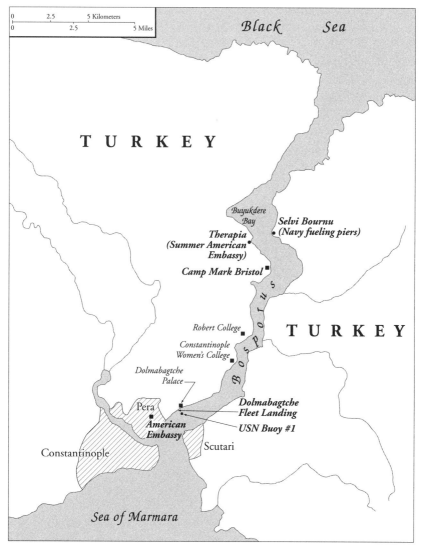

Map 6. Navy and Embassy Sites in and near Constantinople

On one occasion, having barely missed colliding with some merchant ships two hours before in the Sea of Marmara and also being very tired, Capt. Harry Pence of *McFarland* found great difficulty in going alongside *Lawrence* at USN Buoy 2. There was a very strong current, he recorded in his diary, and hence he thought it was touch and go as to whether he would ever make it or not.[26]

American cruisers and other large American naval vessels typically anchored rather than snag the buoys, and normally they lowered the hook a bit upstream of the standard destroyer site. With the swift Bosporus current (as Capt. Pratt Mannix later pointed out), these big ships had to be ever watchful lest they drag anchor.[27] However, at least once the cruiser *St. Louis* moored to a buoy instead of anchoring, only to find the conflicting currents suddenly swing the ship bodily all the way from downstream to up, so that the mooring buoy was caught underneath the cruiser's ram, which sank it. This event quickly brought an alarmed ship's captain to the bridge, though apparently he soon discovered that the anchors attached to the sunken buoy were still holding his ship.[28]

At these same buoys (called "home" by crew members for months on end), a destroyer's in-port watch teams were exercised greatly in performing shipboard protocol. As Dan Gallery recalled, "Every maritime nation in Europe had at least one man'-o'war [in Constantinople], and the British, French, and Italians had squadrons." Hence a ship's watch had to exchange honors with ship after passing ship. Beyond that, "We soon learned never to get caught up on deck at 8 o'clock in the morning. That's when the colors go up and by universal custom the band plays your own national anthem and follows it with those of all nations having warships present in port." In addition to that daily racket, full dress ship and twenty-one-gun noontime salutes were standard for the national holidays of all the several navies present. On such holidays, according to Gallery, the watch could get blisters just hauling the signal flags up and down that were used for dressing ship.[29]

The watch also had to be alert for signals from the duty American station ship typically moored further south, between a buoy and the seawall at Tophany, near the meeting of the Bosporus with the Golden Horn,[30] and also to watch for boats coming alongside that might carry dignitaries. Quick recognition of national uniforms was particularly important in such a cosmopolitan port as Constantinople, so that one might refrain from piping honors for some gaily decorated junior officer climbing the ladder who represented a country no one had ever heard of. (Ashore, a sailor or officer might be tempted to salute the gorgeously dressed Turkish *kavass*—a doorman.[31])

Another challenge for the watch was to make sure liquor was not being brought aboard. If a crew member thought it too dangerous to attempt to sneak a bottle by the watch on the quarterdeck, he might try to purchase some from a visiting bumboat. Hence destroyer standing orders often required the importunate small craft to be kept off and even driven away with fire hoses, if necessary.[32] Ensuring that stowaways were not somehow smuggled into the ship occasionally became a concern at refugee ports (where pity for the local unfortunates could work greatly on bluejackets' feelings), though apparently not at Constantinople.

Quarterdeck watches also helped manage the Navy boats that were operating. In the lower Bosporus, Navy boats from the destroyers or larger ships were sent to and from Dolmabagtche landing at regular intervals, and captain's gigs had to be kept ready as well. This landing comprised "fleet's landing" for the American naval vessels and was heavy with traffic. Hence Turkish boatmen would also be standing by, so if you missed the regular run of the Navy boat, you could usually hire your way out to your ship by native caique. At other ports, though, particularly the smaller ones, Navy people depended almost entirely on ships' boats for transport from anchored or moored destroyer to shore and back.

Whether moored in the Black Sea, the Aegean, or the Mediterranean, in-port watches had to watch for a variety of boat-handling problems. Once when *Smith Thompson* was anchored out at Beirut, four of its officers who had been on the beach got into the ship's wherry (a small passenger boat) and began to row back to the ship, but they broke an oar while still some two miles off. Ultimately, the boat's passengers made a makeshift oar by lashing the tiller to the loom of the broken oar, and they resumed rowing slowly. Aboard the ship, the quarterdeck watch was directed to man the ship's big searchlight. Before long, the watch found the boat, and the quartermaster held it in the searchlight's blinding glare. Being spotlighted in such a compromising situation became even more embarrassing when the four officers realized that among the spectators was a pacing ship's captain who had become very much concerned about the absence of half his officers.[33]

Even in daylight there could be problems. Once, on what appeared to be an ordinary, calm day, Commander Field of the *Goff* and two of his officers were invited to enjoy Thanksgiving dinner with the American missionaries at the Turkish port of Trebizond. Upon their arrival, his host felt obliged to warn Field that a yearly storm that the locals called "the falling of the leaves" was expected on that very date. However, Field had seen no indications of any weather while aboard ship that morning, nor was there a ripple to be seen in the harbor. So the ship's captain shrugged off the homespun weather forecast. Greeted warmly by the missionaries, the officers settled in to a Thanksgiving dinner that included turkey, cranberry sauce, two pies, plum pudding, and ice cream. However, the serving of the ice cream had to be interrupted when Field noticed whitecaps in the harbor, and once the officers reached the landing, they found seas breaking over the pier. Field ordered the *Goff* to send a boat to the inner harbor, and once it arrived, "It took fifty minutes with two officers and six men pulling continuously, to row the short half mile to windward to the ship. Even then our difficulties were not over. With the boat dashing up and down with the waves it was necessary for each man to watch his opportunity to jump for the sea ladder and get over the side quickly enough to avoid being crushed against the ship by the boat." Finally, these officers and men all managed safely to scramble up the destroyer's side.[34]

While in port, on occasion a ship would have to move to another buoy or to get under way for some other reason, perhaps to fuel. In the Black Sea, the DDs visited fueling tanks at Constanza, Romania, but after Bristol had made logistical arrangements, the destroyers more regularly used the Standard Oil fueling piers at Selvi Bournu, located across from Therapia on the Asiatic side of the Bosporus. In addition, sometimes the ships took fuel from a visiting fleet oiler. Interestingly, on one occasion (in bad weather) an American destroyer gave fuel to a battleship. Harry Pence's diary records *McFarland* giving oil to *Utah* during the latter ship's visit to the region; *McFarland* filled back up at Selvi Bournu a couple of days later.[35] Originally, the American destroyers had frequently taken fuel from the British (who had brought tankers along to fuel the many cruisers and battleships they kept in the straits). For instance, when it arrived at Constantinople low on fuel in February of 1920, *Smith Thompson* went directly alongside the British tanker SS *Perthshire* to fuel. It may have been when he learned that the British would no longer guarantee to provide oil to his ships that Bristol initiated his local arrangements with Standard Oil.[36]

Incidentally, although all the destroyers burned oil, several of the older ships burned coal, including *Scorpion* and all the American cruisers ordered to Bristol for duty. Coaling ship was an "all-hands" evolution (including most officers) that typically took twelve hours or more, and could literally exhaust a crew, making tempers short into the bargain. Injury was also a possibility. One of Lieutenant Olsen's men was working in a lighter close aboard *St. Louis* when two 800-pound coal sacks fell on him from ten feet up. Both of his legs were broken in several places. Sympathetic, Olsen wrote his wife that "this little Italian kid," an excellent worker, was suffering terribly.[37]

Bristol, by the way, sometimes had the coal-fired *Scorpion* steam up to Constanza, where teams of Romanians (many of them women) were hired to shovel coal aboard while the yacht's crew and officers took a couple of days off to visit Bucharest. When the Navy people returned, their yacht would not only have been coaled, but also would be "all prettied up, all shined up, and all ready to go again."[38]

Another standard evolution that temporarily took the destroyers away from their buoys was dry docking. This seems always to have taken place at the Armstrong-Vickers dry dock, located deep in the Golden Horn behind the moveable Galata Bridge and behind an inner bridge as well. (The transit beyond the bridges required putting one's ship in the hands of a Turkish pilot, which typically provoked considerable anxiety on the part of a destroyer captain.) Sometimes a ship would dry-dock for repairs: on one dry docking, *Smith Thompson* was said to need the stem straightened, the propeller guard repaired, and the bearings relined. However, dry docking to have the bottom scraped and painted by a crew of Turks was also standard before a destroyer's yearly full-power run.[39]

The goal of such a run was to ensure the ship would conform to naval requirements, the standard for most four-pipers being thirty-five knots. *Smith Thompson* achieved this standard during a full-power run in the Sea of Marmara just before leaving Constantinople to visit the Mediterranean. Fireman Berthelsen was thrilled to witness the event: "With all four cans lit and throttles wide, safety valves tightened a bit, and the revolution counter registering 450 turns per minute—well, there's life below decks, and how! What a thrill to stand on deck and watch our knife-like bow, driven by thirty thousand horsepower,

The commanding and executive officers of *Whipple* (Lt. Cdr. Richard Bernard and Lt. John Waller) pose in front of their destroyer, which rests at drydock deep in the Golden Horn harbor. Whipple *cruise book*

cut through the choppy seas! When the safety valves lifted to release the excessive pressure, a blue, hot blast of steam would burst out of the exhaust lines with the report of a cannon, and the roar would be so deafening as to make it impossible to hear on the bridge until they reseated."[40] During *McFarland's* full power run, Harry Pence was most pleased to note that his three-year-old ship not only completed all of its runs successfully, but that it also made more speed than it ever had before.[41]

While in port, both destroyers and cruisers sometimes left harbor for yet one other evolution: yearly gunnery exercises. Work on the guns took place even while a vessel was moored at the buoys or was anchored, of course. Olsen on *St. Louis* once wrote his wife that he was working on a couple of guns that had their air holes stopped up with mud and dirt from the air compressors. "Before we can fire . . . these holes must be clear to blow out the powder gases and burnt powder bags." Nothing to date had solved the problem, and Olsen was now planning to connect an air hose to the line and attempt to blow the dirt out backwards.[42] A couple of years later, Dan Gallery recorded in his diary the *Pittsburgh's* carrying on gunnery drills at anchor one day, and the next day getting under way for the annual exercises. As we've already seen, ships practiced their gunnery just off the island of Prinkipo in the Sea of Marmara.[43]

For *Pittsburgh*, the exercises consisted of one day spent rehearsing, another day clearing for action and boresighting, and a third day shooting for record. The success of his ship's rehearsal made Gallery think that the cruiser might "surprise everyone & turn in a high score." Two days later, Gallery penned this entry in his diary: "Well, we certainly knocked all the dope gallery [seamen's predictions] west today, and all the targets too. The results were infinitely better than anyone had dared to hope. Many of the targets are utterly ruined and everyone conducted themselves as if they had been brought up since early childhood as a member of a guns crew. The broadside guns raised merry hell with every target put up for them and turret two only got 12 hits out of 12 shots! Everyone of the ship is going around tonight with their chests stuck out so far that they can't see their feet at all." A day after that, Gallery reported that four of his cruiser's guns (two 3-inch and two 6-inch guns) had been awarded Navy Es for excellence, which letters their crews immediately stenciled on the respective gun mounts. "They are all painted on already, in fact they were half an hour after the dope was checked over. Best thing for morale that has happened yet." Adding to the morale was the $1,700 in prize money that the ship immediately distributed to the crews of the best guns.[44]

Pittsburgh's gunnery trials had been umpired by officers from destroyers in port, and these vessels began their own gunnery exercises the next day. The DDs alternated at towing targets for each other and making practice firing runs.

During official rehearsals, one of *Gilmer's* guns also did well enough to earn the Navy E, and the whole ship did well, too, as did the *Hatfield* and *Overton* a day later. However, rough weather shut down operations and extended the time spent anchored or making firing runs to as many as three weeks. In the end, several of these destroyers returned to the States without having completed their annual exercises.[45]

Sometimes a ship's boats (rather than a ship itself) would be asked to leave the buoys to conduct an errand somewhere about the harbor. When refugees overwhelmed the city, Navy people could be tasked to use their boats to deliver food to local refugee camps or refugee ships, or simply to send teams as manpower for soup kitchens. In case of a crisis, the embassy made detailed plans to evacuate Americans from Constantinople (making lists of the addresses of all Americans in the city), although the destroyers never had to execute them. An in-port activity that did occasionally require a Constantinople-based ship or its boats to get under way was firefighting.

Sands once shifted from its buoy to Selvi Bournu to help fight fires in the oil storage area there.[46] On another occasion, a building that was filled with refugees caught fire. It was located near the berth of the large American naval repair ship *Denebola*. Hence Captain Mannix sent away the ship's fire-and-rescue party in a large motor sailing launch, and followed the launch in his gig. Under the captain's direction, *Denebola's* team got the refugees out of the building and tossed their bundles of clothing out as well, and soon the ship's launch had landed "handy billies" attached to fire hoses and got them working. Large streams of water from the pumps soon extinguished the fire and kept neighboring buildings from igniting. (Meanwhile, when the local Turkish excuse for a fire department arrived, it could only provide a stream of water about the size of that from a garden hose, and the Turks' hose was not long enough to reach the fire anyway.)[47]

Individuals from moored naval vessels might be sent on a variety of duties around the port; various ships' crews were sent regularly on shore patrol, for example. In considering the local situation at Constan, Commander Field of the *Goff* thought the permanent American shore patrol organized by the embassy and manned by ships in the harbor "not only kept our liberty-men straight but also protected them from the dangers which naturally lurked in such a city."[48] The Italian soldiers helping to occupy Constantinople posed some of the dangers. As Fireman Berthelsen commented, "The dagos have cultivated a violent dislike for us and our officers—the casualties to date: one American dead and two injured by bayonets. Everyone except an American goes ashore armed with either a bayonet or a pistol; [but] we have to use our fists to combat the pistol-totin' dago."[49]

The day-to-day violence, to be sure, was multifaceted. Note the unique ship's inspection described in a letter to his wife by Lieutenant Olsen: "This afternoon we had an inspection of everybody on board for bite marks on the jaw. A Filipino steward was robbed last night ashore and during the scuffle he bit the man in the jaw. We had two or three men with bites on their necks, gotten in an entirely different way. Ha! We did not locate the man."[50] Olsen further wrote Edna that his ship's dentist, a man named Pebico, had been attacked without provocation while on the way to the Russian Easter service by a drunken Spaniard and slashed across the face from his temple to under his jaw. "He did not know he was cut at first and ran after the man and began beating him. The crowd soon beat [the man] up too and then the English patrol took charge of him. 'Pebico' sure is cut badly and will carry a scar although the doctors took very fine stitches. Constantinople!"

As is evident here, drink was the main devil at hand, and drink could be found everywhere. Olsen at one point was chagrined that a bottle had just been found among *St. Louis's* General Court-Martial prisoners! Anyway, so comparatively large a task could shore patrol impose on the ship's personnel that Charles once lamented to Edna that *St. Louis* was mainly employed in "being the Radio Traffic ship and patrolling the city to pick up drunken sailors."[51]

Of course, men working aboard Navy ships had many other in-port tasks, among them all the repair and maintenance needed to keep the ships steaming. Berthelsen mentions his boiler division relining the fire boxes before the ship proceeded from Constantinople to Manila, for example. And when *Pittsburgh* got sudden orders to speed to Constantinople from Gibraltar, Dan Gallery's boiler division had half the boilers torn apart for maintenance. His people had to put the boilers back together and the ship had to take on coal, too, before the ship could proceed.[52] The engineers could be kept doing repair work even under way, of course; in the midst of the Smyrna crisis, the *Edsall* was down to two boilers when it blew out a gasket in the feed line of one of the remaining boilers, and when that was repaired, it blew two or three tubes in that same boiler and had to limp into port at fifteen knots. Even on the return to Smyrna, *Edsall's* boilermen were kept busy repairing the one boiler and rebricking another at the same time,[53] but the engineers saw to it that the ship completed all its underway assignments.

In engineering, just as in the gunnery work that we have spoken of above, by the way, competition could be involved: Orin Haskell mentioned in a letter to his wife his hope that the *Bainbridge* might win the Navy's engineering *E* award; at that time, only one other destroyer was ahead of his ship in the fleet ratings.[54]

Otherwise, in-port maintenance for the deck crew included such tasks as "painting, scraping and red-leading, cleaning and repairing boats, overhauling rigging, making fenders, cleaning the battery or torpedo tubes, overhauling torpedoes, rousing and wirebrushing the chain cable," according to Lt. John Cross aboard *Smith Thompson*. "These items [were] as a drop in the bucket of a day's work for the deck force," he added.[55]

Paperwork tasks like administration and record keeping took a good deal of time in port, especially the time of officers, yeomen, and the senior enlisted men within a division. A paperwork evolution still familiar today was annual performance reports, written on officers and enlisted alike. Another kind of paperwork was prepared only by officers: fleetwide promotion exams. In his diary, Dan Gallery outlined the series of tests he had to pass before being promoted to lieutenant junior grade, exams (and preparations for them) that took the better part of two weeks. Included were six-hour exams each in the following topics: "steam" (engineering), international law, ordnance, "juice" (electricity), celestial navigation, navigation and piloting, seamanship, strategy and tactics, and military law.[56] It is clear that these challenging exams were taken quite seriously by both officers and the Navy's personnel bureau: at one point two of the *Pittsburgh*'s officers were ordered home for a reexam for promotion, thus finding their European cruise at a sudden end.[57] Even those holding the rank of commander, like Harry Pence, had to take promotion exams, as one of his diary entries indicates.

Other kinds of paperwork that officers and radiomen would regularly find themselves involved in were writing, coding, and decoding naval messages.

As for "general drills"—these included fire, collision, abandon ship, general quarters, man overboard, and landing force drills—they seem to have been conducted as frequently in port as they were while under way.[58] Actually, standard drills like these were sometimes neglected during time at sea because of the rush of events or bad weather, so the in-port drills could be quite important.[59] Otherwise, much work while tied up at the buoys or anchored was simple drudgery: being assigned to working parties to get food and other stores aboard, coaling ship (on a coal-burner), daily sweeping, washing, and cleaning ship (Captain Mannix later claimed that *Denebola* "was kept up like a gentleman's yacht and you could have eaten your meals off her deck" when he commanded the destroyer tender[60]), and particularly field days incident to captain's or admiral's inspection.

Captain's inspection was a routine event typically held weekly (when a ship was in port), but the much-less-frequent admiral's inspection was a very important evolution requiring much preparation. On December 28, 1920, when the officers of *St. Louis* were directed to form Admiral Bristol's inspection board to inspect the cruiser *Chattanooga*, which was in Constan over the holidays, Charles Olsen found he would have over a hundred questions to fill out just on that ship's after division. The next day Olsen and his team went aboard at 8:00 a.m. and inspected the *Chattanooga*'s men at quarters; then they conducted bag and hammock inspections. On the latter, *Chattanooga* scored very well, but the cruiser fell down at the general drills that succeeded them. "At man overboard, we dropped two life preservers over the stern, and it took 8 minutes and 27 sec to get the last preservers. . . . It takes about 1 min. and 30 sec for us to do it—30 sec. for us to lower the life boat fully manned into the water. In everything, sweetheart, we stand so far above them that there was no comparison." On the other drills, *Chattanooga* also performed poorly. Olsen thought the vessel had been let off the hook with the overall grade of 3.0 it was eventually assigned.[61]

Whether the admiral actually came along on this particular inspection is unclear. However, Admiral Bristol did personally inspect *Smith Thompson*; indeed, he had his two-starred flag run up the mainmast immediately upon boarding the destroyer at 8:00 a.m., and then, "not failing to catch the most minute detail," took the whole morning to inspect (first inspecting the crew, of course, and then the ship). The crew was elated to receive an average of 3.5 and to be told they were "the finest ship in the Near East," or so Berthelsen records. And "Why not?" the sailor-turned-writer added, gleefully: "Ain't we got the best wardroom gang in the Navy? And doesn't the crew stick together, even though there is devilment afoot at all times? I'll say!"[62] It's interesting to note that although Ensign Olsen is frequently disconsolate (partly from being apart from Edna for so long) and Berthelsen is usually upbeat, each of them is equally proud of his own ship's performance.

Of course, work never took all the time in port. We have already described the kinds of recreation ashore (particularly sports) in which crew members and officers participated. However, sometimes a ship was in a port where there was nothing doing locally, and of course even in Constantinople there was always a duty crew aboard. Besides performing one's duties and sleeping, what else might help pass the time? Of course, officers and men alike wrote many letters home. Some made this a very regular employment. For instance, if Charles Olsen didn't write each day he would apologize to Edna for not doing so.

Occasionally, reading might capture a young officer's fancy. Dan Gallery read from books on history by H. G. Wells and Francois Guizot while en route to or in port in Constantinople, and he later studied Greek in a grammar text given him by a female friend ashore. This officer, by the way, would read a few novels and other books while aboard the *Pittsburgh* on its cruise throughout Europe, but while in port at Constantinople itself, he was almost always ashore after duty hours—as there was usually an open gangway when your work was done.[63] As for other activities, bridge was quite popular, especially with officers. For a smaller number, chess appealed; more popular than both, though, was "the Mexican game"—shooting the bull. If time *really* was passing slowly, one might barter with the insistent bumboats.

For most of the crew, movies (at least new or good movies) were the high point of shipboard recreation. From the southern Turkish port of Mersina (where the captain of *Bainbridge* once kept the whole crew aboard lest the local Turkish officials try to create an incident), Orin Haskell would write home: "About our only amusement in a port like this is bridge and the movies at night. We brought twelve complete shows along with us from Constantinople, and have a fairly good show every night." Each of these shows consisted of a newsreel, a two-reel comedy, and a feature picture.[64] Haskell was his ship's "amusement officer." Similarly, on its way over from the States, Pratt Mannix's *Denebola* had shown "Douglas Fairbanks in *Robin Hood*, the Gish sisters in *Orphans of the Storm*, *Blood and Sand* with Rudolph Valentino and *The Prisoner of Zenda* with Alice Terry and Lewis Stone"—or at least previews of them, the captain remembered.[65] In his diary, Dan Gallery recorded at one point that *The Sheik* (also starring Valentino) was being shown on *Pittsburgh*.[66]

Finally, a captain might allow the crew members to adopt a pet or two. Someone on *Smith Thompson* captured a dog from a British tanker that had given them fuel, for example. A bit later, a ship's storekeeper on that same vessel decided that a pig might even be fun to have around: "The hog made a pet, all right, but it never learned to walk on steel decks. It could get about a bit by following the seams where the steel overlapped. Then one day, somebody gave it a swim and didn't retrieve it." Another dog that the same ship's crew had taken aboard saw a fellow dog on the pier when the ship was docking, jumped too quickly, fell in the water and drowned. However, the dog from the dock quickly trotted aboard to take its place.[67]

In Constantinople, monkeys and other animals sometimes became pets aboard naval vessels. Aboard the anchored *St. Louis*, Captain Leahy was informed one day that a *bear* was approaching the officer's gangway. Leahy arrived on deck just in time to see a large bear clamber up the ladder, arrive at the quarterdeck, and shake water out of its fur. After that, it shuttled forward—while startled sailors and marines jumped up ladders and ducked behind hatches—where it eventually found the crew's quarters, sat down in a corner and made itself at home. A midshipman shortly arrived from HMS *Iron Duke*, reporting that one Mr. Bear was absent without leave and had reportedly been seen aboard *St. Louis*, and asked leave to take the bear back in a ship's boat. With Leahy's permission, a party of British sailors tugged and shoved and cursed and finally wrapped a line around the bear's midriff and dragged it to a boat alongside and shoved off. The next day the British admiral sent an apology for Mr. Bear presuming to use the officer's ladder on the American vessel.[68]

And a six- or eight-year-old orphan was adopted by *St. Louis,* given a hammock, Navy uniforms, a sea bag and ditty box, and was treated in many respects like a member of the crew. He was even hauled up to captain's mast when out of line. This young fellow had to leave *St. Louis* when the ship was ordered home, but according to Dan Gallery, he might have had a spot on *Pittsburgh,* too, except that by the time the latter ship arrived, the boy had quite a racket going for him ashore—"begging, running errands, pimping, fencing for thieves and peddling their loot," also pickpocketing, guiding foreign tourists in Constantinople, and loaning American sailors money at outrageous interest.[69]

—◆—

Unlike stateside duty with its frequent squadron and fleet exercises, when Bristol deployed his destroyers, he typically had them steam independently from port to port, and they were always operating in relatively unfamiliar waters. Such employment placed considerable stress on the destroyers' navigation teams.

In Near Eastern waters, navigators typically would use dead reckoning, piloting by landmarks and navigation lights rather than depending on celestial navigation, for whether in the Black Sea or Eastern Mediterranean, one was seldom more than 150 miles from land. Nevertheless, navigators encountered a variety of troubles. Arriving at Constantinople from the States at the moment of a crisis in southern Russia, for example, *Smith Thompson* was ordered the very next day to find its way even further out of its navigator's comfort zone—specifically, to Novorossisk, east of the Crimea. After transiting the Bosporus and crossing the Black Sea overnight, the next morning the bridge watch sighted the Russian coast. A fog bank obscured the land, however, and it took several hours for the fog to lift and the Skipper to orient himself before the ship could enter the harbor. On another Black Sea trip several months later, this one to Varna, Bulgaria, a gale and snowstorm caused the same navigational team to miss that port's lighthouse, so they had to backtrack. Eventually, a lessening of the wind and snow helped them make a good landfall.[70]

In the same southwestern corner of the Black Sea, Cdr. Harry Pence of *McFarland* was once ordered by "STANAV" (the embassy) to start back from Constanza to Constan overnight, but on departing that Romanian port, he found his ship rolling 50 degrees to starboard and 30 degrees to port in a fierce gale: "Wow!! What weather!" his diary exclaims. (Actually, the *pitching* on these destroyers could often be worse to endure than the rolling, especially if one's berth was in the forecastle.) After a couple of hours' steaming, the bridge watch mistook a light on the beach for the lightship that marked the entry to the Bosporus and headed directly ashore. When Pence discovered *that* mistake, he turned the ship around and headed out "for the middle of the Black Sea" until daylight. In the morning, they eventually found their way into the Bosporus, having arrived at a "Welcome haven and appropriate Thanksgiving day. Lord help the two cattle steamers which put to sea about the same time we did," Pence's entry concludes. On another occasion, Pence reported that Cdr. Harry Knauss of *Simpson* had relieved him six hours late at Novorossisk because Knauss had missed his proper landfall.[71]

Possibly Knauss' navigational problem had also been caused by bad weather (there had also been high seas on that occasion), although that episode had occurred during the summer. *Winter* weather near the Russian ports could confound many a navigator, and many a ship handler, too. On Webb Trammell's remark one January to a Soviet official that the Novorissik weather seemed one continuous storm, the official replied (the two spoke in French) that they didn't call it a storm there until it began to blow the boxcars off the track. A couple of days later Trammell noted in his ship's war diary, "The wind continues with force of 8 or better and holds the ship to the dock. Spray continually comes on board the *Fox* and freezes, and a few hands are kept busy chopping ice." A couple of weeks later, *Fox* headed for Batoum, and Trammell expected to arrive about noon, but an Easterly gale raised such a heavy sea that the ship could not make headway against it at a speed slower than twelve knots. Trammell had his ship buck the sea for a while, but "after several fixtures had carried away on the forecastle and two of the forward compartments had filled with water, I changed course to the West and lay to before the wind." It was not until the next day that they "made the lee of the land" and so were enabled to enter Batoum. They were twenty-four hours late.[72]

One October *Smith Thompson* was out in a Black Sea storm that had sent green water over the bridge just as the vessel was leaving the Bosporus. The ship continued to "roll and pitch unmercifully—smashing forward as only a destroyer can," Bert Berthelsen wrote. It was belaboring so badly that an admiral of the old Russian navy who happened to be aboard for the trip was apprehensive as to how long the ship's hull would be able to stand the pounding.[73]

At midnight an enormous sea broke over the ship with "a terrific jar" that threw everyone sleeping on bunks in the wardroom onto the floor. One officer reported later that, as his folding bunk jammed him against the bulkhead, he saw another junior officer in his underwear with a coat in one hand and a necktie in the other racing out of the wardroom passageway, only to be temporarily blocked by the wardroom steward who was ahead of him carrying a pair of shoes and a Bible.[74] It took a while for everyone to decide that the ship was not going to sink, and for the young officer who had run so madly out of the wardroom to return with the excuse that he had simply been going out to help calm the crew.[75]

Weather might affect a ship anywhere in the Black Sea, whether at sea or in port. At the Turkish Black Sea ports, you usually had to anchor, for there were few docking facilities (and often no real harbor, either). While dedicating Camp Mark L. Bristol, the sailors' camp at Yeni Keuy, Bristol mentioned some of the hardships the American sailors had to suffer, with their "destroyers lying in open roadsteads, rolling as if they were at sea and not being able to land for sometimes several days as well as [suffering] severe cold and tempestuous weather."[76] Presumably the camp was intended to provide some compensation for the sailors' difficulties.

Perforce, the destroyers also exercised a great deal at anchoring. The young officer Renwick McIver (then on *Gilmer*) once wrote home, "My job takes me to the forecastle, with the anchors, each time we anchor or get underway, so I spent some cold, cold hours on deck. But it was worse when we got underway Wednesday. It took two hours altogether to get up anchor, and when we finally got her in we found an old ship's cable snarled around it, which was the cause of all the difficulty. However, we cleared the Dardanelles that morning, and made twenty-five knots down in order to get in here [at Smyrna] before sunset."[77] At Batoum *Gilmer*'s anchor engine could not get its anchor up one evening, so the captain was unable to get the ship under way at midnight as he had planned. Having waited till morning, he then signaled *Smith Thompson* to come alongside to help so as to add another ship's power to *Gilmer*'s. That did no good either: "Her anchor [still] refused to turn loose; then we surged back and forth, but no soap." However, "A few old buoys came up, giving evidence that her anchor was fouled in the now famous submarine net that had claimed no less than twenty anchors of American, French and British men o' war. We saw no hope in releasing her hook, so we let go and returned to our berth. The *Gilmer* slipped her cables and abandoned forty-five fathoms of chain as she cleared port that afternoon."[78] Besides submarine nets, the destroyers encountered many a minefield also left over from the Great War. Coming in or leaving port at Samsun or Batoum, for instance, you had to make sure to maneuver around the local minefield.[79] At Odessa you had to hire a pilot to guide you.[80]

We speak in other chapters of the varied employment of the destroyers during their Turkish-region tour of duty: serving Admiral McCully's needs in Russia, standing by to rescue refugees during a crisis, escorting the Russian grain ships, reporting on an apparent genocide, enabling communication with inland officials at Angora, and so on. Beyond these things, what other purposes might your ship be serving on all these trips from Constantinople to Russia or Romania, or to the northern ports of Turkey—or even south, to Smyrna and Mersina and back?

As we've seen before, transporting passengers was one regular occupation of the destroyers. Sometimes (as when the White Russian general Wrangel was given a ride from one Russian port to another), such transport might be the prime reason for a trip. More often, the destroyer gave civilians or foreigners a ride to a port since the ship was going there anyway. After commenting that they had just taken two Americans aboard the *Bainbridge* on their trip from Constantinople to Alexandria—a doctor and an antique collector—Orin Haskell complained, "Any civilian can bum a ride over here but at home we cannot take our own families."[81]

Bert Berthelsen's memoir *Tin Can Man* is so detailed that one can identify something of the variety of passengers to whom *Smith Thompson* gave a ride during the ship's Turkish-area service, which stretched from March of 1920 to May of 1921 (much longer than most destroyer Near Eastern tours). On its journeys, this naval vessel transported:

- A Russian general, a YMCA lady, and two Red Cross people from Constan to Samsun, Batoum, and the Crimea;
- Seven passengers on a trip from Smyrna to Mersina, Beirut, and Jerusalem (three of them left the ship at Mersina for a mission school);
- The Michigan professor of archaeology Francis Kelsey and his family from Alexandria, Egypt, to the Greek island of Patmos (Kelsey would examine ancient manuscripts at the ancient monastery there);
- The White Russian general Peter Wrangel, the American admiral Newton McCully, and McCully's aide, Lt. Cdr. Hugo Koehler from Sebastapol to Yalta;
- "An array of Russian generals, colonels, majors and whatnots" from Varna, Romania, to Constantinople;
- The American charge d' affaires at Piraeus, Greece. and his wife from Piraeus to Constan;
- That same diplomatic couple, a Russian admiral, and a diplomat on a trip from Constan to Varna to Constanza to Sebastopol in the Crimea;

at Varna they picked up a Russian requesting transportation to Russia as well as the Boston professor (and Constantinople resident) Thomas Whittemore, with a load of schoolbooks for the South Russia Mission;

- An Armenian member of the American Foreign Trade Corporation, a professor from Constantinople's Robert College, and a Mr. and Mrs. King, connected with the American Tobacco Company in Samsun, on a trip from Batoum to Constantinople via Samsun;

- The wife of the American consul in Baghdad and a NER official from Alexandria to Smyrna;

- Nine passengers from Constan to Gallipoli, Lemnos, Salonika, and Smyrna. These included a Russian official and his interpreter; one "Major D." [Major Claflin Davis] who was the head of the Constantinople office of the Red Cross; and additional Red Cross workers who were inspecting the condition of the various refugee camps along the Dardanelles and on the Island of Lemnos.

After Lemnos, Berthelsen comments (with relief) that the ship got under way from Smyrna *"with only two passengers!"*[82]

By this time the officers and sailors of *Smith Thompson* had become exasperated with some of their passengers, particularly those who tended to make themselves at home "at the expense of the officers and crew, whose accommodations are just large enough for them as it is!" Major Davis of the Red Cross seemed to touch off this particular criticism, for this irritating and officious (though dedicated and efficient) individual—really just a civilian, despite his Red Cross rank—"took charge of the ship the moment he came aboard! He attempted to give orders to the quartermaster, messenger, and boatswain's mate of the watch. In this he was unsuccessful and it irritated him no little." After quoting the naval regulation against transportation of civilians except in exceptional circumstances, Berthelsen goes on in his memoir to comment that all these passengers were "recipients of a great privilege, but to see some of them come aboard with a self-satisfied, conceited, and commanding air is quite disgusting, and all hands pray for a head sea and twenty-five knots to let them know what destroyer service means."[83] (It is clear from the memoir that many passengers became sick even during moderate seas.)[84]

Over their fourteen months of service, the only passenger this ship's crew seems really to have appreciated was the White Russian general they carried on their very first trip, a man named Gurko (son of a great Russian field marshal of the same name from the Russo-Japanese War). General Gurko was billeted with the officers in the wardroom. A quite well educated and widely experienced officer from the czar's army, who spoke Russian, English, German, and French, he made friends on board with officers and enlisted men alike and was a "remarkable conversationalist," Bert commented. "He had a great sense of humor, and his infectious laughter seemed to keep the wardroom merry the whole two weeks" he was with them. General Gurko was touring Russian ports to see "how the land lay for future campaigns" against the Bolsheviks, should there be any. Members of the crew not only talked to the general at the time, but also later at the Tokalian hotel in Constantinople.[85]

On one final trip with passengers, *Smith Thompson* took "36 missionaries and sixty trunks, heavy as lead" from Samsun to Constantinople. (The reason for this large party of American missionaries departing Samsun all at once is unknown.)[86]

Besides passengers, you were always carrying mail, of course, either dropping some off to a ship or picking up whatever letters that ship itself had to send (assuming you were likely to reach the Bosporus before they did), or both. As a constituent part of "The Black Sea Express and Mail"—again, this was one of several local nicknames for Bristol's runabout ships[87]—a destroyer might be ordered to Samsun, say, for a three-week stay, but before it steamed there, it would first stop by the station destroyers at Varna, Odessa, and Novorossisk with the latest ships' mail from home.

Navy people of all ranks would curse when mail failed to arrive for days or even weeks at a time. Of course there could be tension at the other end, too. Charles and Edna Olsen took to numbering the letters they wrote so as to try to keep them in order (they were often received out of order) and probably also to ensure their loved one that they had indeed written regularly. Just after the holidays, on January 4, 1921, Charles wrote his wife, commenting on *both ends* of this postal chain:

> Thank the Lord some mail has arrived to you, at last. I was beginning darling to think that the mail from Constantinople was not getting to you dear heart. Honey bunch two wonderful letters today, the first in three weeks. Oh darling heart what a joy it is to know that you have received some of my letters, and by now you must have received many more. What is strange to me dear heart are the letters I had mailed from Italy by a destroyer. They should have arrived before those from Turkey. Mail leaves here by every which way, boat, train, or any way it can leave in. We are sending mail ashore every day now to put in the first available route. Some of it may catch a tramp steamer and those letters of a later date reach you first. Anyhow, sweet heart, I am so glad that my mail is getting to you. I have letters 63 and 64 and one is so lonely dear heart it makes me just want to pack up and come back to you and the other has made me determined to get back any way possible and as soon as possible. The sooner the better. I think that if I stay here, that you will have to come to me that is all.[88]

One glimpses in this letter some of the great importance of reliable mail service when sailors and officers were overseas. Note, too, that Olsen's cruiser mainly stayed in port in Constantinople; mail service to destroyers on duty in the Black Sea for a month or more (or on a cruise to the Levant) was even more problematic. Hence Bristol's excellent practice of sending a destroyer to all the Navy's ships on station duty in the Black Sea with the latest mail before it assumed its own station—or merely to deliver the mail and then return to Constantinople.

Occasionally, a destroyer would also carry money. At one point, *Smith Thompson* carried a bag with $10,000 in gold from Smyrna to Constantinople for the American Tobacco Company, for instance. Clearly, given the conditions ashore in Turkey throughout this period, it would be much safer to transport the cash by destroyer than by any other method. Just getting the money from an office to a ship moored at the same city could sometimes be a problem.

On another occasion *Smith Thompson* carried Near East Relief money from Constantinople to Batoum.[89] And on his long-anticipated trip to Egypt, Commander Pence of *McFarland* was first required to deliver $150,000 in Turkish lire to American businessmen at Smyrna. "Just another little peace time effort of the Navy to promote American business interests," Pence noted in his diary.[90] Note that, by regulations, the Navy ship's captain was typically entitled to a small cut of the sum transported.

Another general purpose of sending the ships out to Turkish or Russian ports was to gather intelligence. Typically, a destroyer captain in Samsun or Trebizond would designate a junior officer to keep a record of all the shipping that touched at or anchored out in a port while the destroyer was on station there. Depending on conditions ashore, the ship's intelligence officer (a junior officer with no special training in intelligence) might snoop around a bit further. Renwick McIver, then a junior officer aboard *McFarland*, once wrote home that he had been made his ship's intelligence officer, "in which capacity I make reports on the political, social, military, etc. features of all ports visited. You may laugh, but I manage to break out some interesting dope at times. I've been running around Brindisi all afternoon scaring up information on railroads, fortifications, shipyards, cables, landmarks, waterworks, and what-not." McIver's ship had been sent on a quick trip from Constan to the Italian port, where things seem to have been pretty relaxed as compared with the situation at ports in Turkey or in Russia.

Often communication between ship and shore in the latter ports was restricted or totally cut (except for visits by a ship's captain; on rare occasions, even the captain could not get ashore), and junior officers could not do much overt snooping there. Lack of language facility also had to hamper a junior officer's efforts (McIver was handicapped in Brindisi during the visit noted above, for example, for he knew no Italian and hardly anybody in the city seemed to speak English).[91] However, in conversation with local Turkish and Russian officials (often via interpreter or in French), and particularly when talking with local American and European missionaries, relief workers, diplomats, and businessmen, ship captains could and did gain much valuable information for dispatch back to Constantinople. It was an important part of their job to do so.

A kind of "intelligence" the ships always sought was the circumstances of the American businessmen, relief workers, and missionaries who were scattered all over Turkey. (Some were in Russia, too.) One of Bristol's primary responsibilities in a local emergency was to rescue any Americans who might be in trouble, and there was much trouble in both the huge Turkish and Russian regions. Of course, information about others could also be of much interest. (Were the Greeks being deported? Was the White Russian army retreating? Would the Turkish Nationalists have to abandon Angora?) The specific reasons a ship might be stationed at a particular port took priority in a ship's investigations. For example, in Smyrna in the fall of 1919, the destroyers were supporting the Allied team investigating the Greek occupation of that city earlier that same year. Hence much of the information sought and reported had to do with how the local Turks were being treated.

Most of the special missions being reported on by a ship's captain or other officers are treated in other chapters of this text. These include the chapters already presented about the White Russian collapse, the deportations from the Pontus, and America's response to the Russian Famine in 1922–23. Chapters still to come will describe the actions of American Navy ships and servicemen during the burning of Smyrna and its aftermath. However, right now it will be useful to describe a couple of more general kinds of activities the destroyers occasionally got involved in. These were the landing of an armed team ashore and the rescue of derelict ships or boats at sea.

On select occasions in both Russia and Turkey, the destroyers had to provide a "landing force," a team of armed men carrying arms and ready to use force if required. For instance, while American naval vessels were helping American admiral McCully, besides protecting American citizens and property, the destroyers were also ready to send small forces to the aid of endangered British and French in southern Russian ports. At those same sites, they also were to go to the aid of White Russian refugees. To be effective, these landing teams had to be prepared to use force if necessary.

True, in Turkey or in Russia, Admiral Bristol gave general orders to his officers to stay neutral and not get too involved with the British and French, let alone with ethnic minorities. Rescuing the local Americans and protecting American property always were to constitute their main priorities. The naval forces were also ordered never to get involved in a shooting war. However, in both Turkey and Russia, the destroyers did end up sending landing forces to various sites at the order of the on-scene commander.

At Novorossisk in early March of 1920, for instance, when the Bolsheviks were marching on General Denikin's forces, Admiral McCully ordered *Smith Thompson* to be ready to join the cruiser *Galveston* in sending landing forces to rescue the Americans in that city, if necessary, and to succor other Allied civilians as well. Lt. John Cross was detailed to lead this small force, and about his specific instructions, the lieutenant recorded this comment in his diary: "When the signal is given to evacuate, the American forces will land with the British and French to aid in keeping order and escorting the refugees safely to the transports that are to take them away. . . . The temporary campaign orders state that we are to use persuasion unless we meet with armed resistance, and then we are to shoot to kill!"[92]

In the event, it was American property rather than its citizens they were actually sent to guard. Not long after its arrival, Cross' destroyer was ordered to land a small landing party armed with pistols and nightsticks on the dock where the American steamship *Jacona* lay. A few nights later, intelligence suggested an attack was imminent, so several more men were sent along, armed with rifles and machine guns. Lieutenant Cross deployed his men in a line across the inboard end of the dock and set up the machine guns so they could sweep the approach. Meantime, at the head of the neighboring dock, where SS *Sangamon* was tied up, *Galveston* had deployed thirty marines, twenty-five sailors, and eleven machine guns.

Perhaps because of this American preparation, the local Bolsheviks did not attack, and the crisis evaporated.[93]

In November of that year, when the Bolsheviks invaded the Crimea over the frozen marshes and put the White Russians on the run for good, *Overton* put ashore a landing force at Sebastopol to help local Americans remove commercial wares at nearby warehouses. Despite threats from local Bolsheviks, they succeeded in evacuating nearly $400,000 worth of goods. Moving on to Yalta, *Overton* put men ashore again who, in cooperation with French sailors, policed the docks and kept mobs from interfering with the refugee evacuation.[94]

We'll see much more in the next chapter about the American landing forces in the crisis at Smyrna, and while discussing those events, we will speak more directly of the adverse effects of Bristol's orders on that occasion *not* to intervene on behalf of the refugees.

Finally, many a destroyer found itself using its seaborne facilities to rescue a vessel in distress. In October of 1920, *Whipple* saw distress signals from the Greek steamer *Thetis*, which, the Americans discovered, had just gone aground off Constanza. Although the destroyer's crew handled their ship well in rough seas and shoal waters, it still took *Whipple* ten hours of hard work to float the steamer.[95] A couple of years later, the destroyer *Sands* received a letter of commendation from Admiral Bristol for rescuing a barge loaded with Russians that had become stranded somewhere in the Black Sea.[96]

And while en route from Samsun to Batoum, the steaming watch aboard *Smith Thompson* once sighted flares and distress signals from a sailing vessel dead in the water. They investigated and found forty refugees aboard this vessel, an auxiliary schooner. These Russians had left Batoum upon the Bolsheviks' approach, only to have some of the vessel's engines break down and to find themselves drifting back toward the same port. Since they had also failed to load supplies and water, some passengers aboard had not taken a drink for forty-eight hours—though, ironically, the vessel's hold was filled with champagne! *Smith Thompson* gave the passengers water and towed the vessel into Trebizond, although this task had not been completed before the ship's surgeon had been called over to help deliver a new child into the world.[97]

In all their steaming and seamanship, the destroyers naturally suffered a few collisions and other untoward events, not many of them, actually—particularly when one considers all the steaming these ships did in such unfamiliar seas—but some. For instance, *Overton* gained the distinction of being the first American naval vessel ever to go aground in the Danube, when a storm drove the ship onto the mud near Galatz, Romania. The ship got itself unstuck without assistance.[98] On another occasion, a small boat from *Simpson* somehow caused the sinking of a Turkish caique, and one imagines there was probably a good deal of inadvertent sinking of Turkish small craft, more at any rate than was reported.[99]

A much more threatening event occurred during a midwatch aboard *McCormick* while it was steaming toward Constantinople in the Sea of Marmara. On this occasion, Officer of the Deck Dolly Fitzgerald was warned by the starboard lookout that a darkened ship was heading toward them, a ship that seemed to be steaming at high speed. Fitzgerald backed his engines full and turned, but ended up hitting the approaching ship in the side. *McCormick* then "followed after this shadowy thing," and when the watch switched on the searchlights, they discovered the vessel in question was a French destroyer. Neither ship needed the other's assistance to get back into port (*McCormick* had only suffered a bent bow), and the *McCormick*'s captain, Admiral Bristol, and the

French authorities seem to have hushed up the whole event (the French may have paid for *McCormick's* repairs). Officer of the Deck Fitzgerald was pleased to receive a letter of commendation for his alert handling of the *McCormick* in an unusual, dangerous situation.[100]

Finally, one evening in a snowstorm and gale, Captain Mannix's large repair ship *Denebola* was anchored in the Bosporus. While stepping out on his ship's bow to make sure his ship's anchor was not dragging, Mannix noticed a Spanish collier rushing down the straits completely out of control. By ordering *Denebola* to heave on its anchor cable, Mannix veered his ship out of the way, and the captain was impressed to see the British ship next to him fully alert and performing the same maneuver. However, the collier then slammed into an unprepared French vessel anchored a bit further on, smashed one of its guns and a whole line of its ports, and also crushed and sank a big motor sailing launch that had been lying alongside, before disappearing down the strait.[101]

<hr />

So much for a quick survey of the in-port routine and of some of the typical navigational and ship-handling difficulties taken on by Bristol's destroyers and other ships in the region. In chapters to come (particularly the chapter about the burning of Smyrna), we will discuss some very dramatic events in which the destroyers and their men were to figure most heavily. However, to fill out the general picture of destroyer operation, below are snapshots of some typical short-term destroyer deployments.

During early 1922, Bristol employed the six or eight destroyers then on station principally on a circuit of Black Sea ports. For several months now, three ports had become regular stations at which his destroyers would anchor or moor for maybe two or three weeks before being relieved by another vessel and speeding on. Typically *Childs*, *Bulmer*, or *McFarland*, say, would rotate clockwise from Odessa to Novorossisk and then steam down to the Turkish coast of the Black Sea and spend maybe three weeks at Samsun before returning to Constantinople for a couple of weeks' rest. The destroyers would also stop occasionally at less important ports when so ordered, some of these stops (like Theodosia in the Crimea and Trebizond in Turkey) very brief though regular port visits. Meanwhile, another destroyer might make a quick trip through three-quarters of the circumference of the Black Sea, stopping at each port that harbored an American destroyer, to deliver and receive mail and official reports and passengers. Then the latter vessel would steam back to Constantinople or perhaps would itself join the slow rotation of station ships.

The destroyer *Bulmer*, moored in the Bosporus, with Galata and Pera (Constantinople's European quarters) as backdrop. This site was "home" for the American destroyers throughout their service in the Black Sea region. *The Naval History and Heritage Command*

The ports visited did change over time. On Admiral McCully's initial assignment to southern Russia back in January of 1920, one of a series of destroyers had been regularly assigned as his personal flagship and communications center, and this duty destroyer then steamed on to whatever other Russian port McCully directed it: Odessa, Novorossisk, or Sebastapol, typically. With the final White Russian evacuation of the Crimea in late 1920, McCully's assignment ended and the regular Navy assignment to Russian ports lapsed, but as we have seen it would resume with the arrival of the Hoover grain ships in early 1922. For about a year and a half, American destroyers regularly provided coordination at Odessa and Novorissisk, and also often visited Theodosia and Sebastapol briefly, and sometimes even Yalta.

Meanwhile, since 1919, American destroyers had regularly been stopping at Black Sea ports further south. Early on, one common destination was Batoum, the port at the Black Sea's southeastern corner. This city was traditionally Russian, although for the short time that the "jazz republics" (the jazz-age republics) of Georgia, Armenia, and Azerbaijan lasted right after World War I, it served as the major seaport of the Republic of Georgia. In 1919 Batoum was the key seaport enabling Westerners to get to Armenia and into the Caucasus generally. Once taken to Batoum by an American destroyer, relief officials and journalists would entrain for Georgia's capital, Tiflis, a couple of hundred miles east, from which they would take another train south, up into the worst sites of starving Armenia. From late 1920 on, after the Bolsheviks took over there (and the jazz republics collapsed), destroyers would visit Batoum less frequently, but the American ships sometimes still had occasion to stop there briefly.

Turkish ports that the DDs regularly visited were Trebizond and Samsun, as we have seen both of them located on the Black Sea coast of the northern region of Anatolia called the Pontus. Not only did these two cities feature permanent American missionary and relief stations, but they were also the standard Black Sea entry ports to the rest of Asiatic Turkey. (In late 1922 and 1923, these two cities would also become the standard Black Sea *exit* ports for tens of thousands of ethnic Greek and Armenian refugees!) As for American missionaries, they typically traveled inland by whatever commercial ships might be available, but Bristol's wide support of America's relief operations meant that many relief workers, some missionaries and many businessmen, a few American diplomats, and even some Turkish officials rode the destroyers from Constantinople to and from these two Turkish cities.

Samsun and Trebizond had different profiles. Recognizing the importance of the Nationalists long before the British and other allies did, early on Bristol placed a destroyer as station ship at Samsun to facilitate diplomatic and business contacts with Mustapha Kemal and other Nationalists at Angora, which lay some two hundred miles (several days' overland travel) inland. This seems to have been the quickest or most convenient route for Americans to get to the Nationalist capital, because travel there overland from Constantinople would mean transiting the battle lines between the Greek and Turkish armies. Besides the decades-old American mission station at this city (at which much relief work was carried on in the years following World War I), Samsun also featured "three or four soft speaking Carolinians, engaged in buying Samsun and Bafra tobacco for blending in American cigarettes."[102]

In contrast, the port of Trebizond (some two hundred miles east) had been famous for centuries as the terminus of a camel caravan route, one that still saw some twenty or thirty camels arriving about twice a week from Persia.[103] During and before World War I, an American consul (or consular agent) had also been stationed at Trebizond, but just after the war the consul had been withdrawn, and now Trebizond typically only saw a destroyer for one or two days' visit at a time. At Samsun, in contrast, the destroyers typically would stay for two or three weeks.

Down in the Aegean or eastern Mediterranean as opposed to the Black Sea, destroyers had only made a regular station at Smyrna for a few months following the Hellenic army's occupation of that place in May 1919. After that, until events in Smyrna heated up in the fall of 1922, ships visited Smyrna only occasionally. A destroyer was sometimes kept at Beirut (particularly early on) to enhance communications with Beirut, Palestine, and Syria, particularly on the chance that Americans needed to be evacuated from these locations. Very occasionally, a passing naval vessel might stop at the Turkish port of Mersina, partly because that city featured an American mission and relief station, and also because Mersina had rail communication with the interior.

Anyway, stationing a ship in a particular port (either tied up at a dock, which was customary in Russian ports, or anchored out in the harbor at the Turkish Black Sea port cities, especially Samsun, which had a totally open roadstead)[104] provided ready naval communication facilities at each site, facilities that occasionally were used by consuls, relief directors, missionaries, and other American officials ashore who needed to communicate quickly with Constantinople. Such facilities also allowed Admiral Bristol immediate access to all the local Americans via his ship captains. Indeed, because a destroyer's commanding officer directly represented Bristol, that officer would become, in essence, the local American in charge, except perhaps in Smyrna, where Consul George Horton's independent position complicated this informal command structure somewhat.

Besides enabling communication and coordination, these specific stations also provided the American intelligence input already mentioned above. From firsthand observation, from investigation on the quiet by one's junior officers, and particularly by frequent meetings with local officials as well as local Americans and Europeans, a ship's captain could discover a good deal regarding military movements, humanitarian crises, and other information. Bristol directed each destroyer's commanding officer to record such information in his ship's war diaries. A war diary was a standard wartime genre of the era by which Bristol's officers outlined local conditions and operations at a level of detail sometimes reaching to three or four single-spaced typed pages daily. For scholars, these more generalized documents penned from the viewpoint of vessel commanders are for most purposes more useful than a tedious study of ships' logs, which typically record the minutiae of courses and speeds and orders to the helm rather than the broad picture; in the early 1920s, the admiral found these documents highly useful for similar reasons. A captain would submit his current war diary to the embassy staff on return to Constantinople or by another destroyer speeding that way—in any case, usually within a couple of weeks of the latest entries. Sometimes, if intelligence discovered or events occurring were thought to be especially important, events were described by instantaneous naval message.

Nor was this information only read and filed in Constantinople. In the most important "station" ports—Samsun in Turkey, Novorossisk, and eventually Odessa, in Russia—a chronological file of war diaries from all the destroyers that had served at that particular port was kept *on station,* being turned over from ship to ship upon the prescribed "contact relief." In such a way, on arrival at a particular port, each oncoming commanding officer would receive an up-to-date, in-depth intelligence briefing on local events and circumstances (and on local personalities, too) that stretched back *months.* Such a file would be particularly useful for commanders newly reporting to one of these foreign stations, substantially augmenting the briefings these captains would have received from embassy officials in Constantinople, and augmenting as well whatever additional information might be available via a ship's message circuit.[105]

As for those message circuits, because of adverse atmospheric conditions in the region, a radio relay ship was almost always needed to pass messages from Constantinople to Vienna and to destroyers on the south coast of the Black Sea.[106] Therefore, as we have seen, from the beginning of his tour of duty, Admiral Bristol regularly stationed a destroyer at Varna, Bulgaria, or Constanza, Romania, to do communication work.

Finally, sooner or later Bristol's ships would be sent independently to Alexandria, Egypt, and Haifa in Palestine, so that ship's crew and officers could visit the pyramids and the Holy Land. To his credit, Bristol saw to it that virtually every one of his destroyers (and his larger vessels, too) made the latter great trip before steaming home. By so doing, he observed the naval tradition continuing to this day of partially offsetting difficult duty and the stress of long deployments by affording specially attractive port visits to ships that were operating overseas.

Typically, any destroyers not at one of the above-named sites would be moored in the Bosporus, awaiting events. In September of 1922, enormous events were about to come.

CHAPTER 10

THE BURNING OF SMYRNA

*Three quarters Smyrna either ashes or flames . . . flames drove nearly
entire Christian population on to quay screaming praying to overcrowded
harbor craft of every description. Looting and shooting first three days
Turkish occupation now seem incidents . . . the catastrophe has arrived.*

—H. C. Jaquith, by message via USS *Litchfield*

In the late summer of 1922, things were going along pretty much as usual.
The Bristols entertained on *Scorpion* and the destroyers continued their
rounds of Black Sea ports. The grain ship relief to Russia was winding
down, and since most of the local Greeks had by now been deported from the
Pontus or massacred outright, even that controversy had quieted somewhat.

However, on the evening of September 3, while *Edsall* was anchored off
Samsun, the city suddenly erupted with fireworks, rifle shots, and cheering,
after which hundreds of people paraded the length of the city by lantern.
Edsall's officers were told the next day of a great Turkish victory on a broad
front, at Eskishehir. The Greek army was retreating in complete disorder; it
appeared to be the decisive battle of the war. One Turkish column was said to
have advanced as far as the Meander River, about a hundred miles from the site
of the Greek army's original incursion into Anatolia: the city of Smyrna.

Though *Edsall*'s commanding officer, Cdr. Halsey Powell, continued shooting pheasant, touring orphanages, and talking to local relief officials (the local
Americans said they were not uneasy during the shooting, for by now very few
Greeks were left in Samsun!),[1] decisive events had, in fact, occurred, and cata-
clysmic events would soon follow. The Greek army would leave Asia Minor
entirely (except for thousands of soldiers captured by the Turks), the great city
of Smyrna would burn, hundreds of thousands of ethnic Greeks and Armenians

would be expelled from Turkey, and untold tens of thousands would ultimately lose their lives.

The standard work on the burning and evacuation of Smyrna is that of Marjorie Housepian Dobkin in her fine 1971 book, *The Smyrna Affair* (titled *Smyrna 1922: The Destruction of a City* when published in London in 1972), since reissued with a new introduction.[2] Not only is that book the only comprehensive study of the burning of Smyrna, but also one of its exceptional features is the author's thorough exploration of all the most important American naval documents. These are vital reports, because American naval officers and enlisted men were ashore in Smyrna virtually throughout the crisis, as was an American relief team sent by Admiral Bristol, and soon after the event both naval officers and civilian officials recorded in detail what they had seen and experienced. (One should also note, by the way, that Dobkin manifests a very good understanding of the American Navy, whereas other scholars who otherwise write very well about Smyrna—like Giles Milton, in his 2008 book *Paradise Lost: Smyrna, 1922*, written from the standpoint of the Levantines and other residents—betray a lack of understanding of such fundamental things as the difference between a sailor and a marine.)[3] Beyond official reports and published accounts of all sorts, Dobkin unearthed many additional recollections of American naval officers and enlisted men who had been at Smyrna, studied letters and other memoirs from American civilians who had been on the ground there, and by interviews, searched into recollections of people of various other nationalities who had been at the city, including refugees.

However, several additional accounts have been published in the forty years since Dobkin's book appeared, other firsthand documents have surfaced, and additional perspective and some corrections can be supplied.

I present below a new, continuous account of the Smyrna story, primarily from the American naval perspective, one that is necessarily much briefer than Dobkin's book and much more heavily centered on the American Navy throughout. I base this narrative primarily on a fresh reading of firsthand documents in American archives and libraries, but I have also reexamined Dobkin's own account and those of many others, and have considered books, articles, and some memoirs published since Dobkin's book was prepared. Focusing particularly (although not exclusively) on reports by naval officers and other American officials, in the limited space of this chapter I will narrate the story chronologically, in the process sketching the roles American naval and civilian officials took on, discussing their key decisions, recording their overall views as to what had happened, and connecting all these events with what had occurred before and with the actions and opinions of Admiral Bristol back in Constantinople.

—◆◆◆—

Upon news of the Greek defeat, Consul Horton asked Bristol for support, and the admiral ordered *Litchfield* and *Simpson* and a bit later *Lawrence* to proceed to the port. (At the very height of the crisis, *Edsall* would also be sent down.) The American destroyers joined French, Italian, and British warships (including Allied *battleships*) and some merchant vessels. Aboard *Lawrence* (which arrived on the morning of September 9) would be H. C. Jaquith of the Near East Relief and Maj. Claflin Davis of the American Red Cross; these two Constantinople-based officials would constitute the base of the civilian American relief team at Smyrna. Also riding *Lawrence* down were two American journalists and Bristol's chief of staff, Capt. A. J. (Japy) Hepburn.

Captain Hepburn was a conscientious officer of considerable experience and talent who would, in 1936, pin on four stars as commander in chief, U.S. Fleet, then the second highest position in the United States Navy. However, in September of 1922, Captain Hepburn had been at Constantinople less than six months and had served primarily as an embassy administrator. He had never been "in country" in Anatolia, nor did he have any personal knowledge of the region.[4] His views were necessarily conditioned by Bristol's, though along with his other indoctrination, he had heard of Marsovan, the Ward and Yowell reports, and the Armenian deportations of 1915.

Meeting Hepburn in Smyrna were destroyer captains John Butler Rhodes (commanding officer of *Litchfield*) and Harry Knauss (CO of *Simpson*), along with Bristol's current intelligence officer, Tip Merrill. Hepburn was briefed that much of the Greek army had been evacuating by troopship, but some Greeks were fighting a rearguard action nearby, an action that Lieutenant Commander Knauss and several others immediately went off to observe. Greek army troops were reportedly torching all the cities along the line of their retreat, committing a host of atrocities as they went. Also, ethnic Greek civilians from the interior were thronging the roads into the city, many of them reportedly furious that the Hellenic army had forced them to leave their homes behind and then burned those same homes, although some said these civilians were committing atrocities themselves.[5] Throngs of pitiable refugees either walked along or rode wagons, donkeys, mules, even camels. Confusion was "indescribable." Dead animals, sewing machines, and baby carriages lay alongside the road.[6]

Knauss sighted the maneuvers of the opposing forces, ducked a few bullets, and quickly returned to Smyrna. The town itself he found orderly, though refugees and soldiers were flooding the famous large quay and hurriedly boarding the few Greek ships still dockside. Several horses had been turned loose on the city's streets, while pack saddles, trunks, and other debris cluttered the harbor's waters.[7] Residents mostly remained in their homes. More of those residents might have left Smyrna except for a Turkish rule whereby one's property reverted to the government if one "abandoned" it.[8] In the early hours of September 9, cafés and stores were well patronized. Older residents, however (who Hepburn thought would best have known what to expect), manifested a nervousness verging on panic.[9]

Besides the American consulate, a stone's throw from the waterfront, and the YMCA, a couple of blocks away, American institutions in Smyrna included the YWCA buildings and courtyard several blocks into the city; a girl's school called the American Collegiate Institute, which was located in the heart of the Armenian district; the International College, a ten-acre campus three miles south of Smyrna, located in the suburb of Paradise; and the Standard Oil tanks and storehouses on the north side of the bay. It was to these several sites that Hepburn parceled out his meager shore patrol forces, somewhere between hundred and a hundred and fifty men in all, and maybe fewer; he had to leave smaller sites unguarded.[10] Consul Horton had directed Americans (including naturalized Americans—at the time, a great distinction was regularly made between American-born citizens and naturalized ones) who felt endangered to come to the Smyrna Theater, which was right on the quay near the consulate; for several days, this theater became American naval headquarters in the city. So far, only a few had come.

About 11:30 a.m. on the 9th, however, Hepburn heard shots and watched a stampede of refugees. A Turkish cavalry column had arrived. While marching down the quay with banners flying, this column was assaulted by an individual (some said it was an Armenian) launching a bomb or grenade. Return fire from the Turkish military downed six or eight people and cleared the street.[11] More and more Turkish army units entered the city as the day wore on.

Though storefronts soon shut up, Hepburn thought the initial panic had subsided quickly. Late that afternoon, he sought out the senior Turkish officer, who assured him order would be established as soon as possible. Coincidentally, a handbill was passed out promising execution for anybody killing a Christian.[12] However, Harry Knauss, now heading up the shore patrol, found that the Armenian quarter had quickly become infested with "shooting parties," Turkish civilians armed with rifles and shotguns. There, according to the destroyer captain, "the real killing" had already begun. "On nearly every street were lying bodies of men of all ages and conditions, most of [whose] wounds were from rifles and close ranged shots as they were invariably shot in the face or in the back." Knauss personally witnessed three executions that day.[13]

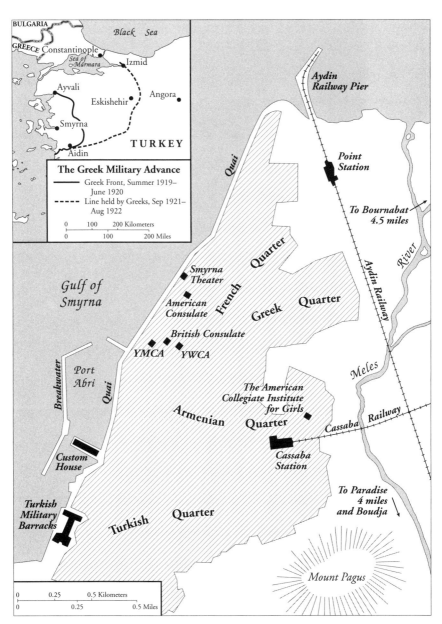

Black Sea

GREECE Constantinople

Sea of Marmara

Izmid

Ayvali

Eskishehir

Angora

Smyrna

TURKEY

Aidin

The Greek Military Advance

—— Greek Front, Summer 1919–
        June 1920

----- Line held by Greeks, Sep 1921–
        Aug 1922

0   100   200 Kilometers

0   100   200 Miles

Aydin
Railway Pier

Quai

Point
Station

To Bournabat
4.5 miles

River

Gulf of
Smyrna

Smyrna
Theater

Quarter

French

Greek   Quarter

American
Consulate

Aydin Railway

British Consulate

YMCA   YWCA

Meles

Port
Abri

The American
Collegiate Institute
for Girls

Breakwater

Quai

Armenian   Quarter

Cassaba   Railway

Custom
House

Cassaba
Station

To Paradise
4 miles
and Boudja

Turkish
Military
Barracks

Turkish   Quarter

Mount Pagus

0   0.25   0.5 Kilometers

0   0.25   0.5 Miles

Map 7. Smyrna, including the American Institutions

Spurred by such activities, mobs of refugees began to push their way into every building that flew an American flag. By nightfall a thousand people had forced their way into the American Collegiate Institute, and five hundred were at the YWCA (with its large courtyard). The sailors guarding these places had their hands full just keeping additional refugees out. Although wholesale massacres were rumored, Hepburn found nothing that justified that description. Overnight, he heard occasional gunfire from his ship.[14] Myrtle Nolan at the YWCA said gunfire was "incessant" during the day but also reported the night was quiet until about midnight. Then heavy rifle fire broke out nearby, followed by doors being broken down and buildings being looted, activities which continued for two hours. But she thought the days were worse than the nights.[15]

By the next day (the 10th), the Smyrna Theater was crowded with naturalized Americans, and Captain Hepburn began considering their evacuation. Rumors confused the situation. A hysterical Armenian priest reported the impending massacre of six thousand refugees in a churchyard, but American journalists who eagerly rushed to the scene returned "visibly disappointed": the churchyard was all quiet.[16] Lieutenant Merrill visited the Americans throughout the city and found them in good spirits, although he considered the "chicken-livered" refugees were all in a "blue funk."[17] That day Hepburn surveyed his officers and found that they had counted altogether only fifty-eight dead, and he projected estimates based on these figures.[18] Apparently he did not talk to Knauss, who personally had counted over a hundred dead on that day and had watched four more people killed in cold blood.[19]

By now many more regular Turkish troops had arrived, and Vice Consul Maynard Barnes reported that both regular soldiers and officers were looting and killing. A reliable American had reported asking of a Turk whether there was security in the Armenian quarter. The Turk had responded, "Not for the Armenian."[20] From the nearby Collegiate Institute on one of these early days, several people witnessed a woman who lived in a building across the street being surrounded by Turkish soldiers. The soldiers robbed her and tore her rings from her fingers. When they finished, one of the Turks stepped back and cut off one of her hands with his sword. She was never seen again.[21]

That night, fewer shots were heard, and Americans who gathered at the consulate the next morning thought that order had been reestablished, but an investigation discovered that bayonets and knives had simply supplanted guns. By day, looting and killing continued, and now Americans reported that Greeks and Armenians were being collected in groups by military authorities and being marched out of the city to face firing squads.[22] Barnes wrote in his diary that Turks had taken all the bodies away from the important streets of the Armenian quarter, but then fifty more suddenly appeared. He also reported an estimate that, by nightfall, seven of ten houses in that part of the city had been looted, and many of their inhabitants had been killed.[23] A sailor named Cahall told Knauss about watching over the wall of the American Collegiate Institute and seeing a family detained. A girl of fifteen was taken from her parents into an alley, after which her shrieks were clearly audible. The Turks returned, and before leading the parents away, one of them wiped a bloody knife on the mother's forearm.[24]

In the Greek quarter, Major Davis found several hundred Turkish troops looting the houses. However, they acted quite courteously to the Americans, even politely pushing their loot wagons aside so the Americans could pass by.[25]

Although Hepburn's estimates for the 11th do not reflect the severity of the situation manifested in the reports of Barnes and Knauss, the captain still found the continuing disorder ominous; troubling too was the decision of the British, Italians, and French to evacuate their nationals. What should the Americans do? Hepburn had asked Merrill to arrange a meeting with the Turkish military governor so he could learn the attitude of the Turkish authorities.[26] The new governor was the same man, it turned out, who had orchestrated the widespread Pontus massacres and deportations: Noureddin Pasha.

—◆—

According to a French account, the day before he met Hepburn, Noureddin had released Greek archbishop Chrysostom to a mob and urged them to murder him. They had immediately complied, after first ripping out the archbishop's beard, gouging out his eyes, and cutting off his ears and his nose. According to the Turkish biographer of Mustapha Kemal, Noureddin's giving Chrysostom up to a mob was a virtual "invitation to mob rule."[27] Now, at the beginning of his conversation with the Americans, Noureddin wanted to make sure they had brought no "priests" along. To the general, the real villains were the American missionaries. Noureddin explained that he had closed Marsovan College because of the political propaganda he had found in the president's letters, and because the Americans there had favored Armenians and Greeks orphans over Turkish ones. Red Cross official Davis assured the general that the Americans in Smyrna would give relief to anybody who needed it (Noureddin doubted that), and then Davis put Admiral Bristol's position before the general, the admiral's naïve views that the refugees should be restored to their homes immediately "under full protection to life and property."[28]

The general was adamant. Because of the atrocities committed by the Greek army during its retreat, were the refugees to return home they would all be killed. They should be taken away, instead. "Bring ships and take them out of the country. It is the only solution." He promised that the Turks would let all the refugees go, and without interference.[29] When Davis asked what would become of the refugees if they could not be evacuated (means were quite uncertain), Noureddin said that he did not know, and that he did not care, either; the Turks certainly could not feed them.[30] The general and his officers seemed much more interested in things happening outside their window than in refugee problems. Six thousand Greek army prisoners marched past, for instance, each unit of them shouting a well-coached "Zito Mustapha Kemal" ("Long Live Mustapha Kemal"). This was in imitation of the "Zito Venizelos" that several groups of Turkish prisoners had been forced to shout to the Greeks during the Greek army's occupation of Smyrna three years before.[31] Also fascinating to Noureddin was the superb appearance of his own Turkish troops. The general pointed out in great pride that, over three years, they had never tasted wine and had prayed five times a day. They also had ridden twenty-five miles each of the past ten days and were still in splendid condition.[32]

Major Davis cabled Bristol his belief that, in the general's insistence for the refugees to leave the country, he had heard the Nationalists' final decision.[33] And in fact, he had. However, it took almost two weeks for anybody to implement Noureddin's solution, and by then not only had thousands more refugees lost their lives, but the Turks had appended some devastating conditions to Noureddin's suggestion.

Bristol's urgent insistence that the Christians not flee the country but stay under Turkish rule no doubt inhibited Hepburn from taking early action.[34] Such a directive was characteristic of Bristol's positions in earlier episodes (when he resisted the Armenians evacuating Cilicia), but the order was to become more and more injurious in the face of the actions and intentions of the Turkish troops (including, more and more, Turkish irregulars or bandit groups) as time went on. Other circumstances also played a part. For instance, Hepburn was not quite sure about Noureddin's attitude. For several minutes during the interview, his American translator (a former missionary) had argued in Turkish with the general about Marsovan, and otherwise he did not translate literally enough for the captain fully to understand their discussion. Hepburn began seeking more cooperative views from other Turkish officials.[35]

However, if the captain had consulted George Horton, America's consul in Smyrna, ironically he would have heard the very same advice as Noureddin's: *get ships and take the refugees away*. On the 12th, Horton was cabling the State Department: "There is one point which I wish to make very plain and to vouch for on my absolute knowledge and authority. These people can never return to their homes." Horton knew the racial antagonisms and the Turkish modus operandi far too well to have any doubts—but now in addition to Turkish history immediately prior to 1919, there had been the three-plus years of the Hellenic Greek occupation of much of western Turkey and the very recent burning of Turkish villages by retreating Greek troops. After pointing out the devastation perpetrated by the Greek army on its retreat and mentioning Noureddin's position, Horton concluded, "Here is then the big humanitarian task in which there is no reason, political or otherwise, that America should not take a hand." He went on to outline a specific plan for assembling the refugees fourteen miles outside of Smyrna as a staging place for their evacuation—a plan that had already been drawn up by American relief workers at Smyrna, who also seem to have manifested considerable prescience as well as human feeling, unlike either Hepburn or Bristol.[36]

The consul's years of experience and intimate knowledge of Smyrna should have been decisive. But if Hepburn heard Horton's position, he discounted it, and there were reasons for this. On the day the Navy captain came to Smyrna, he noted that Horton "had about reached the limit of his physical endurance."[37] Besides writing cables and trying to organize to protect Americans, Horton had been besieged for days by residents wanting visas and telling horrible stories. One old woman, for instance, came screaming to Horton, crying, "'My boy! My boy!' The front of her dress was covered with blood. She did not say what had happened to her boy, but the copious blood told its own story."[38] Although his strenuous efforts were credited with saving hundreds of lives,[39] by this time the consul was near breaking down. Moreover, at the very end of the cable mentioned above, Horton undermined his own credibility by urgently requesting reassignment to another diplomatic post. In conversations with American officers, his frustration was also evident: to Harry Knauss he confessed he was "fed up" with the country.[40] Hepburn decided to send the consul to Athens along with the first refugees. Horton kept cabling, though, and his later cables do not betray the same personal consternation.

———◆———

Horton's departure would put diplomatic affairs into the hands of Vice Consul Barnes, an official with much less experience in the region than Horton, and with a very different outlook. Horton acknowledged many faults among the local Greek people but also pointed to their great industry, and he admired the comparatively civilized and praiseworthy regime of the Greek governor of Smyrna, the stern Aristedes Sterghiades.[41] Some at the time disputed the nature of this Greek administration,[42] but since returning to Smyrna in May of 1919, Horton was in position to know.

As for the Turks, the consul had not forgotten the deportations and massacres for which they had been responsible during the Great War, which he pointed out were the responsibility both of the government that had issued the orders, and, often overlooked, the people who carried them out. Besides the persecution of Armenians (most of which persecution did not occur at Smyrna itself), Horton pointed specifically to the forcible wartime exile from the Asia Minor coasts of 450,000 resident Greeks and noted that the Greeks who had been exiled had been an intensive agricultural class that, over generations, had produced a flourishing community.[43] During their absence, however, "their villages and houses were all torn down by the Turks and their vineyards largely dug up and the roots of the vines used as firewood." Since then, those Greek farmers were rebuilding their property and planting their vineyards, only to find them again "doomed to destruction."[44] From such firsthand witness, and moreover, from his thirty years of experience in the Middle East, the consul would not be easily convinced that the habits of the Turks had changed overnight, nor that the Middle Eastern races were all alike (Bristol's position). However, Horton was on his way out.

On the 12th, the day after Hepburn's meeting with Noureddin, the officers of the merchant ship *Winona* watched through glasses as a band of Turkish irregulars chased six Greeks or Armenians to the water, shooting as they ran: "In order to make death sure, the Turks repeatedly bayoneted the bodies."[45] Hepburn thought order could have been established "within two hours" had the Turks wanted to,[46] but today the captain was told that *chettes* (again, *chettes* were irregulars; bandits) had severely beaten the president of the American university (a British subject named Alexander MacLachlan) and an American chief petty officer, Louis Crocker. These men had also been stripped of their clothing, and MacLachlan had lost consciousness. They were saved from death by Chief Crocker's coolness, the pleas of a Turkish student from the college who stepped in to help save MacLachlan, and the fortuitous arrival of a responsible Turkish officer.[47]

About the same time, Knauss found that, in the Armenian quarter, it had become "the day of greatest slaughter yet." Noticing a Turkish officer manifest particular interest in the refugees taking shelter at the Collegiate Institute, Knauss took care to keep the officer out till the refugees could all be hidden.[48] Barnes himself reported, "All semblance of public safety and order seemed to disappear in certain sections of the city." Astonishingly, however, the vice consul blamed the *refugees* for much of this: "Many of those who lost their lives . . . might be living today had they been more responsive to the desires of the Turks and less positive in their opposition."[49]

On the Smyrna quay a couple of days later, the vice consul himself would see how little an Armenian's attitude might matter to his fate. Circulating among the terrorized refugees on the quay were four or five groups of Turkish civilians armed with clubs covered with blood: "I saw one of these groups fall upon an Armenian . . . and club him to death. The proceeding was brutal beyond belief. We were within ten feet of the assailants when the last blow was struck and I do not believe there was a bone unbroken in the body when it was drug to the edge of the quay and kicked into the sea. In this group were boys [of] no more than twelve or thirteen years of age, each with his club, participating in this horrible killing as heartily as did the more mature individuals." Stunned by this, Barnes admitted in his report what he now found indisputable—that the Turk was capable of a "vandalism essentially medieval." But he quickly added in his report that, of course, all Eastern races were capable of committing atrocities.[50]

On the 13th, fires began being set in the Armenian quarter, near the Collegiate Institute. American sailors at the place believed they had been set to drive the thousand refugees sheltering there into the streets, thus offering further victims for attack and plunder.[51] With a strong wind blowing from the southeast toward the quay and the rich European areas (and away from the Turkish district), the fire grew quickly. By 5:00 p.m. the blaze had become such a holocaust that it was clearly destined to reach the foreign consulates at the water's edge.[52] Every living thing—Greek peasants from the interior, local Greek and Armenian merchants, European residents, frantic horses and mules, and herds of sheep—fled to the waterfront. From there the refugees began to plead with anyone in the consulates or with sailors out in the warship anchorage to save them from the fire. But each country was busy saving its own.

On the early evening of the 13th, this was the spectacle as it appeared to Captain Hepburn on the stern of the *Litchfield*: "The broad waterfront street appeared to be one solidly packed mass of humanity, domestic animals, vehicles and luggage. Beyond, still separated from the crowd by a few short unburned blocks, the city was a mass of flame driving directly down upon the waterfront before a stiff breeze. Mingled with the noise of the wind and flames and the crash of falling buildings were the sounds of frequent sharp reports, such as might have been made either by rifle fire or the explosion of small-arms ammunition and bombs in the burning area. High above all other sounds was the continuous wail of terror from the multitude."[53] The fire grew throughout the night. Lieutenant Merrill had taken a quick trip on a destroyer to Constantinople and back. The following scene presented itself to Merrill and the American Navy people as their ship entered the harbor an hour before dawn: "The entire city was ablaze and the harbor was light as day. Thousands of homeless were surging back and forth along the blistering quay—panic-stricken to the point of insanity. The heartrending shrieks of women and children were painful to [h]ear. . . . To attempt to land a boat would have been disastrous. Several boats tried it and were immediately swamped by the mad rush of a howling mob."

Merrill thought those on the quay were lucky there was a sea breeze, or they would have been "roasted alive." Four cars and two trucks parked at the doorway of the Smyrna Theater were burned to cinders. Packs belonging to refugees caught fire, "making a chain of bonfires the length of the street," and if the pack on a horse's back began to burn, the horse would stampede at top speed through the mass, flinging injury and death, and raising terror to yet another level.[54] Barnes, who estimated there were two hundred thousand along the waterfront, found their shrieking and pleading unendurable. "Walled in by fire and water, [the refugees'] plight seemed hopeless," he wrote. "Many threw themselves into the sea."[55]

A few of the latter were out of their wits, while others were forced off the quay by all the push and shove. Some plunged in on purpose to swim out to the ships, though apparently few actually reached them.[56] Those who swam to American and British warships on the 13th often found themselves unwelcome. The British actually poured hot water down upon many swimmers to discourage them.[57]

Turkish soldiers shot others. Horrified American relief workers on board an American ship saw a man fling himself into the water and swim out toward them, only to have his head blown off by a Turkish soldier who had fired his rifle over the shoulder of a British "marine" (probably a sailor) standing on the pier.[58] Small watercraft of all descriptions attempted to load refugees and help them escape the fire, but many were capsized when a clot of panicked people jumped on board; one of these capsizings of a vessel the size of a large cabin cruiser took place right in front of an American destroyer, and existing photos show the capsizing in dreadful sequence (Those photos are framed in the foreground by an oblivious sailor working in a small ship's boat flying the American flag.) Some peasants who had never been in the water before simply drowned when they fell into the sea.[59]

On the 14th, Oran Raber (an American passenger on an Italian steamer, anchored out) saw his first floating body. He later pointed out it was an exaggeration to say (as some did) that there were so many bodies in the harbor that they blocked traffic. On the 16th, however, he counted ten bodies drifting by his ship in the space of a half hour. And "the ocean is big and human bodies are small."

A large boat capsizes at the Smyrna quay from too many refugees rushing on board. In the foreground, an American seaman works on a ship's boat belonging to *Litchfield*, from which this photo was taken. *Thomas Kinkaid collection, The Naval History and Heritage Command*

About this time, a Greek man who had left a hiding spot in a graveyard and made his way to the quay found so many bodies floating in the water that he thought if he fell in he wouldn't sink, for the bodies would keep him from the water. He also noticed dozens of young Turkish boys swimming amongst the corpses, searching them for anything of value.[60]

According to another report, several hundred refugees crowded onto a lighter alongside the quay, hoping somebody would tow them out into the harbor, only to have Turks cover them with oil or kerosene and burn them all to death. This event might seem incredible, yet separate reports about it came from several witnesses, including Emily McCallam, who saw some of the charred bodies; from a young Armenian woman who witnessed Turkish soldiers pouring the kerosene, after which the "raft" with its human cargo became a blazing torch;[61] and from an Italian who told of witnessing the event in a letter he wrote the American secretary of state.

The latter individual was Theodore Bartoli, a businessman from Smyrna. In his letter, besides describing the lighter's burning, Bartoli also expressed his gratitude to Secretary Charles Evans Hughes for the efforts of two American sailors who had helped him bury both his mother (who had been hit by a stray bullet while embarking on an Italian merchant ship), and his two sisters, who had committed suicide when Turks broke into their house, rather than be raped and killed. "What I saw, what I lived through during 25 days is horrible," he wrote, "I saw young girls of 15 years to 20, have their throats cut at the sea-shore. I saw innocent adolescents have their eyes put out. I saw hundreds of refugees throw themselves into the sea, while they fled from the conflagration, finding a worse death. All this was accomplished before the eyes of the powers represented by officers [and] marines of the battleships anchored close by." Equally bitter in later recollection was the young Armenian woman mentioned above who had seen the blazing raft. Not only did she notice the British pouring boiling water down on swimmers (she and her companions could see the steam rising), but, in addition, she saw that "the Americans were lined up on their [destroyer] decks, their movie cameras turning." She was not the only person to react in disbelief at the latter sight.[62]

As the flames first started eating up the city blocks, officials at the threatened American institutions had collected American staff members and driven them to the consulate in trucks, leaving most native faculty and students behind. Dean Minnie Mills of the Collegiate Institute refused to leave her students, but sailors bundled her into a truck anyway. One American petty officer at the Institute played pied piper, with hundreds of native staff, students, and refugees attempting to stay behind him as he tried to find his way to the quayside consulate, which was, however, all the way across town. The way was blocked much of the time, and many of his followers lost their way.[63]

By now, Hepburn had decided to evacuate naturalized Americans to Athens. Bound by Bristol's orders to be neutral, "restricting naval activity to the protection of American lives and property," he was holding the line there: *only citizens*. An American teacher named John Kingsley Birge reached *Simpson* by boat and Hepburn invited him on board, but finding the man had brought along some female Armenian students and teachers, the captain ordered all the latter sent back. A subordinate officer insisted that he would be sending these women to their deaths, and Hepburn finally gave in. He had the women sent below.[64]

A bit later, ashore at the theater, Hepburn personally stood in the way of Birge's wife Anna, who had brought along with her eight male Greek and Armenian students from the American college south of the city. When Captain Hepburn argued that these boys could not all be *her* children and insisted that only American families could be evacuated, Anna Birge convinced eight families standing nearby to "adopt" one lad apiece. With such a determined challenge to the captain, she managed to get her boys out to the *Simpson* and to collect them there.[65] About 7:45 p.m. on the 13th, just after Consul Horton joined the vessel, Captain Knauss ordered the *Simpson* under way toward Athens.[66]

Also that evening, "on the score of humanity," Hepburn put another two hundred American "retainers" on board the *Winona*, an American merchant ship still in the harbor. Having done so, Hepburn believed he had carried out his orders. The Navy men and the other Americans remaining on board the destroyers now had leisure to gaze at (and photograph) the terrible sight in front of them.[67]

To observers, the fire imposed itself frightfully on virtually every sense, and at almost any distance. The heat, for instance, could be felt on the destroyers though they had moved two hundred yards away from the pier to escape it. The screams of the frantic mob were oppressive at least a mile away.[68] To the naked eye, "an unbroken wall of fire, two miles long" was presented, one in which "twenty distinct volcanoes of raging flame are throwing up jagged, writhing tongues to a height of a hundred feet"—this according to British writer G. Ward Price, looking on from the quarterdeck of the British battleship *Iron Duke*.[69] The purser of the *Winona* would write that "the blaze was reflected bloodred on the calm surface of the water for more than two miles out," and while his destroyer steamed toward Athens, Harry Knauss reported that the flames and the glow of the burning city were visible for over fifty miles.[70] Several days after the fire, ship passengers on the Sea of Marmara would mistake the huge clouds of smoke for a great range of mountains.[71] They were 140 miles from Smyrna.

Of course the fire and the refugees' terror were most horrific at close range. The terrible screams, in particular, made you want to do something, anything to help. Before the fire, American relief officials led by Jaquith and Davis had been doing their best to feed several groups of thousands of refugees. Now, watching in anguish from the decks of a destroyer, Major Davis and Mark Prentiss, a commercial attaché from Constantinople who had been sent to Smyrna as Bristol's special Near East Relief representative, asked Hepburn to let them take a boat in. Perhaps they might move a large lighter over to the pier, put refugees on it, and tow a group to safety. Hepburn demurred; the *Litchfield*'s one motor sailor could hardly handle that lighter, and to put the small powerboat itself along the quay would merely invite disaster. Well, Davis continued, maybe Hepburn could get the French or British to send their many large boats to the rescue. (Again, those countries both had *battleships* present, not just dinky destroyers!) Not unwilling, but no doubt keeping in mind Bristol's desire that the Americans go their own course and not cooperate with the Allies (nor displease the Turks), Hepburn sent Davis to offer the British this "delicate proposition."[72] Davis had no luck with the French, and at first the British admiral Osmand Brock also refused to do anything. He had assured Noureddin of Britain's absolute neutrality, Brock replied. "He could not—and would not—allow his men to take part in the rescue of Greek and Armenian civilians." However, the British chief of staff argued with such vehemence that Admiral Brock eventually changed his mind.[73]

When he did, there was nothing half-hearted about the British response. Navy man Hepburn found the subsequent action quite moving: "It was evidently a squadron signal for 'Away all boats,' and the manner in which it was performed made a stirring spectacle. In spite of the lateness of the hour—well past midnight—it was only a few minutes after Major Davis' return on board that the first boats came sweeping in, all pulling boats large enough to be of service as well as power launches, crews in uniform, and boat officers of all ranks from Captain to Midshipman."[74] The British "pulling boats" (oared launches) and powerboats began making a regular run between the ships in the harbor and the pier. Throughout the night and far into the morning, exhausted oarsmen would stop by *Litchfield* for rest and coffee before resuming their ferry work. They would put almost seven hundred refugees on *Litchfield* itself and others on the American merchant *Winona*, but they would load many more thousands on board European ships in the harbor till the latter could literally take no more. Together, they saved thousands; Dobkin estimates twenty thousand.[75]

It had taken a while to get about it. After listening to all the screaming and watching people push themselves into the sea, Oran Raber judged it a lasting shame to all the nations present that they had not begun rescuing people during the afternoon, when the danger was already evident.[76] Even with the British effort, the rescue had barely dented the black mass of refugees ashore.

The next day, as the fire continued to rage, Hepburn transferred his seven hundred refugees to *Edsall* (just arrived from Constantinople with thirty tons of flour) and sent them on to Salonika, hoping they would find a welcome there. At the plea of reliefer Jaquith (note again the initiative being taken by American reliefers rather than Navy officials), Hepburn agreed to a further deviation from strict neutrality and put hundreds of orphans and various other refugees who had been under the protection of American agencies on board *Winona*, whose captain had signaled that his ship could take even more.[77] This vessel would eventually sail for Piraeus with almost two thousand refugees.

The same day, through glasses, Hepburn himself saw a man in civilian clothes apprehended by a squad of Turkish soldiers, handled brutally, searched, bound, thrown over the seawall, and shot. The impression of Americans ashore who talked to the captain was that every "able-bodied" Armenian man was being hunted down and killed.[78] On the other hand, some rumors were exploded. Two sailors contradicted accounts about Turks using machine guns to drive the refugees toward the flames. They had been surprised to see some Turkish soldiers leading refugees to safety on the "Konak grounds," bringing them water and treating them kindly.[79]

— ◂◆▸ —

In their official reports and discussions with the news media (both at the time and later), Americans attempted to assess the cause of the fire. Several noted then or later that ethnic Greeks or Armenians had beforehand threatened to burn the city, were the Turks ever to take it,[80] but no American seems to have witnessed the Christians acting on such threats. Several Americans (and several locals) did report seeing *Turkish* incendiaries. About noon on the 13th, a bluejacket at the Collegiate Institute drew Minnie Mills to the window to watch Turks setting fires in nearby houses. Together they watched regular Turkish soldiers in sharp uniforms carrying tins of petroleum into house after house. Soon after they left each building it would burst into flames.[81] That night, two American sailors stationed in the Armenian quarter (they were serving as chauffeurs) witnessed Turks running down the street throwing oil-soaked rags in windows.[82]

With the fire approaching the quay, Major Davis was standing in the doorway of the American consulate with the naval guard. He saw a Turkish soldier pouring a liquid in a long stream from the quay toward the fire. Davis tasted the liquid, and found it either gasoline or kerosene.[83] Barnes reported this same or a similar act near the consulate, and the next night he and Jaquith from the deck of a destroyer anchored not far off from the quay watched somebody take twenty minutes to fire the passport control office.[84] Though they could not identify the man, Turkish soldiers were stationed at the place and many were passing right by. Both Americans were convinced that whoever carried this out had to be in sympathy with the Turkish authorities.[85]

Despite the witness of his own eyes, Vice Consul Barnes thought it illogical to conclude that Smyrna was destroyed by the Turks. And even if individual soldiers had contributed, "surely it was not fired by the order of the authorities or with their cognizance," he would argue.[86] In a message to Bristol a month after the fire in which the possibilities of future commercial relations with the Turks figured prominently, Barnes claimed that the majority of the Americans in Smyrna believed the city had been torched by the Armenians. However, by the time he wrote that letter, almost all the Americans who had actually been at Smyrna during or just before the fire had long since left the place.[87]

Bristol's intelligence officer, Tip Merrill, radioed to Bristol on September 14 his belief that the Turks had burned the city to get rid of the Christian minorities.[88] Others thought the Turks' motive was to hide evidence of looting and murders.[89] An American who was convinced the Turks had burned the city was Major Davis, the Constantinople Red Cross chief, who had been in Smyrna from the moment the Turks arrived. He reported that there was only one authentic case of an Armenian using a bomb on Turkish troops (probably he was referring to that initial attack), and he said the looting only began when the Turks were well established. Back in Constantinople, Davis also described the "vigilance" committee of Turks with red armbands pillaging madly and shooting right and left, and the marching of gangs of civilians into the interior. Davis reported he had been refused Turkish permission to visit outlying Greek villages (apparently also consumed by fire) to see if help was needed. Therefore he refused to believe that the *Greeks* had burned them up.[90]

Despite such American witness, officials like Captain Hepburn and Vice Consul Barnes remained convinced that the Armenians had probably set the fire. Hepburn based his conviction partly on the denial of responsibility on the part of Turkish authorities in Smyrna (denials that he and others somehow found credible), and partly on the great savagery the Turks had manifested toward the Armenians *afterward*—as if Turks had never savaged the Armenians without specific provocation before.

Hepburn thought Merrill's notion, that the Turks might have fired the city so as to rid the country of non-Muslims, was far-fetched.[91] However, the latter motive—like the plowing of the Christian graveyards at Marsovan—could have been, by now, simple habit. In 1919 at Samsun, an American naval officer had reported seeing the Greek and Armenian villages practically wiped out there, the villagers having all been driven into the interior by ethnic Turks during the Great War. Not only were their houses burned and leveled, this officer had reported, but "even in some cases the trees were cut down so as to make the destruction of the villages more complete."

Who had reported such thorough attempts permanently to rid the area of the Christian minorities? Hepburn's boss: Mark Bristol.

That the motive behind the Turkish destruction of Smyrna by fire was to rid the country of the minorities for good has recently been argued by a Turkish scholar, who takes an unusual slant on the vexed issue.[92] Really, though, in the face of the Turks' overwhelming power in Smyrna, especially after several days of brutal Turkish occupation, the notion that an organized body of Greeks or Armenians could have found the freedom to start, restart, and spread the fires (still sometimes argued in print and often on the Internet) seems simply absurd. As Consul Horton pointed out, "the Turks had been in full, complete and undisputed possession of the city for five days before the fire broke out."[93] Even Barnes and Hepburn (who argued that minorities had set the fires) admitted that the Turks were culpable in the end, for they certainly *could* have kept order had they so desired—they had all the power. As Barnes put it, "the blame must ultimately rest upon the Turks."[94]

While the fire burned itself out, Hepburn once again began to walk the fine line of neutrality, though now for a different reason. He had increasingly (though very belatedly) come around to Horton's and the relief workers' initial opinion, that a massive international evacuation was the only answer to this awesome humanitarian tragedy. He wanted to get the Allies to endorse the idea and to help execute it. (Bristol was always insisting that the Allies take the lead.) Also, Hepburn thought the goodwill of the Turks essential to perform such an evacuation (by then it certainly was), and he feared to offend them.[95] On Friday the 15th, Hepburn sent an officer south to the International College at Paradise (far from the fire) both to check on conditions there and to let the remaining Americans know that the naval guard would soon have to leave. Any Americans wanting to leave Smyrna would be taken away by destroyer. Once again, even though he had allowed exceptions before, Hepburn was insisting that only *American citizens* could be evacuated. Hence it happened that when a truckload of male Armenian students from the college was also brought along (the officials at the college believing that no one would have the heart to leave these young men behind), an angry Hepburn had them all sent back on the same truck.[96]

Yet even as these students returned to Turkish control, which in the event meant death for most of them, as interviews with survivors were to indicate,[97] the number of refugees within sight of the ships had begun to dwindle dramatically, a phenomenon that had baleful implications not only for ethnic males, but also for young women of possible interest to the Turks. Although some of the refugees were being taken to camps a few miles inland, others were obviously being "conducted into the interior." Merrill radioed Admiral Bristol on the 14th that, the way things were going, within a week there *would be no relief problem*, a chilling conclusion widely agreed upon by relief officials.[98] On the 15th, Barnes reported that maybe 40,000 had already begun "their grim march" inland.[99] Davis recognized that the new Turkish proclamation that all male Greeks and Armenians between the ages of eighteen and forty-five would be held as "prisoners of war" not only meant that combatants and noncombatants were to be treated alike, but since the Turks were judging ages, many males between fifteen and sixty would be seized as well.[100] The announced deadline for the evacuation itself produced great panic among the refugees, for posters proclaimed that, regardless of sex or age, anyone who was left after September 30 would also be deported.[101]

Despite reporting all this at a local Allied conference, Hepburn found he was getting no real cooperation. Frustrated, on the 16th Hepburn left for Constantinople to lay the great evacuation needs before Admiral Bristol.

—◆◆◆—

The destroyer ride from Constantinople to Smyrna took about fifteen hours. At the embassy the next afternoon, Bristol talked with Hepburn and a few other eyewitnesses just returned from Smyrna. Each of them apparently had not only been greatly moved by the suffering, but also had been greatly offended by the atrocities he had seen the Turks mete out. European Standard Oil official L. I. "Irving" Thomas, for example, one of Mark Bristol's closest friends, was to complain later that he had always been pro-Turk; now, however, after seeing the killing and brutality against the refugees on the Smyrna quay, he had no use for the Turks at all.[102] Despite several such "indignant" reports,[103] Bristol remained unmoved. In December Henry King (of the 1919 King-Crane Commission) was to write Bristol and express sympathy. He supposed that Bristol's involvement with Smyrna and the refugees must have been heartbreaking.[104] On the contrary, in Bristol's September war diaries there is little indication that the tales of murder and terror and starvation and all the duress being suffered by the refugees at Smyrna had penetrated to the admiral's psyche at all.

Instead, the admiral reported he was more and more coming to the position (despite his visitors' horrible recital) that the loss of life at Smyrna was really rather small; he had actually expected the Turks to do much more than they had. Though the Turks no doubt set the fires in the Armenian and Greek quarters in reprisal for supposed or actual wrongs, Bristol thought the fires probably got away from them accidentally, and now, "like children," the leaders were undoubtedly sorry for the loss they had caused themselves to sustain. He thought all the eyewitnesses from Smyrna were overwrought. Once emotions were calmed, everyone would realize that, comparatively speaking, Smyrna was a minor affair.[105]

Moreover, although to his credit Bristol had sent several Constantinople relief people to Smyrna very early on, from the beginning of his conversations about the events there, he was adamant that the Greeks and Allies should take the initiative and bear the main evacuation responsibilities, because they had caused the refugee problems in the first place.[106] Back in 1920, when Bristol had heard from McCully that the Bolsheviks were overrunning the Crimea, Bristol had gone to general quarters and ordered under way every vessel he had. Now he dragged his feet. He purposely delayed meeting with the Allies about taking the refugees to safety, lest they try to get the Americans to lead.[107] Even after hearing his own chief of staff, fresh from the scene, call for a massive immediate evacuation, Bristol insisted on pressing the Allies to take *their* share.

In the American relief committee meeting on the 18th, the utterly patient missionary head William Peet finally grew impatient with Bristol's rhetoric and pointed to the great needs of the present circumstances. Yes, of course, the admiral then admitted, America must take instant steps, and a general evacuation was the only thing to do. He claimed he had already ordered his destroyers to start. Despite their limited capacity, these ships would immediately begin shuttling refugees to islands in the Aegean Sea. Meanwhile members of the committee would seek help from the Armenian and Greek patriarchs and see about getting ships from Constantinople down to Smyrna.[108]

Simpson did take some refugees away from Smyrna on the 18th, and three days later, the *Litchfield* transported some orphans and college students and staff to Constantinople.[109] However, having once delivered its refugees, *Simpson* was not sent back to Smyrna. Embassy officials seem to have done virtually nothing toward getting American merchant ships down from Constantinople (though the British would soon commandeer and send down a number of British merchant ships), nor did the admiral bother to transfer to Smyrna any destroyers from the Black Sea ports, although his own records indicate some were available. American relief was winding down at Odessa, for example, and the officers on the station ship at Samsun were passing the time hunting more pheasant.[110] In fact, there was no naval shuttle such as the admiral had promised. A final indication of the relatively casual attention Bristol paid to this truly unprecedented human tragedy is that once Chief of Staff Hepburn came back to Constantinople—with no evacuation in sight—Bristol kept him there.[111]

At one point, some six hundred boys from an American orphanage were rescued from the Smyrna quay and taken to Constantinople by an American destroyer. Note all the white hats. *Thomas Kinkaid collection, The Naval History and Heritage Command*

American command in Smyrna thus passed to the next senior naval officer present, the commander of *Edsall*, Halsey Powell. On the 17th, the day after Hepburn left, Powell found that the deportations inland that had been observed before were still going on and now were being openly acknowledged by the Turks.[112] Harry Knauss reported on the 18th (just before his destroyer left the port) that not only males but some women and children too were now were being driven toward the interior, and that measures were being taken to keep these deportees out of sight of the Americans and Europeans at the harbor.[113] Meantime, such disorder was taking place on the streets away from the quay that it was often not safe for Americans to go into the city, even under guard.[114] Knauss noticed a large number of bodies being stacked a block away from the consulate, and that in the city's interior the smell of burning human flesh was clearly noticeable, something also mentioned by Powell.[115] Major Davis's report of the 19th recorded his belief that a Greek church was being used by the Turks as a "crematorium," but it was blown up as he was on his way to inspect it.[116] Meanwhile, the Turks had initiated a house-to-house search, looking for men of draft age, "making a good allowance on each side of the limit 18 to 45."[117] At the concentration camps inland to which many refugees had been herded, men were also being seized. After this, those camps were closed, and the refugees remaining there (now almost exclusively women, children, and old men) fled back to the city. Soon the numbers on the quay began to swell again.[118]

After the fire, American relief officials had been doing their best to continue to bake bread and distribute rations, but many obstacles hindered them, including the lack of water and fuel, the fire's destruction of ovens and bakeries, and someone's having turned off the water at the bakeries. Although the relief workers quickly got the baking going again,[119] they became increasingly frustrated with military inaction: "We did what we could in the way of distributing food and medical aid, but it was sickening to see a dozen warships idly riding at anchor while the people on shore were dying of exposure or starvation," recalled missionary doctor Wilfrid Post.[120] Commander Powell was frustrated, too. He would note on the 21st that if an evacuation did not take place in a very short time, there would be very few left to evacuate.[121]

Meantime, Major Davis and Commander Powell had met with Turkish patriot Halide Edib, now in Smyrna, to discuss the relief work taking place. On Davis bringing up the probable need for relief work in the interior, Edib went into detail about the Greek atrocities there, and, by the way, "took it for granted" that the two Americans understood that Smyrna had been burned by the Greeks and Armenians.[122] Earlier, on his taking over from Hepburn, Powell

had begun meeting with Turkish officials on another topic: the possible evacuation of the refugees. Powell, by the way, had been considering the chances of
getting Turkish permission for Greek transports to enter the harbor ever since
he had taken refugees to Salonika.[123] However, when he got back to Smyrna he
was told that Mustapha Kemal (the most powerful man in Turkey) "could not
take the responsibility of allowing the Greek ships into Smyrna but would have
to consult the Government at Angora."[124] Eventually, Commander Powell and
some of the Allies would get the Turks to agree on an evacuation. However,
apparently nobody in authority had gone to the effort of talking to the *Greeks*
about this. Consequently, for days, other than an occasional chartered British or
Italian vessel, no transports appeared.

Not every American was content with doing relief work. Just after the fire,
two businessmen named Archbell and Griswold found intact some three thousand tons of tobacco, organized a partnership, set themselves up as shipping
agents, and solicited vessels to take the cargo. Though Powell passed the word
on, he was careful to advise the two men that, until the refugee situation was
handled, nothing but human cargo was likely to be shipped.[125] In this warning, at least, the commander had his priorities in order, unlike his boss back
in Constantinople. Even as hundreds of thousands of refugees still stood or
died in the stench of the Smyrna pier, and as the Turkish army was threatening
Constantinople, Bristol would encourage Col. St. J. Greble to travel to Smyrna
to pursue locomotive business with the Nationalists. And so he did. In other
words, it appears that Admiral Bristol was already back to promoting business
as usual.[126]

—◆◆◆—

And so it was that the initiative for dealing decisively with the disaster passed
for a while from all the naval authorities in Constantinople or on the site in
Smyrna to an American civilian who really did find the refugees' predicament
"heartbreaking." The story that follows has been told before, but deserves telling again.

Asa Jennings was a YMCA "boys' worker" (and an ordained minister) who
had arrived in Smyrna with his wife and two boys only a month or so before
the fire. He only stood five foot two but was "a bundle of nerves and energy."[127]
Although he had only been working in Turkey a short time, he immediately
understood the dangers the Armenians faced. When he found an Armenian
YMCA worker who was frantic about the Turks' approach, Jennings hired
this man as a servant for his family, and in this way enabled him to escape.[128]
More significantly, during the fire and afterward, Jennings took the initiative to

protect some of the most helpless among the refugees, despite the doubtful attitude of naval commanders. For instance, as the fire burned itself out, Jennings
gathered into a house on the quay the many refugee women who were about
to give birth.

Initially, Commander Powell worried that Jennings' project would antag-
onize the Turks, particularly as the American sailors guarding the house were
acting, as Powell called it, "irresponsibly." The enlisted men there had allowed
two Greek priests being chased by Turkish cavalry to enter the house for asylum. (Lieutenant Commander Knauss happened to be present, and he had the
two doff their gowns and hats and duck out the back way.) However, eventually even Powell became infected by the American sailors' sympathy, and later
spoke approvingly of Jennings having gotten as many as four hundred refugees into that building.[129] Several of the latter were young Armenian or Greek
women American bluejackets or their officers had rescued from Turkish soldiers as the latter (or Turkish officers) were leading the girls down the street.
Years later, Red Condon was to recall as a young American naval officer escorting fifty young Armenian women to a safe haven in Smyrna, probably to this
very house. To protect them while en route, Condon and his fellows had the
girls fashion their hair and dress as if they were children of eight, though they

American sailors at Smyrna rescue a young Armenian woman in evening dress. According
to the photograph's caption, "She swam a mile out" to the destroyer to escape the Turks and
the fire. *Thomas Kinkaid collection, The Naval History and Heritage Command*

were, in fact, close to fifteen, and hence in substantial danger. The naval party succeeded in getting the girls to safety.[130]

Powell thought the Navy might be able to evacuate Jennings' refugees, as long as all the Christian males (desperate men fleeing what were, essentially, death sentences) could be kept from barging into the place.[131]

As the days wore on, though, and more and more refugees returned from distant camps to the quay, and transports did not arrive (the British brought two ships in on the 19th that would take away a few thousand, but that just tantalized the great throng),[132] Jennings found his soul increasingly tormented. "I have seen men, women and children whipped, robbed, shot, stabbed, and drowned in the sea, and while I helped save some it seemed like nothing as compared with the great need. It seemed as though the awful, agonizing, hopeless shrieks for help would forever haunt me."[133] A religious man, Jennings frequently prayed, but *he also acted*. At one point, when a young woman was seen swimming near an American destroyer whose sailors would do nothing to save her—they explained that they could not act without orders, and their officers would not issue any (a prime example of the utter enfeeblement created by Bristol's insistence on neutrality)—Jennings erupted: "Well, I'll order it: push off that boat!" The sailors quickly rescued the girl.[134]

On the 20th, Jennings awoke, determined to do *something*. Seeing a French ship anchored out in the harbor, Jennings decided to ask that vessel to take on some refugees and got Powell to give him a boat. The French captain refused. So Jennings climbed aboard an Italian ship called the *Constantinopoli*, which was moored at a wharf. Though this captain was also reluctant, shortly Jennings offered a sum (probably from relief funds) and the captain agreed to take a group. Now, would the Turks allow the evacuation? Yes, they would, he was told, but no draft-age males. Jennings and others worked all night. In the morning the Americans found a squad of Turkish soldiers delegated to scan the refugees as they boarded the vessel. Some minority men who had disguised themselves were detected right on the dock, and the grief of the families as the men were marched away was heartrending. However, as Jennings later pointed out, "It was either play the game as the Turks said, or not play it at all."[135]

The ship sailed the following afternoon with two thousand refugees. To help ensure all of them could be landed at nearby Mytilene, the ship's captain had insisted that Jennings ride the ship there. Upon boarding, the relief worker could hardly make his way through the crowd. "They fell at my feet in gratitude. They kissed me. Old men got on their knees, kissing my hands and feet, tears steaming down their faces." Jennings fought his way on to his cabin, fell onto his berth, and wept. Then he got down on his knees and prayed.[136]

But the *great* rescue had not yet begun. About midnight, when the slow steamer finally sighted Mytilene (it is the capital city of the Greek island of Lesbos), the astonished passengers began cursing. There in the harbor, just a few hours' steaming from Smyrna, lay some twenty Greek passenger ships, all riding high.[137] These were the vessels that had recently transported much of the retreating Greek army away from the Turkish coast. After he landed the refugees, Jennings approached the Greek general Frankos who was present, described the terrible need, and asked if those Greek ships could return to Smyrna. The general wanted assurance that the ships would be protected. After all, the Turks had no navy. Would the Turks commandeer the vessels and then sail them off to capture all the Greek islands? The American's oral assurance was not enough for the Greek general, so, boarding *Litchfield* (which Powell had ordered to go pick Jennings up[138]), Jennings sped back to consult with Powell and returned a few hours later with a written authorization from the American commander. Not only had the Turks authorized the Greek ships to come, but American destroyers would accompany the ships into the harbor.

Frankos was still reluctant. Jennings again promised to ride the ships. But on Jennings pressing the issue—"Will you, or won't you, give us these ships?"—Frankos still waffled.[139]

Jennings stomped out, convinced the general would never agree. Then he noticed in the harbor what looked like an American battleship. And indeed it was . . . or once had been. Years before, America had sold the old *Mississippi* to the Greeks, and now the renamed and reflagged *Kilkis* stood anchored before him. With faith that somehow God would make things come right, Jennings found a boat to take him out to the warship. The ship's captain agreed to help Jennings send a message to Athens. American citizen Asa Jennings had decided to go over General Frankos' head and appeal directly to the Greek government.[140]

The response of Athens to his initial message explaining the situation and asking for ships was, quite naturally, who on earth was Asa Jennings? "The head of American relief at Mytilene," Jennings signaled back. And perhaps he was, though he was also the only American at the place. Another message from Athens announced that even though the cabinet was not in session, Jennings' request had been submitted to the prime minister; a later reply said the prime minister would consult the cabinet at 9:00 a.m. the next day. In those messages and in the cabinet's eventual response were several questions to which the answers were, in fact, quite uncertain. What protection would be offered the ships? Would the Americans fight if the Turks tried to take the vessels? The Greek cabinet (only a few days from its own fall) seemed even more cautious than the local general. Jennings negotiated back and forth by coded signal until four on the afternoon of the 23rd, but found himself increasingly frustrated.

Finally, recollecting all "those poor folks awaiting certain death there on the quay," Jennings decided to try the last: an ultimatum. Unless the cabinet ordered the vessels to Smyrna, he threatened to wire openly without code to whoever might listen, that despite many American guarantees, the Greek government had refused to release their own ships to save tens of thousands ethnic Greeks facing certain death.[141]

It was an astonishing bluff, and even the captain of *Kilkis* (perhaps worried about his own part in this episode) attempted to get Jennings to go below and get some sleep.[142] But Jennings stuck to his program. At about six that evening, he received this wire back: "ALL SHIPS IN AEGEAN PLACED YOUR COMMAND REMOVE REFUGEES SMYRNA." Asa Jennings had just effectually been made an admiral in the Greek navy and placed in charge of a fleet of some fifty transports.[143]

With such authorization, the problems that arose afterward were soon disposed of. Jennings agreed to several Greek conditions, including the stipulations that the ships be escorted into the Smyrna harbor by an American destroyer, that the Greek ships not fly their flags, and that Jennings himself would ride the first ship (even though the only thing he knew about ships was "to be sick on them"). Jennings also got the governor of Mytilene to agree to accept the refugees, to open a hospital and a warehouse, and so on—providing Jennings could provide the refugees food. The relief worker then returned to Smyrna (again he traveled on *Litchfield*—there seems to have been no other reliable way for Jennings to communicate with Powell than in person).[144] Once they checked things through on that end, Powell sent Jennings back to Mytilene again on *Litchfield* (which this time was en route to Constantinople, and dropped Jennings off along the way), to finalize the transport. When several of the Greek merchant captains announced they had developed engine trouble or needed more sailors or required additional provisions, the captain of *Kilkis* threatened to inspect every ship and prepare court-martial charges for any captain who was misrepresenting his vessel's condition. In the end, ten vessels got under way on the 24th, with Jennings riding the lead ship. Having first stowed their Greek flags, they steamed toward Smyrna under escort of *Lawrence*.[145]

When his fleet arrived at the harbor, Jennings was still on the bridge, a bit green from the journey, but able to appreciate the terrific vista. From one aspect it was the most desolate and fearsome scene he had ever witnessed: only smoking ruins where Smyrna's handsome business district had once stood, and at the water's edge an apparently lifeless black mass. But he knew that the black mass was a living body, one that had for days been "waiting, hoping, praying for ships." As his transport approached the pier, Jennings found the air filled with "cries of such transcendent joy that the sound pierced to the very marrow of my bones."[146]

From this time forward, Jennings would be known among the Americans in the region as "Admiral" or "Commodore" Jennings, and even Admiral Bristol would smile at the appellation.

———◆◆◆———

Besides Jennings and the other relief workers and all the naval personnel, a few other Americans had come to the city and were living on the Navy ships. Unlike Jennings, some of these people were as interested in furthering their own careers as they were in supporting the refugees.

Take the journalists, for instance. As has been noted, Constantine Brown's social ties to Admiral Bristol were very strong, and his offer to use his *Chicago Daily News* articles about the Ward and Yowell reports as propaganda tools for Bristol speaks to an obvious bias. In contrast, John Clayton's report from inland Harput about all the Pontic Greeks marching and dying there had showed an independent streak. Still, when Bristol sent these two men to Smyrna on *Lawrence* early on, both of them agreed that, since they were going by Bristol's permission and by his destroyer, they had to protect the admiral's interests.[147] Hence it not surprising that while aboard an American destroyer in the harbor, George Horton heard one of them say distinctly, apparently throwing up his hands while typing a telegram to his paper, "I cannot send this stuff, it will queer me at Constantinople."[148]

Clayton's series of stories is particularly instructive. His early reports might seem to indicate a pro-Turkish slant. On the 11th, he wrote that there had been very few killings, fewer than anybody had expected (except for the shooting of some looters and snipers, and, well, some "executions"; he had seen the bodies). The journalist added that the discipline of the Turkish troops was excellent, and given the circumstances, this was "nothing short of remarkable." The next day he reported that while there were many more executions of Greeks and Armenians, nevertheless relief work was proceeding well, and overall Smyrna was quieting down. On Wednesday the 13th, Clayton got a huge scoop, an interview with Mustapha Kemal himself, an important interview in which Kemal spoke to the freedom of the straits, the safety of Constantinople, European access to oil, suggestions for an "exchange of populations," and the status of Thrace. Kemal also assured the journalist that there had been no massacres in Smyrna, nor would there be. It was difficult to control an army in such a situation, "But control we will," said Kemal. "You can say order has been completely restored from to-day. . . . We are not here to regulate past accounts."

In the same article, Clayton reported that the streets were being swept, shops were being opened and "Smyrna has settled down to normal life again."[149] And, indeed, the trams on the quay had begun operating that morning; a few cafés had even opened.[150]

With the outbreak of the fire, however, which had begun making headway even as the reporter was meeting Kemal on Wednesday, Clayton's stories became very different. A cable with Clayton's byline dated "Smyrna, Thursday" reported that Smyrna was in flames, and that the Turks seemed to be responsible. According to this piece, it was impossible to number the Greek and Armenian dead, many of them having been burned in their houses. And the "Smyrna, Friday" story that Clayton wrote on the 15th seemed to complete the journalist's about-face: Three-fifths of Smyrna was in ashes, the loss of life was impossible to compute, the streets were littered with dead, and the problem of the minorities had been solved for all time: "Thus, despite Kemal Pasha's assurances, Turkey has 'regulated' past accounts."[151]

And so one might think that despite Bristol's warning, Clayton's instinct for truth in journalism had now taken over again. However, when Clayton wrote these last two stories (and even on the 17th, when the journalist penned a story about *plague* breaking out in the city) *he was not even in Smyrna*. According to the memoir of fellow journalist Brown, Clayton had ridden *Simpson* to Athens with Consul Horton and several other evacuating Americans (probably to ensure the filing of his interview with Kemal). That destroyer had left Wednesday night just as the fire was reaching the quay. Clayton based his portrait of the fire's aftermath on an intercepted wire story of Brown's and on recollected details about the city. The only authentic detail in these stories was his citation of reports about the origins of the fire, the latter given by Minnie Mills and others from the Collegiate Institute. These people had taken the *Winona* out of Smyrna, and were now with Clayton in Athens. Yet as late as 2008, one of Clayton's stories was being cited as firsthand evidence of what was then going on in Smyrna.[152]

Another American writing from Smyrna had a stronger connection to the embassy than either Clayton or Brown. With the blessing of the embassy and the Navy (which handled his wires),[153] NER representative Mark Prentiss had become a special representative for the *New York Times*. His articles to that paper soon took on both a pro-Turkish and a pro-Prentiss slant. For instance, as Halsey Powell would later report at length, prior to the evacuation on the Greek ships the Turks had erected five different barricades that each refugee had to pass, and Turkish soldiers robbed the refugees regularly at almost every one of them. This practice would be mentioned and deplored by Commander Powell and several others.[154] However, by reading Prentiss's *New York Times* article on this topic, one would learn only of the refugees' "present[ing] money in various sums for special privileges," as if the chief evil was the refugees' offering of bribes, which proved too much for the poor Turkish soldiers to resist.

And who solved this bribery problem? No other than the writer himself! In his story's first paragraph, Prentiss claimed that the chartering of the ships and their ferry service was being conducted "under my direction." A bit later he referred again to "my personal direction of the embarkation." Further on he pointed out that, in quieting panic, his own helmet and police whistle were "everywhere identifiable." No wonder that at the specific request of this awesome figure, the Turkish officers had immediately stopped that iniquitous Christian bribery.[155]

Halsey Powell would later point out that the whole of the evacuation was actually handled by the Turks and by naval forces. While one relief committee member did come to assist, Powell commented, "as it was an entirely military affair, his services could be of little value."[156] Also, as Dobkin points out, not only did Prentiss' journalism over this period shift radically from being anti-Turk to anti-Greek, but eventually he was being escorted around the city by a Turkish major.[157]

Among the two or three other journalists present, a British writer who arrived at the beginning of the last week was often assumed to be an American, because Halsey Powell was lodging her aboard his own ship. This person was also furthering her own interests while at Smyrna. Her interests, however, at this historic moment, were not so much in the line of journalism—as in *art*.

———◆———

Clare Sheridan was a quite fascinating person. A painter and sculptor of about thirty-five, she had sculpted her first cousin, Winston Churchill, in 1920, and then greatly embarrassed that same statesman by traveling to Russia and sculpting Marxist revolutionaries Vladimir Lenin and Leon Trotsky, too. Sheridan published her diary of this "mad escapade"[158] first in *the London Times* and later in book form.[159] Trotsky reportedly conceived a passion for this attractive, golden-haired widow, and asked her to accompany him on his travels throughout famine-stricken Russia. Sheridan decided against that, but on her tour of the United States the next year, journalists discovered her living in tents in a eucalyptus grove in California with silent film actor Charlie Chaplin and spread that story worldwide.[160]

After sculpting Chaplin, too, Sheridan took an assignment with the *New York World* to write twenty-five stories about Europe.[161] Toward the beginning of this assignment, she published an interview with British writer Rudyard

Kipling in which she claimed Kipling had disparaged America's part in the war effort and its soulless love of money. (Kipling denied it all.) Then she heard of the Anatolian crisis and immediately took passage from Geneva to Constantinople on the Orient Express. Meeting her in the capital the morning she arrived, John Clayton found Sheridan "garbed in flaming orange." He wrote his paper that she insisted on the accuracy of her interview with Kipling and that she was also intent on quickly moving down to Smyrna.[162]

Sheridan then met with Admiral Bristol, who found the British woman tall, well proportioned, and good-looking. "She has a very direct and expressive way of talking and looks you squarely in the eye when she does it."[163] A sympathetic Turkish official provided the journalist with identification papers, after which she took passage on a French ship on its way to Beirut.[164] On this ship's stop in Smyrna's harbor, Sheridan was told there was no safe place for a woman ashore. Her steamer was almost on its way again when a friendly reporter (Constantine Brown?) took her in a boat to *Edsall*. He introduced her to Halsey Powell as "an American correspondent," though not a citizen. So addressed, Powell puzzled briefly, but then told Sheridan she could stay aboard the destroyer until she found a place ashore. One of his lieutenants would give up his cabin. But what was in that tin she was carrying? "Clay," she said. Clay that she had bought from a pipemaker in Constantinople. She planned to sculpt Mustapha Kemal.

The officers on the *Edsall* all erupted in laughter.[165] But the Americans treated her kindly, as a kind of "ship's mascot," Sheridan would later write.[166] They confessed it was excellent for *Edsall's* morale to have a woman aboard, and no doubt it was, especially a woman as charismatic as this one. They also enabled her quixotic enterprise. The next day, commandeering a Ford from the consulate, Powell sent Sheridan under officer escort to see Kemal, who was then housed at a Levantine villa outside town, in the suburb of Bournabat.[167]

Kemal was unsmiling, but extremely polite. Sheridan could not fathom him. He pointed out that since he had already discussed the political situation, any further interview along those lines would be useless. Eventually, he offered Sheridan jam and water and smiled slightly, seeing she did not know how to eat it. He would send for the "lady of the house." Sheridan tried to forestall the latter courtesy by showing Kemal some photographs of her work. He gazed long at Lenin and said that, in Turkey, Bolshevism could take no root, for "Turks are not industrialists, and the peasants own the land." Then Sheridan asked directly: Could she do Kemal's bust? He would be delighted . . . but not the next day. He had little time. (His armies, after all, were even then being shifted toward Constantinople!) Sheridan pressed the issue. Even Caesar, Alexander the Great, and Napoleon, she suggested, had somehow found the time. "You have clean-cut features and the expression of a sphinx. I would like to do you in your tall fur kalpak. *It would be good!*"[168] At just this moment, a short and thick-set young woman entered and confronted Sheridan with a stare of "insolent contempt." The hostility Sheridan felt from Latife' Hanum (who Kemal was shortly to marry, and three years later, to divorce) successfully opposed Sheridan's great charisma, and the sculpture was off.[169]

Although Sheridan's effort failed, another important "artistic" description of Smyrna's terrors ultimately succeeded, to the point of ultimately reaching wide literary attention. Ernest Hemingway was then working for the *Toronto Star*, and upon the news of the events in Smyrna and the obvious Turkish threat to Constantinople, the paper immediately sent him to the capital. Perhaps the only document now widely read about the Smyrna tragedy is the lead piece from Hemingway's 1930 edition of *In Our Time*. "On the Quai at Smyrna" is a fictional monologue of a British officer pictured as having served on a warship in Smyrna's harbor. It begins this way: "The strange thing was, he said, how they screamed every night at midnight. I do not know why they screamed at that time. We were in the harbor and they were all on the pier and at midnight they started screaming. We used to turn the searchlight on them to quiet them. That always did the trick. We'd run the searchlight up and down over them two or three times and they stopped it."[170] This piece is often taught in literature classes today. However, few readers realize that, perhaps because Hemingway apparently designed it as an introduction to a "senselessly brutal universe,"[171] the author has intentionally dehistoricized the circumstances. Consequently, like the British officer, usually neither professors nor students have a clue as to what the refugees are screaming *about*.

Observers who were actually on the quay did know about those screams, however. One of them was Esther Lovejoy, an American doctor representing the American Womens Hospitals service who had come to the city upon hearing of the fire and related crisis, and who spent her days delivering babies and otherwise attempting to help as best she could, meanwhile being immersed in the terrible sights, sounds, and odors of dead beasts and human excrement of the refugees. As for her nights, rather than sleep in an officer's bunk on a destroyer, Lovejoy took a room with other relief workers in a still-undamaged house on the quay whose balcony overlooked the mass of refugees. Because of this immersion in the refugee problem, Lovejoy could both describe the "terrible sounds" she heard in horrified sleeplessness right out her bedroom window *and* identify their cause: "Night after night blood-curdling shrieks, such as Dante never imagined in Hell, swept along that ghastly waterfront. From my room-mate I knew what these cries meant. When the Turkish regulars or irregulars, under cover of darkness, came through the ruins to the quay for the purpose of robbing the refugees or abducting their girls, the women and children, a hundred thousand or more in concert, shrieked for light, until the warships in the harbor would throw their searchlights to and fro along the quay, and the robbers would slink back into the ruins." In this context (not provided by Hemingway, who had neither been at Smyrna nor had taken care to portray the reality underlying the refugees' fear), the British officer seems simply clueless. One could argue, though, that as a character, he realistically resembles many an oblivious naval officer through history who, upon visiting a strange, troubled port, does not bother to take the effort to understand what is happening in the darkness just beyond what he can see from his ship's deck.

At the same time, from her position ashore, Lovejoy was able to point out yet another kind of willful ignorance on the part of the navies present: their attempt to seal themselves away from the terror by playing records on their ships' Victrolas. In the nights, Lovejoy says, the strains of "Humoresque," for instance, or Caruso singing "Pagliacci" were clearly audible throughout the harbor. Apparently they were being played so that some at least of the Allied forces present might continue to sleep rather than have their slumbers recurrently interrupted by "that frightful chorus of shrieks from the Smyrna quay."[172]

— ◆◆◆ —

Although tens of thousands continued to suffer terror and depredation both day and night as long as they remained on the quay, the rescue arranged by Jennings finally began.

When Powell had initially inquired to make doubly sure that the Greek transports would be allowed in the harbor, a Turkish official had replied by writing that while the ships would be allowed to come, they could not lie alongside the quay or piers, but must transfer the refugees to the ships by boats or lighters.[173] Fortunately, however, the American businessman Griswold cajoled the Turkish harbormaster into allowing the Greek steamships to come alongside the Aydin railroad piers at the northern end of the quay instead of requiring they board passengers while moored out in the harbor. At these railroad piers the refugees might be embarked by two, three, or four ships simultaneously rather than depend on the complicated operation of scarce lighters working a seaborne transfer.[174] Powell adopted this plan (which no doubt saved maybe days of work and maybe hundreds of lives), and, having passed the word via Jennings to the Greek captains, also organized the steamships' arrival and departure at the piers so that as some ships were getting under way or docking, the others could keep boarding passengers.

Commander Powell also accepted the offer of the British admiral Sir William Nicholson to send British sailors to help with the embarkation. Given the poisoned relations between the British and the Turks (not only had the two nations been combatants during the Great War, but the British all along had been the chief European power supporting the Hellenic Greek incursion into Turkey), the Turks asked that the British contingent stay away from the Turks. So the British officials directed that their sailors help the refugees only when they reached the end of the pier; they would also help stow the refugees on the ships themselves. Powell coordinated communications between Turkish and British authorities and directed that American officers and sailors organize operations at the last barrier the refugees had to pass, and also handle any pier-side interactions with the Turks.[175]

As mentioned before, on the way out to the ships, there were five gates or barriers through which the refugees would have to pass; they were to be herded all the way along and checked at each of these gate by Turkish military forces; the American sailors (and, after them, the British) would take over only after the refugees had passed through the very last gate. The refugees by this time were not only psychologically exhausted after their long ordeal, but most were terrified by the Turks and were frantic to get to the ships before becoming subject to that terrible September 30 deportation order. Hence, Powell thought the use of Turkish troops was necessary to get the refugees to behave, for his own people would not be rough enough with them.

In support of his view, Powell noted that when the gates opened, "the crowd became a mob; women were knocked down, were walked over, children were torn from their arms by the crush," and to control them, the Turkish soldiers "used their bayonets, butts of rifles, belts and canes; in some cases they knocked them down and kicked then. This was the only restraint that the refugees paid any attention to whatever."[176] Of course, the Turks continued to ensure that no draft-age ethnic Greeks or Armenian males got through the lines, and they made liberal allowance in estimations of age. Consequently, over the six days of embarkation, many hundreds (E. O. Jacob says thousands) of ethnic Greek and Armenian males, not a few of whom had attempted to disguise themselves, were taken even at the very last gate.[177]

As they had done throughout the Smyrna crisis, in the week of the embarkation itself, the American sailors did their best to make themselves useful. Upon arriving at the port, they had been sent to guard the major American schools and YMCA/YWCA properties, the Standard Oil property, and the consulate. They also led some refugees from the Collegiate Institute to the quay, operated launches in the harbor, carried foodstuffs ashore from arriving vessels, shepherded young ethnic Greeks and Armenians away from Turkish plundering and rape, and drove American relief workers on scarce automobiles from place to place in the city—besides a thousand miscellaneous missions. An

American sailor who was driving Dr. Post to a pharmacy did shoot a Turkish soldier who attempted to seize their car and apparently killed him[178]—but most of the sailors' work was less dramatic. When the Greek transports arrived, the sailors working at the gates carried stretchers burdened with the helpless or sick, aided the weak to stand and walk, carried the refugees' bundles, loaded the bundles and the stretchers onto the railway carts, comforted children who had been parted from their mothers, and even caught babies that desperate mothers dropped over the fences to them.

In a few cases (before or during the loading of the transports), sailors helped smuggle young men to the waiting ships. Moved by the plea of family members who said their brother was "already in America," for example, one sailor let an Armenian family board the lighter, which was supposed to carry "only Americans" to a waiting vessel out in the harbor. Another helped a movie producer (who somehow had gotten to Smyrna) smuggle a couple of young Greek men past the gate guards. At least one such attempt misfired, however, again because an American officer felt he was bound strictly to obey Bristol's orders.

For six straight days, American sailors like these worked to evacuate some 200,000 refugees from Smyrna, this after a lowly American YMCA worker named Jennings finally found and brought some Greek transports to Smyrna, something that nobody else had managed to do. *Esther Lovejoy,* Certain Samaritans, *2nd ed. (New York: Macmillan, 1933)*

That is, toward the end of the evacuation, a sailor told a young Greek boy who had been working with the relief workers to carry Doctor Lovejoy's suitcase aboard the lighter, which was going out to the destroyer *Litchfield.* (The doctor had decided to return to the States to raise funds for her organization.) The doctor overheard the sailor's whisper: "Take this suitcase aboard for the lady and don't come back. Listen! Don't come back." The destroyer captain noticed the young man boarding, however, and perhaps influenced by the presence of the American vice consul, he ordered the boy back ashore, to a very uncertain fate.[179]

Once the transports arrived, twenty sailors were ordered by Powell to "assist in patrolling and in preventing undue violence."[180] However, at this point, the ability of the sailors to help anyone was severely limited. The several gates of inspection not only allowed the Turks to keep the refugees under control and help them to spot draft-age men, but they also enabled Turkish soldiers to rob the refugees again and again on their way out of Turkey. Moreover, as the lines of tens of thousands of refugees were organized, they were shaped so as to snake back into the ruins of the city, where many terrible things might occur.

At the gates themselves, the horrible reality of the embarkation would impress itself upon Clare Sheridan, who, after being turned down by Kemal, decided to visit the pier daily and try to help. Her first visit to the refugee lines was particularly traumatic. Sheridan was originally pro-Turkish to the hilt, thinking the Greek fear "most absurd,"[181] and she was utterly unprepared for the degree of their desperation. Again, the deadline of September 30th that the Turks had set had spread expectations of massacre, and while Sheridan herself had heard Kemal say the deadline would be extended, she discovered it was quite another thing to convince the "hysterical maniacs" in front of her. There was worse than hysteria. Standing next to her was a Greek man who had just been arrested. Suddenly, Sheridan clutched an American standing by and cried out in terror, "There's a man cutting his throat." The American told her to get hold of herself. Failing to cut his jugular vein, the apprehended Greek threw himself down and dashed his head against a stone. When that failed to kill him, he leaped into the water, already thick with rotting corpses. As his movements finally stilled, a Turk waded out, took off the man's coat and searched his pockets before dropping the corpse back in.[182]

Though shaken, Sheridan stayed on the pier. She saw refugees fight to get through the gates only to get whipped and trampled on; she watched women drop their children over the spiked fence and get beaten back themselves; she handled babies "until my arms ached, dirty, half-dead babies covered with scurvy, sucking at their mothers' empty breasts." She saw a young boy fall from the quay and drown, with no one except his mother taking notice. She noted that when refugees were found to have died, their bodies were simply toppled into the sea.[183]

Several witnesses (Sheridan included) described the "systematic" robbery that took place at each barrier.[184] Powell pointed out that the looting was so widespread that eventually most of the refugees had been stripped of everything before they even got to the gates. Certainly if they had anything left by then, they lost it at those barriers.

Occasionally, a Turkish officer's approach would stop the looting. Powell, for example, reported seeing a Turkish officer beat a soldier so fiercely that his cane broke, so Powell loaned him his.[185] However, Lovejoy found a similar performance on the part of a Turkish officer a bit "too emphatic." After this officer got on the case of a Turkish soldier for looting (in the presence of the Americans), she kept watching until the officer walked further down the pier, casually stopped an old man ripe for the picking, led him away, and robbed the man himself, "incidentally giving an impressive demonstration" of thoroughness.[186]

Nevertheless, the doctor thought the worst thing happening at those "infernal gates" of the Smyrna pier, the "greatest crime against humanity with which I am personally familiar," was the separation of families. "As family after family passed those gates, the father of perhaps 42 years of age, carrying a sick child or other burden, or a young son, and sometimes both father and son, would be seized. . . . In a frenzy of grief, the mother and children would cling to this father and son, weeping, begging and praying for mercy, but there was no mercy. With the butts of their guns, the Turkish soldiers beat these men backward into the prison groups and drove the women toward the ships." Once, at Lieutenant Commander Rhodes' request, a Turkish officer relented and allowed the brother of some beautiful girls (who spoke perfect English) to pass through the gates to safety, and then accommodated Lovejoy's plea for another young fellow. But those were the only exceptions among many hundreds of separations. Lovejoy reported that the biblical prophecy, "Their wives shall be widows and their children orphan" had been fulfilled on the Smyrna railroad pier.[187]

A few Greek men recognized that they could not get through the Turkish barriers and determined to try another method. One evening, apparently the only night that refugees were taken aboard the Greek ships after dark, Sheridan watched while Turks standing right alongside both British and American naval officers began shooting at two swimmers caught in the cone of a searchlight; the swimmers were making for a warship in the harbor. The water was very smooth, and everyone ashore stood spellbound. There was no noise, no screaming. The shots at first went wide, but the splashes got closer and closer. Then one of the swimmers stopped swimming. At that point, Commander Powell protested and offered to send a boat to pick up any swimmers. Because America was neutral, he said he neither could take them to the British destroyers nor to the Turks, so he would land them back on the quay. The Turks agreed, and the spectacle ended—though not the desperation.[188]

The day after the shooting of the swimmer described above, Lovejoy accompanied a woman who was in labor to the door of one of the few buildings still standing, and after pounding insistently, they were let in. The place was full of troubled people, all terrified of the Turks. The doctor tended to the expectant mother, but as she was leaving, a woman took her upstairs and showed her several young men "lying flat on their chests looking out through peepholes under the eaves."[189] Knowing they could not pass the Turkish guards at the gates, the men were measuring the watery gauntlet they would shortly have to brave. Their mothers were in anguish after witnessing the terrible drama of the preceding night. The woman asked Lovejoy to help.

But the doctor knew she could do nothing, despite knowing what Sheridan also would admit, that for most, this terrible separation of males from their families was permanent. After all, that was what deportation in Turkey had always meant, particularly for Greek and Armenian men: "a short life sentence to slavery under brutal masters, ended by mysterious death."[190] And of course it meant this still, for it was far less likely now (given the Nationalist triumph) than it had even been before that a disinterested European or American force would interfere in the interior of Turkey. The inaction of all those ships in the harbor proved that.

And failing outside interference, who in Anatolia itself was going to stop the long-ingrained privileges of loot, rape, and slaughter after a victory? Not commanders like Noureddin Pasha, who made it very clear he could not have cared less, nor Mustapha Kemal, either, who had earlier okayed the Pontus deportations (or at least helped cover them up) and who was heard to utter, when Smyrna was in flames, "Let it burn, let it crash down."[191] It is possible that Kemal might have wanted to stop the killings and he might have preferred to stop the fire, too, but he would have been powerless against public feeling that had been aroused by all the years of the war, by all the burning Turkish villages, and by the relentless Turkish propaganda the Nationalists had themselves promoted for years. Beyond that, he was already about other things: elements of his army were already streaming toward the Dardanelles.

—◆◆—

Nevertheless, thanks in great part to YMCA workers like Asa Jennings (above all); relief workers like Major Davis, H. C. Jaquith, and Esther Lovejoy; Commander Halsey Powell; and (especially) all the American sailors and officers present on their ships and ashore in Smyrna's streets and piers, during these final days a magnificent evacuation did take place. In the week following the arrival of the first ten of Jennings' ships, nearly two hundred thousand ethnic Christians were taken away from Smyrna proper. Most of these refugees would survive to begin life again in Greece. Jennings kept the Greek ships coming; Powell did the necessary coordination between officials; American sailors tended the refugees on the piers and shepherded them toward the ships; and, well separated from contact with the Turks, British sailors helped the refugees board those same vessels. Through the whole three weeks of the crisis, America had the only relief committee working in Smyrna (again, they had been sent by Bristol even before the fire), and, by providing food and water and medical help, the relief workers helped keep most of the women and children and old men alive till their embarkation. That American "mascot" from the British aristocracy got her hands dirty too. And Bristol's long-term policy of neutrality certainly had at least this good effect: the Turks trusted the Americans to supervise the pier side of the embarkation and to provide the Greek ships protective escort in and out of Smyrna's famous harbor.

On September 30, a few hours before the Turks' fearful deadline (which at the last minute was extended), the great evacuation from Smyrna itself was completed. The massive expulsion of Christian minorities from Turkey, however, had just begun.

CHAPTER 11

THE EXPULSION OF THE MINORITIES
AND CONSTANTINOPLE'S LAST FLING

*The holocaust at Smyrna marked the beginning of a general exodus of
the Christian people from Asiatic Turkey. With one accord, they fled to the
nearest ports in a frenzy of fear.*

—Dr. Esther Lovejoy

*Constantinople is certainly the gayest place I have ever seen. They never
turn in here. The dizzy pace keeps up all night long.*

—Ens. Dan Gallery

W hile swimming to a warship might get you *out* of Turkey, it could
also get you *to* the place. At the request of Admiral Bristol upon
the Turkish threat to Constantinople itself (the threat posed by
movements by the Turkish Nationalist army toward the old Ottoman capital even
before the Smyrna crisis had ended), the Navy ordered twelve more destroyers
to Turkey in late September of 1922. At Norfolk, all sorts of bluejackets sought
to go on the ships.

A man named Christenson was suffering in sick bay on a repair ship when
he heard that his destroyer had been ordered east, and immediately he got up
to swab the decks. A doctor ordered him back to bed. The next morning he
was found polishing the sick bay's brass, but once more the doctor was unim-
pressed. That night, Christenson went over the side, swam to the *Bainbridge* and
hid himself in a cold boiler till his destroyer was well out to sea.[1] With similar
alacrity, even as multitudes desperately fled Turkey, over the next several weeks
American destroyermen and journalists alike jumped at the chance to get to
the place.[2] In no other period was the mixture of tragedy and playground
so pronounced.

— ◆◆◆ —

The journalists came first, most of them arriving just now at the threat to Constantinople. Sent from Paris by the *Toronto Star*, Ernest Hemingway arrived on September 30 to a city hung with red Turkish flags, menaced by large Turkish armies, and finding its ethnic Greeks evacuating in the tens of thousands. In several articles, including one headlined "Waiting for an Orgy,"[3] Hemingway reported that even those Greeks who had decided to stay were arming and talking desperately. Their fear, he noted, was "sickening, cold, crawling." In contrast, newly arrived correspondents like himself were feeling the thrill of a pitcher stepping onto the mound in a world series game. They hoped to find some great stories.[4]

Hemingway was not venturing far from his hotel to get them, though. Palavering at the restaurants and nightclubs, he hit it off, among others, with Charles Sweeney, a soldier of fortune on assignment for the *New York World*. Sweeney is said to have supplied some facts to Hemingway when the latter writer contracted malaria, and he also wrote articles of his own. Yet according to Sweeney's biographer, while in Constantinople he was mainly working as a spy for the French, providing yet another example of a reporter bent on something less than simple, impartial journalism.[5] Hemingway's own professional conduct while on this assignment was also problematic. Besides writing for the *Toronto Star*, he was sending some cables on the sly to the International News Service, thus violating his exclusive contract with the Canadian paper.[6]

Also in the city and attending American and British news conferences (and, one hopes, just doing their own work) were Constantine Brown of the *Chicago Daily News*, James A. Mills of the Associated Press, Carl von Wiegand for the Hearst newspapers, and representatives of the *New York Times* and United Press.[7] As for John Clayton of the *Chicago Tribune*, in order to celebrate a $2,000 bonus from the newspaper's publisher that he had received for the story he wrote about Smyrna's fires (which, as we have seen, he had actually written while at Athens), about the 1st of October Clayton put on a swank dinner for those reporters and naval officers who had stayed on at Smyrna when he took a ship out of the place. At a craps game afterward, his comrades shared further in the writer's good fortune by relieving him of some of it.[8]

While Hemingway and other newsmen whiled away the time in the city, some ersatz reporters were out in the field. At the very end of September, Turkish authorities at Smyrna invited Cdr. Halsey Powell to send some Americans into the interior along with three European journalists, a few Turkish writers, and a Turkish movie man. They were to ride a train under Turkish escort along the route of the retreating Greek army, looking to document how the Greeks in their retreat had ravaged the Turks.[9] Powell sent Lt. (jg) E. B. Perry of the *Edsall*. By naval arrangement (no doubt Bristol's), this young officer was to be a correspondent for the *New York Herald*.

— ◆◆◆ —

In his official report, Perry expressed skepticism about the Greek atrocities that were being spoken of at every stop. Though the burning of "acres" of cities that the group traveled through was authentic enough, at Manemen and Magnesia the party heard and saw no real evidence of atrocities beyond that. To Perry it appeared to be a "propaganda trip, well laid out and all of the actors coached in their various parts." Similarly at Cassaba and Alashehr: there was evidence of catastrophic fire and maybe an unidentified body or two, but only unverified accounts of raping and looting and killing and such. "We were still looking for concrete evidence and were not finding it."

Finally, though, after they started retracing their steps, at a burned town called "Salikli" (Salihli), the group was presented with several dozen witnesses whose translated stories of shootings, rapings, beatings, beheadings, and lootings performed by Greek soldiers upon Turkish civilians they could not help but believe. These stories tipped the scale for Perry. Although he had originally been anti-Turk, and still had no doubts that the trip had been arranged for Turkish propaganda, he now thought the Turks had a good case that should be told to the world.[10] Admiral Bristol heard from Perry and later listened to Mark Prentiss, who had also taken this trip, and concluded that, beyond the widespread burning, there was some evidence of Greek atrocity, although nothing "on a wholesale scale." The main problem was that thousands of Turks were now homeless with winter approaching. Later, Bristol would regularly use the figure of half a million Turkish homeless.[11]

During the same week that Perry and Prentiss were on their Turkish propaganda trip, one more evacuation episode was even then taking place on the Aegean coast of Turkey, an evolution that, except for a story picked up secondhand by a journalist in Athens, went almost wholly unreported (and apparently completely unobserved) by the press. As he completed the evacuations at Smyrna, Asa Jennings warned that great numbers of additional refugees had assembled at nearby cities and villages, and that many of them were starving.[12] Hence, beginning on September 29 and 30, Jennings' ships were ordered to various smaller ports, under escort of the American destroyer *MacLeish*.

At a place called Vurla Skala, the five transports that *MacLeish* was accompanying began evacuating ten thousand refugees. As these women and children were marched down to the docks by Turkish soldiers, according to *MacLeish*'s captain, Cdr. Herbert Ellis, "the usual raping went on," until a Turkish officer stationed a strong guard to stop it. All these refugees were in very bad shape. Fifty of them died right on the beach, for instance, and others succumbed during the embarkation or upon boarding the transports. At another port, Chesme, the refugees had been kept in churches and fed by the Turks, and conditions were better. At Aivali, though, despite the wretched condition of another 15,000 Greek refugees, the Turks had kept them inland for several days, well out of sight of the coast. When they were finally released for evacuation (after systematic looting), the separation of men from the women was especially pitiable. Forced to leave her husband behind, for instance, a lone woman with quadruplets boarded a ship with two babies under each arm.

The vessels *MacLeish* escorted would eventually evacuate over 27,000 refugees from ports other than Smyrna, but Ellis still shook his head, thinking they were not accomplishing much. He was convinced that many more Greeks along these coasts were dying, for Turkish officials admitted to him a policy of deporting their coastal populations. "It is a strange thing that civilized nations do not protest against this making non-combatants [into] prisoners of war," he further lamented. Ellis argued that such criminalizing of noncombatants and the associated deportations were "savage practices." Hence, the Turks should be forced to *stop it all* before anybody treated them as equals by sitting at conference with them.[13] Ignoring such niceties, the Allies were already conferencing with the Turks at Mudania, a small city on the Sea of Marmara.

The enterprising John Clayton "scraped and bribed his way" into the Mudania conference, though journalists were not supposed to be allowed.[14] Actually, despite the blackout, even an American journalist back at Constantinople got a scoop about the Mudania agreement. Hemingway's later story in the *Toronto Star* shows the Constantinople-based correspondent hard at work.

> Constan stayed up all night. Every big newspaper story that broke came after midnight in the nightclubs of Pera. It was in one of these, the Pele Mele . . . that an excited young officer just back on a destroyer from Mudania confided the news of the signing of the armistice to a Russian countess who was acting as a waitress.
>
> The officer, who was present at the signing, told the countess in greatest secrecy because he had to tell someone. He was so excited. She recognized the value of the story and told an American newspaperman whom she liked much better than she did the officer.
>
> In an hour, through means of his own, the newspaperman verified the report, and put it on the cable to New York.[15]

Clearly, the long hours of eating, drinking, and befriending titled Russian wait-resses (from one of whom, by the way, Hemingway bought an antique amber necklace for his wife)[16] had their journalistic uses.

Among the more important provisions of that Mudania armistice was the decision that Eastern Thrace (the area along the Aegean just to the west of Constantinople), ceded to the Greeks in 1920, was to be returned to the Turks. The Greek army would have to leave within a month. At word of this, Hemingway and several other reporters finally got out to the site of some action. There, they found hundreds of thousands of ethnic Greeks frantically abandoning their cultivated fields and fleeing the Turks, even though Greek civilians were not required to leave the country. "If asked where they are going, they shrug their shoulders. If one asks why they are going, they draw their right hand across their throats," a British journalist explained.[17]

The Thracian exodus was comparatively well covered by the press, which was present in numbers there as it seldom was anywhere else. Journalists noted that since the Greek army was doing the herding in Thrace rather than Turks, the ethnic Greek peasants were not being robbed and separated. Yet, as Hemingway pointed out, because the main stream of refugees was far from the coast, on this journey typically there was no welcome succor from America's Near East Relief.[18] Nor were any American naval vessels nearby, American lives not being at risk. In the end, Western Thrace could not hold these three or four hundred thousand peasants, and most of them eventually were dumped by transports down into Greece.

Although he kept some of the more powerful details he observed for his fiction (for his portrait of the retreat from Caporetto in *A Farewell to Arms*), Hemingway described this exodus well. Indeed, all of his journalistic accounts about Constantinople are interesting and provide good "local color." However, partly because the writer spent such a short time in Constantinople and never got near Turkey's interior, his *Toronto Daily Star* journalism does not go very deep. In fact, his stories get the reader little further toward real historical under-standing than the broad generality he penned on the authority of a few days in the city, some bar conversation, and a few military press conferences, at least one of which, significantly, had been given by Bristol himself. Indeed, the admiral himself might have penned what Hemingway wrote then: "The fact is that atrocities are always followed by counter-atrocities in these countries and have been since the siege of Troy."[19]

Besides journalists, a host of additional officers and sailors soon swelled the numbers of Americans in Constantinople. The twelve additional destroyers from Norfolk, greeted by waving sheets and pillowcases and whistling and cheering as they steamed by America's Robert College,[20] arrived on October 22, adding over twelve hundred destroyermen to the region. Another 650–700 men and officers came aboard the two naval support ships (the repair ship *Denebola* and the stores ship *Bridge*), which arrived about the same time as the destroyers and which stayed moored in the Bosporus for nearly a year.[21] And after the armored cruiser *Pittsburgh* dropped anchor in mid-November, its 680 sailors remained at Constantinople for almost six months.[22] So, although several of the newly arrived destroyers were immediately ordered on to Russian or Anatolian ports, every day hundreds of additional American Navy men enthusiastically flooded Pera's already-crowded streets.

Meanwhile, throughout Anatolia, Greeks and Armenians were also flooding the coastal cities, but of course with a very different temper. Turkish authorities had now set a deadline of November 30 for permission for Christians in Anatolia to leave the country. In early November, Bristol would argue that much of the resulting panic was the fault of the Christians, for he did not understand the Turkish "permission" for Greeks and Armenians to leave ports in the Black Sea to mean that the Christian population had been ordered to leave.[23]

In fact, of course, it meant exactly that. On the ground at Samsun, Cdr. Harry Pence had the following "definitive" understanding: that the evacuation was not compulsory, but all Christians remaining as of December 1 would suffer the penalty of deportation![24] According to NER cables, everywhere in Anatolia the Turkish invitation was considered "a massacre and evacuation order," and it initiated "the wildest scenes" of hysteria and terror among the Christian populace. Relief officials anticipated that virtually all the remaining Christians in Anatolia would, at best, be forced to leave the country.

They were already streaming toward the ports. By November 14 some ten thousand refugees had reached the shores of the Black Sea, and thousands more were within two days' march of Samsun. All the males were still being detained, a NER telegram said; the refugees were, again, mainly women, children, and old men.[25] On Turkey's southern border, things were much the same. At the end of November, Consul Jackson reported that 35,000 refugees had arrived at Aleppo from the Turkish interior, having been coerced both by the "permission" orders from Angora and by widespread threats uttered by individual Turks or printed in Turkish newspapers. Jackson added that since none of these refugees had been allowed to sell anything of value, practically all were destitute.[26] As another observer commented, the circumstances of such deportees typically included "leaving homes in midwinter, hasty flight, arduous road for many days or weeks, with danger and terror all the time." No wonder these mostly igno-rant villagers started the long journey with their morale thoroughly broken and proved easy prey to disease, plunder, and abuse while en route.[27]

By late November, a conference was being held in Lausanne, Switzerland. to settle problems between the Europeans and the triumphant Nationalists. Bristol was among the American delegation (to the despair of American mis-sionary leaders there, who were still concerned about the Armenians), and back in Constantinople, Bristol's substitute, Frederick Dolbeare, was cabling the State Department that, despite anyone's wishes, throughout Anatolia "the evacuation is becoming more of a fait accompli every day."[28] These "unilateral expulsions"[29] of the Turkish minorities are not to be confused with the widely used term "exchange of populations." The latter was an expedient agreed on at Lausanne that directed the exchange of ethnic Christian minorities in Turkey and ethnic Turkish populations in Greece. The measure was largely the result of urgings of explorer and humanitarian Fridtjof Nansen, who hoped to mitigate the terrible conditions of refugee multitudes. Signed in mid-1923, it was only actually executed (and then only partially) in 1924. By that time, of course, except for detained males, the vast majority of Christian minorities in Turkey had long since been forced to leave their ancestral homes for Greece.[30]

Beginning in October, at Bristol's orders the American destroyers cooper-ated with Asa Jennings, who now sent his Greek ships throughout the Turkish littoral to effect further evacuations. The naval ships mainly acted in a liai-son role, though this was important enough, to be sure; no doubt the coor-dination and presence of the American Navy ships and officers in the Turkish ports helped saved many thousands of refugee lives. Moreover, Bristol kept his enlarged contingent of destroyers circulating from port to port, even to the smallest ones.

—◆◆◆—

As a result of this mass movement, for months there were continuing huge contrasts between the high life being led by American Navy people and oth-ers in Constantinople, and the awful conditions they and other Americans encountered among the refugees in Asia Minor. A series of examples will illus-trate these contrasts.

Some of the examples recorded below are severe, to be sure, and one might object both that many Americans did not participate in the good times described, and, more important, that by no means all the refugees suffered to the extent that the Anatolian examples reported below might suggest.[31] There would be some truth in such an argument. Some ethnic Greeks and Armenian refugees—the women, children, and old men, that is—made it directly to the coast and were evacuated pretty quickly. However, not a few refugees died on their journeys, which usually were suddenly imposed treks of whole families (minus able-bodied men) of tens, fifties, or even hundreds of miles, and this in early or mid-winter. Actually one historian of the exchange of populations estimates that *tens of thousands* of ethnic Greeks died in the expulsion from Turkey or because of it.[32] Moreover, huge numbers were abused (beaten or raped), most of the million or so Greeks and Armenians expelled were robbed more than once while en route (at the portside gates, if not before; just as at Smyrna, so at other ports the American Navy men mostly could only stand by and watch), and virtually all property owners lost their homes and other properties without compensation.

As for the many tens of thousands of minority males who were detained by the Turks, almost all of them noncombatants, Dobkin says that by October of 1923, most of the males had perished, basing her judgment in part on the awful circumstances described by three Armenian males who had survived being taken inland, with whom she conducted interviews in the late 1960s.[33] More recently, parts of the autobiography of noted Greek author Elias Venezis on his labor battalion experiences have been translated from Greek into English. Venezis was taken inland from Aivali (a coastal town to the north of Smyrna, mentioned above), and with his fellow prisoners he underwent such horrific suffering that, if one regards his reported experiences as authentic, it would not be surprising at all that only twenty-three of the three thousand males taken from Aivali in his group survived until the actual population exchange—which is what the Greek author claims.[34]

Such reference to isolated personal accounts from ethnic Greek and Armenian sources might seem idiosyncratic. However, on this same topic, besides referring to past experience of minority male prisoners in Turkish hands for probabilities (both the experiences of ethnic Armenians in 1915, and in other circumstances like those recounted throughout this book), one can also listen to contemporaneous estimates expressed by Admiral Bristol and by Fridtjof Nansen himself. According to Bristol's war diary account of October 12, 1922, in a conversation involving several high Allied officials, Nansen expressed his opinion that if all the Greek men in labor battalions were not released immediately, few would be left by the spring—that is, the spring of 1923. "This was tacitly agreed to by everyone," Admiral Bristol recorded, "because we all know that the Turks treat prisoners and labor battalions abominably, even if their own people are in the labor battalions." However, under the exchange of prisoners that Nansen negotiated, very few of these detainees were actually released until 1924.[35]

That one's being in a labor battalion in essence amounted to "a death sentence" would no doubt have been the opinion of Greek shipping magnate Aristotle Onassis. Although there are several differing accounts of how Onassis got out of Smyrna (being a Smyrna native of Greek heritage of about eighteen, he was in the greatest danger), perhaps one of the more likely was the account of biographer Peter Evans. He says Onassis was protected from death by a Turkish lieutenant who became the young man's lover. Several weeks after the fire, when things had calmed down a bit, an American vice consul spirited Onassis out to *Edsall* in sailor's garb, and the destroyer took Onassis on to Mytilene. The young man eventually was able to join the women of his family in Greece. In this account, even despite the Turkish officer's and then the American official's help, it had been a close thing. At one point, Onassis had to climb into a large rolltop desk to hide from a Turkish search party, lest he also be sent to the doomed labor battalions, or instead be hanged—which had been the fate of three of his uncles.[36]

Given such circumstances, I would argue that the severity indicated by the following sets of contrasting examples is historically representative.

—◆◆◆—

Consider, to begin with, the general style of the Navy's good times in Constantinople versus what Americans saw in Anatolia, including the general atmosphere, the food and drink consumed, and the treatment of women.

When they first went ashore from the newly anchored *Pittsburgh* on November 16, 1922, the junior officers found the place spectacular. They were dazzled by the nightclubs, the Russian sword dancing, the beautiful Russian waitresses, the great music, and the late hours, all this despite the ubiquitous refugees and the rumors of Nationalist guns being placed (at that very moment) on the Asiatic side of the Bosporus! Of course, helping to fund the high spirits was all the good food and drink. At places like the Muscovite, for instance, you could get an excellent dinner and French champagne, besides a floor show.[37] At all the nightclubs, Scotch and soda simply "flowed like water." Seeing all this, Dan Gallery was convinced that "not even Paris hits as gay a clip."[38]

It is true that a number of American sailors (like sailors from the beginning of time) took advantage of the vice district and streetwalkers, thus often exploiting women of many races, who, desperate for sustenance, had turned to this trade as a last resort. Still, some sailors had genuine feelings for their women, and not a few Americans, officer and enlisted, were romantically inclined. Lt. Cy Olch of the *Pittsburgh* would meet a charming young Russian woman named Ileana Shillenkoff. Then working at an American orphanage in

Constantinople, Shillenkoff had once been a dispatch rider for a White Russian cavalry regiment. Olch and Ileana would marry when they met again in Nice.[39]

In fact, marriages took place throughout the Navy ranks. On the *Goff*— one of the twelve destroyers that arrived in October—a Filipino mess attendant was found to have married a Greek girl after a brief courtship, even though neither spoke the other's language.[40] And before that same squadron's cruise was over, its very squadron commander had married a Russian waitress ("Olga #2") from the Muscovite, the woman "who had kept him up so late so many nights in the past year." Captain C. M. Tozer (a rather august, white-headed personage, according to photographs) would take Olga home with him.[41]

To such good times and romance in the city, on the mainland Americans found several terrible contrasts. From Mersina on the Mediterranean coast of Turkey, for instance, *McCormick* passed along a message that had reached it from an American relief official named Joseph Beach. Beach worked at Caesarea (Kaysari), far inland. He wrote that on November 19 seven hundred Greek women and children had arrived at his relief station, having been deported from villages near Smyrna (over *four hundred miles* west of Caesarea as the crow flies) several weeks before. These people were the remnant of an original group of four thousand deportees. Early on during their trek, the men had been separated out and had not been heard from since; the women and children had been driven along through winter weather without food or shelter. "Their condition may be judged from the following facts," Beach said. "One of our American women brought in to our hospital with a truck twenty-nine who had fallen out on the road and had been left to die. . . . Of these two died before they reached the hospital. . . . Fourteen died in the following ten days. . . . They all cried for bread and suffered the most terrible pain." Beach said there were other groups in a similar state.[42]

In mid-October, Bristol had written a friend that some of the Greeks and Armenians at the time of the Smyrna crisis were said to have been marched inland, but he believed that these people had afterward found their way back to the coast and been evacuated.[43] Hence it was inconvenient to hear via *McCormick* of actual deportations from Smyrna, and he attempted to get this message discounted.

And consider the treatment of refugee women at Mersina. Cdr. Bruce Ware of *Overton*, like most officers who took their lead from the admiral, was originally strongly pro-Turk. However, in the process of evacuating refugees at this coastal city, Ware came to learn of such a series of kidnapping and gang rapes of female refugees (along with brutality, graft, killings, threats, and official obstruction) that his outlook toward the Turks reversed itself. Sometimes three men had committed the rape, sometimes seven; the rapes had typically continued all night. Those who committed these acts included Turkish soldiers and local Arab or Turkish police. From personal observation, Ware cabled to Bristol that the condition of the victims being cared for was "pitiful, comma horrible," and that the whole refugee situation was "critical and frightful."[44] In his war diary entry for the admiral, he made this statement: "I must enter and go on record here in naming the Turk, the Arab from the Mutasarriff and the most well to do man to the little ragged boy on the street, as savages and barbarians; cruel and pitiless. I have frequently read and listened to tales of atrocities committed by Mohammedans; during the past week I have seen them, and it has turned me completely in my sentiments from pro-Turk. It is impossible to place any trust or sincerity in these people. . . . Exclusion from the world; from all social privilege or favor is his due." Just nine days earlier, Ware had verbally belabored two American women relief workers newly arrived at Smyrna from Harput with five hundred orphans. He had lectured them about their evident intense hatred of the Turks. Now Commander Ware had come to feel the same disgust.[45]

——◆◆◆——

A second contrast of American highlife and refugee predicament involves two roughly parallel experiences of young men boarding a ship.

In the wee hours one night in Constantinople, Dan Gallery and his friend, Ash Pleasants, returned to Dolmabagtche landing in a carriage, after a smashing evening in the bars of Galata. As they rode down the hills, just for kicks they took their canes and knocked off every fez they encountered. Naturally enough, at the boat landing they were apprehended by a band of irate Turkish policemen who roughed them up a bit. Eventually, Gallery was loaded into a caique, which was to take him out to his cruiser *Pittsburgh*. Before the boat left the pier, however, the offended Gallery found a boathook lying in the small vessel and slashed at the Turkish sergeant back on the dock with it, forgetting that the boatman was also Turkish. Suddenly, Gallery found himself on his back in the stern sheets of the caique with a knife poised an inch from his throat. Gallery was hauled back to the dock and beaten up some more. Finally, he was released, and allowed to proceed out to his ship.

At the time, Gallery was shaken and angry (not badly hurt, apparently), but later he would delight in retelling this story, typically omitting to mention any offense he had given to the Turks in the first place. It became a simple account of youth and high jinks.[46]

In contrast to this carefree, if mildly irresponsible, episode is the story of the escape of Efthim Couzinos from Turkey. Unlike Gallery's adventure, here lives were very much at stake.

We last saw Couzinos hiding (like Jews evading the Nazis during the Holocaust) in a hole under the floor of the kitchen of the Marsovan College infirmary. He had entered this hiding place in July of 1921. In October and November of 1922, however, upon the perceived ultimatum for Christians to leave Anatolia, the Americans at Marsovan began moving their orphans by *arabas* (carriage) down to Samsun for further evacuation on a transport ship. En route to the city they would pass ethnic Greeks and Armenians who had been walking for days or weeks. At twenty-three, Couzinos was right smack in the "military-aged" population of males forbidden to leave Turkey. Rising from the dead in the infirmary, he tried to disguise his features, but he was still desperately worried that somebody in the crowd of Turks at the college gate would notice him. A newly arrived American relief worker named George Williams learned that some endangered young men were among the students being transported. Riding beside Couzinos' *arabas* as it left the college gate, he flourished a pistol and kept shouting "American property" in Turkish. In such a way he successfully distracted the crowd's attention.[47] Williams was not the only relief worker to help, by the way. Gertrude Anthony rode horseback back and forth alongside a group of endangered Marsovan orphans the whole two days' travel to the coast.[48]

Once at Samsun, the students had to walk two by two from the American orphanage down to the wharf, where large caiques would ferry them to an anchored freighter. (American destroyers seem to have been present at most of these evacuations,[49] but the Americans' observation, coordination, or occasional escort function seems everywhere to have depended on their allowing the Turks to manage things all the way up to the ships themselves.) At the end of each platform on the wharf stood a Turkish gendarme, whose job was to arrest any draft-aged males among the refugees. Though Couzinos tried to slouch by, he suddenly felt a huge hand on his collar and heard the man say (in Turkish), "Where do you think you're going?" He was hauled out of the line of orphans and ordered to stand next to the Turk. He did so for maybe thirty seconds. But when the official stepped away into the crowd of orphans to apprehend another unfortunate fellow, Couzinos leaped into a half-full caique, crawled to the bottom of it, and got some boys to sit on him. Somehow the gendarme failed to notice, and the caique soon cast off lines and took its passengers out to the American-chartered freighter. It had been, according to Couzinos, thirty seconds between life and death.[50]

—◆—

Finally, a third contrast between American good times and refugee trouble was sometimes seen even in Anatolia's ports. During the months after the fire and evacuation at Smyrna, several nations kept a duty warship or two in the harbor, and the equanimity of the American destroyermen there (many of them new to Turkey since the fire) was only occasionally interrupted by reminders of the earlier sufferings. Even during Smyrna's agony, the great warships had kept up their luncheons and formal calls and military flourishes, and Navy bands had played concerts far into the early morning.[51] Now American officers at this same place were kept busy returning formal calls in frock coats or cocked hats upon Dutch or Italian or French ships, playing bridge with Dutchmen and Belgians, and playing tennis with French or British officers either at a French club that was still standing or at an undamaged Swedish court across the harbor that had been appropriated by the British. Despite its horrible past, for the American Navy Smyrna had quickly become, as one destroyer captain remembered, "a very pleasant little social colony."[52]

A few months later a fire would destroy a forty-two-room Armenian palazzo that the new American consul had made into a temporary consulate, and the drunken American tobacco men on hand would pass out bottles of whiskey to the sailors as they helped fight the fire. Unsurprisingly, the building became a total loss.[53] Back in November, though, liquor was scarce and things were more tame. For recreation, sometimes the Americans hiked to Mount Pagus, which overlooked the city. From there they could view both the burned and unburned sectors of the city, along with the famous quay and the harbor and the ancient Roman viaduct. At other times the sailors played baseball or haggled with shopkeepers in the Turkish bazaar, which had not been touched by the fire. The Americans also watched caravans of camels pass by and took photographs of some of the Greek prisoners who were still working in the city under guard. Renwick McIver, a junior officer in *Gilmer*, concluded in a letter home, "We have had quite an enjoyable stay here."[54]

When another destroyer took its place at Smyrna, however, McIver's destroyer had to transport some refugees who were still being collected by the local Near East Relief people out to Mytilene. According to the young officer, the 220 people they took aboard were a "miserable looking lot." The refugees were immensely relieved to get away—those that did get away, for eight of the fourteen men among the refugees were taken by the police as being of military age. The two separations McIver himself witnessed, of a boy from his dad, and of a dignified older man well over forty-five from his grief-stricken wife, were, again, emotionally wrenching. When the destroyer got under way, the sea was choppy, the wind was cold, and it rained. Most of the refugees were topside and were now seasick as well as homeless, and quite pitiable. The bluejackets initially took great delight in tending the unfortunates, passing out hot soup and coffee and giving the children candy. Some sailors gave up their own blankets and raincoats to the poor people. When the ship reached Mytilene, however, the refugees pushed and shoved and became so obsessed with fear that the Americans lost patience. As McIver put it, "We were glad to get rid of the whole jabbering lot."[55]

An epilogue to this particular evacuation at Smyrna manifests the occasional callousness of naval commanders. A Greek cook working for the American YMCA ashore, where the sailors got coffee and donuts, had been hiding her nephew, a young Greek soldier who had escaped from a Turkish prison camp. She persuaded some American sailors to bring a sailor's uniform ashore, dress her nephew in it, and smuggle him up *Gilmer's* brow. The destroyer's officer of the deck saw the Greek fellow come aboard among a group of sailors, and he called the captain to the quarterdeck. The Greek man fell on his knees and begged the captain not to give him back to the Turks.

Back in 1921, at Samsun, an exhausted fourteen-year-old Greek boy had swum to *Sturtevant* to attempt to get food and help for fellow Greeks. Told of the incident, Capt. Bill Leahy of *St. Louis* (then at the port) recognized that if the Navy kept the boy and the Turks heard of it, it might jeopardize American negotiations for the safety of the Greek women and children at Samsun. However, he also knew that the boy would likely be shot as a spy should he be given up. So Leahy ordered him to be dressed as a sailor and taken aboard his own ship. The lad was fed well and was secretly made an honorary member of the crew. It appears he was safely put ashore in Constantinople.[56]

In Smyrna, however, Commander Zogbaum of *Gilmer* had a different outlook. Apparently nobody ashore had taken notice of the Greek soldier being brought aboard. Still, because "all our evacuation of Turkey's enemies had been by arrangement with the Turkish authorities," according to Zogbaum—though of course Turkish officials were causing the expulsions of its own citizens in the first place—Zogbaum considered it a "point of honor" to hand the young man over. Did the captain know the likely consequence? He did. As he reported the stowaway to the Turkish captain of the port, Zogbaum made this noteworthy comment: "If you have to shoot this man please don't do it in the presence of my men."[57]

—◆◆◆—

As a counterbalance to Zogbaum's disgusting act, let us cite one other destroyer captain's unquestionable heroism at about the same time, the only significant episode of its kind through four years of American naval involvement in Turkey.

On the early morning of December 16, 1922, the destroyer *Bainbridge* was in the Sea of Marmara heading toward Constantinople when its officer of the watch noticed a flash of light astern of a vessel off to starboard. Steaming closer, the bridge watch saw that the ship (it turned out to be the French military transport *Vinh Long*) was aflame, with smoke billowing out of its after hatch, boats getting ready to lower, and a varied mass of people milling the decks. *Bainbridge's* skipper, Lt. Cdr. W. Atlee Edwards, ordered his fire and rescue boats away, and then directed that *Bainbridge* itself be brought near the French ship. On approach, he strained to hear the French captain speaking to him through a voice hailer, but then the vessel's after mast was blown skyward with a terrific roar. At about the same time, one of his boats brought a semihysterical fellow back from the transport who was shouting that the French ship was loaded with powder and that if the American destroyer remained close by they would all be blown to bits.

Edwards decided to attempt a rescue anyway. He ordered his ship taken alongside the French vessel and quickly had some lines put over. Then the fire reached *Vinh Long's* after magazine. Another great explosion parted all the lines

Bainbridge (its pilot house seen at right) approaches the burning French transport *Vinh Long* in the Sea of Marmara. The destroyer would rescue the crew and nearly five hundred passengers. *Thomas Kinkaid collection, The Naval History and Heritage Command*

and flung the vessels a ship-length apart, swinging the stern of the *Bainbridge* perpendicular to the *Vinh Long*. Almost thrown to the deck by the concussion, everyone on the bridge of *Bainbridge* was momentarily rendered blind and speechless. When Edwards came to himself, he saw hundreds of people gathered on the forecastle of the French ship.

How could he position his vessel alongside the transport long enough to board the refugees? Edwards' expedient was both unique and dangerous. He determined to ignore any potential damage to *Bainbridge* and its crew (and to his own career) by *ramming* the French vessel, hoping thereby to wedge his ship's bow into the transport, and at the same time maybe flood that ship, thereby stopping the fire. Warning his crew and those aboard the *Vinh Long*, he backed *Bainbridge* a hundred yards, then ordered full steam ahead, directing the helmsman to aim between the ship's bow and its superstructure. The destroyer's bow crunched violently into the transport, with great shrieks of tearing metal, and locked the two ships together. Edwards' maneuver had succeeded. A hurried transfer began over the destroyer's bow, and within twenty minutes Edwards was told that all those who were living had been taken aboard.

Edwards backed away, saw that, fortunately, *Bainbridge* was itself in no danger of sinking, and in the early light turned attention to completing the rescue of the scores of passengers who had leaped over the *Vinh Long*'s side. Then he got up steam toward Constantinople. When he moored to Navy Buoy 2 off Dolmabagtche sometime later, the French admiral Dumesnil boarded from a boat and embraced Edwards on the deck, kissing him on both cheeks. The *Bainbridge* had saved 482 of 495 men, women, and children, mainly dependents of French officers; they had been en route to Constantinople from Bizerte. For this action, Edwards was awarded the Medal of Honor by America, and the Legion of Honor by France.[58]

Chaplain William Maguire was serving in Bristol's Navy then. In a memoir, he would tell about reading the news of Edwards' sudden death one morning at breakfast in 1928. According to Maguire, when the officers in his fleet mess heard the news, they spontaneously delivered "the finest composite eulogy I have ever heard given to a fellow-man." Back in 1923 the chaplain had also admired the fact that Edwards was free of the cynicism about the refugees that possessed many Americans. In particular, Maguire had found that many Navy people damned all the refugees for the manipulativeness of a few, but Edwards continued to sympathize with the suffering Armenians.[59]

One of Edwards' young officers, however, put his ship's captain in a slightly different light, adding the Constantinople high-living touch. In a letter written a few months after the *Vinh Long* episode and just before *Bainbridge* returned home, Orin Haskell wrote that Edwards had become much smitten with an ex-Austrian countess and had recently outdone himself in entertaining the woman (no scandal, to be sure, just total admiration). The captain was "really branching out," Haskell considered, for he had recently invited a Russian prince, an Egyptian princess, and a son of the ex-sultan (besides his countess and other dignitaries) out to the ship for dinner. Moreover, Edwards was not only going to take the Russian prince back to the States, but also was planning to buy a Rolls Royce and carry it across the Atlantic on the destroyer's deck. "When we sail into New York with a prince in tow and ride up Broadway in his Rolls Royce," Haskell penned in amazement, "there will be nothing to [rival] it."[60]

———◆◆◆———

As more and more of the Greek and Armenian refugees were expelled from Anatolia, they finally came knocking on the very back door of what, for many Americans (not only the Navy people), was the grand nightclub of Constantinople.

The ones who arrived in the city came mainly from the Pontic ports. Refugees from Smyrna and points south typically sailed directly to Greece on getting away (maybe via Mytilene), and initially most refugee ships from Turkey's Black Sea coasts also steamed directly to Greece, bypassing the great city on the Bosporus. Then Greece filled up with maybe a million distressed, so many in fact that the Greek government in January told the relief groups temporarily to stop sending more.[61] Hence, in early 1923 many transports offloaded their burdens in Constantinople instead. In early March, Constantinople relief head Harold Jaquith described the circumstances.

> In the harbor crowded with twenty-one warships of seven different nations, are four refugee ships crammed with deportees from Asia Minor, who have waited for days to be landed. Ashore, at eleven different places along the Bosphorus, earlier arrivals are huddled together in windowless, doorless, leaky buildings under conditions beyond description. Afloat and ashore, smallpox, typhus, dysentery and pneumonia are unchecked. . . . Weakened by days of travel, by wagon and foot . . . these wretched people fall easy victims to disease. Many of those who survived their march of terror to the sea died on shipboard and 60 per cent of those who lived through the voyage on filthy, crowded ships, were diseased on arrival here.[62]

At one point there were over thirty thousand Anatolian refugees in the city.[63] Their condition was more than wretched. On one "death ship" in the harbor, Near East Relief personnel saw cases of "smallpox, typhoid, dysentery, pneumonia, and typhus lying a hundred in heaps together"; in this black hole, two hundred had died within three weeks' time.[64] Ashore, until the League of Nations lent its aid, the Greek refugee camp at San Stefano was said to harbor in old, broken-down barracks some twenty-five hundred refugees who were dying at the rate of forty to fifty per day.[65] And when Esther Lovejoy visited the Greek Hospital at Yedi Koule, the camp had been swamped with typhus to such a terrible degree that five of its Greek physicians had died from the disease, including the head of the hospital.[66]

However, by far the worst place of all was across in the suburb of Scutari, ironically at the very location where the nursing profession itself had been founded, that is, at Selimieh Barracks, site of Florence Nightingale's famous achievements. According to Lovejoy, the barracks there was the "worst pest-hole" she had ever seen. It was certainly the worst in the world at that time.[67] Here, ten thousand refugees (again, mainly women and children) suffered from typhus and also from smallpox. At the height of the epidemic a hundred and forty died per day, according to some estimates; others say three hundred a day.[68] Europeans and Americans were at first prevented by Turkish authorities from working here, with the natural result that, according to Doctor Lovejoy, the conditions were worse than anything even Nightingale herself had ever encountered. In early 1923 foreigners were finally allowed into the barracks (and into the stables, too, which itself housed a thousand refugees), to delouse this "colossal incubator of pestilence," clean up the reeking floors, and begin quarantine and feeding.[69]

American relief workers and missionaries were prominent among those risking their lives at Selimieh. Aided by a Turkish interpreter, two American doctors, Wilfred Post (from Konia and Smyrna) and Christopher Thurber (from Sivas), organized the relief efforts. Thurber, who himself had undergone a grave bout with typhus before coming from Sivas with its orphans, cheerily donned a nurse's white costume, put a pipe in his mouth, and began work again.[70] Fresh from trying to keep children alive in Marsovan and elsewhere in Anatolia, Ruth Compton sorted clothing for the refugees that had been sent from the States.[71] The outfit she wore, which featured a bag of mothballs at her neck to keep out the lice, perhaps helped ward off the disease. Two American doctors and a nurse got typhus here, but recovered. Henry Flint, cashier of the American Board in Constantinople, volunteered to run a feeding station, for, of course, here as everywhere Americans were providing bread, soup, potatoes, and rice, which helped save hundreds. Flint himself, however, got the germ and died.[72]

Heroic as these efforts were, their charitable impulse did not reach throughout the American community. This descent of Christian refugees from Turkey on Constantinople differed substantially from the earlier invasion of Russian masses, and not just because of the rampant diseases. The Anatolian refugees who actually stopped in Constantinople composed a much smaller group than the Russians had, for one thing. For another, rather than including many cultured Europeans, most of this new group of forlorn humanity were Turkish-speaking peasants from Asia, which meant they were generally much less interesting to the Europeans and Americans in the city. Moreover, many of the hundreds of thousands of refugees who had preceded this new group were still in the city. For such reasons, this new mass of diseased and dying unfortunates did not impose itself greatly on most Americans' conscience. As writer Bill Ellis commented, "Their fate . . . is outside the range of the ken and interest of the city and its visitors. Only the serious-minded few know or care."[73]

The sailors from the cruiser and destroyers were certainly not among the "serious-minded few." Though they did their Navy jobs well and were encouraged to contribute to the Red Cross, when they went ashore in the city it was not to visit the hospitals or refugee camps. The sailors who had done such a great job at Smyrna or Samsun or Mersina were now to be seen in crowded carriages singing and shouting, on their way to such places as "Dinty Moore's Place for American Sailors" or the "White Thrush." Captain Hepburn would speak of sailors rolling down the Pera and singing "Hail, hail, the gang's all here."[74] Esther Lovejoy's assessment was more sober, even bitter. Although Constantinople was "gay at night," it was also "ghastly in the morning," she noted. In particular, "Sailors on the rampage were common sights."[75]

Young officers probably partied even harder than the enlisted, for their money went further. Naval Academy classmates who had once caroused wildly in New York or Philadelphia now were delighted to discover each other in this astonishing Near Eastern city and to celebrate their renewed friendship at the Pele Mele or Muscovite or Rose Noire or Maxim's, Black Thomas's place being the favorite of all. If called to an official luncheon during the day, they obediently hauled "bricks" around the dance floor, but they were visibly upset if offered only tea to drink rather than spirits. In the evenings many got thoroughly spiked at newly found oases like the Oiseu Bleu or the Dutchmans, and then after dancing with the Russian waitresses or other young women, they got into fights and tore up the bars and walked off with pictures or potted plants.[76] Oil men and journalists remaining in the city frequently joined in the fun. Indeed, military and civilian alike often joined in the "Bosporus Club" too, that select group of revelers who managed somehow, while in their cups, to tumble into the sea.[77]

Even one destroyer captain had to be sent home for his abuse of alcohol.[78] However, usually the senior naval officers and embassy staff (including clerical staff and wives of naval officers or diplomats) enjoyed more sedate recreation. Although the embassy did continue to host refugee benefits, few of these senior people were paying much attention to the desperate Greeks and Armenians (the Russians still held center focus). And just as Bristol had played tennis while the events at Smyrna were transpiring, so during these later months the embassy staff continued about its leisure activities, with picnics across the Bosporus, or swimming parties on Captain Mannix's large repair ship, or excursions to Prinkipo to party and to see the destroyers shoot. At the latter place the embassy people had such a good time that even the junior officers objected: "We have had dinner parties aboard ship and dinner parties ashore until we are all tired of living."[79]

A few final contrasts manifest a degree of ignorance and insensitivity on the part of some Americans. In December of 1922, diplomat G. Howland Shaw wrote Admiral Bristol (still in Lausanne) of lately having cranked a phonograph at the NER personnel house while Refed Pasha, the so-called "Terror of Christians and Scourge of Minorities" and the ranking Nationalist in the city, danced with a pretty Near East Relief girl there. Shaw could not help gloating as he wrote Bristol (who he thought was sure to be "enormously amused") about the potential effects that a photograph of the occasion might have had on relief supporters back home.[80]

The young relief woman would probably not have appreciated being made the subject of such triumphant crassness by an American diplomat. Still, her likely ignorance was nothing to the apparent cluelessness of Professor Edward Fisher of Robert College. In early October Fisher noted in his diary having just attended a lecture on "The Limitations of Nationalism and the Need of Reviving Christendom." The history professor failed to note a huge irony: this lecture was being delivered at his college even as Turkish Nationalist forces were threatening the British at Chanak, and just as the Nationalists were beginning to expel all the Christians within Turkey's borders.[81]

And then there were the Americans on the ocean liners, *Homeric*, *Rotterdam*, and *Mauretania* among them. The passengers on these great ships, which had bypassed Athens because of its huge refugee problems,[82] had wonderful days in Constantinople in the winter of 1922. They dined at the embassy and at the restaurants and attended dances ashore as well. Then they reciprocated with dinners and dances for American naval officers and diplomats and other local Americans on board their own ships. They also visited the famous sites of the city, from Sancta Sophia to the whirling dervishes to the Roman cisterns to the Princes' Islands to the fascinating Grande Bazaar. Yet they remained almost completely oblivious of another equally powerful vista, that is, of those ten thousand women and children suffering and dying behind the imposing walls of Selimieh Barracks, in plain view from their liners, just one more caique trip away. Ironically, though, while the tourists knew nothing of them, those afflicted refugees knew intimately of the high times being enjoyed by the tourists. As Doctor Lovejoy observed, having visited both Selimieh Barracks and *Rotterdam* on the same day, "They saw the big ships during the day tended by hundreds of caiques, and after dark they heard the mocking music from the brilliantly lighted decks, where thousands of God's favored people danced the hours away. The outcasts were included in these dancing parties. In the dead of the night, when Death came reaping along the corridors of their prison house, he came on the orchestral waves of these liners from New York, and frequently to the rollicking tune of 'Yes! We have no bananas, we have no bananas to-day.'"[83]

Nevertheless, even the Americans from the liners visited local Near East Relief headquarters while in Constantinople, as many had contributed to that organization, and few Americans were purposely insensitive. Frequently enough they reached out in generosity even in these confusing days. Sometimes the efforts of a relief worker or doctor or missionary would save a life. Maybe a diplomat's spouse (often Helen Bristol herself) would be moved by somebody's troubles and summon effectual aid, or a destroyer captain would notice an especially troubling situation and do what he could to help. However, perhaps one of the more striking personal touches was provided by the offhand comment of a naval enlisted man, a comment that I choose to regard as characteristic of American naval men performing their ordinary duties in that forgotten day.

We last saw Efthim Couzinos boarding a steamer with his classmates from Anatolia College and thanking God for his escape, the success of his departure from Turkey having been in grave doubt even at the Samsun dock. With him, all the refugees crammed on their steamer were ecstatic to be out of Turkish control. Their happiness did not last long, however. As the transport steamed west through the Black Sea (a body of water, incidentally, that many of the refugees from inland Anatolia had, until now, never seen), the refugees fed on hardtack and drank from the ship's water supply. Unexpectedly, about midnight they drained the water tanks dry. Suddenly they all became tortured with thirst.

What was to be done? That was obvious to the ship's captain: radio an American destroyer. The refugees on Couzinos' steamer would later remember a tiny speck of light appearing somewhere near the Turkish coast . . . which soon became a searchlight . . . which finally illuminated the transport from end to end. The "fast, trim, beautiful ship" came to a stop close by, and the destroyer sent a boat over with a water line.

Acting with characteristic efficiency (after all, it was just one of a thousand such errands of mercy carried out by America's Black Sea Fleet of that period), the enlisted men quickly completed the water transfer. Then, as one of the American sailors turned to go, he happened to notice a group of young women among the ragged refugees. "What pretty girls!" he remarked. One of this group who had learned American English in a mission school demurred: "You should have seen us two years ago. We are refugees now!" The sailor was undeterred. As he stepped down into his motor boat, he replied, "But you are very pretty, just the same!" As Couzinos later wrote, "This sailor might have expressed these same words to any group of girls around the world and have gone unheeded. But the insistence and clarity in the tone of his voice when he said, '*But you are very pretty, just the same*,' was the most encouraging sentence that he could have uttered."

And so it was. It comprised, in fact, "the most rhetorical, deep-seated, inspirational statement" that any human being could give to another, especially in the circumstances: a packed-in shipload of worn-down, frightened, anxious, penniless, filthy, and ragged refugees in the middle of the Black Sea.[84]

CHAPTER 12

The Departure

When you get off in a place like this for seven months and see greed,
avarice, and barbarism, as we see it here, you learn how to appreciate
gentleness, courtesy, love, and home.

—Lt. Orin Haskell

O n the morning of November 17, 1922, Helen Bristol got up early,
and, with the escort of Maj. Sherman Miles (the new American
military attaché), she traveled to the mosque in front of Yildiz Kiosk,
the sultan's current palace. She had been informed that today, at the sultan's
selamlik (a ceremonial appearance to his women), she would receive the "Order
of Chastity, Third Class." This was a standard award for prominent wives of
diplomats. However, Helen had only been persuaded to come by being assured
that third class was the *highest*, not the lowest order.

At any rate, along with many European diplomats there to see her honored,
Helen and the attaché waited for the sultan to appear. As the appointed time
passed, they were told that the sultan was "on his way," and they were served
Turkish coffee (but no food). They waited longer, to be given again the same
assurance, and waited longer yet. After hours they returned to the embassy; Mrs.
Bristol was hungry and upset. The sultan, meantime, was indeed "on his way."
At 8:00 a.m., with his son and a few retainers and servants, he left the palace in
a British vehicle, was driven to a quay, and was taken by a British launch out
to HMS *Malaya*, which carried him on to Malta. After centuries, the sultan
had left Constantinople for good. Meanwhile, hearing that her husband had
known of the plans to use Mrs. Bristol's award as a ruse but had not informed
her about it, reportedly "Ma Bristol" (as she was informally called, though not
in her hearing) would not speak to the admiral for a week.[1]

With the sultan's abdication, and with the expulsion of Christian minorities from mainland Turkey well under way, the writing was on the wall for all those in power in Constantinople. Not only did Turkish armies now control the Asiatic side of the straits, but also even before the sultan left, all of the sultan's ministers had resigned and the Ottoman ministries had been shut down. The Nationalists would soon take over most of the city's government, and the large Turkish population of Constantinople was united on the Nationalist side and quite expectant. Within a year, not only would the Allies and their armadas have to leave the Bosporus, but the American warships would have to go, too.

In some respects the American Navy's departure would be a very natural thing. The grain ships had long since stopped coming, nor was there any need to have destroyers stationed at Samsun to keep in contact with the defiant Nationalists at Angora—the Nationalists were coming to power in Constantinople! Moreover, by the fall of 1923 (when the Allied armies actually departed the city), most of the American relief people and missionaries would have left the Turkish countryside. Hence there would be little need to keep Navy ships on hand to rescue Americans in desperate circumstances, this being one major rationale for having ships on hand. In fact, many American relief workers who had been stationed in mainland Turkey had left with the Smyrna evacuees, although they typically continued to help those desolated peoples in Cyprus, Greece, or elsewhere.

Admiral Bristol argued that American relief efforts should be limited to evacuations per se (from Smyrna or elsewhere in Turkey) and should go no further. As for the multitudes of refugees arriving in Greece, he thought the Greek government "should be made to take charge of the situation and do their own work."[2] Bristol argued this even though most of the hundreds of thousands of refugees arriving in Greece were only ethnically Greek (indeed, a large number were Armenian), most spoke only Turkish, and few had taken any part in the war. The secretary of state declined to restrict the American agencies' efforts. Many individuals and American institutions like the Red Cross would work with the human deluge engulfing Greece itself for months.[3] Those Americans who (unlike the American Navy) stayed in Constantinople would face new conditions, and would have to make significant accommodations.

The Allied ships streamed out of Constantinople and the Bosporus on October 2, 1923. On the day of the Turkish takeover, the city was hung with Turkish flags, sprigs of greenery interlaced with red and white muslin, and Oriental rugs hanging from windows. Turkish troops marched by in their different regiments. Then, after muezzin calls to prayer, crowds of unveiled Turkish women (a startling sight in itself) paraded as did several men's societies, all of them carrying banners. Hundreds of Turkish Boy Scouts and white-robed school girls also marched. The Americans at the colleges thought they should join in. Elizabeth Dodge Huntingdon (the wife of the vice president of Robert College, George Huntington) later remembered walking through the streets with the marching crowds, after which they all watched a beautiful sunset over the city. It was a symbolic "taking part," she wrote, suggesting solidarity with the Turks, and implying, if not approval, perhaps forgetfulness of any untoward events of the past.[4] It would be the first step of accommodation.

The American colleges would make several adjustments to the new situation. For example, America's Constantinople Women's College was soon forced to shut down its emerging medical program (the college had actually been in the first stages of starting a medical school), though its trustees would probably have shut that down anyway because of the financial difficulties the college was beginning to face; with so many Greeks leaving the city, the college's enrollment was plummeting. On the men's side, some alterations were fended off by President Gates, but among unavoidable changes, within a couple of years Robert College would be required to abandon its Greek and Armenian departments. This was a major change, as these programs (in language, history, culture) had been a part of the curriculum since that college's beginning. However, for a time Robert College would retain a mixed population of ethnic groups, as the treaty negotiated at Lausanne in 1922–23 allowed Greeks and Armenians to remain in Constantinople, and many did so.[5]

Despite their troubles, for years after 1923 the American colleges retained the strong support within Constantinople that they had enjoyed for decades. A striking pair of instances that demonstrates the high degree of the two colleges' traditional prestige in Constantinople was that the sultan, before he abdicated, and Mustapha Kemal, after he took over the government of Turkey, both sent their adopted daughters to the American women's college.[6] For a period, the American schools' great traditional prestige continued to buoy them up.

American relief work continued on in Constantinople itself. In late 1922, the Near East Relief in the city evacuated its orphans to Syria and Greece; after that, it kept working both to keep refugees alive at the various evacuation ports, and particularly to provide food, clothing, and medical care when the ships holding refugees stopped in Constantinople before steaming to Greece. (As we have seen, sometimes Greece simply could not handle the masses and asked that the ships temporarily stop coming.)

The times could not have been pleasant for Constantinople NER head Harold Jaquith, who Bristol had "jumped onto" in repeated tirades for such things as bringing Armenian orphans to Constantinople from the interior, where Bristol "knew perfectly well that they were safe," for not helping destitute Turks enough, and for the "propaganda" of his organization's Ward-Yowell reports.[7] (Bristol apparently never learned Jaquith's exact role in the latter events.) Despite such antagonism, the Near East Relief would continue its work for a couple of years even after all the Allied armies and ships left, before closing down its operations in Turkey altogether.

In their dealings with the Turkish government, officials of American relief and civic organizations alike had to adjust to the new order. As just one example, for some time Turkish officials had been objecting to the use of the word "Christian" in the title of the YMCA. Though many Turks admired the organization and its service, anything "Christian" was automatically suspect—whatever that word actually meant. Sometime after Smyrna, when Captain Pratt Mannix was spoken to (in Turkish) by an old Turk, a young Austrian woman standing nearby started to laugh. Mannix asked the woman what the man had said. She answered, "He says that the Turks like [the] Americans but they cannot stand those accursed Christians."[8] When some Westerners proposed that the word "Christian" in the YMCA's title simply be dropped, the parent organization objected. So YMCA secretary Asa Jennings—the same fellow who had somehow found the way to evacuate Smyrna of its remaining hundreds of thousands of ethnic Greek and Armenian refugees when no one else could—formed an organization called the "American Friends of Turkey," a nonsectarian and international group with a Turkish board, which was to do much of the same kind of work as the YMCA.[9]

Imitation can be a form of flattery, and hence while it might have raised eyebrows for a Christian to take the lead, this was a foreseeable development. Indeed, for some time a "Red Crescent" society had operated in the Ottoman Empire, this in imitation of the nominally Christian "Red Cross."

A more problematic kind of accommodation was shown by the American Board of Foreign Missions in its decision "to kiss and make up," as James Barton once put it,[10] which involved a shift of the American Board to "behavioral" rather than "evangelical" Christianity. After the Turkish government passed laws forbidding schools from teaching Christianity, the American Board sent out missionaries who were not to preach or even conduct any formal ministry, but who would simply "live their faith," maintaining their Christian influence only by "personal example and friendly contact."[11] Put in another way, while French and Italian Catholic schools refused to remove their crucifixes from classroom walls and chose to suffer wholesale closure rather than suffer the inability overtly to profess their religion, some American protestants chose to proceed by "unnamed Christianity."[12]

This was, of course, a major accommodation. Christians of all stripes have believed that they should be doers of the word, not just hearers of it (in keeping with James 1:22), but the proclamation of the word itself has always been understood as preliminary and necessary. To say that social workers are preferable to missionaries in overseas work would be a tenable position, of course. (This opinion was often expressed among missionary opponents.) Too, no one would deny that social work and character building can be "good works" in a spiritual sense. However, to practice "unnamed Christianity" could also be understood as becoming a glorified Peace Corps worker rather than a missionary, or being just a good citizen and not necessarily a Christian at all.

As a parallel example, A. C. Ryan, one of the "younger missionaries" of the Bible House in Constantinople, once went to see Admiral Bristol. According to Bristol's summary of their conversation, Ryan "did not seem to feel that baptism or the profession of any particular creed was necessary in order for a Moslem to become a Christian."[13] Accommodation here has reached a kind of zenith.

Bristol found Ryan both progressive and intelligent, and the admiral was quite enthusiastic overall about this change to behavioral Christianity.[14] Actually, in speeches at the colleges and in his conversations with religious authorities, Bristol had long been preaching this very doctrine of "teaching religion by example" instead of "proselyting."[15] Nevertheless, for the admiral to point out as vehemently as he did to committed Christians the way they should proclaim their faith (without proclaiming it) was quite disingenuous. As Bristol once confessed to Gates, he had not darkened a church door for years.[16] When, on Sunday mornings, the people from Bible House were attending the Dutch Chapel in Pera and educators at Robert College were worshiping in their chapel, and while even a few Navy people might be listening to one of the occasionally available chaplains, Bristol was customarily to be found with his wife at home, or perhaps on the *Scorpion*, preparing for the next weekend social function.

Bristol continued to preach the gospel of American business, however. Within two weeks of the last refugee being taken off the Smyrna railroad pier, Bristol was writing American friends, suggesting they should now pursue business with the Nationalists. This "virgin country," he wrote, was now "open to all kinds of developments."[17] Moreover, in the tense period during which everyone in the city could see the Nationalists were placing guns on the hills above Scutari,[18] Bristol could even contemplate optimistically the possibility of new business arrangements in Constantinople itself. As he argued to a Standard Oil friend, "even if the Turks came in and drove out all these Greeks and Armenians that have been here centuries bleeding the country and practicing all kind of business methods[,] I would not consider it the worst thing that could happen to Constantinople." Considerable suffering and unfairness might be involved in the "cleaning out of the population," Bristol thought, but even that did not seem so bad, in comparison to the possibility of business then being built up on more "decent lines."[19]

At the State Department, Allen Dulles was a bit more clear-sighted than Bristol both on the possibilities for commerce and on the nature of decency. "Turkey wants American business but I can't imagine American or other business men risking their capital under present conditions or under a regime where they would be at the mercy of Turkish justice or caprice."[20] In the event, the Turks did not immediately enter Constantinople at the time Dulles' letter was written, in late 1922. Nevertheless, 150,000 ethnic Greeks left the city between 1922 and 1924, and the minorities continued to be expelled from Anatolia till they were virtually all gone. Through such transactions, which cost Turkey its most productive class, for years Turkey suffered "something like an economic paralysis," and for a decade, American trade with Turkey went stagnant.[21]

Eventually, neither fearing "Turkish justice or caprice" nor apparently caring what his actions might imply as to his attitude toward the recent expulsions or earlier atrocities, Bristol and staff members left Constantinople briefly to vacation through western Anatolia. With his wife, Helen; the Kinkaids; diplomat Pierrepont Moffat; and Lt. Julian Wheeler, Bristol took an eleven-day sightseeing junket in April of 1924. They first traveled from Scutari to Eskishehir and then to Angora, and afterward on to Konia and through the Cilician range to Mersina and Adana, much of the trip in a private railway car provided by the Turkish government. According to Kinkaid's biographer, it was a "glorious trip," and Kinkaid's journal (as well as the Kinkaid photos) indicates it was filled with monuments, mosques, mountains, plains, and bazaars.[22] Monuments probably *not* visited were the countless appropriated Armenian homes in Cilician cities; the gravesites or bones of the 1921–22 Pontus deportees, many of whom had come from Konia and some even from as far as Eskishehir, not just from the Pontus;[23] nor any of the numerous Greek labor battalions formed after Smyrna, most of which by now had been disbanded from lack of living membership.

In contrast, within a year of Bristol's trip, that British writer and sculptor and relative of Winston Churchill named Clare Sheridan who had been at Smyrna and witnessed many terrible events firsthand was struck by certain Turkish "monuments" as she made an unescorted journey into Anatolia, traveling down the whole Pontic Coast. The Turkish handiwork she particularly noticed included the defacing of every church in sight. The "jewel of Trebizond," for example, its own Santa Sofia church, smaller but to Sheridan even more beautiful than its namesake in Constantinople, had had its thirteenth-century frescoes chipped by hammer and chisel beyond recognition. "This destruction is deliberate, irremediable, and complete." The mutilation had also occurred in Samsun and in Kerasonde. "Wherever there were Christians there are ruins. Every shrine, every chapel, every church upon the way, is reduced to a mere mass of rubble." The mutilation did not stop there. The Christian *cemeteries* in these cities had suffered the same, or even worse. "The tombstones are broken, the monuments overturned, the mausoleums looted, and human bones lying among fragments of marble carving and iron railings." The Greek cemetery in Samsun had been plowed up and planted with tobacco, apparently with no complaint from the American tobacco firms still doing business at the place. Nor, Sheridan added, was all this desecration the result of a single act of war madness. It had been in gradual process for three years.[24]

Bristol's friendship for the Turks remained strong, and he was retained in Constantinople as a de facto diplomat for four additional years despite the departure of all his Navy arm, reportedly hoping eventually to become the actual American ambassador (something that would never actually occur). With other Americans who remained in the city, Bristol would lobby for the approval of the Lausanne Treaty. When it was rejected (in January of 1927), within weeks Bristol had helped negotiate an exchange of notes that restored diplomatic relations anyway.[25] In that same year, Bristol was ordered to naval fleet command in China. Years before Bristol left Constantinople, of course, not only all his destroyers but even *Scorpion* itself had been ordered away.[26] Virtually all the Navy people had gone with the ships.

Departing famous places is usually not as exciting as arriving at them. Moreover, people seldom write letters describing their journeys home to family members who will be waiting for them on the pier. Still, by referring to naval diaries and a few other documents, one can get across the flavor of American sailors' and officers' departure from Constantinople, thus rounding out the story we began.

When Ens. Dan Gallery heard that the *Pittsburgh* was finally leaving after its six months' stay, he was having drinks on the sly aboard ship with buddies in a junior officer's stateroom. He went on the beach right away, determined to have a big night. He first stopped at the "little chapel" in Pera for confession, considering he had no idea when he would have another such opportunity. Then he stopped by the home of his ex-girlfriend, where she was emotionally bidding farewell to her new boyfriend (who was, again, Gallery's best friend). Moving on, he stopped by the Bear for dinner, where he saw shipmate George Bahm and his Russian girlfriend, Valentina—"another sad farewell, of course." Gallery and the *Pittsburgh* paymaster eventually trooped over to the Hotel Tokatlian at 9:00 to pick up yet another friend, and then they met the whole gang at the Petit Champs. After a couple of hours, some eight or ten junior officers left this place thoroughly drunk and committed some petty vandalism as they proceeded to Maxim's, which they hit "like a West Indian hurricane." More carousing and then off to the Merle Blanc, which Gallery estimated might be repaired in a week. Two of the officers took a flivver at three, and leaving a "wake of destruction" as they went, finally made it back to Dolmabagtche dock.

The ship did not leave till the early evening of the next day, and, under the insistent eye of his executive officer, Gallery had time to settle for damages done on the Pera the night before.[27]

Bert Berthelsen's destroyer squadron had departed Constantinople a couple of years earlier (ending its fourteen-month stint), after it received orders to sail for the Far East via the Suez Canal. For several days the sailors of *Smith Thompson* (and those of the squadron's other three ships) paid bills, took on stores, swept down and cleaned up the ship, and decorated it with colored bunting. The night before leaving, the squadron moored its ships together at USN Buoy 2 for a joint reception, with a Navy dance band playing on one of the destroyers' forecastles. Then off to the city, where the bluejackets' night was wild and replete with sad farewells.

The next day was memorable, too. All the warships in the city (including the great foreign battleships) had dressed ship in the squadron's honor that day, and in the late morning, boats, launches, and caiques began circling the moored destroyers. The sailors' girlfriends in these boats threw kisses and sobbed; some grew hysterical. At 1:00 the ships cast off lines, formed a column, and briefly headed up the strait. Then they turned back south and came up to standard speed. The buglers on the British battleships sounded attention; all their bands struck up "Auld Lang Syne" as the four destroyers passed in line ahead, and the crowds lining the banks waved, cheered, and wept. "It was just too much for any outfit to take!" recalled Berthelsen. On *Smith Thompson*, tears came to the sailors' eyes, and no one noticed if a man stepped out of ranks for one last wave. Indeed, the officers in charge wept right along with the men.[28]

Although Robbie Dunn also left Constantinople on naval orders, apparently it was his freewheeling spy work that had ended his naval duty. Someone in Constantinople complained of Dunn to the State Department, and then an official in the Division of Near Eastern Affairs suggested up the line that the lieutenant be removed. In a long memorandum, Harry Dwight observed

American sailors on the destroyer *Parrott* show off Turkish fezzes and Russian kalpaks obtained while their ship served briefly in America's small Black Sea Fleet. *Courtesy family of Ash Pleasant*

that Dunn's intelligence reports were "too yellow-journalistic" to suit him, far too much like "Levantine coffee-house gossip." He remarked that others had complained of Dunn in the past, including Colonel Haskell on his return from the Caucasus. (Haskell, then the Allied high commissioner for Armenia, had denounced Dunn for abusing his hospitality and evading his instructions.) Dunn's rumored Great War fame of jumping into German trenches with John Reed and taking potshots at the French also came in for criticism (whether he had actually picked up a rifle then or not). To top it off, the jest Dunn had made with the Arabs at the bar in Therapia was taken quite seriously at State: "Cumberland says, corroborated by Mears of Commerce, that the Admiral's intelligence officer has turned Turk, being known in Islam as Mehmed Ali Bey."

Hence, despite Dunn's value to Bristol, the State Department asked the Navy to have Dunn transferred, and immediately the Navy complied by tele-graphing orders.[29] The lieutenant rode *St. Louis* out of Constantinople, and its captain, Bill Leahy, noticed that, as the domes and minarets faded astern, Dunn could not keep tears from his eyes.[30] Actually, even Leahy himself found himself affected, as he noted in his diary. "Stamboul is today in reality an ugly, decrepit, dirty city, with all its ancient glory gone probably beyond recall; but seen from the sea in the evening and from a distance it is transformed by the color of age and romantic history to a strange and a real beauty. No sailor I am sure ever saw it recede into the evening distance without a desire to return some time."[31]

A young officer who made the voyage home just as unexpectedly as Robbie Dunn had but about a year later was Ted Wellings, who had been serving on the destroyer *Litchfield*. One day Dan Gallery heard that Ted was to be married to a White Russian girl. On the way to the wedding, though, he was told that Bristol had talked Ted out of it. Wellings was not the only man to be dissuaded from marriage to a foreign woman on the grounds that it would injure his life or his naval career. As a destroyer's commanding officer remembered, "it was Admiral Bristol's policy to place all reasonable obstacles in the way of sudden and ill-advised marriages between our men and foreign women."[32] Even Mrs. Bristol sometimes got into the act. At one point she made certain that staff lieutenant Julian Wheeler stopped dating the Italian girl he was so smitten with.[33]

At any rate, not only was Ted Wellings' wedding called off, but the young officer also was sent home on the next destroyer, probably to make sure Ted did not change his mind.[34] In the year 2000, though, when the author contacted Wellings' son, Ted Jr., by phone, he was startled to hear him say, "Did you know, Bob, that my mother was a White Russian?" Apparently, Wellings found the money for passage, sent it to Constantinople, and (despite the admiral's wishes) married the Russian girl when she arrived in Boston.[35]

Once Navy people got home, of course, they ran into each other occasionally and shot the breeze about their Turkish experiences. Those officers who had been on the admiral's staff—along with their wives and the diplomatic officials and their families—kept in pretty close contact. Many remembered the Constantinople years as "glorious," with all the terrific social life and their various escapades. In the States they entertained Russian visitors like Baroness Wrangel, still seeking funds for her refugee countrymen, and made snide remarks about Admiral McCully's Russian waifs, though the children themselves seemed quite happy. Margaret Bryan and Admiral Bristol wrote frequently. Soon after she got home, Margaret was startled to receive a fitness report from Bristol. Margaret was identified as "the Junior Aide," and the admiral reported that this officer "can cooperate, if she wants to," and so on. Margaret's letters were very lively, and Bristol once suggested she ought to write a book.[36]

Naval people occasionally did write about their experiences, and of course I have frequently quoted from their writings here. In 1925 Lt. Cdr. Richard Field published two long and informative articles for the Naval Institute's *Proceedings* that described the Near Eastern experiences of USS *Goff*. This ship (which Field had commanded) was one of the twelve destroyers that had steamed to Turkey right after the burning of Smyrna. In the 1960s enlisted engineer Bert Berthelsen wrote his humorous and detailed book about service aboard *Smith Thompson* during its year in Turkey (from 1920 to 1921); it also described his ship's later duty in the Philippines. Berthelsen was aided in this by a diary of his own and by journals kept by one of the ship's officers. Dan Gallery's fascinating diary about his naval service as a junior officer on *Pittsburgh* and other naval vessels of the day has only recently been discovered and published; six months of its pages describe life in Constantinople, particularly life ashore (for the cruiser mostly stayed moored in the harbor, and Gallery and his mates were much happier going ashore than staying aboard). Unfortunately, Gallery never turned his considerable talents at humorous short fiction to the Turkish experience—except briefly, in his autobiography.[37]

As we have seen, a couple of journalists who later were to become famous novelists interacted very briefly with Admiral Bristol while writing for their papers at the one-time Ottoman capital. The articles Ernest Hemingway wrote for the *Toronto Star* about happenings in Constantinople right after Smyrna are quite evocative, but as they were based on less than three weeks' visit (and Hemingway was sick at the time, to boot), they are not probing. Hemingway spoke with Admiral Bristol a couple of times (as recorded in Bristol's war diary) but apparently talked with no other American Navy men—Hemingway typically ran with the British. Similarly, while John Dos Passos was most impressed by the admiral and did observe that meeting of the Commander Houston with the Greek Orthodox patriarch, these two officials seem to be the only American Navy people with whom he interacted. Dos Passos' travel book, *Orient Express*, a small portion of which discusses his three weeks or so in Constantinople, is marvelously impressionistic, but for the most part it touches the Navy hardly at all; moreover, Dos Passos remained ignorant about the real state of things in Turkey.

In contrast, the two hundred pages of Robbie Dunn's book, *World Alive*, that deal with his Turkish experience have, as a root, his two and a half years in the city as a naval officer on Bristol's staff, besides forays deep into the countryside. Published posthumously in 1956 but most of it probably being written not long after the events, the Turkish parts of Dunn's book are wonderfully descriptive of both personality and place, even of twang. They also are highly redolent of the admiral's strong prejudices, some of which Dunn no doubt helped to create.

Most regular naval officers naturally kept their eyes strictly on their naval duty and wrote nothing more public than letters, journals, diaries, and official documents. Several of these men would later become highly successful in the naval service, not only being promoted to admiral at one level or another, but also taking on major jobs and accomplishing important things. After Bristol's chief of staff, Japy Hepburn, for instance, became commander in chief, U.S. Fleet, in 1936, he then headed the "Hepburn Board," which set in motion the massive U.S. defense expansion of the late 1930s. Then, for three years during World War II, he had charge of the Navy's General Board. (Capt. Harry Pence, commanding officer of *McFarland* during two Turkish tours, was a member of that same board.) In that same war, Bristol's one-time assistant chief of staff, Thomas Kinkaid, commanded the 7th Fleet during the New Guinea campaign and the great Battle of Leyte Gulf, while fellow staffer A. Stanton "Tip" Merrill commanded the cruiser-destroyer force that won the Battle of Empress Augusta Bay.

A few people who rode or commanded Navy ships at Constan and in the Black Sea also gained naval fame and public attention during or shortly after World War II. For example, Robert Ghormley, who had commanded the destroyer *Sands* while in Turkish waters, worked his way up in the 1930s to become the vice chief of Naval Operations. In the war to come, Ghormley had command of all the operations in the Southwest Pacific for a time, until being dismissed by Adm. Chester Nimitz for being too pessimistic. Bill Leahy, who had captained *St. Louis* at Constantinople, became chief of Naval Operations in 1937, and although he retired after that assignment, he was brought back to active duty on the outbreak of World War II to become President Franklin

Roosevelt's chief of staff (effectually the first Armed Forces chief of staff), a position he kept throughout that war. And in 1944, the task group that Ens. Dan Gallery commanded carried out successfully Gallery's astonishing plan to capture a German submarine on the high seas. Promoted to rear admiral partly because of this exploit, Gallery did not retire until 1960, by which time he had orchestrated a move to get that same German submarine placed along-side the Museum of Science and Industry in Chicago, where it remains (having recently been moved inside and refurbished) till this day.

A diplomat on Bristol's staff who became particularly prominent after the war was Allen Dulles. He became the first civilian director of central intel-ligence in 1953 and remained in that office until 1961, when he was forced to resign partly because of the notorious failure of the Bay of Pigs invasion of Cuba. Later he served on the Warren Commission that investigated the assassi-nation of John F. Kennedy.

At least two American naval officers eventually went back to Turkey. During World War II, Webb Trammell (who had commanded *Fox* in the Black Sea) and former Bristol staffer Robbie Dunn were ordered to naval duty in the city now called Istanbul. Trammell (now a captain) was assigned as naval attaché, and Dunn (appointed a lieutenant commander upon returning to active duty at age sixty-four) was his assistant. Though an old *kavass* at the embassy gates kissed Dunn's hand, otherwise Istanbul was a "city of ghosts" for the writer. Pera was slovenly, the Grande Rue (now Istiklal Caddesi, or Independence Avenue) was the world's ugliest artery, Dunn thought, and the once bawdy Petit Champs had been turned into a children's playground.[38] (Reportedly, upon their occu-pation of Constantinople in October of 1923, the Nationalists had closed four thousand public houses—and had kept most of them closed.[39])

Dunn's business was still spying, but because of Turkey's neutrality during the later war, the great city seems to have been a pretty dull place compared to earlier years.[40] Dunn left before 1945, the year in which the American Hospital in Constantinople was renamed "Admiral Bristol Hospital,"[41] the name it car-ried for fifty years, and with some justice, for Bristol was probably the hospi-tal's greatest sponsor both while in Turkey and when he returned to the States, as well being as a major friend of the Turks.[42] Not only did some Nationalists regard Bristol as "one of the heroes of their national struggle," by the way, but a few historians also have credited the admiral with helping to lay the foundation for the relatively good relations obtaining between America and Turkey since the late 1940s, and even during the Cold War.[43]

Finally, one naval enlisted man who no doubt would have liked to have gotten away from the Black Sea region, but for some time did not, is worth comment.

In June of 1922, Chief of Staff Hepburn wrote Admiral Niblack in London about Niblack's former steward. This sailor, named Thomas, had been on Niblack's staff while the admiral rode *Utah* into the Bosporus and up into the Black Sea and back, this in 1921. However, Thomas had then transferred to Bristol's navy. In Constantinople (Hepburn wrote) Thomas had accumulated such a list of bills, apparently just from living it up, that Hepburn was taking unusual action. Hepburn was sending him into the Black Sea and ordering him to "remain in that region, transferring . . . from one destroyer to another, until he has saved enough money to pay his debts." If that were possible, Hepburn added, and "if Thomas lives."[44]

One is reminded of Edward Everett Hale's *The Man Without a Country* and of Philip Nolan's being transferred from ship to ship on foreign stations, never to see America again.

Hence, besides all its other missions, at least in this way, Bristol's Black Sea Fleet briefly became a prison of sorts. It was not a bad thing, then, that this small American fleet eventually was dissolved. Otherwise, Steward Thomas might be making the rounds from ship to ship even to this day.

For this study, I make reference to numerous items in the Mark Bristol Collection (MBC) in the Library of Congress; its General Correspondence section I abbreviate as GC. I also refer to a wide variety of files in the National Archives, especially files of the Department of State (NA), and those in the Naval Records Collection, Subject File WT (NR). In the chapter on the burning of Smyrna, I typically note the archival location of reports in the first few chapter endnotes, and afterwards simply refer to those documents as "Barnes report," "Hepburn diary," "*Simpson* war diary," etc., with pagination. Full reference to most magazine articles, oral histories, and books can be found in the bibliography rather than in the notes.

Preface

1. Marjorie Housepian Dobkin's *The Smyrna Affair* was later published as *Smyrna 1922: The Destruction of a City*. See bibliography for details.

Chapter 1. The Arrival

1. Lewis Heck, "Constantinople Embassy," 169.
2. Caleb Frank Gates, *Not to Me Only*, 237; Heck, "Constantinople Embassy," 178.
3. Gates, *Not to Me Only*, 245.
4. Philip Mansel, *Constantinople*, 379; Gates, *Not to Me Only*, 245. Taner Akçam itemizes the warships entering the Bosporus as sixty-seven British, twenty-two French, ten Italian, and one Greek, *A Shameful Act*, 208, but Gates records only thirty-six ships in this fleet, 245.
5. Heck, "Constantinople Embassy," 174.
6. Bert Berthelsen, *Tin Can Man*, 20–29.
7. William R. Braisted, "Mark Lambert Bristol," 340–42, and Buzanski dissertation, 28–31.

8. Charles Olsen letters to his wife, Edna, Sept. 7, 19 and Oct. 4, 12, 1920, Olsen Papers.

9. Charles Wheeler, "Reminiscences," 68–71.

10. Constantine Brown, *The Coming of the Whirlwind,* 109–15.

11. Solita Solano, "Constantinople," 647.

12. George Young, *Constantinople*, 12.

13. Stanley Kerr letter to his mother, Mar. 14, 1919, Kerr Letters.

14. Robert Dunn, *World Alive*, 281.

15. Olsen letter to his wife of Oct. 19, 1920, Olsen Papers.

16. Alexander Powell, *The New Frontiers of Freedom*, 169–72.

17. Alice Keep Clark, *Letters from Cilicia*, 5; unpublished diary of Walter George Smith, 36; Berthelsen, *Tin Can Man*, 28.

18. Robert Shenk, ed., *Playships of the World*, 153; William F. "Dolly" Fitzgerald, oral history, 30.

19. George Young, *Constantinople*, 12.

20. Charles Olsen letter to his wife Edna Olsen, Oct. 19, 1920, Olsen Papers.

21. Stanley Kerr to his mother, Mar. 14, 1919, Kerr Letters.

22. George Young, *Constantinople*, 13.

23. Powell, *The New Frontiers of Freedom*, 173.

24. Charles Woods, "Constantinople after the War," 457.

25. Mansel, *Constantinople*, 288.

26. Ibid., 354; Young, *Constantinople*, 14.

27. Shenk, *Playships of the World*, 153.

28. John Dos Passos, *Orient Express*, 8.

29. E. W. Brigg and A. A. Hessenstein, *Constantinople Cameos*, 83.

30. William White, ed., *Hemingway, Ernest. Dateline Toronto*, 227.

31. Frank Carpenter, *The Alps, the Danube, and the Near East*, 260.

32. Charles J. Wheeler, "Reminiscences," 68.

33. Brigg and Hessenstein, *Constantinople Cameos,* 22.

34. Woods, "Constantinople after the War," 457; Fitzgerald oral history, 29.

35. Eugenia Bumgardner, *Undaunted Exiles*, 1–2.

36. Young, *Constantinople*, 14.

37. (Jeanette Edwards), "Turkish Delight," 328.

38. Berthelsen, *Tin Can Man*, 29; Dunn, *World Alive*, 281.

39. Epigraph to the war diary of the USS *Fox*, DD 234, kept by Trammell, then the *Fox*'s commanding officer.

40. James G. Harbord, "Investigating Turkey and Trans-Caucasia," 37.

41. Dos Passos, *The Fourteenth Chronicle*, 316.

42. Powell, *The New Frontiers of Freedom*, 176; Shenk, *Playships of the World*, 153–54.

43. Berthelsen, *Tin Can Man*, 29.

44. Solano, "Constantinople Today," 647–680, in *National Geographic*, 41:6 (June 1922): 647.

45. Edgar J. Fisher, "From Bad to Worse in Constantinople," *New York Times Magazine*, Jan. 11, 1920, 5.

46. Solano, "Constantinople Today," 651.

47. Berthelsen, *Tin Can Man*, 28.

48. Solano, "Constantinople Today," 647.

49. Lucian Swift Kirtland, "The New Melting Pot on the Bosporus," 8.

50. Mark Twain, *The Innocents Abroad, or The New Pilgrim's Progress*, 238; G. Ward Price, *Extra-special Correspondent,* 38.

51. Isaac Marcosson, "When Constantinople Went Dry," 46.

52. Brigg and Hessenstein, *Constantine Cameos*, 47.

53. Brown, *The Coming of the Whirlwind*, 126.

54. June 30, 1919, entry in Pence diary, Pence Papers.

55. Brown, *The Coming of the Whirlwind,* 126.

56. William Leahy diary, 242.

57. Allen Dulles letter of Dec. 10, 1920, Dulles Papers.

58. Clover Dulles letter to her mother, Dec. 13, 1920, Dulles Papers.

59. Peter Grose, *Gentleman Spy*, 76.

60. Gerald Wheeler, *A Biography of Admiral Thomas C. Kinkaid*, 30–31.

61. Daniel P. Mannix, *The Old Navy*, 263–65.

62. Ibid., 266.

63. Ibid., 267–68.

64. Ibid., 268.

Chapter 2. Turkey in 1919 and the American Commissions

1. This war took place under the presidency of Thomas Jefferson and featured famous American skippers such as Edward Preble and Stephen Decatur. Cf. Thomas Bryson, *Tars, Turks, and Tankers*, 1–19, and standard naval histories, such as E. B. Potter and Chester Nimitz, *Sea Power: A Naval History*, 196–206.

2. Leland James Gordon, *American Relations with Turkey*, 11; John A. DeNovo, *American Interests and Policies*, 18. Porter's descriptions can be found in *Constantinople and Its Environs in a Series of Letters*, 2 vols., 1854, now available in modern editions. See the bibliography.

3. Gates, *Not to Me Only*, 163; William N. Still Jr., *American Sea Power in the Old World*, 37 and note 68, 223. (Farragut's exact role is debated.)

4. Twain, *The Innocents Abroad, or The New Pilgrim's Progress*; Jay Leyda, *The Melville Log: A Documentary Life of Herman Melville, 1819–1891*, vol. 2.

5. DeNovo, *American Interests and Policies*, 8.

6. Buzanski dissertation, 2.

7. Joseph Grabill, *Protestant Diplomacy and the Near East*, 7ff, 33; Dobkin, *Smyrna 1922*, 30.

8. Bernard Lewis, *The Emergence of Modern Turkey*, 214–18; Robert F. Melson, *Revolution and Genocide*, 138, 160–62.

9. Grabill, *Protestant Diplomacy and the Near East*, 50; Lewis, *The Emergence of Modern Turkey*, 214; Melson, *Revolution and Genocide*, 156.

10. Melson, *Revolution and Genocide*, 139; Dobkin, *Smyrna 1922*, 39–40.

11. Dobkin, *Smyrna 1922*, 59.

12. Suzanne Elizabeth Moranian dissertation, 26. Also cf. General Harbord's statements in his report that no more than 20 percent of the Turkish peasants who went to war had returned, that 600,000 Turkish soldiers had died of typhus alone, and that a great lack of supplies and medical treatment had swelled the list of Turkish military dead. Papers Relating to the Foreign Relations of the United States (hereafter cited as FRUS), 1919, vol. 2, 848.

13. Grabill, *Protestant Diplomacy and the Near East*, 11; Dobkin, *Smyrna 1922*, 24.

14. Mark Bristol War Diary, Oct. 29, 1922 (and see the whole passage there), MBC. For Armenians' customary treatment as inferiors, see also Clarence Ussher, *An American Physician in Turkey*, 156–59, and Dobkin, *Smyrna 1922*, 25–28.

15. Grabill, *Protestant Diplomacy and the Near East*, 50.

16. This renaissance occurred among all the Armenians, both those in the Ottoman Empire and those in Russia. See, for brief accounts, Richard Hovannisian, *Armenia on the Road to Independence, 1918*, 61–62, and Melson, *Revolution and Genocide*, also 61–62.

17. Grabill, *Protestant Diplomacy and the Near East*, 60; Vahakn Dadrian, *The Key Elements*, 14–16; and (especially) Ussher, *An American Physician in Turkey*, 234–87. Ussher (*An American Physician in Turkey*, 265, 289) puts the massacre's toll among Armenians outside Van at fifty-five thousand. Conversely, when the

Russians took over, the Armenians, in turn, "burned and murdered; the spirit of loot took possession of them, driving out every other thought" (285).

18. Morgenthau, in "*Henry Morgenthau: Ambassador Morgenthau's Story*, 300, points out that the defense of Van by "revolutionists" was always brought forward by the Turks to justify their later acts. In 1961 Bernard Lewis referred to "a struggle between two nations for the possession of a single homeland," as if the Armenians were organized massively to fight the Turks, *The Emergence of Modern Turkey*, 356. Melson, in *Revolution and Genocide*, refutes this position in his discussion of "The Provocation Thesis," 152–59.

19. See Grabill, *Protestant Diplomacy and the Near East*, 60–64, for a brief account of the massacres and deportations; Dobkin, *Smyrna 1922*, 44–45 and 16, on the orders themselves; and Melson and the references he cites (*Revolution and Genocide*, 143–45) on the general organization of the operation.

20. Actually edited by Toynbee. See James Bryce, "Memorandum by the Editor of the Documents," *The Treatment of the Armenians in the Ottoman Empire, 1915–16*, xxxv ff.

21. Grabill, *Protestant Diplomacy and the Near East*, 75, 101.

22. Dobkin says "over one million Armenians died," *Smyrna 1922*, 45, while Peter Balakian says that "the death tolls from 1915 through 1922 range from over a million to a million and a half"; see his discussion, *The Burning Tigris*, 179–180, and notes.

23. Johannes Lepsius, *Le rapport Secret sur les Massacres d'Arme'nie*, Paris, 1918.

24. Renwick McIver of the *Gilmer* wrote home on Oct. 18, 1922, that he had finished Morgenthau's book, McIver Papers.

25. Heath Lowry, *The Story Behind Ambassador Morgenthau's Story*.

26. Roger W. Smith, "Was Morgenthau a Liar?" 51–52.

27. Lowry, *The Story Behind*, 42–43; 49; 73. Note on the August 14th entry of Morgenthau's diary, his last sentence: "[Enver] told [Lepsius] about the same thing that he had told me" (quoted in Lowry, 73). Lowry's assertion that what the Young Turks had in mind for the Armenians was simply "segregation" rather than destruction (5) is simply not credible. See also Vahakn N. Dadrian's discussion of Lowry in *The Key Elements*, 38–42 and notes.

28. June 1915 message from FRUS 1915 Supplement, 982–84, quoted in DeNovo, *American Interests and Policies*, 99.

29. Ara Sarafian, ed., *United States Official Documents on the Armenian Genocide*, vol. 2, 53.

30. Leslie A. Davis, *The Slaughterhouse Province*, especially 81–87.

31. Morgenthau, *Ambassador Morgenthau's Story*, 328.

32. DeNovo, *American Interests and Policies*, 102–3; Grabill, *Protestant Diplomacy and the Near East*, 77.

33. Moranian dissertation, 210.

34. Grabill, *Protestant Diplomacy and the Near East*, 77.

35. DeNovo, *American Interests and Policies*, 103.

36. The term is used in DeNovo, *American Interests and Policies,* 103.

37. Moranian dissertation, 176.

38. Cf., for example, the report of Captain Emory Niles and Arthur Sutherland (discussed in some detail in Justin McCarthy, *Death and Exile,* 223–30; the report itself is in NA 184.021/175). In early 1919, while investigating the situation in eastern provinces such as Van, Bitlis, and Erzurum, the two officers were astonished to hear complaints at every hand of scorched earth, massacres, and atrocities perpetrated by Armenians against Muslims (rather than the other way about). Given the enormity of the offenses originally perpetrated in these provinces, that furious reprisals were sometimes taken is hardly remarkable. However, for more perspective, see Hovannisian, *Armenia on the Road to Independence, 1918*, 46–47, 122–24, 135, and n. 88 on 257; the Bryce Report, chapters 2–6; Usshur, *An American Physician in Turkey*; and Dadrian, *The Key Elements*.

39. For example, Grabill, *Protestant Diplomacy and the Near East* (164) cites a film shown in fifty American cities called *Ravished Armenia*, which depicted a scantily clad young Armenian woman being dragged by a stallion, a flogging of girls who refused to enter Turkish harems, and twelve Armenian maidens nailed to crosses.

40. Eleanor Francis Egan, "This to Be Said for the Turk," 15.

41. Winston Churchill, *The World Crisis—1918–1928*, vol. 5, 385.

42. Grabill, *Protestant Diplomacy and the Near East*, 200, and Lybyer letters, June 18 and 26, 1919, Lybyer Papers; as for Harbord, besides his official report (to be found in FRUS, 1919, vol. II, 841–74, hereafter cited as Harbord FRUS report), Harbord described his experiences in *The World's Work* and in a *New York Times* article of Feb. 22, 1920. The quotations above and the reference to swimming in the Euphrates are in James G. Harbord, "Mustapha Kemal Pasha and His Party," 176–77, 180.

43. Gates' speech is in the Bristol war diary, filed under a *Scorpion* letter to the force commander of Apr. 29, 1919, 3.

44. Gates' speech, 2–3.

45. Walter George Smith journal, June 11, 1919.

46. Grabill, *Protestant Diplomacy and the Near East*, 227.

47. Walter George Smith journal, June 11, 1919.

48. Interview of Mary Louise Graffam by the King-Crane Commission of Aug. 6, 1919. In Lybyer Papers, Univ. of Illinois at Urbana-Champaign; italics added.

49. Harbord, "Investigating Turkey and Trans-Caucasia," 36.

50. Harbord, "Mustapha Kemal Pasha and His Party," 190.

51. Clipping of article in the *San Antonio Light* of Apr. 25, 1920, Folder 36 of General Harbord collection, Library of Congress; Harbord, "Mustapha Kemal Pasha and His Party," 180.

52. Lybyer letter, July 17, 1919.

53. Harbord FRUS report, 844, 847, 844–45.

54. Ibid., 860.

55. Anna Mitchell, uncorrected letter of June 24, 1922 or 1923, Mitchell Letters.

56. Harbord FRUS report, 860.

57. Ibid., 848. Harbord may be referring here to the Niles/Sutherland report (Cf. footnote 38, above). If so, he chose to condense that report's import to this one line.

58. Ibid., 860.

59. Richard Hovannisian, *The Republic of Armenia*, vol. 2, *From Versailles to London, 1919–1920,* , 345.

60. Harbord FRUS report, 846, 847.

61. Grabill, *Protestant Diplomacy and the Near East*, 203.

62. Harbord, "Mustapha Kemal Pasha and His Party," 185.

63. Ibid., 185–86.

64. Ibid., 186; and see Andrew Mango, *Atatürk*, 246–48, on Nationalist opposition to a mandate.

65. Harbord, "Mustapha Kemal Pasha and His Party," 187.

66. Giles Milton, *Paradise Lost*, 134.

67. Cited in Dobkin, *Smyrna 1922*, 64, referring to Horton letter or cable to State Department of June 7, 1919, NA 763.72/13197. The American ships did no more than lie in the harbor, send some twenty men to guard the consulate, and observe. Capt. J. H. Dayton of the *Arizona* did collect numerous reports from various Americans about the Smyrna occupation and made some observations of his own; some of his comments and those of R. S. Berry, commanding officer of the accompanying destroyer *Manley*, are cited in Giles Milton, *Paradise Lost*, 140, 143, 145, 147. Berry, in particular, was dismayed both by the lack of discipline shown by the Greek troops on their disembarkation and by their utter insensitivity in stacking their arms on reaching the docks and then doing Greek dances around them (140).

68. Dobkin, *Smyrna 1922*, recounts the background to the occupation, 61–64. Taner Akçam argues that this occupation *by Greeks* (not the occupation of Smyrna, per se) is what "ultimately mobilized the Muslim population of western Anatolia," *A Shameful Act*, 321. Dobkin describes a variety of Turkish reaction (68–69), and points out that for Mustapha Kemal (who landed in Samsun four days after the Greek landings at Smyrna), the situation was "riper for a massive rebellion than he could have dreamed. For his purpose, the Council's action in sending the Greeks to Smyrna had provided the ultimate gift," 69.

69. The observations of the captain of the *Arizona* are cited in Giles Milton, *Paradise Lost*, 143–45.

70. I use Dobkin's figures for the casualties in Smyrna itself. (See her citations of passages from Arnold Toynbee, George Horton, and A. F. Frangulis, *Smyrna 1922*, 66, and endnote on 249); for the wider casualties, see Dobkin, *Smyrna 1922*, 65–66, and the documents she references. Note, however, that Giles Milton cites eyewitness estimates of the number of Turkish corpses in the city as somewhere between three and five hundred (144–45). Also pertinent is the report of the Interallied Commission of Inquiry on Smyrna, found in Box 75, "Smyrna Inquiry, 1919," MBC; Dobkin criticizes this inquiry in *Smyrna 1922*, 70–71.

71. Dobkin, *Smyrna 1922*, 69.

72. As just one example, three years later, when speaking to American officers in Smyrna in 1922, General Noureddin Pasha put the figure at *six thousand* dead. Merrill war diary at Smyrna, Sept. 11, 1922, NR, RG 45, Subject File 1911–27; Box 836.

73. Harbord, "Mustapha Kemal Pasha and His Party," 187.

74. Letter to Morgenthau of Aug. 19, 1915, NA 867.4016/148. Many Armenian survivors of the genocide ended up in or near Aleppo. Some implications related to the sudden acquisition of considerable wealth by Turks who took over Armenian property are discussed in Taner Akçam's *Dialogue Across an International Divide: Essays towards a Turkish-Armenian Dialogue* (Zoryan Institute, 2001), as Nergis Canefe reports in his evaluation of three of Akcam's works: "History and the Nation," 237–46, 240.

75. Harbord, "Mustapha Kemal Pasha and His Party," 188.

76. Ibid., 188.

77. Kemal met with correspondent Louis Edgar Browne in Sivas on September 8, Browne being a "freelance go-between" with connections to Admiral Bristol in Constantinople. However, Browne was in no official capacity. See Mango, *Atatürk*, 247.

78. Harbord FRUS report, 873.

79. One confused reader was Bristol's biographer, who thought Harbord's report had not taken a stand on the feasibility of a mandate, Buzanski dissertation, 108.

80. Harbord FRUS report, 874.

81. Ibid.

82. Ibid., 873.

83. Ibid., 871.

Chapter 3. The Admiral, the Embassy, and the Crisis in Cilicia

1. Bristol to Helen while on *Schley*, (Ae)gean Sea, Jan. 26, 1919, Box 13, Family Papers: Jan. 1–30, 1919, folder, MBC.

2. The person who spoke of the moral ignorance of the Middle Eastern races was Harold Bliss of Beirut, Bristol war diary of June 24, 1919. See also Bristol's memorandum to C. Van H. Engert, Apr. 25, 1920, Apr. 1920 GC, MBC, 3.

3. Cf. original of Bristol biographical entry for the *National Cyclopaedia of American Biography*, 256–57, in Nov., 1921 GC, Box 36, MBC; also Buzanski dissertation, 14.

4. Braisted, "Mark Lambert Bristol: Naval Diplomat," 334.

5. Letter of Mar. 23, 1921, to Rear Adm. Andrew T. Long, Mar. 1921 GC, MBC.

6. Clover Dulles letter to her father, Dec. 13, 1920, Dulles Papers; Buzanski dissertation, 16; George Henderson and Paul Ryan, "Naval Watch in the Mideast," 66–75. The latter authors cite diplomats Joseph Grew and Richard W. Child, 71, 72.

7. Henderson and Ryan, "Naval Watch in the Mideast," 72; George Horton, *The Blight of Asia*, 204.

8. Henry P. Beers, "U.S. Naval Detachment in Turkish Waters, 1919–1924," 211; Dunn, *World Alive*, 283; Bristol letter to Adm. R. E. Coontz of Feb. 28, 1920, Mar. 1920 GC, MBC.

9. A memorandum listing warships attached or calling at Constantinople can be found in the June 1920 GC, MBC.

10. Donald Patterson thesis, 69.

11. Robert A. Bachman, "The American Navy and the Turks," 289.

12. Mitchell letter to "Caroline" of July 27, (1921), Mitchell Letters.

13. Buzanski dissertation, 39, 40, 44; Roger Trask, *The United States Response*, 28–29.

14. Mansel, *Constantinople*, 391; Bristol's correspondence in Mar. 1920 GC, MBC.

15. Laurence Evans, *United States Policy*, 328.

16. David Walder, *The Chanak Affair*, 133.

17. Dunn, *World Alive*, 425.

18. Neville Henderson, *Water under the Bridges*, 104.

19. Martin Gilbert, *Sir Horace Rumbold: Portrait of a Diplomat*, 242, 288.

20. Powell, *The New Frontiers of Freedom*, 198. Surely biographer Buzanski's kindred comment is an exaggeration, but it reflects the admiral's mind-set: "When Bristol arrived in Constantinople he had definite opinions on the Near East problem and these views did not change one iota during his nearly nine years' service in Asia Minor," Buzanski dissertation, 20.

21. Laurence Evans, *United States Policy*, 186.

22. Thomas A. Bryson, "Admiral Mark L. Bristol," 450–67, 452.

23. Dunn, *World Alive,* 299.

24. Buzanski dissertation, 235–46.

25. Ibid., 236, but widely manifested in Bristol's correspondence.

26. Bristol war diary, July 1, 1920; Buzanski dissertation, 237.

27. Buzanski dissertation, 245, 225–34; for Chester's ultimately unsuccessful negotiations, cf. Dobkin, *Smyrna 1922*, 80, 152–53, 213–14, 224–25.

28. Buzanski dissertation, 216.

29. See, for example, Berthelsen, *Tin Can Man*, 48, and Earle Kincaid, *History and Cruises of the Whipple,* 87.

30. The visit by embassy staff and their wives to Yalta while embarked on *Scorpion* is noted in the Bristol war diary, July 24–25, 1920, MBC, while a telegram from Bristol to Sec State of Mar. 11, 1924, reports difficult travel conditions, 1919–1923, NA 867.00/1775. One notes that relief workers Elsie Kimball and Alice Keep Clark were allowed to ride destroyers in the Black Sea, as two among many possible examples.

31. Harry Pence diary, Nov. 19, 1921, Pence Papers; Richard Stockton Field, "A Destroyer in the Near East," vol. 51, 402; Bristol war diary, Aug. 25, 1920, MBC; Henderson and Ryan, "Naval Watch in the Mideast," 73.

32. Baldwin letter of Nov. 16, 1921, to Bristol, Nov. 1921 GC, MBC. For a discussion of the importance of business in the development of Bristol's overall viewpoint, see Dobkin, *Smyrna 1922*, 72–83.

33. Nov. 17, 1921, letter in Nov. 1921 GC, MBC.

34. Levon Marashlian points out that "the very skills that Armenians did excel in—finance, commerce and manufacturing—were the very areas into which Bristol wanted American capital to penetrate," "Economic and Moral Influences," 1886.

35. Letter to L. I. Thomas in Buzanski dissertation, 148.

36. Hester Donaldson Jenkins, *An Educational Ambassador*, 143.

37. Buzanski dissertation, 41.

38. Dunn, *World Alive*, 266, 268.

39. Ibid., 268–81.

40. Ibid., 305–18.

41. Ibid., 319.

42. Cited in Richard Hovannisian, *The Republic of Armenia*, vol. 2, *From Versailles to London, 1919–1920*, 352–3.

43. Cited in Moranian dissertation, 177.

44. Buzanski dissertation, 148.

45. Mango, *Atatürk*, 284, 381–84.

46. Phone conversation with Webb Trammell (Junior) on Mar. 23, 2000.

47. See, for instance, Heath W. Lowry, "American Observers in Anatolia," 42–70, esp. 42–46.

48. Lybyer diary, July 24 and Aug. 7, 1919, Lybyer Papers; Mufty-Zade Zia Bey, *Speaking of the Turks*, 199; Edgar Fisher, diary entry of Apr. 17, 1922, Fisher Papers; Joseph C. Grew, *Turbulent Era*, vol. 1, 539; Ahmed Emin Yalman, *Turkey in My Time*, 94, 79. See Buzanski dissertation on Yalman's education, 129, note 98.

49. Bristol war diary, Oct. 25, 1920, MBC.

50. Davis, *The Slaughterhouse Province*, especially his letter report to Morgenthau of Dec. 30, 1915, 178ff.

51. Barton is cited in Moranian dissertation, 474. That the Armenians' motive to leave Cilicia was "absolute distrust of Turkish intentions" is found in a letter from R. S. Stewart to Consul Paul Knabenshue on the occasion of a trip to Cilicia, Dec. 19, 1921, NA 867.00/1475. Bristol later reported an estimated one hundred thousand Armenians had fled Cilicia; see his Jan. 23, 1922, letter to Henry King, Jan. 1922 GC, MBC. On a local view of this forced emigration, see Stanley Kerr, *Lions of Marash*, 247–54. He had been at Marash at the time.

52. The teacher was L. P. Chambers; Moranian dissertation, 465.

53. Bristol letter to Sec State of Oct. 23, 1920, NA 867.00/1361; Bristol war diary, Oct. 25, 1920, MBC.

54. Bristol's report can be found in Senior U.S. Naval Officer, Turkey, to Force Commander, Mar. 28, 1919, NR, RG 45, Subject File 1911–1927, "Samsoun Asia Minor" folder, Box 831.

55. Bristol letter to Helen Bristol, Mar. 13, 1919, Box 13, Family Papers, 1 Feb.–30 Mar. folder, MBC.

56. Letter to Sec State of Dec. 23, 1920, NA, RG 59, 760J.67/58. Levon Marashlian notes the similarity of these statements in "Economic and Moral Influences," 1881.

57. Stanley E. Kerr, *Lions of Marash*, 51. Sixteen thousand Armenians returned to Marash after the war, according to Kerr, to join the six thousand who had stayed in the city. (He notes, however, that the district as a whole had suffered a 75 percent loss.) According to Kerr, some twelve thousand survived the siege, all of whom left Turkey soon afterward, eventually to find asylum in such places as Lebanon, South America, the United States, and Soviet Armenia, 254. (Note: Kerr's way of listing figures is not entirely perspicuous.)

58. Ibid., 62–64. Musa Dagh was to be immortalized by Franz Werfel's *The Forty Days of Musa Dagh*, Viking Press, 1934.

59. Taner Akçam points out that the nationalist forces at the time were "largely composed of bandits who roamed the mountains, military deserters, criminals on the lam, released convicts and adventurers interested in plunder," *A Shameful Act*, 332.

60. Kerr, *Lions of Marash*, 65–71, speaks to the design of using irregulars. Note that in the far-eastern part of Turkey, a successful campaign of forces under Kiazim Karabekir against the forces of the fledgling "Democratic Republic of Armenia" would culminate in late 1920, and the young republic would succumb. By and large the Eastern campaign events do not seem to have involved American naval forces, nor much diplomatic effort; hence I leave them outside the scope of this work.

61. Ibid., 68–69. It appears that several of the large groups of Armenians who collected in churches and elsewhere in the city were guarded by small armed cadres of Armenians as long as their limited supply of ammunition held out. See here Ghevorn Chorbajian, "The 22 Days of Marash: Papers on the Defense of the City Against Turkish Forces Jan.–Feb., 1920," 402–18. Chorbajian had been commissioned a reserve officer in the Turkish army in 1917 but joined his parents when they were sent back to Marash in 1919 by French occupation authorities. (They were being deported just as he was originally drafted, in 1915—but survived.) This diary parallels Kerr's account fairly closely (Kerr had not seen it when he wrote), though it portrays the events mainly from the Armenian perspective.

62. Mabel Elliott, *Beginning Again at Ararat*, 98.

63. Kerr, *Lions of Marash*, 98–99.

64. Kerr outlines the events in *Lions of Marash*, 142–92; the skeletons on the road to Islahiye' (mostly those of Armenians, though some French soldiers also died en route) are mentioned on 196 and 213. Dr. Mabel Elliott described her experiences in this evacuation in *Beginning Again at Ararat*, 115–31.

65. Kerr, *Lions of Marash*, 175, cites Dr. Marion Wilson as fearing a general slaughter, for "each time an Armenian stronghold had been overwhelmed the *che'te'* had annihilated everyone." For instances of individual massacres of Armenians, see 99, 100, 110, 114, 117ff. in Kerr.

66. Ibid., 178–80.

67. Ibid., 205, 207.

68. Ibid., 86.

69. Alice Keep Clark (who had served as a relief worker at the American mission and orphanage at Hadjin during the first part of that siege) mentions the size of the post-deportation Armenian population of Hadjin in *Letters from Cilicia*, 116, and speaks to the massacre, 200. In *At the Mercy of Turkish Brigands,* 284, Mrs. D. C. Eby (a Canadian who had been at Hadjin) noted that some four hundred Armenians fought their way through to Adana—those were the only survivors. Richard Hovannisian says "some 8,000" were at Hadjin, vol. 3, 376, in *The Republic of Armenia (From London to Sevres, Feb.–Aug. 1920)*, 1996.

70. Kerr, *Lions of Marash*, 214.

71. See the accounts of John E. Merrill, "Pen Pictures of the Siege of Aintab," 1–3, and Lorin Shepard, "Fighting the Turks at Aintab," 590–93. Both Merrill and Shepard had been at Aintab.

72. A French withdrawal from Cilicia was negotiated in Oct. 1921, to be executed by Jan. 1922. Kerr, *Lions of Marash*, 236–37.

73. Bristol letter to J. B. Jackson, June 21, 1920, Box 32, June 1920 GC, MBC; also see Report on Marash by Dr. M. C. Wilson, director of Near East Relief at Marash, sent by Paul Knabenshue at Beirut to Admiral Bristol, report dated Aug. 2, 1920, in NR, RG 45, Subject File 1911–27, Box 831, Folder 9, 1, 8–9.

74. For example, see Bristol's dispatch to Sec State of Nov. 19, 1921, "Ottoman Empire, Refugees and Relief, 1921" folder, Box 73, MBC, and other messages in that same folder.

75. Buzanski dissertation, 180–82. Bristol was simmering about this over a year later; see the Bristol war diary, Nov. 2, 1922, MBC.

76. Letter to William T. Ellis of Feb. 26, 1920, Feb. 1920 GC file, MBC.

77. Bristol cable to Sec State of Feb. 26, 1920, NA 867.00/1124.

78. Laurence Evans, *United States Policy,* 258–61.

79. Message to Sec State of Mar. 24, 1920, in Bristol "Ottoman Empire Military, 1920" file, box 73, MBC.

80. Apr. 29, 1921, Bristol letter to Edward Moore of Harvard, Apr. 1921 GC, MBC.

81. Cf. Kerr, *Lions of Marash,* 214–19, and documents to which he refers; also Horton, *The Blight of Asia*, 195–200, which presents the account of an

unnamed American witness who accompanied the French; and Mary Caroline Holmes, *Between the Lines in Asia Minor.*

82. Francis Kelsey letter of Aug. 2, 1920, with attachment, one of them this copy of Holmes' letter from the diary of Harriett A. M. Smith, a nurse who had been at Urfa who Kelsey had met on a ship sailing for Athens, Aug. 1920 GC, MBC. The whole story of Urfa was told a couple of years later, though not with this immediacy, by Holmes in *Between the Lines in Asia Minor.*

83. Letter of Bristol to James L. Barton of Oct. 19, 1920, Oct. 1920 GC, MBC.

84. Dunn, *World Alive*, 307.

85. Ibid., 358–63.

86. Harbord, "The New Nations of Trans-Caucasia," 276, 280. Dr. Mabel Elliott (who went to the Caucasus in 1921) briefly describes the "constant war between Armenian and Tartar villages everywhere in the Caucasus," tracing its czarist instigation in Baku in 1905, *Beginning Again at Ararat*, 332–36. In *Armenia on the Road to Independence, 1918*, Hovannisian discusses the conflict's history and mentions some severe Armenian reprisals against Tartars in 1918. See, for instance, 21–22, 143–45. More generally, Taner Akçam itemizes and discusses massacres conducted by the Armenians of the Caucasus in *A Shameful Act*, 327–31.

87. Harbord Report, Papers Relating to the Foreign Relations of the United States, 860; Harbord, "The New Nations of Trans-Caucasia," 280.

88. Harbord Report, FRUS, 851.

89. Dunn, *World Alive*, 286, 406, 407.

90. Ibid., 348, 290–91. As Dunn's book was published posthumously, it is possible these discrepancies can be traced to his editor, not to Dunn.

91. Barton letter to Bristol of May 6, 1921, May 1921 GC, MBC.

92. Associated Press clipping of Mar. 6, 1920, Folder 36, Papers, General James Harbord, Library of Congress.

93. Halide letter to Bristol of Mar. 1, 1920, misfiled in GC Mar. 1921, MBC.

94. Kerr, *Lions of Marash*, 67, 201.

95. For example, in a letter to C. Van H. Engert at Aleppo, Mar. 20, 1920, Mar. 1920 GC, MBC.

96. Bristol war diary, Feb. 17 and Mar. 4, 1920, MBC.

97. Bristol's hope for American (and European) exertion of moral influence over the Turks was a common theme. See, for example, his war diary entry of Mar. 31, 1921, and Bristol's letter to James Barton of Mar. 28, 1921, Mar. 1921 GC, MBC.

98. See Bristol's brief description of his day, in a letter of Oct. 26, 1921, to Henry Goldthwaite, Oct. 1921 GC, MBC.

99. Letter from Dunn to Bristol of Nov. 29, 1922, in Box 68, "Dunn Papers," MBC.

100. Leahy diary, 243, 248.

101. Sept. 3 and 8, 1921, letters of Clover Dulles to her parents, Dulles Papers.

102. Letter of Allen Dulles to his mother, Jan. 18, 1921, Dulles Papers.

103. May 4, (1921?), Bristol family letters, Box 25, MBC.

104. Helen Ogden letter to mother and father, Apr. 25, 1921, Ogden Papers.

105. (Edwards), "Turkish Delight," vol. 22, 440.

106. Pence diary entry of Nov. 17, 1921.

107. Hovannisian, *The Republic of Armenia*, vol. 2, *From Versailles to London, 1919–1920*, 353.

108. Dunn, *World Alive*, 425.

109. E-mail of Apr. 15, 2000, to the author from Britton Murdoch, Williams' son-in-law.

110. Charles J. Wheeler, "Reminiscences," 75.

111. For the term "indefatigable," see the State Department reference cited in the Buzanski dissertation, 183; for the social life comment, see (Edwards), "Turkish Delight," 329.

112. Henderson and Ryan, "Naval Watch in the Mideast," 72; Horton, *The Blight of Asia*, 205.

113. Informal oral history of Rear Adm. William F. "Dolly" Fitzgerald, 42; Clover Dulles letter to her father of Dec. 13, 1920, Dulles Papers.

114. Dobkin, *Smyrna 1922*, 97; Buzanski dissertation, 188.

115. Buzanski dissertation, 182–85; see "Pontus" chapter.

116. Edward Hale Bierstadt, *The Great Betrayal*, 101.

117. Charles J. Wheeler, "Reminiscences," 80.

Chapter 4. The White Russian Invasion

1. Mansel, *Constantinople*, 398.

2. P. R. Butler, "Grief and Glamour of the Bosphorus," 203–12, 204.

3. Gates, *Not to Me Only*, 276.

4. Butler, "Grief and Glamour of the Bosphorus," 206; Kenneth L. Roberts, "The Constantinople Refugees," 56.

5. Kenneth L. Roberts, *Why Europe Leaves Home,* 127.

6. Alice Keep Clark, *Letters from Cilicia,* 13; Andrew Ryan, *The Last of the Dragomans*, 132.

7. H. H. Fisher, *The Famine in Soviet Russia*, 451.

8. Charles J. Weeks Jr., *An American Naval Diplomat*, 208.

9. C. E. Bechhofer, *In Denikin's Russia,* 212–13.

10. Vernon Duke, *Passport to Paris*, 66.

11. Weeks, *An American Naval Diplomat*, 209.

12. Letter to McCully of Mar. 5, 1920, Mar. 1920, MBC.

13. Duke, *Passport to Paris*, 65.

14. Bechhofer, *In Denikin's Russia*, 212–13.

15. H. H. Fisher, *The Famine in Soviet Russia*, 451.

16. Author's phone interview with Tony Waller, early Apr. 2000.

17. Charles J. Weeks, "A Samaritan in Russia," 12–13.

18. Ibid., 13–15.

19. Cf. P. J. Capelotti, ed., *Our Man in the Crimea*, 1991.

20. Weeks, "A Samaritan in Russia," 16.

21. Bristol Letter to McCully of Mar. 5, 1920, Mar. 1920 GC, MBC.

22. McCully letter to Bristol of Mar. 26, 1920, Mar. 1920 GC, MBC; Berthelsen, *Tin Can Man*, 29–35, 211–12. A smaller evacuation from Theodosia and Sebastopol followed soon after; cf. Berthelsen, *Tin Can Man*, 203, 212–13.

23. Weeks, "A Samaritan in Russia," 16.

24. H. H. Fisher, *The Famine in Soviet Russia*, 451; Eugenia S. Bumgardner, *Undaunted Exiles*, 4.

25. Weeks, *An American Naval Diplomat*, 221.

26. McCully letter to Bristol of May 11, 1920, May 1920 GC, MBC.

27. Weeks, *An American Naval Diplomat*, 213; McCully diary, Feb. 17 to Mar. 9, 1920, McCully Papers, Library of Congress.

28. McCully diary, Apr. through May, 1920.

29. Weeks, *An American Naval Diplomat*, 237–38.

30. Berthelsen, *Tin Can Man*, 68–72.

31. Roberts, "The Constantinople Refugees," 10.

32. Sharp memoir, privately printed, provided to the author by Sharp's son, George.

33. Weeks, *An American Naval Diplomat*, 243; Beers, "U.S. Naval Detachment in Turkish Waters," 216.

34. Weeks, "A Samaritan in Russia," 17; Berthelsen, *Tin Can Man*, 203; McCully diary, Nov. 14–15, 1920, McCully Papers; Beers, "U.S. Naval Detachment in Turkish Waters," 216.

35. Charles Olsen letters to Edna of Nov. 14–16, 1920, Olsen Papers.

36. Ibid., Nov. 15–16, 1920.

37. Ibid., Nov. 17, 1920.

38. Berthelsen, *Tin Can Man,* 205–6.

39. McCully diary, Nov. 18, 19, 1920, McCully Papers.

40. Charles Olsen letter to Edna, Nov. 17, 1920, Olsen Papers.

41. McCully diaries, Nov. 16 and 22, 1920, McCully Papers.

42. Weeks, "A Samaritan in Russia," 17.

43. Charles Olsen letter to Edna, Nov. 21, 1920, Olsen Papers; Vernon Duke, *Passport to Paris,* 70.

44. A report quoted by Bumgardner, *Undaunted Exiles,* 5.

45. Helen Bristol letter to her mother of Nov. 22 and 30, 1920, undated letters, Box 25, MBC, and an article of hers in the Nov. 9, 1921, issue of *Utah* ship's paper called "The Big U," in the first of four files entitled "The Russian Refugees," Box 74, MBC.

46. Roberts, "The Constantinople Refugees," 56.

47. Jak Deleon, *The White Russians in Istanbul,* 49–50.

48. Mansel, *Constantinople,* 399.

49. Eveline Scott, "When the Russians Came to Constantinople," 571; Olsen letter to Edna, Nov. 27, 1920, Olsen Papers.

50. Deleon, *The White Russians in Istanbul,* 28.

51. Bumgardner, *Undaunted Exiles,* 157; Dos Passos, *Orient Express,* 12.

52. Solano, "Constantinople Today," 55.

53. Bumgardner, *Undaunted Exiles,* 148–50.

54. Isaac Marcosson, "When Constantinople Went Dry," 44.

55. Clover Dulles letter to "Dearest Pelican," (c. Apr. 4, 1921), Dulles Papers.

56. James Clay mentioned this to his son; phone interview with his son, James Clay, Oct. 1999.

57. Roberts, "The Constantinople Refugees," 58.

58. Ogden letter of Feb. 13, 1921, Ogden Papers.

59. Letter to the author of Oct. 25, 1999, from John B. Pleasants.

60. Scott, "When the Russians Came to Constantinople," 572; (Edwards), "Turkish Delight," 441.

61. Charles Olsen letter to Edna, Apr. 14, 1921, Olsen Papers.

62. Roberts, *Why Europe Leaves Home,* 136.

63. Roberts, "The Constantinople Refugees," 58.

64. Ibid., 58.

65. Clarence Johnson, *Constantinople To-Day*, 214; Roberts, "The Constantinople Refugees," 58; Bumgardner, *Undaunted Exiles*, 140ff.

66. John Freely, *A History of Robert College*, 241.

67. Author's interview with Erkmen, Istanbul, May 2000.

68. Deleon, *The White Russians in Istanbul*, 81; Gates, *Not to Me Only*, 227; Lynn Scipio, *My Thirty Years in Turkey*, 190–91; Freely, *A History of Robert College*, 241.

69. The author was shown Becker's portrait of Louise Hepburn by Joseph and Lorraine Hepburn Barse, 2000. Bristol records posing for Becker in his war diary of Mar. 22, 1923, MBC.

70. Author's interview with Frank Howell, Cdr. Harry Pence's son-in-law, San Diego, May 2000.

71. Bumgardner, *Undaunted Exiles*, 157.

72. Kenneth L. Roberts, "Drifting Leaves," 366–67.

73 Deleon, *The White Russians in Istanbul*, 25; Roberts, "Drifting Leaves," 369; Duke, *Passport to Paris*, 70.

74. Ogden letters of Feb. 21 and 27 and Mar. 3, 4, and 7, 1921, Ogden Papers.

75. Ogden letter of July 18, 1921, Ogden Papers.

76. Bumgardner, *Undaunted Exiles,* 79.

77. Peter Grose, *Gentleman Spy*, 74.

78. Letters from Clover to various recipients of Jan. 11, Mar. 2, Aug. 9, and Sept. 3 and 8, 1921, Dulles Papers. Bumgardner also mentions Gortchakoff, *Undaunted Exiles*, 156.

79. Grose, *Gentleman Spy*, 78, 84; letter of Clover to her mother ca. Jan. 1922, Dulles Papers.

80. Anna V. S. Mitchell, corrected letter to "Caroline" (her sister, Caroline Green Mitchell Stokes) of Mar. 18, 1922, Mitchell Letters.

81. Ibid., May 20, 1922.

82. See Mark Bristol's letter to a Mr. Vanderlip of Oct. 9, 1922, misfiled in Oct. 1921 GC, MBC; see also the folders on the Russian refugees in Box 74, and Helen Moore Bristol's general correspondence, Boxes 19 and 20, MBC.

83. See Elsie Kimball's letter to her family of Apr. 11, 1920, Kimball Papers.

84. Many of these Turkish refugees had come from Eastern European nations that had recently thrown off the Ottoman yoke. Others, however, were from various places in Turkey itself. Anyway, in a letter to a Turkish paper of June 21, 1921, probably while she was in Angora, relief worker and Bristol representative Annie Allen agreed that it was time to plead to America for Turkish

orphans and pointed out that a small effort had already begun along those lines. See the reply of Miss Annie T. Allen to correspondent "Sekeria," in July 21–31, 1921 GC, General Correspondence folder, MBC.

85. Harriet Welles, "Following the Ship," 118.

86. A. Goodrich-Freer, *Things Seen in Constantinople*, 63.

87. Paul Morand, "Turkish Night," 106.

88. Letters of Margaret Bryan to Helen Bristol of Dec. 20, 1923; Feb. 2, 1924; and Jan. 30, 1923, found in Family Papers, 1923–24, MBC.

89. Philip R. Hepburn, description of a trip to Constantinople, 6, Hepburn Papers.

90. William Maguire, *Rig for Church,* 123–24.

91. Weeks, *An American Naval Diplomat*, 248.

92. Letter to author from John Waller's son Tony Waller, Mar. 29, 2000.

Chapter 5. Death in the Pontus

1. For example, the dispatch of May 29, 1921, sent by *Fox*. Summarized in the *Fox* May 29, 1921, war diary entry, but see especially May 17, 21, 24, and 28 entries; NA 867.00/1426. The *Fox* war diary can be found in the bibliography under "Trammell."

2. Dunn's *World Alive* (427) places the interruption of the Prinkipo party on a Sunday in midsummer, at the ordered deportation of the Greeks in Samsun. However, Bristol's Sunday, May 29, 1921, war diary reports an interruption of a daytime Prinkipo party that closely matches much of Dunn's description. Various documents cited in this chapter indicate that two such urgent messages were sent by destroyer to Bristol; Dunn seems to have confused the second with the first.

3. Oscar Heizer, Apr. 11, 1919, letter to Sec State, NA 867.4016/411. For the apparently widespread use of young Armenian women for sexual pleasure in Trebizond, see Vahakn N. Dadrian's reference to the testimony of Turkish officials, found in "The Armenian Genocide: An Interpretation," in Jay Winter, ed., *America and the Armenian Genocide of 1915*, 83–84. As for Armenians being loaded in boats and thrown overboard into the Black Sea, this came out at the 1919 trials. See Taner Akçam, *A Shameful Act*, 181.

4. Heizer July 28, 1915, letter to Morgenthau, NA 867.4016/128, in Ara Sarafian, *United States Official Documents on the Armenian Genocide*, vol. 1, 24–28. Sir Martin Gilbert quotes from the Italian consul-general's chilling eyewitness account of the Trebizond massacres and concludes that in a two-week period, Turkish troops murdered all but some 100 of the 17,000 Armenians in Trebizond. See "Twentieth-Century Genocides," 15.

5. *Olympia* report of Sept. 9, 1919, especially the portion of that report composed by John B. Bostick, NA 867.00/963.

6. Constantinople Consul's report of Aug. 8, 1919, NA 867.00/923.

7. Ibid., and *Olympia* report, NA 867.00/963. See also the report of an encounter of American naval officers with highly armed Greek bandits near Samsun, the latter very tired of being outlaws and wanting to get back to their regular work; Bristol war diary weekly summary for week ending Oct. 1, 1922, MBC.

8. *Olympia* report, NA 867.00/963; the same frustration on the part of Greeks was also reported by Consul Horton in Smyrna concerning Greeks who had been forced out of the Aegean coasts of Turkey during the Great War and came back only to find their property occupied. See Horton's letter to Bristol of Jan. 23, 19(2)0, in NA 867.00/1168.

9. *Olympia* report, NA 867.00/963.

10. See, for example, the American intelligence report of Nov. 1, 1920, about Greek intrigue in the Pontus, an examination of documents written by Venizelos and others, in NA Box 831, folder 9. Bristol's intelligence officer Robbie Dunn later spoke of the "well established Pontus sedition" (Dunn draft letter to Sec State of July 28, 1921, July 1921 GC, MBC), but his credibility on this topic is suspect. See the skeptical references to Dunn and to a dispatch in part focusing about his dealing with the "Pontus sedition" in an internal memorandum at the State Department, NA 867.00/1495. It seems true, though, that at one point, Premier Venizelos seriously considered a Greek landing at Trebizond. See J. K. Hassiotis, "Shared Illusions: Greek–Armenian Co-operation in Asia Minor and the Caucasus (1917–1922)," 169–71.

11. Everett and Mary Stephens, *Survival Against All Odds*, 40.

12. Ibid., 33–34; Efthimios Couzinos, *Twenty-Three Years in Asia Minor*, 48.

13. Stephens, *Survival Against All Odds*, 33–34, 118–19, 163; also Willard and Gage obituaries seen at the Bible House office in Istanbul. Even in Stephens' book, accounts conflict. I use figures from the Bible House obituaries.

14. George E. White, *Adventuring with Anatolia College*, 107.

15. Ibid., 108; Stephens, *Survival Against All Odds*, 39.

16. Phelps report to Allen Dulles is filed under a July 7, 1922, letter from Charles Fowle to Dulles, NA 867.4016/582, 2–3. See also Annie Allen's outrage at the Turkish claims about Talas, recorded in Dunn, *World Alive*, 418, and Dunn's draft letter to Sec State of July, 28, 1921, July 1921 GC, MBC.

17. Stephens, *Survival Against All Odds*, 39; George E. White, *Adventuring with Anatolia College*, 108.

18. George E. White, *Adventuring with Anatolia College*, 108–9; Dunn draft letter to Sec State of July 28, 1921, in July 1921, MBC; Moranian dissertation, 448–50.

19. George E. White, *Adventuring with Anatolia College*, 111; Moranian dissertation, 449.

20. Mango, *Atatürk*, 331.

21. George E. White, *Adventuring with Anatolia College*, 109.

22. Mar. 31, 1921, Bristol war diary, and weekly report of Apr. 3, 1921, MBC.

23. Hosford statement of Dec. 7, 1921, NA 867.4016/449.

24. Draft letter to Sec State, July 28, 1921, July 1921 GC, MBC and letter of Bristol to Sec State, NA 867.00/1489.

25. Notes of Dunn's second interview with Youssouf Kemal Bey, July 5, 1921, 2, in July 21–31, 1921 GC, MBC.

26. From the paper *Hakimiyeti Milliye* of Angora of June 24, 1921, found in the Annie Allen compilation, July 21–31, 1921 GC, MBC.

27. Mango, *Atatürk*, 330–31.

28. Ibid., 329.

29. Gertrude Anthony report to Sec State of Dec. 12, 1921, transmitting a corrected copy of what she wrote to Admiral Bristol in Constantinople on Nov. 1, 1921, 1–2ff, NA 867.4016/448; also messages of May 26, 1921, and June 2, 1921, from Bristol to Sec State, in "Ottoman Empire, Refugees and Relief, 1921" File, Box 73, MBC.

30. Anthony report to Sec State of Dec. 12, 1921, ibid., 1–2.

31. Ibid., 3–4.

32. *Fox* diary from May 21–28 in report dated May 29, 1921, NA 867.00/1426. See also Joyce's letter to Captain Cotten of June 20, 1921, in which Joyce cites well-authenticated reports that most of the first three parties of deported Greeks were killed, NR, RG 45, Box 832, Folder 2, Box 832.

33. Dunn memo for Bristol, June 9, 1921, June 1921 GC, MBC.

34. Dunn draft of message of May 29, 1921, "Dunn" file in Box 68, MBC.

35. Arnold Toynbee, *The Western Question*, 287, 298; the quotation is taken from Toynbee's letter to Bristol from Smyrna, dated 7/8/21, NA 867.4016/445. See also Bristol war diary, May 27, 1921, for a conversation between the two on this topic.

36. The quotations from the two paragraphs above come from pages 9 and 11, respectively, of the Allied white paper, "Report on Atrocities in the Districts of Yalova and Guemlek and in the Ismid Peninsula," Box 1346 U-1-I, NA. See 3, 4, 6, and 11 of that report on atrocities against Greeks and Armenians in 1915, 1920, and 1921, and also see Michael Llewellyn Smith, *Ionian Vision*, 31, 34, on the massive Turkish deportations of Greek coastal populations during the war. However, the whole Allied report and Smith's brief account of the Marmora activities (209–15) should be consulted for evidence and arguments

on both sides. Also to be consulted is Toynbee's long account in *The Western Question* (259–319), which account documents many atrocities of Greeks against Turks of this period. Toynbee interviewed many Turkish survivors or victims, but he did not seem to look much into the Greek side of this particular issue. Though he quotes the Allied report frequently, the historian omits to notice its conclusion that, on the Ismid peninsula, atrocities committed by the Turks "have been more considerable and ferocious than those on the part of the Greeks," 9. Overall, Winston's Churchill's judgment—that the Greek atrocities were "on a minor scale" when compared to the "appalling deportations of Greeks from the Trebizond and Samsun districts" (which had also taken place in 1921)—is better to be trusted. Cf. *The Aftermath*, vol. 5 of *The World Crisis: 1918–1928*, 430.

37. See, on reprisals, Bristol's war diary account of a discussion with acting British high commissioner Henderson of July 26, 1922. Bristol's message to Sec State of June 2, 1921, incorporating Dunn's comments, can be found in Bristol, "Ottoman Empire Military, 1921," File Box 73, MBC. In a subsequent message of June 7, Bristol did mention the Greek refugee complaints.

38. Mark Bristol war diary for July 20, 1921, MBC; John Dos Passos, *The Best Times*, 91–92.

39. Dos Passos, *The Best Times*, 92. The deck capacity of the destroyers for refugees would be tested several times over the next year or two; on one occasion, an American destroyer would carry eleven hundred refugees. See Charles Merz, "Bristol, Quarterdeck Diplomat," 6.

40. Bristol war diary for July 20, 1921, MBC.

41. Heizer report of June 28, 1915, NA 867.4016/114.

42. *Humphreys* war diary account of June 7, 1921 (6), NR RG 45, Box 832, Folder 2; Dunn memo for Admiral of June 10, 1921, June 1921 GC, MBC.

43. Second interview with Youssouf Kemal Bey; July 5, 1921, July 1921 GC, MBC.

44. July 14 telegrams to Bristol, *Brooks* 71 serial, Ottoman Empire, Military, 1921 folder, Box 73, MBC.

45. Anthony report to Sec State of Dec. 12, 1921, NA 867.4016/448, 4–5.

46. Handwritten letter from G. L. Bristol of *Overton* to Admiral Bristol, July 18, 1921, in GC July 1–20, 1921 GC, MBC.

47. Dos Passos, *Orient Express*, 13.

48. The Bristol war diary of July 22, 1921, MBC, indicates Commander Houston was the man who had met with the archbishop.

49. Quoted in Moranian dissertation, 466.

50. For this fitness report and the two letters attached, see the promotion file for Commander Houston in NA, Record Group 125, Proceedings of the N&MC Examining Board, circa 1890–1941, Box 538, vol. 742 (two folders). Houston failed to be selected for captain, and retired as a commander on June 22, 1926. *Brooks* was in fact not sent home immediately, but was ordered back to the States on Sept. 25, 1921.

51. Message from Bristol to Sec State of July 18, 1921, in Bristol "Ottoman Empire, Military, 1921" file, Box 73, MBC; the text of the report itself can be found following the Aug. 1, 1921, entry in *Overton* war diary, NR, RG 45, Box 832, Folder 2.

52. *Overton* serial 362 message to Stanav, CS, July 20, 1921, Ottoman Empire file, MBC; for the latter, see the July 19, 1921, entry of *Overton* war diary, NR, RG 45, Box 832, Folder 2.

53. Copy of Youssuf Bey's dispatch of July 23, 1921, in *Overton* war diary after Aug. 1, entry, NR, RG 45, Box 832, Folder 2.

54. Anthony report to Sec State of Dec. 12, 1921, NA 867.4016/448, 15; Charles E. Hughes letter to Henry Cabot Lodge of Apr. 22, 1922, NA 867.4016/453. British sources had reported that plans to deport all remaining Christians from Samsun had been postponed, and attributed this change to interventions on the part of "commanders of American vessels in that port." See Yeghiayan Yartkes, *British Reports on Ethnic Cleansing in Anatolia,* 223, 231. These sources would report additional Samsun deportations later, however; see 245, 254–55.

55. Anthony report to Sec State of Dec. 12, 1921, NA 867.4016/448, 5; Carl C. Compton, *The Morning Cometh,* 36.

56. Compton, *The Morning Cometh,* 36; Anthony report to Sec State of Dec. 12, 1921, NA 867.4016/448, 6.

57. Compton, *The Morning Cometh,* 36.

58. Anthony report to Sec State of Dec. 12, 1921, NA 867.4016/448, 2.

59. Ibid., 8, 13.

60. Ibid.; Compton, *The Morning Cometh,* 37.

61. Compton, *The Morning Cometh,* 37.

62. Everett and Mary Stephens, *Survival Against all Odds,* 170.

63. Anthony report to Sec State of Dec. 12, 1921, NA 867.4016/448, 10–11; Hosford report on Marsovan, NA 867.4016/441, 8.

64. Compton, *The Morning Cometh,* 37.

65. Anthony report to Sec State of Dec. 12, 1921, NA 867.4016/448, 11.

66. Compton, *The Morning Cometh,* 38; see a similar incident recorded by Anthony, report to Sec State of Dec. 12, 1921, NA 867.4016/448, 12.

67. Anthony report to Sec State of Dec. 12, 1921, 867.4016/448, 13; Hosford, report on Marsovan, NA 867.4016/441, 8–9; W. Peet, encl. 2 to report to Sec State, Nov. 6, 1921, NA 867.4016/438.

68. Compton, *The Morning Cometh*, 38.

69. Anthony report to Sec State of Dec. 12, 1921, NA 867.4016/ 448, 11; Hosford report on Marsovan, NA 867.4016/441, 11.

70. Compton, *The Morning Cometh*, 40–41.

71. Ibid., 39–40.

72. Couzinos, *Twenty-Three Years in Asia Minor*, 112–14.

73. Compton, *The Morning Cometh,* 41.

74. Gillespie numbers Osman's men at three thousand, 5, in letter to Bristol of Jan. 10, 1922, NA 867.00/1488, NA. The term "cut-throat" is from Andrew Mango, *Atatürk,* 330; for the acclaim see Hosford report of Dec. 6, 1921, NA 867.00/1500. *The London Times* clipping "The Turk at Work" of Oct. 16, 1921, NA 867.4016/438, mentions the Turkish press's treatment of Osman.

75. Gillespie, 5, letter to Bristol of Jan. 10, 1922, NA 867.00/1488.

76. Dunn, Memorandum to Bristol reporting information from Florence Billings on her return from Angora, Aug. 25, 1921, "Dunn Papers," Box 68, MBC.

77. Theda Phelps' report enclosed an envelope featuring this stamp, NA 867.4016/582; Mango, *Atatürk*, 384, speaks of the monument over his grave in Giresun, Osman's hometown.

78. NA 867.4016/449.

79. NA 867.00/1500.

80. Buzanski dissertation, 182–85; Grabill, *Protestant Diplomacy and the Near East*, 260–61.

81. Anthony report to Sec State of Dec. 12, 1921, NA 867.4016/448, 15.

82. Bristol war diary accounts, Aug. 17, 1921 (Marden), and Apr. 15, 1922 (Anthony), MBC.

83. Compton, *The Morning Cometh*, 42.

84. War diaries of *McFarland* of Aug. 31 and Sept. 2, 3, 5, and 8, 1921, NR, RG 45, Box 832, Folder 2; *Williamson* serial 119 message to Stanav, Oct. 9, 1921, Ottoman Empire, Military, 1921 file, Box 73, MBC.

85. Leahy diary, 256 (entry of Sept. 21, 1921).

86. *Fox* war diary, Nov. 14, 17, and 26.

87. Ibid., Apr. 10, 1922.

88. *McFarland* war diary, May 26, 1922, Pence Papers.

89. Charles W. Fowle letter to Sec State of Nov. 17, 1921, with Hopkins' Nov. 16 report as attachment, NA 867.4016/432.

90. Bristol letter of Jan. 23, 1922, Jan. 1922 GC, MBC.

91. Letter of Nov. 8, 1921, Nov. 1921 GC, MBC.

92. Letter to Sec State of Oct. 23, 1920, NA 867.00/1361; Bristol war diary of Oct. 3, 1922, MBC.

93. Bristol letter to Sec State of Feb. 22, 1922, NA 867.00/1497; Gillespie letter of Jan. 10, 1922, NA 867.00/1498. 94. "Jivislik" in original; I use the spelling from Gibbons' newspaper article, referred to below.

95. *Fox* war diary, June 18, 1922.

96. *McFarland* war diary, May 26, 1922, Pence Papers.

97. Letter to Jackson at Aleppo, Apr. 5, 1922, NA 867.4016/454.

98. Supplementary report to the secretary of state of uncertain date, marked for receipt on July 14, 1922, NA 867.4016/575.

99. Bristol war diary, May 27, 1921, MBC.

100. Ibid., May 3 and 24, 1922, MBC.

101. "Personal" letter of H. C. Jaquith to Charles V. Vickery, May 3, 1922, NA 867.4016/489.

102. Bristol war diary account of May 24, 1922, MBC.

103. Ibid., for example, of May 10, May 17, May 23, and July 26, 1922, MBC.

104. Ibid. of May 12, 1922, MBC.

105. May 22, 1922, message from Bristol to Sec State, NA 867.4016/464.

106. "The Explanation of the Ministry of Interior" and other papers, in Bristol letter to Sec State of July 12, 1922, NA 867.4016/588.

107. Even Bristol would later occasionally acknowledge the validity of their reports. Cf. Oct. 7, 1922, war diary, MBC.

108. Extracts from Ward diary, encl. 1 to Bristol's report to Sec State, July 12, 1922, NA 867.4016/588.

109. June 14, 1922, report by Murdoch, encl. 2 to Bristol's letter to Sec State of July 12, 1922, NA 867. 4016/588.

110. Aug. 4, 1922, statement, 5, NA 867.4016/621.

111. See H. G. D.'s (Harry G. Dwight's) memo to Warren Robbins prefacing Anthony's report, which she had laid before Bristol in Constantinople, NA 867.4016/448.

112. July 25, 1922, letter to Bristol, in June–July 1922 GC, MBC.

113. Harry Pence, war diary of *McFarland*, May 26, 1922, Pence Papers.

114. Herbert Adams Gibbons, "Greek Massacres by Turks Continue," in Edward Hale Bierstadt, *The Great Betrayal*, 201–3; also *McFarland* war diary, May 26, 1922, Pence Papers.

115. Herbert Adams Gibbons, "Near East Relief Prevented from Helping Greeks," *Christian Science Monitor,* July 13, 1922, reprinted in Bierstadt, *The Great Betrayal*, 204–12; 205.

116. Cf. the full Clayton report in NA 867.4016/618.

117. Miss Wade report of June 23, 1922, NA 867.4016/619. See also the detailed report by Ruth Woods concerning the early period of deportations at Harput, i.e., from June 5 to Sept. 10, 1921, NA 867.4016/645.

118. See, in this respect, Stanley Kerr's letters sent by Consul Jackson in Aleppo to the State Department about further deportations occurring in Cilicia, NA 860.4016/87. In addition, Andrew Mango reports that "Greeks in areas of western and southern Anatolia under Turkish nationalist control were also deported by order of the Ankara government," *Atatürk*, 331.

Chapter 6. After Dark in Pera and Galata

1. Deleon, *The White Russians in Istanbul*, 69.

2. Scott, "When the Russians Came to Constantinople," 571; Butler, "Grief and Glamour of the Bosphorus," 208.

3. Bumgardner, *Undaunted Exiles*, 135–36, 132.

4. Deleon, *The White Russians in Istanbul*, 65–66.

5. Bumgardner, *Undaunted Exiles*, 133–35.

6. Olsen letter to Edna of Apr. 14, 1921, Olsen Papers; Bumgardner, *Undaunted Exiles*, 133.

7. (Edwards), "Turkish Delight," 441. Jeanette was wrong in her expectations about Vertinsky's short life, however. The singer eventually left for Europe, where he not only continued to sing and compose "novellas-in-song" (Duke would call them "sex serenades") but also acted in films. He returned to Russia in 1943 and died in 1957. See Vernon Duke on Vertinsky in Constantinople in his *Passport to Paris*, 77, and the brief Internet biography by Anastasia Vertinsky accessed Oct. 28, 2001, http://russia-in-us.com/Music/Pop/Vertinsky/.

8. Bumgardner, *Undaunted Exiles*, 130–31; Deleon, *The White Russians in Istanbul*, 50; and Zia Bey, *Speaking of the Turks*, 157–58.

9. Duke, *Passport to Paris*, 78–79; Mansel, *Constantinople*, 399; Rufus Fairchild Zogbaum, *From Sail to Saratoga*, 366; Bumgardner, *Undaunted Exiles*, 130–31.

10. (Edwards), "Turkish Delight," 440.

11. Olsen letter of Dec. 17, 1920, Olsen Papers.

12. Dunn, *World Alive*, 387.

13. Charles J. Wheeler, "Reminiscences," 104.

14. Bumgardner, *Undaunted Exiles*, 127.

15. Deleon, *The White Russians in Istanbul*, 64, 68.

16. Ibid., 67, 69.

17. Ibid., 68.

18. Shenk, *Playships of the World*, 175. Deleon, *The White Russians in Istanbul* (49) mentions a Jan Gilesko, who played the violin.

19. Roberts, "The Constantinople Refugees," 58.

20. Maguire, *Rig for Church*, 116.

21. Jean and Kathy Godfrey, *Genius in the Family*, 213; also D.V. Gallery, "My Pal Arthur Godfrey," 25, 112–14.

22. Zia Bey, *Speaking of the Turks*, 158. Zia Bey's specific reference is to Stella's rather than Maxim's.

23. Deleon, *The White Russians in Istanbul*, 49.

24. The Aquarium reference comes from this website, accessed May 29, 2003: www.kcn.ru/tat_en/university/ahern/493/mod2.htm.

25. Dunn, *World Alive*, 421.

26. Elizabeth Cotten, "In the Days of the High Commissioner," 952.

27. (Edwards), "Turkish Delight," 329.

28. Cotten, "In the Days of the High Commissioner," 952.

29. Daniel P. Mannix, *The Old Navy*, 275. See also Mansel, *Constantinople*, 399, and Marcosson, "When Constantinople Went Dry," 44.

30. (Edwards), "Turkish Delight," 441.

31. Paul Morand, "Turkish Night," 97.

32. Butler, "Grief and Glamour of the Bosphorus," 208; Zia Bey, *Speaking of the Turks*, 155.

33. Roberts, "Drifting Leaves," 370; Bumgardner, *Undaunted Exiles*, 125.

34. Shenk, *Playships of the World*, Nov. 17 and Nov. 30, 1922, 154–56, 164–65.

35. Bumgardner, *Undaunted Exiles*, 107, 106.

36. Roberts, "Drifting Leaves," 370; Bumgardner, *Undaunted Exiles*, 116.

37. Zia Bey, *Speaking of the Turks,* 151–60.

38. Bristol war diary, June 27, 1921, MBC.

39. Appendix to Bristol war diary of Feb. 9, 1919, entry by E.W.Tod, CO, *Scorpion*, MBC.

40. William T. Ellis, "Constantinople Today," 519. Again, Abdul Hamid was the infamous sultan, who, partly in response to provocations by Armenian revolutionaries, had ordered massacres of Armenians not only far away in Anatolia, but even in the city of Constantinople itself; in 1896 some six thousand Armenians were killed there (Mansel, *Constantinople*, 333; Balakian, *The*

Burning Tigris, 103–10). The appellation "Abdul the Damned" is from Sir Martin Gilbert, "Twentieth-Century Genocides," 10.

41. Ships and Shipping Folder, Box 78, MBC.
42. Clarence Johnson, ed., *Constantinople To-Day*, 360.
43. Ibid., 263.
44. Bumgardner, *Undaunted Exiles*, 119–20; Bristol letter to Clarence Johnson of Feb. 15, 1921, Feb. 1921 GC, MBC.
45. Johnson, *Constantinople To-Day*, 356, 359.
46. Duke, *Passport to Paris*, 70.
47. Dunn, *World Alive*, 287–89.
48. Olsen letter to Edna of Dec. 25, 1920, Olsen Papers.
49. Ibid. of Feb. 6, 1921.
50. Ibid. of Dec. 29, 1920.
51. Ibid. of Jan. 2, 1921; Dec. 29 and Dec. 27, 1920.
52. Ibid., Jan. 27, 1921.
53. Ibid., of Jan. 5, 18, and 25, 1921.
54. Ibid., of Apr. 14, 1921.
55. Ibid., of Dec. 29, 1920; Apr. 21, 1921; Jan. 25, 1921.
56. Ibid., of Dec. 28 and 29, 1920; Jan. 21, 27, 29; and Feb. 6, 1921.
57. Ibid. of Jan. 30, 1921.
58. Ibid., of May 9, 1921.
59. Edna's letters to her parents of Oct. 22, 1921, and June 10, 1922, Olsen Papers.
60. Bumgardner, *Undaunted Exiles*, 119.
61. Orin Haskell letter to his wife, Audrey, of Apr. 23, 1923, Haskell Letters.
62. Edna Olsen letter to mother and father of Feb. 19, 1922, Olsen Papers.
63. (Edwards), "Turkish Delight," 329, 442.
64. Bristol war diary, June 24, 1922, MBC.
65. N. Teffi, "Constantinople—The Rusty Door to the East," 567.
66. Letter to Edna of Feb. 7, 1921, Olsen Papers.
67. Letter from John B. Pleasants to the author, Oct. 25, 1999.
68. Leahy diary, 246; Henry H. Adams, *Witness to Power*, 43.
69. Alfons Pacquet, "Constantinople," 260.
70. Marcosson, "When Constantinople Went Dry," 44.
71. Dunn, *World Alive*, 293; correspondence with Winckler's relatives, early 2000.

72. Interview of Feb. 7, 2000, and subsequent correspondence with Edward Jones Jr.

73. Alice Keep Clark, *Letters from Cilicia*, 10; Mitchell, uncorrected letter to her sister Caroline of July 27, 1922, Mitchell Letters; Pence, July 4, 1922, diary entry, Pence Papers.

74. Letter to Edna of Dec. 28, 1920, Olsen Papers.

Chapter 7. The Great Russian Famine

1. Bristol message to Sec State, July 25, 1921, and Sec State response of July 26, 1921, also Bristol message of Aug. 10, 1921, all in Box 73, Ottoman Empire, Refugees and Relief, 1921 folder, MBC; W. L. White, "The Liquidation of Herbert Hoover," 1–2; Dunn, *World Alive*, 390. For Gorky's appeal, see also Bertrand M. Patenaude, *The Big Show in Bololand*, 27. Patenaude's 750-page opus, obviously the standard work on its topic, barely touches on the American Navy's experience of the famine and its assistance in the relief efforts.

2. Commission message to the Associated Press of Sept. 5, 1921, from Tsaritsin, in Aug. 1921 GC, MBC.

3. W. L. White, "The Liquidation of Herbert Hoover," 4.

4. Commission message to "Nearest New York" of Sept. 7, 1921, from Aksai, Astrakhan, in Aug. 1921 GC, MBC.

5. F. A. Mackenzie, *Russia Before Dawn*, 152.

6. Henry Beeuwkes, "American Medical and Sanitary Relief in the Russian Famine, 1921–1923," 26.

7. In addition to Bolshevik requisitions, several other factors helped cause the famine, including inefficient and antiquated agricultural practices under the czar, the wartime mobilization of millions of men and horses, a peasant rebellion, and the great drought of 1920–21.

8. See here Patenaude, *The Big Show in Bololand*, 25–27. Specific figures for relief contributions are cited in H. H. Fisher, *The Famine in Soviet Russia*, 549.

9. Dunn's narration of the initial confrontation can be found in *World Alive*, 390–402.

10. Ibid., 400, 397, 398.

11. Ibid., 402.

12. H. H. Fisher, *The Famine in Soviet Russia*, 184; Herbert Hoover, *An American Epic*, vol. 3, 484.

13. H. H. Fisher, *The Famine in Soviet Russia*, 177–79.

14. Dunn, *World Alive*, 402.

15. Beers, "U.S. Naval Detachment in Turkish Waters, 1919–1924," 9; Patenaude, *The Big Show in Bololand*, 151–52.

16. Trammell war diary, Jan. 19 to Jan. 23, 1922.

17. Ibid., Jan. 29, 1922.

18. Ibid., Feb. 6, 1922. As Bruce Clark points out (*Twice a Stranger*, 66–67), throughout this period North Sea Greeks were fleeing Turkey by boat or ship (however they could), but usually surreptitiously. Reading of a variety of American accounts indicates that untold thousands of Greeks ended up across the Black Sea, at refugee camps in ports stretching from Batoum to Novorossisk in Southern Russia.

19. Trammell war diary, Feb. 6 to Feb. 8, 1922.

20. Ibid., Feb. 9 to Mar. 23, 1922.

21. Trammell, CO of *Fox* and Harry Pence of *McFarland*. Trammell recorded that he kept his files particularly because *Fox* had initiated the "Relief expedition in Russian Waters," and saw it through. Introductory page, entitled "The USS Fox (DD234) in the Black Sea, 1922."

22. Trammell war diary, Mar. 2 and Feb. 27, 1922.

23. Ibid., Feb. 27 and Mar. 1, 1922, though the latter figures may refer only to those in the hospitals; *Williamson* war diary quoted in Patenaude, *The Big Show in Bololand*, 231; Pence war diary of May 4, 1922, Pence Papers.

24. Trammell war diary, Feb. 28, Mar. 2 and Feb. 26, 1922.

25. Pence war diary, Apr. 29 and May 19, 1922, Pence Papers.

26. Pence war diary, May 2, 1922, Pence Papers.

27. The custom is a plot feature in Richard McKenna's fine novel, *The Sand Pebbles*; McKenna based that novel on his experience aboard a naval gunboat in China in the 1930s.

28. Fitzgerald oral history, 32; Patterson thesis, 89.

29. Fitzgerald oral history, 33.

30. Trammell war diary, Feb. 25, 1922.

31. Letter to the author from Robert L. Ghormley Jr., Oct. 22, 1999.

32. E. St. J. Greble letter to Bristol, Apr. 1922 GC, MBC, 6—Greble had probably overheard this from Trammell. See Trammell war diary, Apr. 4, 1922.

33. Trammell war diary entry, Jan. 19 and 22, 1922.

34. Ibid., Jan. 29, 1922.

35. Ibid., Mar. 2, 1922.

36. Translated letter from (Anatole) Potapoff to Eleana Ivanovna and Vladimir Josephovich of Jan. 9, 1923, attached to another earlier letter and filed in Nov. 1922 GC, MBC.

37. Pence war diary, June 18, 1922, Pence Papers.

38. Trammell war diary, Mar. 9–12, 1922; Bristol letter to Edwin Denby, secretary of the Navy, while on the Simplon Orient Express en route Lausanne, Nov. 25, 1922, NR, RG 45, Subj. File 1922–1927, Subject File "Turkey—Conditions—Aug. 1, 1920–21/27," Box 830.

39. Pence diary, May 7–8, 1922, Pence Papers.

40. Ibid., Apr. 29, 1922.

41. Fitzgerald oral history, 32.

42. Trammell war diary, Mar. 10, 1922.

43. Pence diary, Apr. 29, 1922, Pence Papers.

44. Trammell war diary, Feb. 24, 1922.

45. Pence diary, Oct. 30, 1922, Pence Papers; interview with Margaret and Frank Howell, May 2000.

46. "Service in the Early Twentieth Century Navy," Commodore Carlos Augustus Bailey, 13–14, in the short Bailey memoir provided to the author by Eugene H. Farrell, Rear Admiral, USN (Ret.).

47. Pence war diary, May 20, 1922, Pence Papers.

48. Mackenzie, *Russia before Dawn*, 278–79; see also Hoover, *An American Epic*, vol. 3, 439, 440, and Beeuwkes, "American Medical and Sanitary Relief," 20ff.

49. Mitchell uncorrected letter to her sister Caroline, Feb. 18, 1922, Mitchell Letters; spelling regularized.

50. Letter to the author from Robert L. Ghormley Jr., Oct. 22, 1999; also Pence war diary, May 1, 1922, Pence Papers.

51. Recollection of Rear Adm. Matthew Gardner, as told to his son Joel; letter from Joel R. Gardner to the author of June 15, 2000.

52. Trammell war diary, Feb. 25, 1922.

53. Pence war diary, Apr 27, 1922, Pence Papers.

54. Trammell war diary, June 11, 1922.

55. From page 27 of an untitled talk found in box labeled "Books, Clippings, Papers, H. L. Pence, 1907–1920," Pence Papers.

56. Cyril Quinn's phrase was quoted by Patenaude, *The Big Show in Bololand* (309), who discusses several romances and marriages, 302–11.

57. Greble's letter to Bristol, Apr. 10, 1922, in Apr. 1922 GC, MBC.

58. Trammell war diary, Apr. 6, 1922.

59. Ibid.

60. Greble letter to Bristol, Apr. 10, 1922, in Apr. 1922 GC, MBC, 4.

61. Trammell war diary, Apr. 8, 1922; Greble letter to Bristol, Apr. 10, 1922, in Apr. 1922 GC, MBC, 9.

62. Fitzgerald, oral history, 31.

63. H. H. Fisher, *The Famine in Soviet Russia*, 272.

64. Hoover, *An American Epic*, vol. 3, 485.

65. Uncorrected letter to her sister Caroline of Sept. 9, 1922, Mitchell Letters.

66. See W. L. White, "The Liquidation of Herbert Hoover," 8, on the conversion of Hoover into a murderer and saboteur. Patenaude's chapter 38 of *The Big Show in Bololand* (644–53) speaks at length to contemporary Bolshevik efforts to disparage the American efforts.

67. Harry Pence originally reported from Odessa that 50 percent of the grain had been appropriated by government officials or stolen but later reported this was a gross error; in fact, he later said that he thought very little was lost. See his Apr. 27, May 6, and May 20, 1922, war diary entries, Pence Papers.

68. Patenaude, *The Big Show in Bololand*, 196–99, discusses the difficulties of estimating the numbers who died in the famine (estimates range up to ten million) and how many Russians America saved. He quotes various estimates.

69. Beeuwkes, "American Medical and Sanitary Relief," v.

70. H. H. Fisher, *The Famine in Soviet Russia* , 223.

71. W. L. White, "The Liquidation of Herbert Hoover," 8.

72. Pence war diary, June 27, 1922, Pence Papers.

73. They had traveled there on *Scorpion*. Bristol war diary, July 24–25, 1920, MBC.

74. Pence war diary, June 29, 1922, Pence Papers.

Chapter 8. Swimming the Hellespont and Other Naval Recreation

1. Pence war diaries, May 5, 1922, and May 26, 1922, Pence Papers.

2. Field, "A Destroyer in the Near East," vol. 51, 409; Kincaid, *History and Cruises of the Whipple*, 45–46.

3. Holmes, *Between the Lines in Asia Minor*, 172–73; Shenk, *Playships of the World*, June 9, 1921, 105.

4. Olsen letter to Edna, New Year's Day, 1921, Olsen Papers.

5. Olsen letter to Edna, Christmas, 1920, Olsen Papers; Pence diary, Apr. 22 and 28, 1923, Pence Papers.

6. For example, Olsen's letter to Edna, May 1, 1921, Olsen Papers, and a story about the *Utah's* competition with a local YMCA team in *Utah's* ship's paper, *The Big U*, of Nov. 19, 1921, first of four folders entitled "The Russian Refugees," Box 74, MBC.

7. Deleon, *The White Russians in Istanbul*, 41; I was shown the program for the YMCA games by Zafer Toprak in Istanbul in May, 2001.

8. Johnson, *Constantinople To-Day*, 285.

9. Charles Olsen letter to Edna of Apr. 14, 1921, Olsen Papers.

10. Johnson, *Constantinople To-Day*, 159; Ellis, "Constantinople Today," 519.

11. Johnson, *Constantinople To-Day*, 283; G. Ward Price, *Extra-special Correspondent*, 47.

12. Dos Passos, *Orient Express*, 24.

13. Johnson, *Constantinople To-Day*, 269; Dunn, *World Alive*, 403.

14. Dunn, *World Alive*, 320. See also "Richard G. Hovannisian on Lt. Robert Steed Dunn," review note by Heath W. Lowry, "The Journal of Ottoman Studies," vol. 5, 1985 (my source is an offprint).

15. (Lydia A. P. Flint), *Navy YMCA Guide*, 39.

16. Letter to Caroline of May 20, 1922; punctuation and spelling standardized, Mitchell Letters; letter of Helen Ogden to her mother and father, May 16, 1921, Ogden Papers.

17. Leahy diary, July 4, 1921; Mitchell letter to Caroline of July 27, 1922, spelling and punctuation regularized, Mitchell Letters; Charles Olsen letter to Edna, May 9, 1921, Olsen Papers.

18. Thomas Kinkaid, "Scrapbook S-046-A."

19. Brown, *The Coming of the Whirlwind*, 148; Bristol letter to F. L. Belin of Oct. 1921, in Oct. 1921 GC, MBC.

20. Memoir of Philip R. Hepburn, A. J. Hepburn's son, 6, privately held; Allen Dulles letter to his father, Sept. 3, 1921, Dulles Papers.

21. Brown, *The Coming of the Whirlwind*, 147–48.

22. Mitchell letter to Caroline of July 27, 1922, Mitchell Letters.

23. (Edwards), "Turkish Delight," 442; Ogden letter to Aunt Annie and Uncle Bryan of July 6 1921, Ogden Papers.

24. Edna Olsen letter to her folks, Apr. 1920, Olsen Papers.

25. Mitchell letter of Aug. 10, 1922, Mitchell Letters; Mansel, *Constantinople*, 144d, illustration title.

26. Ogden letter to her parents, Mar. 28, 1921, Ogden Papers; Olsen letter to Edna, Jan. 1, 1921, Olsen Papers.

27. Leahy diary, 246.

28. Ogden letter to her parents of Mar. 28, 1921, Ogden Papers.

29. Jeremy Seal, *A Fez of the Heart*, 28.

30. Johnson, *Constantinople To-Day*, 267.

31. Letter of Helen Ogden to her parents of June 13, 1921, Ogden Papers.

32. (Edwards), "Turkish Delight," 442; Edna Olsen letter to her folks of Apr. 1922, Olsen Papers.

33. Olsen letter to her folks of Apr. 1922, Olsen Papers; Mitchell letter to Caroline of Oct. 18, 1922, Mitchell Letters.

34. Zia Bey, *Speaking of the Turks*, 77–79; Leahy diary, 246.

35. Shenk, *Playships of the World*, Dec. 7, 1922, 168–69.

36. Dos Passos, *Orient Express*, 24–26.

37. Uncorrected letter to Caroline of Aug. 10, 1922, Mitchell Letters.

38. Charles J. Wheeler, "Reminiscences," 104–5.

39 Leahy diary, 246.

40. Pence diary, July 9, 1919, Pence Papers.

41. Leahy diary, 246.

42. Dunn, *World Alive*, 425–27.

43. Orin Haskell letters, Apr. 27 and 30, 1923, Haskell Letters; letter of Clover Dulles to her mother of May 4, 1921, Dulles Papers.

44. Letters to Edna, Apr. 27 and 28, 1921, Olsen Papers.

45. Letters of Aug. 15, Sept. 19, and July 11, 1921, Ogden Papers.

46. Informal oral history of Rear Adm. William F. "Dolly" Fitzgerald, 34; Pence diary, July 4, 1919, Pence Papers; diary entry for July 6, 1920, McCully Papers, Library of Congress.

47. Pence diary, July 4, 1919, Pence Papers; Dos Passos, *Orient Express*, 26; Gardner scrapbook, courtesy of Gardner's son, Joel Gardner.

48. Josephus Daniels, "Franklin Roosevelt as I Know Him," 26ff.

49. Dunn, *World Alive*, 351.

50. Weeks, *An American Naval Diplomat*, 79, 236; Capelotti, *Our Man in the Crimea*.

51. Gregory Robert Cunningham, "Winfield Scott Cunningham."

52. Charles J. Wheeler, "Reminiscences," 106; Charles Harington, *Tim Harington Looks Back*, 106; Young, *Constantinople*, 11; Neville Henderson, *Water Under the Bridges*, 105–6.

53. Peter Quennell, *Byron, a Self-Portrait: Letters and Diaries, 1798–1824*, 64, 70, 592.

54. Other Romantic poems that relate to the myth include Byron's "The Bride of Abydos," Leigh Hunt's "Hero and Leander," and Keats' "On a Picture of Leander."

55. Mannix, *The Old Navy*, 155n.

56. Ibid., 290–91; cf. *New York Herald Tribune* article of Monday, Nov. 16, 1925, in Harry Pence papers, box labeled "Books, Clippings."

57. A photograph of this document can be found in Mannix, *The Old Navy,* in the illustrations following page 166.

58. Ibid., 289–91; *New York Herald Tribune* article of Nov. 16, 1925, in Harry Pence papers, box labeled "Books, Clippings"; Gus Townsend, "Richard Halliburton: The Forgotten Myth," *Memphis Magazine On-Line Sections*, April 2001, http://www.memphismagazine.com/backissues/april2001/coverstory2.htm. The latter story first appeared in the *Memphis Magazine,* August 1977.

59. Kelsey diary, Jan. 2, 1920, Kelsey Papers.

60. Trammell diary, Jan, 26, 1922.

61. Message from Hatfield to Naval Station, Constantinople, Oct. 28, 1922, file on "Greek, Political—Refugees, 1922" folder, in Folder 68, MBC.

Chapter 9. Shipboard Life

1. Beers, "U.S. Naval Detachment in Turkish Waters," 209.

2. NavSource Online: "Patrol Yacht Photo Archive: Scorpion (PY 3) ex-Gunboat Scorpion."

3. Mannix, *The Old Navy*, 274.

4. NavSource Online: "Patrol Yacht Photo Archive: Scorpion (PY 3) ex-Gunboat Scorpion."

5. Bristol war diary, July 24, 1920, MBC.

6. NavSource Online: "Patrol Yacht Photo Archive: Scorpion (PY 3) ex-Gunboat Scorpion."

7. Beers, "U.S. Naval Detachment in Turkish Waters," 214.

8. Ibid., 213; Online Library of Selected Images, USS *Noma* (SP-131), 1917–1919, and USS *Nahma* (SP-771), 1917–1919.

9. "The Subchaser Archives: Documents and Stories of the Subchasers in WWI."

10. Berthelsen, *Tin Can Man*, 204.

11. K. Jack Bauer, *Ships of the Navy 1775–1969*, vol. 1, *Combat Vessels*, 127–28, 134, 136–37.

12. See reports found in Bristol's Aug. and Sept. 1919 war diaries, MBC.

13. Dictionary of American Naval Fighting Ships, *Galveston*; Berthelsen, *Tin Can Man*, 34–35.

14. Letter from Admiral Bristol to Admiral Coontz of May 6, 1920, May 1920 GC, MBC.

15. See Admiral McCully diary, Nov. 14–15, 1920, at the Library of Congress. Charles Olsen's letters also chronicle that evacuation (see the chapter on the "White Russian Invasion" earlier in this book), as does the *Whipple* cruise book for 1920, authored by Kincaid, *History and Cruises of the Whipple*, 83–85.

16. The diary can be found in Admiral Leahy's papers at the Library of Congress, and in Special Collections at the Naval Academy.

17. Shenk, *Playships of the World*, 142–207, reproduces Dan Gallery's diary version of life on the *Pittsburgh* while in Constantinople.

18. As an example, see in the June 1920 General Correspondence folder of the Bristol Papers the memorandum entitled "List of United States Vessels (Men-of-War). . . ." This list itemizes over forty American naval vessels that came to the station from Jan. 28, 1919, to May 1, 1920. They included eight subchasers and dozens of destroyers, but also a couple of supply ships and the battleship *Arizona*. Most of these ships spent only a week or so in the Bosporus.

19. Beers, "U.S. Naval Detachment in Turkish Waters," 217.

20. Ibid. names many but not all of these destroyers.

21. John Alden, *Flush Decks and Four Pipes*, 3.

22. The 1920 *Whipple* cruise book (Kincaid, *History and Cruises of the Whipple*, 97–105) names these men and sorts them into gun crews, divisions, etc. Some 113 enlisted men are named, but it is not clear that they all stayed with *Whipple* throughout its cruise.

23. Alden, *Flush Decks and Four Pipes*, 1–5, 30.

24. Donald M. Kehn Jr., *A Blue Sea of Blood,* 14.

25. Field, "A Destroyer in the Near East," 251.

26. Pence diary, Apr. 9, 1923, Pence Papers.

27. Gallery, *Eight Bells and All's Well*, 59; Mannix, *The Old Navy*, 268.

28. Olsen letter to Edna of Jan. 29, 1921, Olsen Papers.

29. Gallery, *Eight Bells and All's Well*, 55–56.

30. Field, "A Destroyer in the Near East," 248–50.

31. Mannix, *The Old Navy*, 269.

32. Berthelsen, *Tin Can Man*, 82.

33. Ibid., 83.

34. Field, "A Destroyer in the Near East," 260–61.

35. Pence diary of Nov. 28 and Dec. 1, 1921, Pence Papers.

36. Berthelsen, *Tin Can Man*, 28; Dobkin, *Smyrna 1922*, 82.

37. Shenk, *Playships of the World*, 151, 167; Olsen letter to Edna of Nov. 14, 1920, Olsen Papers.

38. Fitzgerald oral history, 44.

39. Field, "A Destroyer in the Near East," 410–11; Berthelsen, *Tin Can Man*, 80, 121–22.

40. Berthelsen, *Tin Can Man*, 122.

41. Pence diary, Mar. 10, 1923, Pence Papers.

42. Olsen letter to Edna of Jan. 26, 1921, Olsen Papers.

43. See the preceding chapter on "Recreation."

44. Shenk, *Playships of the World*, 202–3, 199.

45. Pence diary, Apr. 19–May 7, 1923, Pence Papers.

46. Dictionary of American Naval Fighting Ships, *Sands*.

47. Mannix, *The Old Navy*, 280–82. Thanks were subsequently showered on the American ship and its men.

48. Field, "A Destroyer in the Near East," 250.

49. Berthelsen, *Tin Can Man*, 112.

50. Olsen letter of Dec. 28, 1920, Olsen Papers.

51. Olsen letter of May 3, 1921; the incident of the bottle being found among the prisoners is in the Dec. 29, 1922, letter, Olsen Papers.

52. Berthelsen, *Tin Can Man*, 132; Shenk, *Playships of the World*, 150–51.

53. *Edsall* war diary, Sept. 14 and 15, 1922, NA 767.68/407.

54. Letter of Orin Haskell to his wife of Apr. 23, 1923, Haskell Letters.

55. Lt. John G. Cross, "Daily Routine Aboard a Destroyer," 192–202 of the appendix of Berthelsen, *Tin Can Man*, 195.

56. Shenk, *Playships of the World*, 214–17.

57. Ibid., 162.

58. Olsen letter, Dec. 29, 1920, Olsen Papers.

59. Berthelsen, *Tin Can Man*, 125.

60. Mannix, *The Old Navy*, 263.

61. Olsen letters of Dec. 28 and 29, 1920, Olsen Papers.

62. Berthelsen, *Tin Can Man*, 119.

63. Shenk, *Playships of the World*, 152, 163, 176.

64. Haskell letter of Mar. 25, 1923, Haskell Letters.

65. Mannix, *The Old Navy*, 265.

66. Shenk, *Playships of the World*, 151.

67. Berthelsen, *Tin Can Man*, 66, 78, 81, 117.

68. Kincaid, *History and Cruises of the Whipple*, 33; Henry Adams, *Witness to Power*, 43–44.

69. Gallery, *Eight Bells and All's Well*, 57–58.

70. Berthelsen, *Tin Can Man*, 29, 113.

71. Pence diary, entries of Nov. 23, 1921, and July 2, 1922, Pence Papers.

72. Trammell war diary, entries for Jan. 20, Jan. 22, and Feb. 9–10, 1922.

73. Berthelsen, *Tin Can Man*, 95–96.

74. Ibid., 96.

75. Ibid., 97.

76. Bristol war diary for Saturday, May 20, 1922, MBC.

77. Letter of Dec. 16, 1922, McIver Letters.

78. Berthelsen, *Tin Can Man*, 114.

79. Ibid., 113, 126.

80. Field, "A Destroyer in the Near East," 252.

81. Letter of Mar. 22, 1923, Haskell Letters.

82. Berthelsen, *Tin Can Man*, 42, 49, 66, 67–68, 78. 95, 95–97, 100–101, 102, 113, 118, 119, 122–24.

83. Ibid., 123.

84. For instance, ibid., 42.

85. Ibid., 42, 43.

86. Ibid., 130.

87. Ibid., 48.

88. Letter of Jan. 4, 1921, Olsen Papers.

89. Berthelsen, *Tin Can Man*, 101, 126.

90. Pence diary, Jan. 20, 1923, Pence Papers.

91. Renwick McIver letter to his family of Mar. 31, 1923, McIver Letters.

92. Cross is quoted in Berthelsen, *Tin Can Man*, 30–31.

93. Ibid., 30–34.

94. Berthelsen, quoting in his appendix an undated issue of the "Far Seas" newsletter put out by the American embassy at Constantinople, *Tin Can Man*, 207.

95. Kincaid, *History and Cruises of the Whipple*, 71–74.

96. Dictionary of American Naval Fighting Ships, *Sands*.

97. Berthelsen, *Tin Can Man*, 127–28.

98. Alden, *Flush Decks and Four Pipes*, 7.

99. Pence diary, Apr. 17, 1923, Pence Papers.

100. Fitzgerald oral history, 38.

101. Mannix, *The Old Navy*, 276–77.

102. Field, "A Destroyer in the Near East," 265.

103. Ibid., 262.

104. Ibid., 264.

105. Apparently no one kept an official copy of these station files after the stations were dissolved. However, two commanding officers (Cdrs. Pence and Trammell) kept complete copies of their ships' war diaries during the Turkish period.

106. Field, "A Destroyer in the Near East," 408.

Chapter 10. The Burning of Smyrna

1. *Edsall* war diary, Sept. 4–7, 1922. Officers' reports (such as those of ship captains like Halsey Powell) were forwarded by Bristol to the secretary of state and sometimes can be found with his own war diaries; for instance, Bristol sent Powell's diaries (called "*Edsall* war diaries") of Sept. 19–22 with his Sept. 28, 1922, report (NA 867.00/1551) and included those of Sept. 24–29 in his Oct. 5, 1922, report (NA 867.00/1555). Powell's war diaries of Sept. 30 to Oct. 3 were sent with Bristol's report of Oct. 17 (NA 867.00/1559). Other officers' reports including earlier ones of Powell can be found collected in NA 767.68/407. See these sources or sources referenced below for specific reference to key reports of American officers Hepburn, Merrill, and Knauss, and civilians Barnes, Davis, Jaquith, and Horton.

2. Throughout this text, I cite the 1998 reprint of Dobkin's book, based on the Faber and Faber text. Note that my characterization of Dobkin's book as the "standard work" on Smyrna might be denied by scholars such as Heath Lowry (see note 94, below) and Biray Kolluoglu Kirli, but there really is no competition to Dobkin's exhaustively researched text. Moreover, the references to cultural Turkish "silence" about the fire in Kirli's 2005 article and her quoting of eyewitnesses there—"Forgetting the Smyrna Fire," *History Workshop Journal*, 60: 25–44—actually support Dobkin's conclusions as to Turkish responsibility for the fire (see note 92, below). Kirli says that *The Smyrna Affair* is "based largely on the sources utilized by [George] Horton" (in his book *The Blight of Asia*), but this misrepresentation is egregious.

3. As for Christos Papoutsy's 2008 book, *Ships of Mercy: The True Story of the Rescue of the Greeks, Smyrna, September, 1922*, certainly American ships were heavily involved in the ultimate Smyrna rescue, as *Ships of Mercy* narrates, and as I show here. Although the picture of the rescue in his account is generally accurate, Papoutsy is not at all reliable as to details. That is, Papoutsy writes to correct what he says "Greek history" has claimed for eighty years, that although American warships were in the harbor at Smyrna, they provided no help (vii)—and he says Dobkin credited Japanese ships with the actual, heroic

rescue (134). That Dobkin credited Japanese ships with the ultimate rescue is simply not true. Indeed, despite his citing of Dobkin, Papoutsy has apparently not read her book. As a part of her text published forty years ago, Dobkin narrated well *both sides* of the American Navy's involvement at Smyrna, including the undeniable story of many personal tragedies that were caused by Admiral Bristol's policy of utter neutrality (whereby American naval men were stymied in their natural propensity to help the suffering, and sometimes did turn refugees away against their will), *and* the astonishing story of Asa Jennings that so impresses Papoutsy—which story he thinks has been utterly forgotten for eighty years, 216–19. In fact, in her 1971 book Dobkin narrated the Jennings-led rescue in some detail (*Smyrna 1922*, 190–97), as I do here.

4. "Notes on Capt. Arthur J. Hepburn's Service in Constantinople," provided to the author by Hepburn's family.

5. Merrill diary, Sept. 7, 1922, diary from NR, RG 45, Subject File 1911–27, Box 836; George Horton letter to Sec State from Smyrna, Sept. 12, 1922, NA 767.68/449.

6. *Simpson* diary (Simpson's skipper was Harry Knauss) of Sept. 8, 1922, found in NA 767.68/408; John Clayton, *Daily Telegraph* article of Sept. 12, 1922, in Lysimachos Oeconomos, *The Martyrdom of Smyrna*, 55–56.

7. *Simpson* diary, Sept. 8, 1922.

8. Esther Lovejoy, *Certain Samaritans*, 149.

9. Hepburn diary, 3, 6; his diary or report is found in NR, RG 45, Subject File 1911–27, Box 823.

10. Ibid., 4–6.

11. Ibid., 7.

12. Ibid., 8–9; Myrtle Nolan's report, attachment to Bristol's Dec. 6, 1922, letter to Sec State, NA 867.48/1452, 1.

13. *Simpson* diary, Sept. 9, 1922.

14. Hepburn diary, 7–10.

15. Nolan report, NA 867.48/1452, 1–2.

16. Hepburn diary, 12–14.

17. Merrill diary, Sept. 10, 1922.

18. Hepburn diary, 13.

19. *Simpson* diary, Sept. 10, 1922.

20. Barnes, 2; Barnes' report of Sept. 18, 1922, to Sec State is found in NA 767.68/463.

21. Horton, *The Blight of Asia*, 159–60.

22. Barnes, NA 767.68/463, 2; Hepburn diary, 20; *Daily Telegraph* story of Sept. 13, 1922, in Oeconomos, *The Martyrdom of Smyrna*, 63.

23. Barnes, in NA 767.68/463, 2–3.

24. *Simpson* diary, Sept. 11, 1922.

25. Davis report, 5, an attachment to Bristol's Dec. 6, 1922, letter to Sec State, NA 867.48/1452.

26. Hepburn diary, 15–16.

27. From a passage of M. Rene Puaux, *La Mort De Smyrna*, translated and quoted in Bierstadt, *The Great Betrayal*, 24–25; see also Horton letter to Sec State, Sept. 18, 1922, NA 767.68/540; Andrew Mango, *Atatürk*, 345.

28. Davis, 867.48/1452, 6–8; Hepburn diary, 17–18.

29. Hepburn diary, 17.

30. Davis, NA 867.48/1452, 7.

31. Merrill diary, Sept. 11, 1922.

32. Davis, NA 867.48/1452, 7.

33. Ibid., 8.

34. This was a position he had taken about Armenians in Cilicia in 1921 and would insist upon even after Smyrna: Bristol war diary, Oct. 13, 1922, MBC.

35. Hepburn diary, 16–19.

36. Cable to the Sec State, Sept. 12, 1922, NA 767.68/449, 3.

37. Hepburn diary, 5.

38. Horton, *The Blight of Asia*, 137.

39. Dobkin, *Smyrna 1922*, 124–27.

40. *Simpson* diary, Sept. 9, 1922.

41. Cable of Sept. 27, 1922, to Sec State, NA 867.4016/698.

42. These included Arnold Toynbee, who made a trip of a bit less than a week through the area. Cf. Toynbee's letter to Bristol from Smyrna dated "7/8/21," NA 867.4016/445. See also James Bryce bibliographic entry.

43. Horton cable to Sec State of Sept. 12, 1922, NA 767.68/449, 3. Horton notes that these Greeks had been cultivating the Sultana raisin and high grades of tobacco.

44. Ibid.

45. *Winona* article, no author, "Smyrna Under the Greco-Turkish Terror," 38.

46. Hepburn diary, 21.

47. Ibid., 21–22; Horton, *The Blight of Asia*, 138–39.

48. *Simpson* diary, Sept. 12, 1922.

49. Barnes report, in NA 767.68/463, 4, 2.

50. Ibid., 6–8.

51. Hepburn diary, 25.

52. Oran Raber, "New Light on the Destruction of Smyrna," 316.

53. Hepburn diary, 29.

54. Merrill diary, Sept. 14, 1922.

55. Barnes report, in NA 767.68/463. 4.

56. Merrill diary, Sept. 14, 1922; Griswold report, 5, attachment to Bristol's Dec. 6, 1922, letter to Sec State, NA 867.48/1452.

57. Dobkin, *Smyrna 1922*, 161.

58. Horton, *The Blight of Asia*, 159.

59. The cover of Dobkin, *Smyrna 1922*, shows the capsizing craft with the American sailor working in the foreground; see also Merrill diary, Sept. 14, 1922, speaking of men jumping in a boat and having it capsize.

60. Raber, "New Light on the Destruction of Smyrna," 317; Giles Milton, *Paradise Lost*, 339.

61. Horton, *The Blight of Asia*, 160; Veron Dumehjian's story is told by her son, David Kherdian, in *The Road from Home: The Story of an Armenian Girl*, 196.

62. Theodore Bartoli letter answered by Allen Dulles on Dec. 8, 1922, NA 867.4016/773; Kherdian, *The Road from Home*, 196.

63. Dobkin, *Smyrna 1922*, 158.

64. Ibid., 162–63.

65. Ibid., 165.

66. *Simpson* diary, Sept. 13, 1922.

67. Hepburn diary, 28; Dobkin, *Smyrna 1922*, 171.

68. Raber, "New Light on the Destruction of Smyrna," 317.

69. Price, *Extra-special Correspondent,* 129.

70. "Smyrna Under the Greco–Turkish Terror," 38; *Simpson* diary, Sept. 13, 1922.

71. Ward Price, quoted in Dobkin, *Smyrna 1922*, 166.

72. Hepburn was to write, about Davis's proposal, "For several reasons this seemed rather a delicate proposition to be presented to any of the Allied Senior Officers by me in person, or in any manner which might in the future be described as 'official.'" Hepburn diary, 29–30.

73. Merrill diary, Sept. 14, 1922; Milton, *Paradise Lost*, 332.

74. Hepburn diary, 30.

75. Dobkin, *Smyrna 1922*, 172.

76. Raber, "New Light on the Destruction of Smyrna," 317.

77. Hepburn diary, 30; 32–33.

78. Ibid., 33.

79. Merrill diary, Sept. 14, 1922, and Chester Griswold report (6) attached to Bristol's letter to Sec State of Dec. 6, 1922, NA 867.48/1452.

80. For instance, see Merrill's diary, Sept. 6, 1922.

81. See "Miss Mills Blames Turks for the Fire," *New York Times* article of Sept. 27, 1922; Horton, *The Blight of Asia*, 145; and John Clayton, *Daily Telegraph* articles of Sept. 15 and 16, 1922, in Oeconomos, *The Martyrdom of Smyrna*, 65–67. However, see the section found later in this chapter about Clayton's unusual form of journalism.

82. Merrill diary, Sept. 14, 1922.

83. Davis report, NA 867.48/1452, 10.

84. Barnes report, in NA 767.68/463, 6.

85. Jaquith report, 5, attachment to Bristol's Dec. 6, 1922, letter to Sec State, NA 867.48/1452.

86. Barnes report, in NA 767.68/463, 6.

87. Message of Oct. 10, 1922, from Barnes while aboard *Edsall* at Smyrna, Box 78, file on "Turkish Political Situation," MBC. Note that during the days of the fire itself, the *Edsall* had been at sea, or at Athens or Salonika. It pulled into the Smyrna harbor only long enough to board some refugees and then pulled out again, returning to stay on Sept. 16.

88. Merrill diary, Sept. 14, 1922.

89. Hepburn diary, 46.

90. Anna Mitchell heard Davis's opinion in Constantinople in late September, Mitchell letter to Caroline, Sept. 30, 1922, Mitchell Letters.

91. Hepburn diary, 46.

92. Bristol's report on conditions at Samsun can be found in Mar. 28, 1919, NR, RG 45, Subject File 1911–27, Box 231. In her article, "Forgetting the Smyrna Fire," 25–44, Biray Kolluoglu Kirli quotes Turkish eyewitnesses who say that "the fires were started to force the *gavur* inhabitants of the city from their houses" (38, "gavur" meaning "infidel"). As she notes, one of them (journalist Falih Rifki Atay) asked even at the time of the event, "Why were we burning down Izmir? Were we afraid that if waterfront konaks, hotels and taverns stayed in place, we would never be able to get rid of the minorities? When the Armenians were being deported in the First World War, we had burned down all the habitable districts and neighbourhoods in Anatolian towns and cities with this very same fear" (39). Kirli contends that "the Great Fire was an act of punishment, a destruction aiming to purify, to chastise this 'gavur' (infidel)

city" (27). Further, a "vast silence" has swallowed up the fire in Turkish culture. "Not a single Turkish novel, film, or memoir deals with it," nor a single scholarly study. The episode has been wiped from Turkish history, she argues (34), so that a new, non-infidel history of Turkey might be created. Ironically, Kirli's broad argument that "the way in which fire is deliberately overlooked implies the presence of an offence, a violence" (41) essentially puts her on the same side as Dobkin, who (by detailed research into the events) suggests Turkish responsibility for the fire.

93. Horton's argument from *The Blight of Asia* (147ff.) is paraphrased in Constantine G. Hatzidimitriou's introduction to *American Accounts Documenting the Destruction of Smyrna*, 11.

94. Barnes, in NA 767.68/463, 6; Hepburn diary, 47. In *Turkish History: On Whose Sources Will It Be Based? A Case Study on the Burning of Smyrna*, Heath Lowry cites Mark Prentiss's interview with the Turkish fire chief in Smyrna, a man named Grescovich, and the latter's opinion that the Christian minorities set the fire. Dobkin (*Smyrna 1922*) had itemized some of Grescovich's comments in her bibliography (237), but she did not cite this official's opinion in the narrative of her text, indicating apparently that she found the fire chief's remarks less than credible. I will only comment that Grescovich should certainly be regarded as an "interested witness": any fire chief of a city utterly destroyed by fire might have many reasons to invent things in his report.

95. Hepburn diary, 37.

96. Ibid., 35–36; Merrill diary, Sept. 15, 1922; Dobkin, *Smyrna 1922*, 179–80.

97. Cf. typical personal accounts, Dobkin, *Smyrna 1922*, 219–22.

98. Merrill diary, Sept. 14, 1922.

99. Barnes report, in NA 767.68/463, 7.

100. Davis report, NA 867.48/1452, 14; Barnes report, in NA 767.68/463, 7.

101. Lovejoy, *Certain Samaritans*, 150.

102. Bristol war diary, Sept. 21, 1922, MBC.

103. Ibid., Sept. 19, 1922.

104. King letter of Dec. 4, 1922, GC Dec. 22, MBC.

105. Bristol war diary, Sept. 17, 1922, MBC.

106. Ibid., Sept. 12, 1922.

107. Ibid., Sept. 19, 1922.

108. Ibid., Sept. 18, 1922.

109. Dobkin, *Smyrna 1922*, 188; *Edsall* diary, Sept. 21, 1922.

110. Bristol war diary: Weekly Summary for Week Ending Oct. 1, 1922, MBC.

111. Hepburn went for one last conference with Powell on the 22nd but was immediately called back to Constantinople; cf. *Edsall* diary, Sept. 22, 1922. Bristol

may have been concerned with possible eventualities in Constantinople itself, but no evacuation of the remaining hundreds of thousands on the Smyrna quay was in sight when Bristol had Hepburn return for good.

112. *Edsall* diary, Sept. 17, 1922.

113. *Simpson* diary, Sept. 18, 1922.

114. *Edsall* diary, Sept. 17, 1922.

115. *Simpson* diary, Sept. 17, 1922; *Edsall* diary, Sept. 17, 1922.

116. Davis report, NA 867.48/1452, 15.

117. *Edsall* diary, Sept. 20, 1922.

118. Ibid., Sept. 21, 1922

119. Ibid., Sept. 20, 1922.

120. Quoted in Moranian dissertation, 477.

121. *Edsall* diary of that date.

122. Ibid., Sept. 20, 1922.

123. Ibid., Sept. 14, 1922.

124. Ibid., Sept. 17, 1922.

125. Ibid.

126. Bristol war diary, Sept. 25 and Oct. 2, 1922, MBC. Dr. Esther Lovejoy (an American doctor who we will discuss later in this chapter) ran into this fellow at Smyrna, who confessed that he could not stay long on the pier because he could not stand the suffering of the children. "'Besides,' he added, as he turned away, 'my business is to sell locomotives.'" Lovejoy concluded bitterly, "That was the core of the whole wicked game. It was a case of every man for himself, and every company and country for that matter." *Certain Samaritans*, 174–75.

127. Bristol war diary, Nov. 8, 1922, MBC.

128. R. W. Abernethy, "The Great Rescue," 174.

129. *Edsall* diary, Sept. 17, 1922; *Simpson* diary, Sept. 17, 1922.

130. A letter of July 15, 1965 from Arthur D. ("Red") Condon to Editor, Naval Academy Alumni magazine *Shipmate*, along with a review of Alden, *Flush Decks and Four Pipes*. Filed in alumni papers in the Naval Academy Library archives.

131. *Edsall* diary, Sept. 17, 1922; "death sentence" is a term that was used by one of those who was deported but fortunate enough to survive: see Dobkin, *Smyrna 1922*, 179–80.

132. *Edsall* diary, Sept. 19, 1922.

133. Undated report to Dr. D. A. Davis of YMCA, NA 767.68/605, cited in Dobkin, *Smyrna 1922*, 190.

134. Abernethy, "The Great Rescue," 195–99; William T. Ellis, "Jennings of Smyrna," 232.

135. Abernethy, "The Great Rescue," 176–77.

136. Ibid., 177–78.

137. Ellis, "Jennings of Smyrna," 232.

138. *Edsall* diary, Sept. 21, 1922.

139. Abernethy, "The Great Rescue," 182.

140. Ibid., 184.

141. Ibid., 184–88; Ellis, "Jennings of Smyrna," 232–34.

142. Bristol war diary, Nov. 8, 1922.

143. Abernethy, "The Great Rescue," 162.

144. Ibid., 188; *Edsall* diary, Sept. 22, 1922.

145. Abernethy, "The Great Rescue," 189; *Edsall* diary, Sept. 24, 1922 (in a letter report dated Sept. 23).

146. Abernethy, "The Great Rescue," 191.

147. Bristol war diary, Sept. 5, 1922, MBC; Dobkin, *Smyrna 1922*, 117.

148. Horton's Sept. 18, 1922, report to the State Department, NA 767.68/450.

149. *Daily Telegraph* articles (by arrangement with the *Chicago Tribune*) of Sept. 13, 14, and 15, Oeconomos, *The Martyrdom of Smyrna*, 62–65.

150. Raber, "New Light on the Destruction of Smyrna," 316.

151. *Daily Telegraph* articles of Sept. 15 and 16, Oeconomos, *The Martyrdom of Smyrna*, 65–67.

152. Brown, *The Coming of the Whirlwind*, 162–63; Milton, *Paradise Lost*, 324–25.

153. Prentiss' cable of Oct. 10, 1922, to the *New York Times-London* in Box 78, "Turkish Political Situation," MBC.

154. See, for instance, Lovejoy, *Certain Samaritans,* 157–63. For the barriers, see Halsey Powell's report, i.e., the *Edsall* report of Oct. 9, 1922, and the fully annotated large diagrams of the piers, barriers, etc., which can be found in NR, RG 45, Subject File 1911–1927, Box 833, Folder #1.

155. "Hasten Evacuation of Smyrna Hordes," *New York Times*, Sept. 27, 1922, 2.

156. *Edsall* report of Oct. 9, 1922, 4.

157. Dobkin, *Smyrna 1922*, 202.

158. A comment from a relative, quoted in Anita Leslie, *Clare Sheridan,* 129.

159. Bristol war diary, Sept. 21, 1922, MBC.

160. Clare Sheridan's dealings with Trotsky and Chaplin are described in her memoir, *Naked Truth*, and in Anita Leslie's biography, *Clare Sheridan.*

161. Bristol war diary, Sept. 21, 1922, MBC.

162. John Clayton, "Kipling Said It, Woman Insists," *Chicago Tribune*, Sept. 20, 1922, 1.

163. Bristol war diary, Sept. 21, 1922, MBC.

164. Sheridan, *Naked Truth*, 304.

165. Leslie, *Clare Sheridan*, 199–200.

166. Sheridan, *Naked Truth*, 305.

167. Milton, *Paradise Lost*, 344–45, describes the villa where Kemal was staying.

168. Leslie, *Clare Sheridan*, 201.

169. See Sheridan, *Naked Truth,* 306–9, for the whole interview.

170. Ernest Hemingway, *In Our Time*, 9.

171. Peter A. Smith, "Hemingway's 'On the Quai at Smyrna' and the Universe of *In Our Time*," 160.

172. Lovejoy, *Certain Samaritans*, 156.

173. *Edsall* diary, Sept. 22, 1922.

174. Papoutsy, *Ships of Mercy*, 61, citing a diary of E. O. Jacob, a traveling YMCA secretary who had been at Smyrna and kept a diary of events.

175. *Edsall* diary, Sept. 26, 1922.

176. Ibid., Sept. 24, 1922.

177. Ibid., Sept. 26, 1922; Jacob is cited by Papoutsy, *Ships of Mercy*, 62.

178. This event is briefly described by Edward M. Fisher (who had been director of the YMCA of Smyrna) in the Associated Press report recorded at "Constantinople, September 19," reproduced in Hatzidimitriou, *American Accounts*, 88–90.

179. Dobkin, *Smyrna 1922*, 161–62, 204–5; Lovejoy, *Certain Samaritans*, 173–75.

180. *Edsall* diary, Sept. 24, 1922.

181. Sheridan, *Naked Truth*, 305.

182. Ibid., 310–11.

183. Ibid., 312–13.

184. Ibid., 312.

185. *Edsall* diary, Sept. 28, 1922.

186. Lovejoy, *Certain Samaritans*, 161–62.

187. Ibid., 162–63; Dobkin*, Smyrna 1922*, 204.

188. Sheridan, *Naked Truth*, 315; Lovejoy, *Certain Samaritans*, 166; *Edsall* diary, Sept. 26, 1922.

189. Lovejoy, *Certain Samaritans*, 165–66.

190. Ibid., 150; Sheridan, *Naked Truth*, 312.

191. Mango, *Atatürk*, 346.

Chapter 11. The Expulsion of the Minorities and Constantinople's Last Fling

1. Field, "A Destroyer in the Near East," 247.

2. Field reported that "the European duty was very popular with officers and men alike. Our allowed complement was 106 men. We might have taken twice that number if immediate availability of hands had been the only consideration," 247.

3. In fact, some fifteen thousand Constantinopolitan Greeks left during October alone (usually they evacuated to Greece). Alexis Alexandris, *The Greek Minority of Istanbul*, 82.

4. *Toronto Daily Star* stories of Oct. 18 and 19, 1922, William White, *Hemingway, Ernest. Dateline Toronto*, 227–31.

5. Donald McCormick, *One Man's Wars*, 1972, 120–25.

6. Scott Donaldson, "Hemingway of *The Star*," 93–95. Hemingway identified himself to Admiral Bristol as writing for both the *Star* and the INS: Bristol War Diary, Oct. 3, 1922, MBC.

7. Oct. 2 and 3, Bristol war diary, MBC.

8. Brown, *The Coming of the Whirlwind*, 163.

9. *Edsall* war diary, Sept. 29, 1922.

10. Attachment to Bristol's letter to the Sec State, Nov. 8, 1922, NA 867.00/1573.

11. Bristol war diary, Oct. 10, 1922; letter of Oct. 18, 1922, to Admiral Niblack, Oct. 1922 GC; Bristol letter to G. M. Tisdale, Dec. 21, 1922, Dec. 1922 GC, MBC.

12. *Edsall* diary, Sept. 24, 1922.

13. Ellis's comments are found in *MacLeish*'s "Report of Movements" from Sept. 27 to Oct. 8, 1922, especially entries for Oct. 6 and 7; NR, RG 45 File 1911–1927, Box 1206, Folder #4 (WT 2). See also Otis Swift's interview with American relief worker Alfred Brady in "Greek Flight from Asia Minor," *Daily Telegraph*, Oct. 14, 1922, in Oeconomos, *The Martyrdom of Smyrna*, 170–72.

14. Michael Reynolds, *Hemingway: The Paris Years*, 76.

15. "European Nightlife: A Disease," *Toronto Star Weekly*, Dec. 15, 1923; William White, *Hemingway, Ernest. Dateline Toronto*, 404–9.

16. Baker, *Ernest Hemingway*, 131.

17. H. J. Greenwall, "Greek Flight to the West," *Daily Express*, Oct. 24, 1922, in Oeconomos, *The Martyrdom of Smyrna*, 192–93.

18. "A Silent, Ghastly Procession," 232, in William White, *Hemingway, Ernest. Dateline Toronto*.

19. "Constantinople, Dirty White, Not Glistening and Sinister," TDS of Oct. 18, 227–29, in William White, *Hemingway, Ernest. Dateline Toronto*. Bristol's war diary indicates Hemingway attended Bristol's conference on Oct. 3, 1922; Hemingway along with other journalists also met with Bristol on the 7th and the 10th.

20. Letter of Renwick McIver to his mother, Nellie McIver, McIver Letters.

21. Manning figures for *Denebola* and *Bridge* are minimal estimates drawn from online naval entries.

22. Shenk, *Playships of the World*, 143.

23. Bristol war diary, Nov. 2, 1922; dispatch of Nov. 6, 1922, to *Overton,* in "Turkish Refugee Situation, 1922" file, MBC.

24. Pence war diary, Nov. 8, 1922, Pence Papers, 7.

25. Messages from Charles Fowle to Charles Vickery of Nov. 14 and 17, 1922, NA 867.4016/736 and 740.

26. Message to Constantinople, Nov. 27, 1922, in "Turkish Refugee Situation, 1922" file, Box 78, MBC.

27. Executive Committee of NER report dated Apr. 12, 1923, comments by "Morris," NA 867.48/1463.

28. Dolbeare message to Sec State, Nov. 26, 1922, Turkish Refugee Situation, 1922 file, MBC; also NA 867.4016/759.

29. The term is that of Bruce Clark, in *Twice a Stranger*, 60.

30. Lovejoy, *Certain Samaritans*, 183, 200–201; Dobkin, *Smyrna 1922*, 218–19; and Stephen P. Ladas, *The Exchange of Minorities*, 17, 724.

31. One should note, in particular, that few reporting officers are as vehement as Commander Ware, who is quoted further on in this chapter; many simply report an evacuation, without much comment or complaint.

32. Ladas, *The Exchange of Minorities*, 724.

33. Dobkin, *Smyrna 1922*, 219–22.

34. Speros Vryonis, "Greek Labor Battalions [in] Asia Minor," 284.

35. Ladas, *The Exchange of Minorities*, 430–31; Dobkin, *Smyrna 1922*, 219.

36. Cf. Peter Evans, *Ari: The Life and Times of Aristotle Socrates Onassis*, 32–47, for his account of the Smyrna episode.

37. Zogbaum, *From Sail to Saratoga*, 366.

38. Shenk, *Playships of the World*, diary entry for Nov. 18, 1922.

39. Correspondence with Judy Meiselman and Banice Webber, Cy Olch's niece and nephew.

40. Field, "A Destroyer in the Near East," 411–12.

41. Zogbaum, *From Sail to Saratoga,* 379; Pence diary, May 4, 1923, Pence Papers.

42. From *McCormick* war diary of Dec. 2, 1922, NA 867.00/1606. See also *Overton* message of Nov. 22, 1922 in Turkish Refugee Situation, 1922 file, MBC, referring to reports of NER official Moore, who on his trip to Mersina from Konia passed many Smyrna refugees being deported into the interior, as well as many other refugees heading to the seaports.

43. Letter of Oct. 18, 1922, to Rear Adm. A. P. Niblack, Oct. 1922 GC, MBC.

44. War diary entries for Nov. 27 and 18, in *Overton's* message report/war diary of Nov. 16 to Dec. 2 (at Smyrna from Nov. 16 to Nov. 21, first page dated Nov. 16; at Mersina from Nov. 22 to Dec. 2, first page dated Nov. 22); NA 867.00/1606.

45. *Overton* war diary entry for Nov. 28, 1922 (while at Mersina); war diary entry for Nov. 19, 1922 (while at Smyrna); see preceding footnote. In the latter passage, Ware noted that one of these relief workers expressed enmity that "even extended to the Destroyers and to the Admiral."

46. Dan Gallery, *Eight Bells and All's Well*, 59–60, as corrected by a letter of Oct. 15, 1999, to the author from John B. Pleasants, Ash Pleasants' son. See also Shenk, *Playships of the World*, May 18, 1923, entry.

47. Couzinos, *Twenty-Three Years in Asia Minor*, 130.

48. Stephens, *Survival Against All Odds*, 170.

49. Clark, *Twice a Stranger,* 68.

50. Couzinos, *Twenty-Three Years in Asia Minor*, 136–37.

51. Dobkin, *Smyrna 1922,* 183.

52. McIver letters of Oct. 28 and Nov. 2, 1922, McIver Papers; Field, "A Destroyer in the Near East," vol. 51, 406.

53. Zogbaum, *From Sail to Saratoga*, 375–77.

54. Letters from Smyrna of Oct. 28, Nov. 2, and Nov. 5, 1922, McIver Papers.

55. McIver letter of Nov. 15, 1922, from Constantinople. See also McIver's informal oral history, 71–80, McIver Papers.

56. Leahy diary, 257; also cf. Adams, *Witness to Power*, 44–45.

57. Zogbaum, *From Sail to Saratoga*, 371–72.

58. Fitzhugh Green, "Stand by to Ram!" 19, 49; Newton W. Parke, "Inferno at Sea," 138–41.

59. Maguire, *Rig for Church*, 131–33.

60. Orin Haskell, Apr. 30, 1923, letter to his wife, Audrey McDougall Haskell, Haskell Letters.

61. Message from Frederick Dolbeare to Sec State of Jan. 4, 1923, in Bristol File #78, Turkish Refugees, 1923, MBC; see also Ellis, "Constantinople To-day," 518.

62. Letter to Vickrey in New York, Mar. 12, 1923, cited in Lovejoy, *Certain Samaritans*, 267.

63. Jaquith, in Lovejoy, *Certain Samaritans*, 267.

64. Executive Committee of NER report dated Apr. 12, 1923, comments by "Morris," NA 867.48/1463.

65. S. Lawford Childs, League of Nations official, to "Johnson," June 19, 1923, MBC; June 1923 GC, MBC.

66. Lovejoy, *Certain Samaritans*, 272; Edgar Fisher diary of Mar. 8, 1923 (addition found under Tuesday, Feb. 27, 1923, entry), Fisher Papers.

67. Lovejoy, *Certain Samaritans*, 266.

68. James L. Barton, *Story of Near East Relief*, 160; Compton, *The Morning Cometh*, 51; Melville Chater, "History's Greatest Trek," 559.

69. Lovejoy, *Certain Samaritans*, 272–73.

70. Barton, *Story of Near East Relief*, 158–60.

71. Compton, *The Morning Cometh*, 50–51.

72. Barton, *Story of Near East Relief*, 159, 196, 339.

73. Ellis, "Constantinople To-day," 518.

74. Hepburn diary at Smyrna, 43.

75. Lovejoy, *Certain Samaritans*, 263–66.

76. Shenk, *Playships of the World*, Nov. 16, 1922, to May 20, 1923.

77. Ibid., Nov. 18, 1922; Dunn, *World Alive*, 425.

78. Letter from Admiral Long to Bristol, Jan. 15, 1923, in Jan. 1–19, 1923 GC file, MBC.

79. Orin Haskell letter to Auddie of Apr. 27, 1923, Haskell Letters.

80. Letter to Bristol of Dec. 19, 1922, Dec. 1922 GC, MBC.

81. Fisher letters of Oct. 1 and 2, 1922, Fisher Papers.

82. Lovejoy, *Certain Samaritans*, 199.

83. Ibid., 273–74.

84. Couzinos, *Twenty-Three Years in Asia Minor*, 143–45.

Chapter 12. The Departure

1. Brown, *The Coming of the Whirlwind,* 164–66. Brown calls Miles "Herman." See also Mansel, *Constantinople*, on the sultan's departure, 407–8.

2. Bristol war diary, Oct. 13, 1922, MBC.

3. Hughes to Bristol, Sec State #189 of Oct. 13, 1922, in Bristol file #78, Turkish Refugees, 1923, MBC. The Red Cross, for instance, fed 860,000 refugees daily in Greece through the winter of 1922–23; Robert L. Daniel, *American Philanthropy*, 167.

4. Elizabeth Dodge Huntingdon Clarke et al., *The Joy of Service*, 169.

5. Robert L. Daniel, *American Philanthropy*, 181; Mary Mills Patrick, *Under Five Sultans*, 334; Bristol war diary, Dec. 6, 1922, MBC. Actually, as early as Jan. 25, 1923, Adnan Bey had told Gates that the medical department would not be allowed. Cf. Dolbeare message to American Mission, Lausanne, "Turkish Political Situation" file, Box 78, MBC. For the Armenian and Greek departments being shut down (and other issues), see John Cecil Guckert dissertation, "The Adaptation of Robert College," 152–61.

6. Patrick, *Under Five Sultans,* 341; Clarke et al., *The Joy of Service*, 213–14.

7. For example, see the Bristol war diary entry of Oct. 13, 1922, MBC.

8. Mannix, *The Old Navy*, 286.

9. Robert L. Daniel, *American Philanthropy*, 185.

10. Grabill, *Protestant Diplomacy and the Near East*, 296.

11. Ibid., 282; Trask, *The United States Response*, 150.

12. Grabill, *Protestant Diplomacy and the Near East*, 282; Trask, *The United States Response*, 15.

13. Ryan interview filed with the Bristol war diary of July 10, 1922, MBC.

14. Grabill, *Protestant Diplomacy and the Near East*, 282.

15. Bristol's authorities were Howard E. Bliss and J. Stanley White, especially Bliss in a pamphlet called "The Modern Missionary," Bristol war diary, Mar. 31, July 8, and July 14, 1921, MBC. An address of Bristol's to the Robert College student body that refers to this concept can be found in his 1921 war diary, filed near the date it was delivered, on Apr. 15, 1921, MBC.

16. Bristol war diary, Apr. 4, 1923, MBC.

17. Oct. 9, 1922, letter to H. Mason Day, Oct. 1922 GC, MBC and Oct. 9, 1922, letter to Frank A. Vanderlip, misfiled in Oct. 1921 GC, MBC.

18. Letter to Vanderlip, misfiled in Oct. 1921 GC, MBC, 3.

19. Bristol war diary, Oct. 14, 1922, MBC.

20. Letter from Dulles to Bristol, Dec. 28, 1922, Dec. 1922 GC, MBC.

21. Mansel, *Constantinople*, 407; Ladas, *The Exchange of Minorities*, 728; Bryson, "Admiral Mark L. Bristol," 464–65.

22. Gerald A. Wheeler, *A Biography of Admiral Thomas C. Kinkaid*, 35; *Journal* in Kinkaid Papers, Operational Archives, Naval History Division, Washington,

D.C. (a very spare diary); photos found in Kinkaid scrapbook (see Bibliography); and Charles J(ulian) Wheeler, "Reminiscences," 80–82.

23. Clayton report, NA 867.4016/618.

24. Clare Sheridan, *A Turkish Kaleidoscope*, 197, 192, 199, 182–86. See also Sheridan on similar events in Buyukdere (83–83).

25. Trask, *The United States Response*, 37–51.

26. *Scorpion* left Turkey with the other ships in September of 1923. For four years it continued to operate in the Mediterranean until being sent home in 1927 for decommissioning.

27. Shenk, *Playships of the World*, May 18–19, 1923.

28. Berthelsen, *Tin Can Man*, 133–34.

29. NA 867.00/1495, with prefatory note. The principal memo of "October (4?), 1921" is signed by "H. G. D.," or Harry G. Dwight; an attached, prefatory note of Oct. 10, 1921, by "W. R.," or Warren Robbins, to Robert Bliss comments that "[Dunn] is an ex-newspaper man of apparently little judgment and moral standing. . . . If you see fit I should like to suggest to the Assistant Secretary of the Navy that Mr. Dunn be transferred." Next to other initials appended is the comment, "do it personally," with the follow-on circled comment: "done WR Oct 11/21." (In different handwriting, "Telegram sent!" also appears at the bottom of the note).

30. Leahy's diary (258) indicates Dunn was aboard *St. Louis* as it left the city on Oct. 5, 1921. Apparently Dunn had seen the writing on the wall, and left Constantinople voluntarily. In *World Alive*, 428–29, Dunn attributes his departure to "'I' commissions in the regular navy expiring on New Year's."

31. Leahy diary, 258.

32. Field, "A Destroyer in the Near East," 412.

33. Charles J. Wheeler, "Reminiscences," 77–78.

34. Shenk, *Playships of the World*, May 10–11, 1923.

35. Phone conversation of the author with Timothy F. (Ted) Wellings in Apr. 2000.

36. See letters from Margaret Bryan, Helen Moore Bristol correspondence, Box #20, folder labeled Jan–July 1923, MBC. The fitness report is described in her letter of Apr. 25, 1923.

37. Gallery's best collection of humorous naval short stories is *Now Hear This!* (Paperback Library, 1966), and subsequent editors.

38. Dunn, *World Alive*, 459.

39. Goodrich-Freer, *Things Seen in Constantinople*, 153.

40. Dunn, *World Alive*, 457–70.

41. Robert L. Daniel, *American Philanthropy*, 186.

42. Upon the admiral's retirement, the Bristols sponsored a fund-raising effort to construct and equip a modern hospital; Scipio, *My Thirty Years in Turkey*, 189.

43. Yalman, *Turkey in My Time*, 79; Bryson, "Admiral Mark L. Bristol," 451, 466; Buzanski dissertation, iii–iv.

44. Letter of Hepburn to Vice Adm. A. P. Niblack, June 20, 1922, in Jun–Jul 1922 GC, MBC.

BIBLIOGRAPHY

For additional archival reference, see the preface to "Notes." On personal papers and interviews with family members of American servicemen, see individual references in the notes and my comments in the "Preface."

Abernethy, R. W. "The Great Rescue." In *The Spirit of the Game. A Quest by Basil Mathews and Some Stories by A .E. Southon and R. W. Abernethy*. New York: Doran, n.d., 159–200.

Adams, Henry H. *Witness to Power: The Life of Fleet Admiral William D. Leahy*. Annapolis: Naval Institute Press, 1985.

Akçam, Taner. *A Shameful Act: The Armenian Genocide and the Question of Turkish Responsibility*. New York: Henry Holt, 2006.

Alden, John. *Flush Decks and Four Pipes*. Annapolis: U.S. Naval Institute, 1965.

Alexandris, Alexis. *The Greek Minority of Istanbul and Greek-Turkish Relations, 1918–1974*. Athens: Center for Asia Minor Studies, 1983.

Bachman, Robert A. "The American Navy and the Turks." *The Outlook* (October 18, 1922): 288–89.

Baker, Carlos. *Ernest Hemingway: A Life Story*. New York: Charles Scribner's Sons, 1969.

Balakian, Peter. *The Burning Tigris: The Armenian Genocide and America's Response*. New York: HarperCollins, 2003.

Barton, James L. *Story of Near East Relief (1915–1930): An Interpretation*. New York: Macmillan, 1930.

Bauer, K. Jack. *Ships of the Navy 1775–1969*, vol. 1, *Combat Vessels*. Troy, NY: Rensselaer Polytechnic Institute, 1969.

Bechhofer, C. E. *In Denikin's Russia and the Caucasus, 1919–1920*. London: W. Collins Sons, 1921.

Beers, Henry P. "U.S. Naval Detachment in Turkish Waters, 1919–1924." In *Administrative Reference Service Report No. 2*. Office of Records Administration,

Navy Department. June 1943. Reprinted in *Military Affairs* 7, no. 4 (Winter 1943): 209–20. (All paginal reference is to the reprinting.)

Beeuwkes, Henry. "American Medical and Sanitary Relief in the Russian Famine, 1921–1923." *American Relief Administration Bulletin* 2, no. 45 (April 1926).

Berthelsen, Bert. *Tin Can Man: Memoirs of Destroyer Duty after World War I.* New York: Exposition Press, 1963.

Bierstadt, Edward Hale. *The Great Betrayal: A Survey of the Near East Problem.* New York: Robert M. McBride, 1924.

Braisted, William R. "Mark Lambert Bristol: Naval Diplomat Extraordinary of the Battleship Age." In *A Navy Second to None: The Development of Modern American Naval Policy,* edited by George Theron Davis, 331–73. Westport, CT: Greenwood Press, (1971), c. 1940.

Brigg, E. W., and A. A. Hessenstein. *Constantinople Cameos.* Constantinople: W. Dudavsky, 1921.

Bristol, Mark L. Papers. The Library of Congress. Cited as MBC. "GC" means "General Correspondence" section.

Brown, Constantine. *The Coming of the Whirlwind.* Chicago: Henry Regnery, 1964.

Bryce, James, Viscount. *The Treatment of the Armenians in the Ottoman Empire, 1915–16,* compiled by A. Toynbee. London: British Government Document Miscellaneous, 1916.

Bryson, Thomas A. "Admiral Mark L. Bristol, an Open-Door Diplomat in Turkey." *International Journal of Middle Eastern Studies* 5 (1974): 450–67.

———. *Tars, Turks, and Tankers: The Role of the United States Navy in the Middle East, 1800–1879.* Metuchen, NJ: Scarecrow Press, 1980.

———. *Walter George Smith.* Washington, DC: Catholic University of America Press, 1977.

Bumgardner, Eugenia S. *Undaunted Exiles.* Staunton, VA: The McClure Company, 1925.

Butler, P. R. "Grief and Glamour of the Bosphorus." *Blackwood's Magazine* (February 1921): 203–12.

Buzanski, Peter M. "Admiral Mark L. Bristol and Turkish-American Relations, 1919–1922." Diss. University of California, 1960.

———. "The Interallied Investigation of the Greek Invasion of Smyrna, 1919." *The Historian* (May 1963): 325–43.

Canefe, Nergis. "History and the Nation; The Legacy of Taner Akçam's work on Ottoman Armenians." *South European Society & Politics* 12, no. 2 (2007): 237–46.

Capelotti, P. J., ed. *Our Man in the Crimea: Commander Hugo Koehler and the Russian Civil War.* Columbia: South Carolina University Press, 1991.

Carpenter, Frank G. *The Alps, The Danube, and The Near East*. Garden City, NY: Doubleday, 1924.

Chater, Melville. "History's Greatest Trek." *National Geographic* 48, no. 5 (November 1925): 533–90.

Chorbajian, Ghevorn. "The 22 Days of Marash: Papers on the Defense of the City Against Turkish Forces Jan.–Feb., 1920," Part III, "A Diary of the Events in Marash," trans. Nishan DerBedrosyan. *The Armenian Review* 31, no. 4 (1979): 402–18.

Churchill, Winston S. *The World Crisis—1918–1928*, vol. 5, *The Aftermath*. New York: Charles Scribner's Sons, 1929.

Clark, Alice Keep. *Letters from Cilicia*. Chicago: A. D. Weinthrop, 1924.

Clark, Bruce. *Twice a Stranger: The Mass Expulsions that Forged Modern Greece and Turkey*. Cambridge, MA: Harvard University Press, 2006.

Clarke, Elizabeth Dodge Huntingdon, Elspeth McClure Clarke, and Court Carroll Walters. *The Joy of Service*. New York: National Board of the Young Women's Christian Association, 1979.

Compton, Carl C. *The Morning Cometh: 45 Years with Anatolia College*. New Rochelle, NY: Aristide D. Caratzas, 1986.

Cotten, Elizabeth. "In the Days of the High Commissioner." *Asia and the Americas* 23 (December 1923): 900–902, 951–52.

Couzinos, Efthimios N. *Twenty-Three Years in Asia Minor (1899–1922)*. New York: Vantage Press, 1969.

Cunningham, Gregory Robert. *Cunningham*. "Winfield Scott Cunningham," http://www.monticellowi.com/RichlandCo/Ancestors/ CunninghamWinfredScott.htm, accessed December 22, 2001.

Dadrian, Vahakn N. *The Key Elements in the Turkish Denial of the Armenian Genocide: A Case Study of Distortion and Falsification*. Cambridge, MA: The Zoryan Institute, 1999.

Daniel, Robert L. *American Philanthropy in the Near East: 1820–1960*. Athens: Ohio University Press, 1970.

Daniels, Josephus. "Franklin Roosevelt as I Know Him." *Saturday Evening Post* 205 (September 24, 1932): 26ff.

Davis, Leslie A. *The Slaughterhouse Province: An American Diplomat's Report on the Armenian Genocide, 1915–1917*, edited by Susan K. Blair. New Rochelle, NY: Aristide D. Caratzas, 1989.

Deleon, Jak. *The White Russians in Istanbul*. Istanbul: Remzi Kitabevi Publications, 1995.

DeNovo, John A. *American Interests and Policies in the Middle East, 1900–1939*. Minneapolis: University of Minnesota Press, 1963.

Dictionary of American Naval Fighting Ships. *Galveston*, http://www.history.navy .mil/danfs/g1/galveston-i.htm, accessed June 17, 2009.

———. *Sands*, http://www.history.navy.mil/danfs/s5/sands-1.htm, accessed June 18, 2009.

Dobkin, Marjorie Housepian. *The Smyrna Affair*. New York: Harcourt Brace Jovanovich, 1971, published with corrections by Faber and Faber in London in 1972 as *Smyrna 1922: The Destruction of a City*. This edition was reprinted by Kent State University Press with a new introduction by Dobkin in 1988, and then by Newmark Press in New York in 1998 (all quotation is from this edition).

Donaldson, Scott. "Hemingway of *The Star*." In *Ernest Hemingway: The Papers of a Writer*, edited by Bernard Oldsey, 89–107. New York: Garland Publishing, 1981.

Dos Passos, John. *The Best Times: An Informal Memoir*. New York: New American Library, 1966.

———. *The Fourteenth Chronicle: Letters and Diaries of John Dos Passos*. Edited and with a Biographical Narrative by Townsend Ludington. Boston: Gambit Inc., 1973.

———. *Orient Express*. New York: Harper & Brothers, 1927.

Duke, Vernon. *Passport to Paris*. Boston: Little, Brown & Co., 1955.

Dulles, Allen and Clover. Papers. Princeton University.

Dunn, Robert. *World Alive: A Personal Story*. New York: Crown Publishers, 1956.

Eby, Mrs. D. C. (Charlotte). *At the Mercy of Turkish Brigands: A True Story*. New Carlisle, OH: Bethel Publishing, 1922.

Edib, Halide. *Memoirs of Halide Edib*. New York: The Century Co., 1926.

———. *The Turkish Ordeal. Being the Further Memoirs of Halide Edib*. New York: The Century Co., 1928.

(Edwards, Jeanette). "Turkish Delight: As It Appears to an American Girl in Constantinople." *The Outlook* 22 (October 25, 1922, and November 8, 1922): 328–29 and 440–42, respectively.

Egan, Eleanor Francis. "This to Be Said for the Turk." *Saturday Evening Post* 192, no. 25 (December 20, 1919): 14ff.

Elder, John. "Memories of the Armenian Republic." *Armenian Review* 6 no. 1 (March 1953): 3–27.

Elliott, Mabel Evelyn. *Beginning Again at Ararat*. New York: Flaming H. Revel, 1924.

Ellis, William T. "Constantinople To-day." *The American Review of Reviews* 67 (May 1923): 517–20.

———. "Jennings of Smyrna." *Scribner's* 84 (August 1928): 230–35.

Evans, Laurence. *United States Policy and the Partition of Turkey, 1914–1924*. Baltimore: Johns Hopkins Press, 1965.

Evans, Peter. *Ari: The Life and Times of Aristotle Socrates Onassis*. New York: Summit Books, 1986.

Fenton, Charles A. *The Apprenticeship of Ernest Hemingway: The Early Years*. New York: Viking, 1954.

Field, Richard Stockton. "A Destroyer in the Near East." *Naval Institute Proceedings* 51 (February 1925 and March 1925): 246–67 and 400–23, respectively.

Fincanci, May. *The Story of Robert College Old and New: 1863–1982*. Istanbul: Trustees of Robert College of Istanbul, 1983.

Fisher, Edgar J. Diary, in Papers. Rare Books and Manuscripts Library. Ohio State University. A very detailed diary during his professorship at Robert College in Constantinople.

Fisher, H. H. *The Famine in Soviet Russia, 1919–1923: The Operations of the American Relief Administration*. Stanford, CA: Stanford University Press, 1927.

Fitzgerald, William F. "Dolly." Rear Adm., USN. Informal oral history, the portion covering the years 1922–1924. In possession of the family. Used by permission.

(Flint, Lydia A. P.) *A Guide for the Personally Conducted Sight Seeing Trips by the American Navy Y.M.C.A.* Constantinople: YMCA, 1922. Located in the Pence Papers.

Freely, John. *A History of Robert College, the American College for Girls, and Bogaziçi University (Bosporus University)*, vol. 1. Istanbul: Türkiye'de Arastirmalari Enstitüsü, 2000.

Gallery, Daniel V., Rear Adm., USN. Diary. Papers of Admiral Daniel V. Gallery. Special Collections. U.S. Naval Academy.

———. *Eight Bells, and All's Well*. New York: W. W. Norton, 1965.

———. "My Pal Arthur Godfrey." *Saturday Evening Post* (19 July 1952): 25ff.

Gates, Caleb Frank. *Not to Me Only*. Princeton, NJ: Princeton University Press, 1940.

Gilbert, Martin. *Sir Horace Rumbold: Portrait of a Diplomat, 1869–1941*. London: Heinemann, 1973.

———. "Twentieth-Century Genocides." In *America and the Armenian Genocide of 1915*, edited by Jay Winter, 9–36. New York: Cambridge University Press, 2003.

Godfrey, Jean and Kathy. *Genius in the Family*. New York: G. P. Putnam's Sons, 1962.

Goodrich-Freer, A. (Mrs. Spoer). *Things Seen in Constantinople*. London: Seeley and Service, 1925.

Gordon, Leland James. *American Relations with Turkey, 1830–1930: An Economic Interpretation*. Philadelphia: University of Pennsylvania Press, 1932.

Grabill, Joseph L. *Protestant Diplomacy and the Near East: Missionary Influence on American Policy, 1810–1917.* Minneapolis: University of Minnesota Press, 1971.

Green, Fitzhugh. "Stand by to Ram!" *Collier's* 78 (November 6, 1926): 19, 49.

Grew, Joseph C. *Turbulent Era: A Diplomatic Record of Forty Years, 1904–1945,* vol. 1. Freeport, NY: Books for Libraries Press, 1952.

Grose, Peter. *Gentleman Spy: The Life of Allen Dulles.* Boston: Houghton Mifflin, 1994.

Guckert, John Cecil. "The Adaptation of Robert College to Its Turkish Environment, 1900–1927." Diss. Ohio State University, 1968.

Harbord, Maj. Gen. James G. "Investigating Turkey and Trans-Caucasia." *The World's Work* 40 (May 1920): 35–47.

———. "Mustapha Kemal Pasha and His Party." *The World's Work* 40 (May 1920): 176–92.

———. "The New Nations of Trans-Caucasia." *The World's Work* 40 (May 1920): 272–80.

Harington, General Sir Charles. *Tim Harington Looks Back.* London: John Murray, 1940.

Hartunian, Abraham H. *Neither to Laugh nor to Weep: A Memoir of the Armenian Genocide,* translated by Vartan Hartunian. Boston: Beacon Press, 1968.

Haskell, Orin. Letters. Special Collections. U.S. Naval Academy.

Hassiotis, J. K. "Shared Illusions: Greek-Armenian Co-operation in Asia Minor and the Caucasus (1917–1922)." In *Greece and Great Britain During World War I,* 169–71. Thessaloniki: Institute for Balkan Studies, 1985.

Hatzidimitriou, Constantine G., ed. *American Accounts Documenting the Destruction of Smyrna by the Kemalist Turkish Forces, September, 1922.* New York: Aristide D. Caratzas, 2005.

Heck, Lewis. "Constantinople Embassy." *The American Foreign Service Journal* 12 (March 1935): 130–34, 166–69, 174–78.

Hemingway, Ernest. *In Our Time.* New York: Scribner's, 1925.

———. *The Short Stories of Ernest Hemingway.* New York: Scribner's, 1956.

Henderson, George W., and Paul B. Ryan. "Naval Watch in the Mideast." *Naval Institute Proceedings* 103, no. 7 (July 1977): 66–75.

Henderson, Neville. *Water Under the Bridges.* London: Hodder & Stoughton, 1945.

Hepburn, Arthur Japy. Papers. In possession of the family. Used by permission.

Holmes, Mary Caroline. *Between the Lines in Asia Minor.* New York: Fleming Revell, 1923.

Hoover, Herbert. *An American Epic,* vol. 3. Chicago: Henry Regnery, 1961.

Horton, George. *The Blight of Asia.* Indianapolis, IN: Bobbs-Merrill, 1926.

Hovannisian, Richard G. *Armenia on the Road to Independence, 1918.* Berkeley: University of California Press, 1967.

———, ed. *Remembrance and Denial: The Case of the Armenian Genocide.* Detroit: Wayne State University Press, 1998.

———. *The Republic of Armenia,* vol. 2. *From Versailles to London, 1919–1920.* Berkeley: University of California Press, 1986.

———. *The Republic of Armenia,* vol. 3. *From London to Sevres, Feb–Aug. 1920.* Berkeley: University of California Press, 1996.

———. *The Republic of Armenia,* vol. 4. *Between Crescent and Sickle: Partition and Sovietization.* Berkeley: University of California Press, 1996.

Howard, Douglas A. *The History of Turkey.* Westport, CT: Greenwood Press, 2001.

Howard, Harry N. *The King-Crane Commission: An American Inquiry in the Middle East.* Beirut: Khayats, 1963.

Jenkins, Hester Donaldson. *An Educational Ambassador to the Near East: The Story of Mary Mills Patrick and an American College in the Orient.* New York: Fleming H. Revell, 1925.

Johnson, Clarence Richard, Director. *Constantinople To-Day, or The Pathfinder Survey of Constantinople: A Study in Oriental Social Life.* New York: Macmillan, 1922.

Kehn, Donald M. Jr. *A Blue Sea of Blood: Deciphering the Mysterious Fate of the USS Edsall.* New York: Basic Books, 2008.

Kelsey, Francis. Diary. Kelsey Papers. Bentley Historical Library, University of Michigan.

Kerr, Stanley E. *The Lions of Marash: Personal Experiences with American Near East Relief, 1919–1922.* Albany, NY: SUNY Press, 1973.

Kerr, Susan E. "Letters of Stanley E. Kerr: Volunteer Work with the 'Near East Relief' among Armenians in Marash, 1919–1920." History Honors Thesis, Oberlin College, 1980.

Kherdian, David. *The Road from Home: The Story of an Armenian Girl.* New York: Greenwillow Books, 1979.

Kimball, Elsie. Kimball Letters. In Kimball Papers. Archives and Special Collections, Mount Holyoke College, South Hadley, MA.

Kincaid, Earle H. *The History and Cruises of the United States Ship Whipple, Destroyer Number 217,* vol. 1. Privately printed, 1920.

Kinkaid, Thomas. "Scrapbook S-046-A" (of Kinkaid's tour on the U.S. Naval Detachment, Turkish Waters) in general photo collection. Operational Archives, Naval History Division, Washington, D.C.

Kirli, Biray Kolluoglu. "Forgetting the Smyrna Fire." *History Workshop Journal* 60 (2005): 25–44.

Kirtland, Lucian Swift. "The New Melting Pot on the Bosporus." *Travel* 38, no. 1 (November 1921): 3–8.

Ladas, Stephen P. *The Exchange of Minorities, Bulgaria, Greece and Turkey*. New York: Macmillan, 1932.

Leahy, William. Diary. In Papers. The Library of Congress. Also to be found at Special Collections, U.S. Naval Academy.

Lecouras, Peter. "Hemingway in Constantinople." *The Midwest Quarterly* 43, no. 1 (2001): 29–41.

Leslie, Anita. *Clare Sheridan*. Garden City, NY: Doubleday, 1977.

Lewis, Bernard. *The Emergence of Modern Turkey*. 2nd ed. London: Oxford University Press, 1961.

Leyda, Jay. *The Melville Log: A Documentary Life of Herman Melville, 1819–1891*, vol. 2. New York: Harcourt, Brace, 1951.

Lovejoy, Esther. *Certain Samaritans*. New York: Macmillan, 1933.

Lowry, Heath W. "American Observers in Anatolia ca. 1920: The Bristol Papers." In *Armenians in the Ottoman Empire and Modern Turkey (1912–1926)*. Istanbul: Boğaziçi University Publications. 1984.

———. *The Story Behind Ambassador Morgenthau's Story*. Istanbul: Isis Press, 1990.

———. *Turkish History: On Whose Sources Will It Be Based? A Case Study on the Burning of Smyrna*. Istanbul: n.p., 1989.

Ludington, Townsend. *John Dos Passos: A Twentieth Century Odyssey*. New York: Dutton, 1980.

Lybyer, Albert. Papers. University Archives, University of Illinois at Urbana-Champaign, Urbana, IL.

Mackenzie, F. A. *Russia Before Dawn*. London: T. Fisher, 1923.

MacLachlan, Alexander. "A Potpourii of Sidelights and Shadows from Turkey." http://www.levantineheritage.com/note14.htm, accessed Jan. 4, 2012.

Maguire, William A. *Rig for Church*. New York: Macmillan, 1942.

Mango, Andrew. *Atatürk: The Biography of the Founder of Modern Turkey*. Woodstock and New York: The Overlook Press, 2000.

Mannix, Rear Adm. Daniel P., III. *The Old Navy*, edited by Daniel P. Mannix, IV. New York: Macmillan, 1983.

Mansel, Philip. *Constantinople: City of the World's Desire 1453–1924*. New York: St. Martin's, 1995.

Marashlian, Levon. "Economic and Moral Influences on U.S. Policies Toward Turkey and the Armenians 1919–1923." *Türk Tarih Kongresi* 11 (1990): 1873–944.

Marcosson, Isaac. "When Constantinople Went Dry." *Saturday Evening Post* 196 (March 8, 1924): 40, 43–44, 46, 48.

McCarthy, Justin. *Death and Exile: The Ethnic Cleansing of Ottoman Muslims, 1821–1922.* Princeton, NJ: Darwin, 1995.

McCormick, Donald. *One Man's Wars: The Story of Charles Sweeny: Soldier of Fortune.* London: Arthur Barker, 1972.

McCully, Newton A. Diaries. The Library of Congress.

McIver, Renwick. Letters and other papers. In possession of the family. Used by permission.

Melson, Robert F. *Revolution and Genocide: On the Origins of the Armenian Genocide and the Holocaust.* Chicago: University of Chicago Press, 1992.

Merrill, John E. "Pen Pictures of the Siege of Aintab." *Envelope Series* (Published by American Board of Commissioners for Foreign Missions) 34, no. 3 (October 1920): 1–24.

Merz, Charles. "Bristol, Quarterdeck Diplomat." *Our World* 2 (December 1922): 3–9.

Meyers, Jeffrey. "Hemingway's Second War: The Greco-Turkish Conflict, 1920–1922." *Modern Fiction Studies* 30, no. 1 (1984): 25–36.

Milton, Giles. *Paradise Lost: Smyrna, 1922; The Destruction of a Christian City in the Islamic World.* New York: Basic Books, 2008.

Mitchell, Anna V. S. Letters. Olivia Stokes Hatch Papers. Bryn Mawr College Library. Bryn Mawr, PA.

Morand, Paul. "Turkish Night." In *Fancy Goods; Open All Night / Stories by Paul Morand,* translated by Ezra Pound and edited by Breon Mitchell, 96–107. New York: New Directions, 1984.

Moranian, Suzanne Elizabeth. "The American Missionaries and the Armenian Question, 1915–1927." Diss. University of Wisconsin-Madison, 1994.

Morgenthau, Henry. *Henry Morgenthau: Ambassador Morgenthau's Story.* Garden City, NY: Doubleday, 1918.

NavSource Online. "Patrol Yacht Photo Archive: Scorpion (PY 3) ex-Gunboat Scorpion," 2005, first photo, "At the New York Navy Yard, Brooklyn, New York, circa April 1898," http://www.navsource.org/archives/12/1303.htm, accessed June 8, 2009.

Oeconomos, Lysimachos. *The Martyrdom of Smyrna and Eastern Christendom.* London: George Allen & Unwin, 1922.

Ogden Lowrie, Helen. Ogden Papers. University Archives. University of Illinois at Urbana–Champaign. Urbana, IL.

Olsen, Charles and Edna. Papers (chiefly letters). In possession of the family. Used by permission.

Online Library of Selected Images. USS *Nahma* (SP-771), 1917–1919, www.history .navy.mil/photos/sh-usn/usnsh-n/sp771.htm, accessed June 8, 2009.

———. USS *Noma* (SP-131), 1917–1919, http://www.history.navy.mil/photos/ sh-usn/usnsh-n/sp131.htm, accessed June 8, 2009.

Papoutsy, Christos. *Ships of Mercy: The True Story of the Rescue of the Greeks, Smyrna, September, 1922.* Portsmouth, NH: Peter E, Randall, 2008.

Paquet, Alfons. "Constantinople." *The Living Age* 315 (November 4, 1922): 259–64.

Parke, Newton W. "Inferno at Sea." *Naval Institute Proceedings* 144, no. 1 (January 1988): 138–41.

Patenaude, Bertrand M. *The Big Show in Bololand: The American Relief Expedition to Soviet Russia in the Famine of 1921.* Stanford, CA: Stanford University Press, 2002.

Patrick, Mary Mills. *Under Five Sultans.* London: Williams and Norgate, 1930.

Patterson, Donald. "Admiral Mark L. Bristol and American Naval Involvement in Turkey, 1919–1923." Master's Thesis. Old Dominion College, 1968.

Pence, Harry. Personal papers, including personal diary (cited as Pence diary). In possession of the family. Used by permission.

———. War diary of USS *McFarland*, 1922–23 (cited as "Pence war diary"). Papers. Mandeville Special Collections, University of California, San Diego.

Peterson, Merrill. *"Starving Armenians": America and the Armenian Genocide, 1915– 1930 and After.* Charlottesville: University of Virginia Press, 2004.

Porter, David. *Constantinople and Its Environs in a Series of Letters . . . By an American, Long Resident at Constantinople,* 2 vols., 1854, reprinted by the British Library, 2011, and available in other editions as well.

Potter, E. B., and Chester Nimitz. *Sea Power: A Naval History.* Englewood Cliffs, NJ: Prentice-Hall, 1960.

Powell, E. Alexander. *The New Frontiers of Freedom: From the Alps to the Aegean.* New York: Charles Scribner's Sons, 1920.

———. "The New Frontiers of Freedom: III. Will the Sick Man of Europe Recover?" *Scribner's* 67 (March 1920): 284–96.

Price, G. Ward. *Extra-special Correspondent.* London: George G. Harrap, 1957.

Punton, John. *Reminiscences of a Recent Visit to the Near East.* Kansas City: Punton Brothers, 1923.

Quennell, Peter. *Byron, a Self-Portrait: Letters and Diaries, 1798–1824.* Oxford, United Kingdom: Oxford University Press, 1990.

Raber, Oran. "New Light on the Destruction of Smyrna." *Current History* 18 (May 1923): 312–18.

Reynolds, Michael. *Hemingway: The Paris Years*. New York: Norton, 1989.

Roberts, Kenneth L. "The Constantinople Refugees." *Saturday Evening Post* 194 (July 16, 1921): 10ff.

―――. "Drifting Leaves." *Harper's* 144 (February 1922): 364–72.

―――. *Why Europe Leaves Home*. Indianapolis: Bobbs-Merrill, 1922.

Ryan, Andrew. *The Last of the Dragomans*. London: Geoffrey Bles, 1951.

Sarafian, Ara, ed. *United States Official Documents on the Armenian Genocide*, vol. 1. *The Lower Euphrates*. Watertown, MA: Armenian Review, 1993.

―――. *United States Official Documents on the Armenian Genocide*, vol. 2. *The Peripheries*. Watertown, MA: Armenian Review, 1994.

Scipio, Lynn A. *My Thirty Years in Turkey*. Rindge, NH: Richard R. Smith, 1955.

Scott, Eveline. "When the Russians Came to Constantinople." *The Living Age* 312 (March 11, 1922): 570–73.

Seal, Jeremy. *A Fez of the Heart: Travels Around Turkey in Search of a Hat*. New York: Harvest (Harcourt Brace), 1995.

Shenk, Robert, ed. *Playships of the World. The Naval Diaries of Admiral Dan Gallery, 1920-24*. Columbia: University of South Carolina Press, 2008.

Shepard, Lorin. "Fighting the Turks at Aintab." *Current History* 14 (July 1921): 590–93.

Sheridan, Clare. *Naked Truth*. New York: Harper, 1928.

―――. *A Turkish Kaleidoscope*. New York: Dodd, Mead and Company, 1926.

Slonimsky, Nicolas. *Perfect Pitch: A Life Story*. Oxford, United Kingdom: Oxford University Press, 1988.

Smith, Michael Llewellyn. *Ionian Vision: Greece in Asia Minor, 1919–1922*. London: Allen Lane, 1973.

Smith, Peter A. "Hemingway's 'On the Quai at Smyrna' and the Universe of *In Our Time*." *Studies in Short Fiction* 24, no. 2 (1987): 159–62.

Smith, Roger W. "Was Morgenthau a Liar?" *Ararat* 32 (Autumn 1991): 51–52.

Smith, Walter George. "Journal of a Journey to the Near East." The Smith Collection. Archive of the American Catholic Historical Society, St. Charles Seminary, Philadelphia, PA.

"Smyrna Under the Greco-Turkish Terror." (No author listed.) *Literary Digest* 75 (28 October 1922): 34–38.

Solano, Solita. "Constantinople Today." *National Geographic* 41, no. 6 (June 1922): 647–80.

Stephens, Everett and Mary. *Survival Against All Odds: The First 100 Years of Anatolia College*. New Rochelle, NY: Aristide D. Caratzas, 1986.

Still, William N. Jr. *American Sea Power in the Old World: The United States Navy in European and Near Eastern Waters, 1865–1917.* Westport, CT: Greenwood Press, 1980.

"The Subchaser Archives: Documents and Stories of the Subchasers in WWI," www.subchaser.org/home, accessed June 17, 2009.

Tarbuck, Raymond D., Rear Adm., USN. "The Reminiscences of Rear Admiral Raymond D. Tarbuck, U.S. Navy, Retired." Annapolis: U.S. Naval Institute, 1973.

Teffi, N. "Constantinople—The Rusty Door to the East." *The Living Age* 312 (March 11, 1921): 365–69.

Thomas, Thelma K. "Dangerous Archaelogy: Francis Willey Kelsey and Armenia (1919–1920)." Catalog of an exhibition presented at the Kelsey Museum of Ancient and Mediaeval Archaeology, University of Michigan, September 1990–February 1991.

Townsend, Gus. "Richard Halliburton: The Forgotten Myth." *Memphis Magazine On-Line Sections,* April 2001, http://www.memphismagazine.com/backissues/april2001/coverstory2.htm, accessed December 7, 2001.

Toynbee, Arnold. *The Western Question in Greece and Turkey.* London: Constable and Company, 1922.

Trammell, Webb. War diary, USS *Fox*, DD 234. Sept. 1921 to June 1922. In possession of the family. Used by permission.

Trask, Roger R. *The United States Response to Turkish Nationalism and Reform 1914–1939.* Minneapolis: University of Minnesota Press, 1971.

Twain, Mark. *The Innocents Abroad, or The New Pilgrim's Progress.* New York: Airmont, 1967.

Ussher, Clarence D. *An American Physician in Turkey: A Narrative of Adventures in Peace and War.* Boston: Houghton Mifflin, 1917.

Vryonis, Speros Jr. "Greek Labor Battalions [in] Asia Minor." In *The Armenian Genocide: Cultural and Ethical Legacies,* edited by Richard Hovannisian, 275–90. New Brunswick, NJ: Transaction Publishers, 2007.

Walder, David. *The Chanak Affair.* London: Hutchinson. 1969.

Weeks, Charles J. Jr. *An American Naval Diplomat in Revolutionary Russia: The Life and Times of Vice Admiral Newton A. McCully.* Annapolis: Naval Institute Press, 1993.

———. "A Samaritan in Russia: Vice Admiral Newton A. McCully's Humanitarian Efforts, 1914–1920." *Military Affairs* 52, no. 1 (January 1988): 12–17.

Welles, Harriet. "Following the Ship." *Woman's Home Companion* 54 (December 1927): 118ff.

Wheeler, Charles J., Rear Adm., USN. "The Reminiscences of Rear Admiral Charles J(ulian). Wheeler, U.S. Navy, Retired." Annapolis: U.S. Naval Institute, 1970.

Wheeler, Gerald. *A Biography of Admiral Thomas C. Kinkaid, U.S. Navy*. Washington, D.C.: Naval Historical Center, 1995.

White, George E. *Adventuring with Anatolia College*. Grinnell, IA: Herald-Register Publishing Co., 1940.

White, W. L. "The Liquidation of Herbert Hoover." Offprint from *The Reader's Digest*, May 1960 issue.

White, William, ed. *Hemingway, Ernest. Dateline Toronto: The Complete Toronto Star Dispatches, 1920–1924*. New York: Charles Scribner's Sons, 1985.

Winter, Jay, ed. *America and the Armenian Genocide of 1915*. New York: Cambridge University Press, 2003.

Woods, H. Charles. "Constantinople after the War." *The Fortnightly Review* 115 (March 1921): 457–66.

Yalman, Ahmed Emin. *Turkey in My Time*. Norman: University of Oklahoma Press, 1957.

Yartkes, Yeghiayan, compiler. *British Reports on Ethnic Cleansing in Anatolia, 1919–1922: The Armenian-Greek Section*. Center for Armenian Remembrance, 2007.

Young, George. *Constantinople*. London: Methuen, 1926.

Zia Bey, Mufty-Zade K. *Speaking of the Turks*. New York: Duffield, 1922.

Zogbaum, Rufus Fairchild. *From Sail to Saratoga: A Naval Autobiography*. Rome: Tipographia Italo-Orientale, n.d., c. 1960.

INDEX

A

Abdul Hamid II: despotic rule, 48; massacre of Armenians, 21

Aintab: correspondence between Jackson and Bristol, 58–59; Nationalist attack, 58

Allied powers: fleet enters the Bosporus, 2, 12; fleet leaves the Bosporus, 272; Greeks to occupy Smyrna, 37; Greeks to proceed further, 69; occupation of Constantinople, 45, 69; opposition to Bristol, 44–45

American commissions: faults with, 29; origin of, 28–29. *See also* Harbord, James; King-Crane Commission

American embassy in Constantinople: Bristol moves into, 42; conflict in leadership, 44; description, 42; diplomatic secretaries, 66; disaster relief committee, 76, 79; help to White Russians, 79, 83, 122; insularity, 68; interview of Black Thomas, 125; lesser attention to Greeks, 268–69; plan for evacuating Americans, 187; radio circuits, 42; recreational trips, 169; social life, 64–65; sponsoring of dances and concerts, 80, 122; summer palace, 161; welcome for Turks,

65. *See also* Bristol, Helen; Bristol, Mark

American idealism after World War I, 39–40

American missionaries: American Board, 21; Armenian converts, 21, 204; departure from Anatolia, 272; excellent image of Americans, 39; Harbord impressed by, 32–33; missionaries as villains, 51, 215; reports of deportations to Morgenthau, 27; risking lives at Selimieh Barracks, 266; taking orphans out of Cilicia, 59; transport by destroyers, 47, weather interrupting dinner, 183–84; "unnamed Christianity," 274–75

American Red Cross: effort at Smyrna, 211, 215; relation with Bristol, 44, 64; work with Greek refugees, 267, 272; work with Russian refugees, 71, 74, 78–79, 81–82, 196. *See also* Davis, Claflin

Armenian genocide: Aegean displacements, 218; Bristol's excuses for Turks, 54–55; Bryce's report, 24; consular reports, 19, 26–27; death marches during, 15; genocide queried, 15; Harbord's conclusions, 34; Morgenthau's memoir, 25–27;

ABOUT THE AUTHOR

ROBERT SHENK is a professor of English at the University of New Orleans and a retired captain in the U.S. Naval Reserve.

Shenk's previous Naval Institute Press books include *The Naval Institute Guide to Naval Writing*, now in its third edition; *Authors at Sea: Modern American Writers Remember Their Naval Service*, a History Book Club selection; and *Admiral Dan Gallery: The Life and Wit of a Navy Original*, a biography Shenk coauthored with Professor Herb Gilliland of the U.S. Naval Academy. In 2008 the University Press of South Carolina published Shenk's edition, *Playships of the World: The Naval Diaries of Admiral Dan Gallery, 1920–1924*.

As a naval officer, Shenk initially served as communications officer of the USS *Harry E. Hubbard* (DD-748) on service that included two deployments to the South China Sea (1966–68); he also spent a year on river patrol boats in the Mekong and Vam Co Tay Rivers of Vietnam (1968–69). Besides inactive Reserve service, he later spent three years apiece teaching English at the U.S. Air Force Academy and Naval Academy, on voluntary recall to active duty (1979–85).

The Naval Institute Press is the book-publishing arm of the U.S. Naval Institute, a private, nonprofit, membership society for sea service profession-als and others who share an interest in naval and maritime affairs. Established in 1873 at the U.S. Naval Academy in Annapolis, Maryland, where its offices remain today, the Naval Institute has members worldwide.

Members of the Naval Institute support the education programs of the soci-ety and receive the influential monthly magazine *Proceedings* or the colorful bimonthly magazine *Naval History* and discounts on fine nautical prints and on ship and aircraft photos. They also have access to the transcripts of the Institute's Oral History Program and get discounted admission to any of the Institute-sponsored seminars offered around the country.

The Naval Institute's book-publishing program, begun in 1898 with basic guides to naval practices, has broadened its scope to include books of more gen-eral interest. Now the Naval Institute Press publishes about seventy titles each year, ranging from how-to books on boating and navigation to battle histories, biographies, ship and aircraft guides, and novels. Institute members receive sig-nificant discounts on the Press's more than eight hundred books in print.

Full-time students are eligible for special half-price membership rates. Life memberships are also available.

For a free catalog describing Naval Institute Press books currently available, and for further information about joining the U.S. Naval Institute, please write to:

Member Services
U.S. Naval Institute
291 Wood Road
Annapolis, MD 21402-5034
Telephone: (800) 233-8764
Fax: (410) 571-1703
Web address: www.usni.org